THE
BOOK ®

Renault 5
Service and Repair Manual

A K Legg LAE MIMI

(1219-256-2Y7)

Models covered

Renault 5 models, including special/limited editions, Van and GT Turbo
956 cc, 1108 cc, 1237 cc, 1390 cc, 1397 cc and 1721 cc petrol engines

Covers most mechanical features of Extra Van
Does not cover Diesel engine models

Printed in the USA

ABCDE
FGHIJ
KLMNO
ST
3

Haynes Publishing
Sparkford, Nr Yeovil, Somerset BA22 7JJ, England

Haynes North America, Inc
861 Lawrence Drive, Newbury Park, California 91320, USA

Editions Haynes S.A.
Tour Aurore - La Défense 2, 18 Place des Reflets,
92975 PARIS LA DEFENSE Cedex, France

Haynes Publishing Nordiska AB
Box 1504, 751 45 UPPSALA, Sweden

© Haynes Publishing 1996

A book in the **Haynes Service and Repair Manual Series**

ISBN **1 85960 099 9**

British Library Cataloguing in Publication Data
A catalogue record for this book is available from the British Library.

Contents

LIVING WITH YOUR RENAULT 5

Roadside Repairs

Routine Maintenance

Contents

Introduction to the Renault 5

Available in France from late 1984 and the UK from February 1985 the new Renault 5 incorporates many innovations compared with its forerunner. Front-wheel drive is retained, but with a transverse engine and gearbox instead of the in-line previous arrangement. This has not only improved front wheel traction owing to a greater concentration of weight over the wheels, but has also resulted in additional interior space. Many components both mechanical and body have been subjected to weight saving in order to improve economy and performance, one example being the gearbox which is now of light alloy instead of cast iron. The MacPherson strut front suspension replaces the previous torsion bar and wishbone type, and the bodywork incorporates improved aerodynamics giving it a sleeker look.

A choice of 956 cc, 1108 cc and 1397 cc overhead valve engines is available, ranging from 42 brake horse power to 115 brake horse power for the Turbo version. A 1721 cc overhead cam engine became available in 1987: this and other later model changes are covered in Chapter 12.

The car is quite conventional in design and the DIY home mechanic should find most work straightforward.

Acknowledgements

Thanks are due to Champion Spark Plug who supplied the illustrations showing spark plug conditions. Certain other illustrations are the copyright Renault Limited (UK) and are used with their permission. Thanks are also due to Sykes-Pickavant Limited, who supplied some of the workshop tools, and to all those people at Sparkford who helped in the production of this manual.

We take great pride in the accuracy of information given in this manual, but vehicle manufacturers make alterations and design changes during the production run of a particular vehicle of which they do not inform us. No liability can be accepted by the authors or publishers for loss, damage or injury caused by any errors in, or omissions from, the information given.

Renault 5TL (three-door)

Working on your car can be dangerous. This page shows just some of the potential risks and hazards, with the aim of creating a safety-conscious attitude.

General hazards

Scalding

• Don't remove the radiator or expansion tank cap while the engine is hot.
• Engine oil, automatic transmission fluid or power steering fluid may also be dangerously hot if the engine has recently been running.

Burning

• Beware of burns from the exhaust system and from any part of the engine. Brake discs and drums can also be extremely hot immediately after use.

Crushing

• When working under or near a raised vehicle, always supplement the jack with axle stands, or use drive-on ramps. *Never venture under a car which is only supported by a jack.*
• Take care if loosening or tightening high-torque nuts when the vehicle is on stands. Initial loosening and final tightening should be done with the wheels on the ground.

Fire

• Fuel is highly flammable; fuel vapour is explosive.
• Don't let fuel spill onto a hot engine.
• Do not smoke or allow naked lights (including pilot lights) anywhere near a vehicle being worked on. Also beware of creating sparks (electrically or by use of tools).
• Fuel vapour is heavier than air, so don't work on the fuel system with the vehicle over an inspection pit.
• Another cause of fire is an electrical overload or short-circuit. Take care when repairing or modifying the vehicle wiring.
• Keep a fire extinguisher handy, of a type suitable for use on fuel and electrical fires.

Electric shock

• Ignition HT voltage can be dangerous, especially to people with heart problems or a pacemaker. Don't work on or near the ignition system with the engine running or the ignition switched on.

• Mains voltage is also dangerous. Make sure that any mains-operated equipment is correctly earthed. Mains power points should be protected by a residual current device (RCD) circuit breaker.

Fume or gas intoxication

• Exhaust fumes are poisonous; they often contain carbon monoxide, which is rapidly fatal if inhaled. Never run the engine in a confined space such as a garage with the doors shut.
• Fuel vapour is also poisonous, as are the vapours from some cleaning solvents and paint thinners.

Poisonous or irritant substances

• Avoid skin contact with battery acid and with any fuel, fluid or lubricant, especially antifreeze, brake hydraulic fluid and Diesel fuel. Don't syphon them by mouth. If such a substance is swallowed or gets into the eyes, seek medical advice.
• Prolonged contact with used engine oil can cause skin cancer. Wear gloves or use a barrier cream if necessary. Change out of oil-soaked clothes and do not keep oily rags in your pocket.
• Air conditioning refrigerant forms a poisonous gas if exposed to a naked flame (including a cigarette). It can also cause skin burns on contact.

Asbestos

• Asbestos dust can cause cancer if inhaled or swallowed. Asbestos may be found in gaskets and in brake and clutch linings. When dealing with such components it is safest to assume that they contain asbestos.

Special hazards

Hydrofluoric acid

• This extremely corrosive acid is formed when certain types of synthetic rubber, found in some O-rings, oil seals, fuel hoses etc, are exposed to temperatures above 400°C. The rubber changes into a charred or sticky substance containing the acid. *Once formed, the acid remains dangerous for years. If it gets onto the skin, it may be necessary to amputate the limb concerned.*
• When dealing with a vehicle which has suffered a fire, or with components salvaged from such a vehicle, wear protective gloves and discard them after use.

The battery

• Batteries contain sulphuric acid, which attacks clothing, eyes and skin. Take care when topping-up or carrying the battery.
• The hydrogen gas given off by the battery is highly explosive. Never cause a spark or allow a naked light nearby. Be careful when connecting and disconnecting battery chargers or jump leads.

Air bags

• Air bags can cause injury if they go off accidentally. Take care when removing the steering wheel and/or facia. Special storage instructions may apply.

Diesel injection equipment

• Diesel injection pumps supply fuel at very high pressure. Take care when working on the fuel injectors and fuel pipes.

⚠ *Warning: Never expose the hands, face or any other part of the body to injector spray; the fuel can penetrate the skin with potentially fatal results.*

Remember...

DO

• Do use eye protection when using power tools, and when working under the vehicle.

• Do wear gloves or use barrier cream to protect your hands when necessary.

• Do get someone to check periodically that all is well when working alone on the vehicle.

• Do keep loose clothing and long hair well out of the way of moving mechanical parts.

• Do remove rings, wristwatch etc, before working on the vehicle – especially the electrical system.

• Do ensure that any lifting or jacking equipment has a safe working load rating adequate for the job.

DON'T

• Don't attempt to lift a heavy component which may be beyond your capability – get assistance.

• Don't rush to finish a job, or take unverified short cuts.

• Don't use ill-fitting tools which may slip and cause injury.

• Don't leave tools or parts lying around where someone can trip over them. Mop up oil and fuel spills at once.

• Don't allow children or pets to play in or near a vehicle being worked on.

For information applicable to later models, see Supplement at end of manual

Dimensions

Overall length:
  Three-door .... 3591 mm (141.4 in)
  Five-door .... 3651 mm (143.7 in)
Overall width .... 1584 mm (62.4 in)
Overall height:
  Non-Turbo .... 1397 mm (55.0 in)
  Turbo .... 1367 mm (53.8 in)
Ground clearance .... 120 mm (4.7 in)
Track:
  Front .... 1320 mm (52.0 in)
  Rear .... 1290 mm (50.8 in)
Wheelbase:
  Three-door .... 2400 mm (94.5 in)
  Five-door .... 2460 mm (96.9 in)
Turning circle (between kerbs) .... 9800 mm (385.8 in)

Weights

Kerb weight:
  TC .... 710 kg (1565 lb)
  TL (three-door) .... 730 kg (1609 lb)
  TL (five-door) .... 735 kg (1620 lb)
  GTL (three-door) .... 740 kg (1631 lb)
  GTL (five-door) .... 745 kg (1642 lb)
  TS .... 720 kg (1587 lb)
  Auto (three-door) .... 770 kg (1698 lb)
  Auto (five-door) .... 775 kg (1709 lb)
  TSE .... 755 kg (1664 lb)
  GT Turbo .... 830 kg (1830 lb)
Maximum roof rack weight .... 60 kg (132 lb)
Maximum towing weight:
  TC .... 550 kg (1213 lb)
  TL .... 650 kg (1433 lb)
  GTL, TS and TSE .... 750 kg (1653 lb)
  Auto .... 450 kg (992 lb)
  GT Turbo .... 800 kg (1764 lb)

Capacities

Engine oil (excluding filter):

Non-Turbo	3.0 litre (5.3 Imp pt)	
Turbo	3.7 litre (6.5 Imp pt)	

Oil filter:

Non-Turbo	0.50 litre (0.9 Imp pt)	
Turbo	0.25 litre (0.4 Imp pt)	

Manual gearbox:	**Steel filler plug**	**Plastic filler plug**
Four-speed units	3.25 litre (5.72 Imp pt)	2.75 litre (4.84 Imp pt)
Five-speed units	3.40 litre (5.98 Imp pt)	2.90 litre (5.10 Imp pt)

Automatic transmission (refill after draining) .... 2.0 litre (3.52 Imp pt)
Cooling system (total) .... 5.5 litre (9.7 Imp pt)
Fuel tank:
  Non-Turbo .... 43.0 litre (9.5 Imp gal)
  Turbo - main .... 43.0 litre (9.5 Imp gal)
  Turbo - auxiliary .... 7.0 litre (1.54 Imp gal)

Puddles on the garage floor or drive, or obvious wetness under the bonnet or underneath the car, suggest a leak that needs investigating. It can sometimes be difficult to decide where the leak is coming from, especially if the engine bay is very dirty already. Leaking oil or fluid can also be blown rearwards by the passage of air under the car, giving a false impression of where the problem lies.

Warning: Most automotive oils and fluids are poisonous. Wash them off skin, and change out of contaminated clothing, without delay.

Identifying leaks

HAYNES HiNT *The smell of a fluid leaking from the car may provide a clue to what's leaking. Some fluids are distinctively coloured. It may help to clean the car carefully and to park it over some clean paper overnight as an aid to locating the source of the leak.*

Remember that some leaks may only occur while the engine is running.

Sump oil

Engine oil may leak from the drain plug...

Oil from filter

...or from the base of the oil filter.

Gearbox oil

Gearbox oil can leak from the seals at the inboard ends of the driveshafts.

Antifreeze

Leaking antifreeze often leaves a crystalline deposit like this.

Brake fluid

A leak occurring at a wheel is almost certainly brake fluid.

Power steering fluid

Power steering fluid may leak from the pipe connectors on the steering rack.

Jacking and towing

To change a wheel, remove the spare wheel and jack, apply the handbrake and chock the wheel diagonally opposite the one to be changed. On automatic transmission models, place the selector lever in P. Make sure that the car is located on firm level ground and then slightly loosen the wheel bolts with the brace provided. Locate the jack head in the jacking point nearest to the wheel to be changed and raise the jack using the other end of the brace. When the wheel is clear of the ground remove the bolts (and trim) and lift off the wheel. Fit the spare wheel using two diagonally opposite wheelbolts and moderately tighten them, then locate the large holes of the trim over them and fit the two remaining wheelbolts. This trim is only fitted to steel wheels and has two large and two small holes to allow prior fitting of two bolts. Lower the car and then tighten the bolts fully. With the spare wheel in position, remove the chock and stow the jack and tools.

When jacking up the car to carry out repair or maintenance tasks position the jack as follows:

If the front of the car is to be raised, position the jack head under a stout wooden beam placed transversely across the underside of the car and in contact with the front subframe side rails. Supplement the jack with axle stands which can be placed under the subframe or under the load bearing members of the underbody.

Jack and brace location

Turn nut (1) to lower spare wheel

Spare wheel carrier retaining hook

On steel wheels two wheel bolts can be fitted before fitting the trim

To raise the rear of the car, jack up each side in turn with the jack head positioned under the load bearing underbody members adjacent to the rear suspension bearing brackets.

To raise the side of the car place a block of wood under the side sill and located centrally under the front door. Place the jack head in contact with the block and raise the car. Shape the wooden blocks as necessary to avoid damaging the sill edges and supplement the jack with axle stands positioned under the jacking points. Never work under, around or near a raised car unless it is adequately supported in at least two places with axle stands or suitable sturdy blocks.

The car may be towed for breakdown recovery purposes only using the towing eyes positioned at the front and rear of the vehicle. These eyes are intended for traction loads only and must not be used for lifting the car either directly or indirectly. If the car is equipped with automatic transmission the following precautions must be observed if the vehicle is to be towed. Preferably a front end suspended tow should be used. If this is not possible, add an extra 2 litres (3.5 Imp pints) of the specified automatic transmission fluid to the transmission. The car may now be towed for a maximum of 30 miles (48 km) at a speed not exceeding 18 mph (30 kph). The selector lever must be in the N position during the tow. Drain off the surplus transmission fluid on completion of the tow.

Rear towing eye

Front towing eye

Axle stand positions

Cha. 280-02

Use a beam between the subframe side rails to raise the front of the car

Cha. 280-02

Raising the side of the car

Jump starting

When jump-starting a car using a booster battery, observe the following precautions:

✔ Before connecting the booster battery, make sure that the ignition is switched off.

✔ Ensure that all electrical equipment (lights, heater, wipers, etc) is switched off.

✔ Make sure that the booster battery is the same voltage as the discharged one in the vehicle.

✔ If the battery is being jump-started from the battery in another vehicle, the two vehcles MUST NOT TOUCH each other.

✔ Make sure that the transmission is in neutral (or PARK, in the case of automatic transmission).

HAYNES HiNT
Jump starting will get you out of trouble, but you must correct whatever made the battery go flat in the first place. There are three possibilities:

1 *The battery has been drained by repeated attempts to start, or by leaving the lights on.*

2 *The charging system is not working properly (alternator drivebelt slack or broken, alternator wiring fault or alternator itself faulty).*

3 *The battery itself is at fault (electrolyte low, or battery worn out).*

1 Connect one end of the red jump lead to the positive (+) terminal of the flat battery

2 Connect the other end of the red lead to the positive (+) terminal of the booster battery.

3 Connect one end of the black jump lead to the negative (-) terminal of the booster battery

4 Connect the other end of the black jump lead to a bolt or bracket on the engine block, well away from the battery, on the vehicle to be started.

5 Make sure that the jump leads will not come into contact with the fan, drive-belts or other moving parts of the engine.

6 Start the engine using the booster battery, then with the engine running at idle speed, disconnect the jump leads in the reverse order of connection.

For modifications, and information applicable to later models, see Supplement at end of manual

Maintenance is essential for ensuring safety and desirable for the purpose of getting the best in terms of performance and economy from your car. Over the years the need for periodic lubrication has been greatly reduced if not totally eliminated. This has unfortunately tended to lead some owners to think that because no such action is required the items either no longer exist, or will last forever. This is certainly not the case; it is essential to carry out regular visual examination as comprehensively as possible in order to spot any possible defects at an early stage before they develop into major expensive repairs.

The following service schedules are a list of the maintenance requirements and the intervals at which they should be carried out. Where applicable these procedures are covered in greater detail throughout this manual, near the beginning of each Chapter.

Every 250 miles (400 km) or weekly - whichever comes first

☐ Check the engine oil level and top up if necessary (Chapter 1, Sec 2)
☐ Check the coolant level in the expansion tank and top up if necessary (Chapter 2, Sec 2)
☐ Check the brake fluid level in the master cylinder reservoir and top up if necessary (Chapter 8, Sec 2)
☐ Check and adjust the tyre pressures (Chapter 9, Sec 29)
☐ Visually examine the tyres for wear or damage (Chapter 9, Sec 29)
☐ Check the operation of all interior and exterior lamps, wipers and washers (Chapter 11, Sec 3)
☐ Check, and if necessary top up, the washer reservoir adding a screen wash
☐ Clean the windscreen and windows
☐ Clean the headlamps

Every 6000 miles (10 000 km) or six months - whichever comes first

☐ Change the engine oil (Chapter 1, Sec 2)
☐ Check the water pump/alternator drivebelt for condition and tension and adjust if necessary (Chapter 2, Sec 12)
☐ Check and adjust the idling speed (Chapter 3, Secs 15 and 38)
☐ Check the exhaust system for leaks and deterioration (Chapter 3, Sec 20)
☐ Check condition of contact breaker points where fitted and clean or renew (Chapter 4, Secs 3 and 4)
☐ Renew the spark plugs (Chapter 4, Secs 10 and 20)
☐ Check the gearbox/automatic transmission oil level and top up if necessary (Chapter 6, Secs 2 and 8)
☐ Check the driveshaft rubber bellows for damage and leaks (Chapter 7, Sec 2)
☐ Check bodywork for damage and deterioration (Chapter 10, Sec 2)
☐ Check and if necessary top up the electrolyte level in the battery (except on maintenance-free type) (chapter 11, Sec 3)
☐ Check the operation of all equipment checking for oil, water and fuel leaks

Every 12 000 miles (20 000 km) or 12 months - whichever comes first

In addition to the 6000 mile service

☐ Renew the oil filter (Chapter 1, Sec 2)
☐ Check and if necessary adjust the valve clearances (Chapter 1, Sec 47)
☐ Renew the air filter (Chapter 3, Sec 3)
☐ Check disc pad and brake shoe lining wear without removing components (ie using inspection hole for rear brakes) (Chapter 8, Secs 3 and 6)
☐ Lubricate all door hinges and locks (Chapter 10, Sec 6)

Every 30 000 miles (50 000 km)

In addition to the 6000 mile service.

☐ (Check and adjust the idling mixture (Chapter 3, Secs 15 and 38)
☐ Renew the fuel filter (in-line type) (Chapter 3, Sec 28)
☐ Change the gearbox/automatic transmission oil (Chapter 6, Secs 2 or 10)
☐ Check disc pad and brake shoe lining wear by removing (Chapter 8, Secs 3 and 6)
☐ Renew the brake fluid (Chapter 8, Sec 18)
☐ Renew the brake servo air filter (Chapter 8, Sec 25)
☐ Check suspension and steering components for condition and wear (Chapter 9, Sec 2)
☐ Check and if necessary adjust the front wheel alignment (Chapter 9, Sec 28)

Every 40 000 miles (60 000 km)

☐ Change the antifreeze (Chapter 2, Secs 2, 3, 4, 5 and 6)

Engine compartment (GTL, 1397 cc model)

1 Washer reservoir
2 Accelerator cable
3 Speedometer cable
4 Crankcase ventilation hoses
5 Rear engine mounting
6 Electronic ignition computer module
7 Lower suspension arm inner pivot
8 Clutch cable
9 Coolant expansion tank
10 Radiator filler cap
11 Engine/gearbox mounting
12 Ignition timing marks and inspection hole
13 In-line fuel filter
14 Fuel pump
15 Engine oil level dipstick
16 Distributor
17 Alternator
18 Oval plate
19 Top hose bleed screw
20 Choke cable
21 Engine oil filler cap
22 Heater hose bleed screws
23 Throttle return spring
24 Carburettor
25 Brake fluid reservoir
26 Earthing cable

View of rear underside of car (GTL, 1397 cc model)

1 Rear towing eye
2 Exhaust rear mounting
3 Brake pressure regulating valve
4 Spare wheel carrier and hook
5 Spare wheel
6 Rear bumper mounting
7 Fuel tank filler neck
8 Rear shock absorber lower mounting
9 Rear brake backplate
10 Connecting hose
11 Rear suspension trailing arm
12 Rear suspension bearing bracket
13 Rear axle
14 Fuel tank
15 Rigid brake hydraulic pipe
16 Flexible brake hydraulic hoses
17 Handbrake cables
18 Anti-roll bar
19 Exhaust intermediate mounting
20 Exhaust intermediate section
21 Rear jacking pad
22 Handbrake cable mounting bracket
23 Exhaust rear section

View of front underside of car (GTL, 1397 cc model)

1 Steering gear
2 Gearchange rod
3 Exhaust intermediate section
4 Exhaust front pipe
5 Subframe mounting
6 Anti-roll bar
7 Track rod end
8 Driveshaft inner joint
9 Front suspension lower balljoint
10 Front lower suspension arm
11 Brake caliper
12 Horn
13 Engine oil drain plug
14 Radiator location grommet
15 Engine-to-gearbox steady rod
16 Radiator
17 Front towing eye
18 Gearbox drain plug
19 Anti-roll bar mounting on lower suspension arm
20 Front subframe

Tyre conditon and pressure

It is very important that tyres are in good condition, and at the correct pressure - having a tyre failure at any speed is highly dangerous. Tyre wear is influenced by driving style - harsh braking and acceleration, or fast cornering, will all produce more rapid tyre wear. As a general rule, the front tyres wear out faster than the rears. Interchanging the tyres from front to rear ("rotating" the tyres) may result in more even wear. However, if this is completely effective, you may have the expense of replacing all four tyres at once! Remove any nails or stones embedded in the tread before they penetrate the tyre to cause deflation. If removal of a nail does reveal that

the tyre has been punctured, refit the nail so that its point of penetration is marked. Then immediately change the wheel, and have the tyre repaired by a tyre dealer.

Regularly check the tyres for damage in the form of cuts or bulges, especially in the sidewalls. Periodically remove the wheels, and clean any dirt or mud from the inside and outside surfaces. Examine the wheel rims for signs of rusting, corrosion or other damage. Light alloy wheels are easily damaged by "kerbing" whilst parking; steel wheels may also become dented or buckled. A new wheel is very often the only way to overcome severe damage.

New tyres should be balanced when they are fitted, but it may become necessary to re-balance them as they wear, or if the balance weights fitted to the wheel rim should fall off. Unbalanced tyres will wear more quickly, as will the steering and suspension components. Wheel imbalance is normally signified by vibration, particularly at a certain speed (typically around 50 mph). If this vibration is felt only through the steering, then it is likely that just the front wheels need balancing. If, however, the vibration is felt through the whole car, the rear wheels could be out of balance. Wheel balancing should be carried out by a tyre dealer or garage.

1 Tread Depth - visual check

The original tyres have tread wear safety bands (B), which will appear when the tread depth reaches approximately 1.6 mm. The band positions are indicated by a triangular mark on the tyre sidewall (A).

2 Tread Depth - manual check

Alternatively, tread wear can be monitored with a simple, inexpensive device known as a tread depth indicator gauge.

3 Tyre Pressure Check

Check the tyre pressures regularly with the tyres cold. Do not adjust the tyre pressures immediately after the vehicle has been used, or an inaccurate setting will result.

Tyre tread wear patterns

Shoulder Wear

Underinflation (wear on both sides)
Under-inflation will cause overheating of the tyre, because the tyre will flex too much, and the tread will not sit correctly on the road surface. This will cause a loss of grip and excessive wear, not to mention the danger of sudden tyre failure due to heat build-up.
Check and adjust pressures
Incorrect wheel camber (wear on one side)
Repair or renew suspension parts
Hard cornering
Reduce speed!

Centre Wear

Overinflation
Over-inflation will cause rapid wear of the centre part of the tyre tread, coupled with reduced grip, harsher ride, and the danger of shock damage occurring in the tyre casing.
Check and adjust pressures

If you sometimes have to inflate your car's tyres to the higher pressures specified for maximum load or sustained high speed, don't forget to reduce the pressures to normal afterwards.

Uneven Wear

Front tyres may wear unevenly as a result of wheel misalignment. Most tyre dealers and garages can check and adjust the wheel alignment (or "tracking") for a modest charge.
Incorrect camber or castor
Repair or renew suspension parts
Malfunctioning suspension
Repair or renew suspension parts
Unbalanced wheel
Balance tyres
Incorrect toe setting
Adjust front wheel alignment
Note: *The feathered edge of the tread which typifies toe wear is best checked by feel.*

H9623

Component or system	Lubricant type/specification
1 Engine	Multigrade engine oil, viscosity range 10W/40 to 20W/50, to API SG/CD
2 Manual gearbox Non-Turbo models Turbo models	 Gear oil, viscosity SAE 80W Gear oil, viscosity SAE 75W/90S
3 Automatic transmission	Dexron type ATF
4 Brake fluid reservoir	Hydraulic fluid to SAE J1703F, DOT 3, or DOT 4
5 Cooling system	Ethylene glycol based antifreeze
6 Power steering	Dexron type ATF

Chapter 1 Engine

For modifications, and information applicable to later models, see Supplement at end of manual

Contents

Degrees of difficulty

| Easy, suitable for novice with little experience | | Fairly easy, suitable for beginner with some experience | | Fairly difficult, suitable for competent DIY mechanic | | Difficult, suitable for experienced DIY mechanic | | Very difficult, suitable for expert DIY or professional | |

Specifications

To avoid conversion inaccuracies, most specifications are given in metric values only, as specified by the manufacturers

General

Type	Four cylinder In-line, overhead valve			
Firing order	1 - 3 - 4 - 2 (No 1 cylinder at flywheel end)			
Designation	C1C	C1E	C1J	C2J
Bore	65.0 mm	70.0 mm	76.0 mm	76.0 mm
Stroke.	72.0 mm	72.0 mm	77.0 mm	77.0 mm
Capacity	956 cc	1108 cc	1397 cc	1397 cc
Compression ratio	9.7 : 1	9.5 : 1	9.25 : 1*	9.25 : 1

Turbo models 7.9 : 1

Crankshaft

Number of main bearings	5
Main journal diameter.	54.795 mm
Main journal minimum regrind diameter	54.545 mm
Crankpin journal diameter	43.98 mm
Crankpin journal minimum regrind diameter	43.73 mm
Crankshaft endfloat	0.05 to 0.23 mm

Connecting rods

Small end side-play	0.31 to 0.57 mm

Cylinder liners and pistons

	C1C and C1E	C1J and C2J
Liner protrusion	0.04 to 0.12 mm	0.02 to 0.09 mm (less seal)
Liner base seal type	Excelnyl	O-ring
Liner base seal thickness	1.15 to 1.35 mm	
Blue	0.08 mm	
Red	0.10 mm	
Green	0.12 mm	
Piston fitted direction	Arrow on crown towards flywheel	
Gudgeon pin fit in piston	Hand push-fit	
Gudgeon pin fit in connecting rod	Interference	

Piston rings

Number	Three (two compression, one oil control)	
Piston ring end gaps	Supplied pre-set	

Thickness:	C1E	C1C, C1J and C2J
Top compression	2.0 mm	1.75 mm
No 2 compression	2.0 mm	2.0 mm
Oil control ring	3.5 mm	4.0 mm

Camshaft

Number of bearings	4
Endfloat	0.05 to 0.12 mm

Valves

Seat angle	45°
Valve guides:	
Bore diameter in cylinder head (nominal)	11.0 mm

Fitted height above valve seat:	C1C and C1E	C1J and C2J
Inlet	26.5 mm	30.5 mm
Exhaust	26.2 mm	25.2 mm
Valve springs:		
Free length	42 mm	

Valve timing at valve clearances of 0.35 mm (inlet), 0.50 mm (exhaust):

	Inlet opens	Inlet closes	Exhaust opens	Exhaust closes
C1C and C1E	12° BTDC	48° ABDC	52° BBDC	8° ATDC
C1J and auto C2J	12° BTDC	56° ABDC	56° BBDC	12° ATDC
Manual C2J	12° BTDC	62° ABDC	65° BBDC	25° ATDC

Valve clearances (except C1J Turbo):	
Cold - inlet	0.15 mm (0.006 in)
Cold - exhaust	0.20 mm (0.008 in)
Hot - inlet	0.18 mm (0.007 in)
Hot - exhaust	0.25 mm (0.010 in)
Valve clearances (C1J Turbo):	
Cold - inlet	0.20 mm (0.008 in)
Cold - exhaust	0.25 mm (0.010 in)
Hot	Not specified

Cylinder head

Maximum permitted warp	0.05 mm
Maximum permitted refacing cut	0.5 mm

Lubrication system

Oil type/specification	Multigrade engine oil, viscosity range 10W/40 to 20W/50, to API/SG
Oil filter type:	
Non-Turbo models	Champion F101
Turbo models	Champion F124
Oil pump:	
Gear-to-body clearance	0.2 mm (maximum)
System pressure:	
Idling	0.7 bar (minimum)
Running (at 4000 rpm)	3.5 bar (maximum)

Torque wrench settings

	Nm	lbf ft
Cylinder head bolts	60	44
Rocker shaft pedestal nuts and bolts	20	15
Main bearing cap bolts	65	48
Big-end bearing cap nuts:		
C1C and C1E	35	26
C1J and C2J	45	33
Flywheel retaining bolts	50	37
Torque converter driveplate retaining bolts	70	52
Camshaft sprocket retaining bolt	30	22
Engine mounting nuts and bolts	40	30
Crankshaft pulley retaining bolt	110	81

Fig. 1.1 Cut-away view of the C1E and C1C engine (Sec 1)

Fig. 1.2 Cut-away view of the C1J engine (Sec 1)

C2J Engine has different carburettor and manifolds.

1 General description

The engines are of four-cylinder, in-line overhead valve type, mounted transversely in the front of the car. Apart from the cylinder liner bore diameter, the crankshaft stroke and minor detail differences, all engine types are virtually identical in design and construction.

The cast iron cylinder block is of the replaceable wet liner type. The crankshaft is supported within the cylinder block on five shell type main bearings. Thrust washers are fitted at the centre main bearing to control crankshaft endfloat.

The connecting rods are attached to the crankshaft by horizontally split shell type big-end bearings, and to the pistons by interference fit gudgeon pins. The aluminium alloy pistons are of the slipper type and are fitted with three piston rings, two compression rings and a scraper type oil control ring.

The camshaft is chain driven from the crankshaft and operates the rocker arms via pushrods. The inlet and exhaust valves are each closed by a single valve spring and operate in guides pressed into the cylinder head. The valves are actuated directly by the rocker arms.

A semi-closed crankcase ventilation system is employed, and crankcase gases are drawn from the rocker cover via a hose to the air cleaner and inlet manifold.

Lubrication is provided by a gear type oil pump driven from the camshaft and located in the crankcase. Engine oil is fed through an externally mounted full-flow filter to the engine oil gallery, and then to the crankshaft, camshaft and rocker shaft bearings. A pressure relief valve is incorporated in the oil pump.

Fig. 1.3 Cross-section of C1J and C2J engine (Sec 1)

Fig. 1.4 Engine lubrication system (Sec 1)

2.1A Showing the engine oil level notches on the dipstick

2.1B Topping-up the engine oil level

2.3 Engine oil drain plug on the sump

2 Routine maintenance

At the intervals specified in the "Routine maintenance" section in the front of the manual carry out the following procedures.
1 Check the engine oil level with the car on a level surface and the engine cold. Remove the dipstick and wipe it clean then fully insert it and withdraw it again. The oil level should be on the Maximum notch on the dipstick except during the running-in period of a new engine when it should be half way between the minimum and maximum notches. Top up the level if necessary, through the filler neck in the rocker cover (photos).
2 Visually inspect the engine joint faces, gaskets and seals for any sign of oil or water leaks. Pay particular attention to the areas around the rocker cover, cylinder head, timing cover and sump joint faces. Rectify any leaks by referring to the appropriate Sections of this Chapter.

Fig. 1.5 Using a special tool to remove the oil filter (Sec 2)

3 Place a suitable container beneath the oil drain plug on the sump. Unscrew the plug and allow the oil to drain (photo). Refit and tighten the plug after draining, then refill the engine with the correct grade and quantity of oil.
4 Move the bowl to the front of the engine, under the oil filter. Using a strap wrench, or filter removal tool, slacken the filter and then unscrew it from the engine and discard. Wipe the mating face on the cylinder block with a rag and then lubricate the seal of a new filter using clean engine oil. Screw the filter into position and tighten it by hand only, do not use any tools. With the engine running, check for leaks around the filter seal.

3 Major operations possible with the engine in the car

The following operations can be carried out without having to remove the engine from the car:
a) Removal and refitting of the cylinder head
b) Removal and refitting of the timing cover, chain and gears
c) Removal and refitting of the sump
d) Removal and refitting of the connecting rods, pistons and liner assemblies
e) Removal and refitting of the oil pump
f) Renewal of the engine mountings

4 Major operations requiring engine removal

The following operations can only be carried out after removal of the engine from the car:
a) Removal and refitting of the camshaft
b) Removal and refitting of the crankshaft and main bearings
c) Removal and refitting of the flywheel
d) Removal and refitting of the crankshaft rear oil seal

5 Methods of engine removal

The engine is removed upwards and out of the engine compartment. Although it is possible to remove the engine together with the gearbox or transmission, subframe and front suspension downwards this method involves additional work only worthwhile when changing a bodyshell or carrying out similar major procedures.
The engine may be removed on its own or in unit with the gearbox or transmission except in the case of 1986 on automatic transmission models, where it must be removed together with the transmission, then separated on the bench. (Also see Chapter 12).

6 Engine - removal without gearbox or automatic transmission

1 Disconnect both battery leads with reference to Chapter 11.
2 Remove the bonnet as described in Chapter 10.
3 Remove the radiator as described in Chapter 2.
4 Remove the air cleaner or inlet duct as applicable with reference to Chapter 3.
5 On Turbo models remove the anti-percolation device with reference to Chapter 3.
6 Remove the starter motor as described in Chapter 11.
7 Unscrew the nut and remove the engine earth strap from the body.
8 Disconnect the throttle cable, choke cable and vacuum pipe from the carburettor with reference to Chapter 3.
9 Disconnect the wire (brown) from the temperature gauge sender unit at the water pump.
10 Disconnect the brake servo hose from the inlet manifold.
11 Disconnect the two heater hoses from the

6.12 The fuel supply and return pipes below the water pump. Note cylinder block coolant drain plug (arrowed)

6.17A Engine-to-gearbox steady rod at engine, showing distance spacer

6.17B Engine-to-gearbox steady rod on gearbox

water pump, remove the bracket from the rocker cover, and tie the hoses to one side.

12 Disconnect the fuel supply and return pipes (photo).

13 Disconnect the exhaust downpipe from the manifold or turbocharger with reference to Chapter 3.

14 Remove the water pump/alternator drivebelt as described in Chapter 2, then adjust the alternator fully against the engine.

15 Disconnect the HT lead and where applicable the LT leads from the distributor and oil level sensor wires.

16 Raise the car on a ramp or jack up the front of the car and support on axle stands. Apply the handbrake.

17 Unscrew the retaining bolts and remove the steady rod connecting the gearbox to the engine. Note the position of the distance spacer (photos).

18 Unscrew the bolts and lift off the cover plate at the base of the gearbox bellhousing (photo).

19 Turn the crankshaft as necessary until the notch on the flywheel or torque converter is in line with the TDC timing mark on the bellhousing timing scale. Make a reference mark on the cylinder block in line with the TDC mark for use when the engine has been removed.

20 Undo the bolt and remove the washer securing the crankshaft pulley to the pulley hub. To lock the engine while the bolt is undone, firmly apply the handbrake and engage top gear. On cars with automatic transmission, wedge a screwdriver between the starter ring gear teeth and the bellhousing through the starter motor aperture. With the pulley bolt removed, lift off the pulley and withdraw the pulley hub by carefully levering it off using two screwdrivers.

21 Where fitted remove the ignition angular position sensor from the bellhousing with reference to Chapter 4.

22 On automatic transmission models rotate the crankshaft as necessary to provide access, and undo the bolts or nuts securing the torque converter to the driveplate. Retain the torque converter in position on the transmission, using a flat strip of metal

secured to the bellhousing with one of the coverplate bolts.

23 Undo all the bellhousing-to-engine retaining bolts accessible from under the car.

24 Place a jack with an interposed block of wood under the gearbox or transmission and just take the weight of the unit.

25 Attach a suitable hoist or crane to the engine using chains or rope slings, or by attaching the chains or ropes to the engine lifting brackets. Raise the hoist to just take the weight of the engine.

26 Undo all the bellhousing-to-engine retaining bolts accessible from above and additionally the two nuts, one each side of the engine. To provide sufficient clearance for engine removal, both these studs must be removed. To do this lock two nuts together on the exposed threads and undo the studs using the innermost nut.

27 Unscrew the bottom nut from the right-hand engine mounting. Alternatively remove the two bolts from the mounting.

28 Raise the engine and gearbox or transmission very slightly and withdraw the engine from the gearbox or transmission bellhousing. The engine may be tight owing to the locating dowels. Check that the right-hand driveshaft joints are not pulled apart.

29 Move the engine as far as possible to the right until it is completely clear of the gearbox or transmission and then lift the engine slowly, turning it as necessary to clear any

6.18 Flywheel (or driveplate) cover plate

obstructions. As soon as the engine is high enough, swing it over the front body panel and lower the engine to the floor.

7 Engine - removal with gearbox or automatic transmission

1 Disconnect both battery leads with reference to Chapter 11.

2 Remove the bonnet as described in Chapter 10.

3 Remove the radiator as described in Chapter 2.

4 Drain the gearbox oil or fluid as described in Chapter 6.

5 Remove the air cleaner or inlet duct as applicable with reference to Chapter 3.

6 On Turbo models remove the anti-percolation device with reference to Chapter 3.

7 Where fitted remove the ignition module or transistor assistance unit with reference to Chapter 4.

8 Disconnect the wiring to the reversing lamp switch on the gearbox at the connector.

9 On manual gearbox models disconnect the clutch cable with reference to Chapter 5.

10 Disconnect the main engine wiring

Fig. 1.6 Remove studs A and B to provide clearance for engine removal (Sec 6)

1

7.10 Main engine wiring harness connector

7.11A Earth strap located near the expansion tank

7.11B Earth strap located on the right-hand bulkhead

harness connector near the expansion tank location (photo).

11 Unscrew the nut and remove the engine earth straps from the body (photos).

12 Disconnect the speedometer cable from the gearbox with reference to Chapter 11.

13 Disconnect the throttle cable, choke cable and vacuum pipe from the carburettor with reference to Chapter 3.

14 Disconnect the wire (brown) from the temperature gauge sender unit at the water pump.

15 Disconnect the brake servo hose from the inlet manifold.

16 Disconnect the two heater hoses from the water pump, remove the bracket from the rocker cover, and tie the hoses to one side.

17 Press out the grommet and pull the

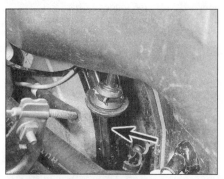

7.17 Pull the positive battery lead through the bulkhead

battery positive lead through the bulkhead (photo).

18 Disconnect and plug the fuel supply and return pipes.

19 Disconnect the exhaust downpipe from the manifold or turbocharger with reference to Chapter 3.

20 Remove the water pump/alternator drivebelt as described in Chapter 2, then adjust the alternator fully against the engine.

21 Disconnect the LT and HT leads from the ignition coil where necessary, also the oil level sensor wiring.

22 Raise the car on a ramp or jack up the front of the car and support on axle stands. Apply the handbrake.

23 Remove the splash shield from under the subframe (photos).

24 If a manual gearbox is fitted, slide back the rubber cover and undo the nut and bolt securing the gearchange rod to the gearbox fork control shaft. Slide the rod off the shaft and recover the distance sleeve.

25 If automatic transmission is fitted, disconnect the transmission selector control rod from the bracket and bellcrank. Also disconnect the wiring and hoses as necessary with reference to Chapter 6 and disconnect the fluid cooler pipes.

26 On Turbo models unbolt and remove the engine steady bar.

27 Remove both front wheels.

28 From under the car drive out the roll pin securing the right-hand driveshaft inner joint

to the differential stub shaft. Note that the roll pin is in fact two roll pins, one inside the other.

29 Unscrew the bolts securing the left-hand driveshaft inner joint bellows and retaining plate to the side of the gearbox or transmission.

30 Unscrew and remove the bolts securing the right-hand suspension strut to the upper part of the stub axle carrier noting that the bolt heads are facing forward. Pull the stub axle carrier to disconnect it from the stub shaft taking care not to damage the bellows, and support it in this position without straining the flexible brake hose.

31 Unbolt the left-hand brake caliper with reference to Chapter 8 and tie it to one side.

32 Disconnect the left-hand steering track rod from the stub axle carrier with reference to Chapter 9.

33 Unscrew and remove the bolts securing the left-hand suspension strut to the upper part of the stub axle carrier noting that the bolt heads are facing forward. Pull the stub axle carrier to disconnect the inner joint from the differential and support it in this position.

34 Unscrew the nut from the rear engine mounting and where fitted, remove the small support bracket (photos).

35 Remove the shield from the left-hand side of the engine compartment (photo).

36 Check that all cables and pipes have been disconnected then attach a hoist and take the weight of the engine and gearbox.

37 Unscrew the nuts and bolts from the left, right and front engine mountings.

7.23A Engine splash shield side clip

7.23B Engine splash shield rear screw

7.23C Engine splash shield front bolt

7.34A Rear engine mounting

7.34B Rear engine mounting with nut and bracket removed

7.35 Engine compartment left-hand side splash shield

38 Slowly lift the engine and gearbox or transmission assembly, moving it around as necessary to clear all obstructions. When high enough, lift it over the front body panel and lower the unit to the ground (photo).

39 If the car is to be moved refit the stub axle carriers to the struts and fit the wheels.

8 Engine - separation from manual gearbox or automatic transmission

1 With the assembly removed from the car disconnect the wiring harness from the alternator, oil pressure switch and starter and remove it.

2 Unscrew the retaining bolts and lift off the cover plate at the base of the transmission bellhousing.

3 Turn the crankshaft as necessary until the notch on the flywheel or torque converter is in line with the TDC timing mark on the bellhousing timing scale. Now make a reference mark on the cylinder block in line with the flywheel or torque converter notch. This will provide a useful reference because, once the gearbox or transmission is removed, the timing marks go with it, and it then becomes difficult to determine the TDC position of the engine.

4 If automatic transmission is fitted, undo the bolts or nuts securing the torque converter to the driveplate. Using a strip of metal as a suitable bracket, retain the torque converter on the transmission by securing the bracket to one of the cover plate bolt holes.

5 Undo the support bracket bolt and the three bellhousing bolts securing the starter motor in position. Lift off the starter noting the location of the dowel in one of the bolt holes.

6 Undo the two bolts securing the steady rod to the engine and gearbox or transmission. Lift off the rod, noting the location of the distance spacer.

7 Undo the bolts and the two nuts securing the engine to the gearbox or transmission bellhousing. Support the engine then withdraw the gearbox or transmission from it (photo).

9 Engine dismantling - general

1 If possible mount the engine on a stand for the dismantling procedure, but, failing this, support it in an upright position with blocks of wood placed under each side of the sump or crankcase.

2 Drain the oil into a suitable container before cleaning the engine or major dismantling.

3 Cleanliness is most important, and if the engine is dirty it should be cleaned with paraffin or a suitable solvent while keeping it in an upright position.

4 Avoid working with the engine directly on a concrete floor, as grit presents a real source of trouble.

5 As parts are removed, clean them in a paraffin bath. However, do not immerse parts with internal oilways in paraffin as it is difficult to remove, usually requiring a high pressure hose. Clean oilways with nylon pipe cleaners.

6 It is advisable to have suitable containers to hold small items, as this will help when reassembling the engine and also prevent possible losses.

7 Always obtain complete sets of gaskets when the engine is being dismantled, but retain the old gaskets with a view to using them as a pattern to make a replacement if a new one is not available. Note that in many instances a gasket is not used, but instead the joints are sealed with an RTV sealant. It is recommended that a tube of CAF 4/60 THIXO paste, obtainable from Renault dealers be obtained as it is specially formulated for this purpose.

8 When possible, refit nuts, bolts and washers in their location after being removed, as this helps to protect the threads and will also be helpful when reassembling the engine.

9 Retain unserviceable components in order to compare them with the new parts supplied.

10 The operations described in this Chapter are a step by step sequence, assuming that the engine is to be completely dismantled for major overhaul or repair. Where an operation can be carried out with he engine in the car, the dismantling necessary to gain access to the component concerned is described separately.

10 Ancillary components - removal

1 With the engine separated from the gearbox or transmission the externally-mounted ancillary components, as given in the following list, can be removed. In most cases removal is straightforward, but further information will be found in the relevant Chapters.

Inlet and exhaust manifolds and carburettor, also Turbo components where applicable (Chapter 3)

7.38 Lifting the engine and gearbox assembly from the car

8.7 Separating the gearbox from the engine

1

11.7 Undo the bolt (A) and remove the alternator adjustment arm from the pump at (B)

Fuel pump, except on Turbo models (Chapter 3)
Alternator (Chapter 11)
Spark plugs (Chapter 4)
Distributor (Chapter 4)
Water pump (Chapter 2)
Clutch (Chapter 5)
Oil filter (Section 2 of this Chapter)
Engine front mounting bracket (Section 22 of this Chapter)
Fuel supply and return pipes

11 Cylinder head -
removal with engine in car

1 Disconnect both battery leads with reference to Chapter 11.

11.11 Disconnect the brake servo vacuum hose

11.17 Undo the nuts and lift off the rocker cover

11.8 Disconnect the heater hoses . . .

2 Refer to Chapter 2 and drain the cooling system.
3 Remove the air cleaner or inlet duct as applicable with reference to Chapter 3.
4 On Turbo models remove the anti-percolation device and turbocharger with reference to Chapter 3.
5 Disconnect the HT leads at the spark plugs, release the distributor cap retaining clips or screws and remove the cap and leads.
6 Disconnect the lead at the water temperature gauge sender on the water pump.
7 Slacken the alternator mountings and adjustment arm bolt, push the alternator in towards the engine and slip the drivebelt off the three pulleys. Undo the bolt securing the alternator adjustment arm to the water pump and swing the alternator clear of the engine (photo).

11.13 Disconnect the fuel inlet pipe at the carburettor

11.18 Undo the nuts and bolts arrowed and withdraw the rocker shaft assembly

11.9 . . . and the radiator top hose at the water pump

8 Release the hose clips and remove the two heater hoses from the water pump (photo). Also remove the support bracket from the rocker cover.
9 Release the hose clip and remove the radiator top hose from the water pump (photo).
10 Disconnect the throttle cable, choke cable and vacuum pipe from the carburettor with reference to Chapter 3.
11 Disconnect the brake servo hose from the inlet manifold (photo).
12 Undo the nut and washer on the inlet manifold and on the cylinder block and lift off the heat shield where fitted.
13 Disconnect the fuel inlet pipe and the crankcase ventilation hose at the carburettor (photo).
14 Disconnect the distributor LT lead (where applicable) at the wiring connector.
15 Undo the bolt and release the retaining clip securing the cable and hose guide to the side of the cylinder head.
16 Undo the two bolts and withdraw the tension springs securing the exhaust front section to the manifold.
17 Undo the nuts and remove the rocker cover, complete with gasket, from the cylinder head (photo).
18 Undo the two bolts and two nuts securing the rocker shaft pedestals to the cylinder head (photo). Lift the rocker shaft assembly upwards and off the two studs.
19 Lift out each of the pushrods in turn using a twisting action to release them from their cam followers (photo). Keep them in strict

11.19 Take out the pushrods and keep them in order

11.22 Free the cylinder head from the gasket then lift the head, complete with manifolds and water pump, off the engine

order of removal by inserting them in a strip of cardboard having eight numbered holes punched in it. Note that No 1 should be the pushrod nearest the flywheel.

20 Slacken all the cylinder head retaining bolts half a turn at a time in the reverse order to that shown in Fig. 1.28. When the tension has been relieved remove all the bolts, with the exception of the centre bolt on the distributor side.

21 Using a hide or plastic mallet, tap each end of the cylinder head so as to pivot the head around the remaining locating bolt and unstick the gasket. Do not attempt to lift the head until the gasket has been unstuck, otherwise the cylinder liner seal at the base of each liner will be broken, allowing water and foreign matter to enter the sump.

22 After unsticking the cylinder head from the gasket, remove the remaining bolt and lift the head, complete with water pump, manifolds and carburettor, off the engine (photo). Note the crankshaft must not be rotated with the head removed, otherwise the liners will be displaced. If it is necessary to turn the engine (eg to clean the piston crowns), use bolts with suitable washers screwed into the top of the block to retain the liners (photo 35.11).

12 Cylinder head - removal with engine on the bench

The procedure for removing the cylinder head with the engine on the bench is similar to that for removal when the engine is in the car, with the exception of disconnecting the controls and services. Refer to Section 11 and follow the procedure given in paragraphs 7, 12 and 15, then 17 to 22.

13 Cylinder head - dismantling

1 Extract the circlip from the end of the rocker shaft, then remove the springs, rockers arms and pedestals, keeping each component in its original fitted sequence.

Fig. 1.7 Exploded view of the cylinder head components (Sec 13)

1 Rocker cover	6 Rocker	11 Split collet	16 Cylinder head bolt
2 Gasket	7 Bolt	12 Retainer	17 Cylinder head
3 Circlip	8 Pedestal	13 Spring	18 Cylinder head
4 Rocker shaft	9 Adjuster	14 Washer	gasket
5 Spring	10 Pushrod	15 Valve	19 Manifold gasket

2 Remove the valves from the cylinder head. Compress each spring in turn, with a valve spring compressor until the collets can be removed. Release the compressor and remove the spring, spring retainer and thrust washer.

HAYNES HiNT *If, when the valve spring compressor is screwed down, the valve spring retaining cap refuses to free to expose the split collet, do not continue to screw down on the compressor, but gently tap the top of the tool directly over the cap with a light hammer. At the same time hold the compressor firmly in position with one hand to avoid it jumping off.*

3 It is essential that the valves are kept in their correct sequence unless they are so badly worn that they are to be renewed. Numbering from the flywheel end of the cylinder head, exhaust valves are 1-4-5-8 and inlet valves 2-3-6-7.

4 The valve springs and collets should also be kept in their correct sequence as the inlet and exhaust valve components differ.

14 Sump - removal

1 If the sump is to be removed with the engine in the car, first carry out the following operations:

14.2 Undo the retaining bolts and remove the sump

a) *Jack up the front of the car and support on axle stands, remove the splash shield, the unscrew the two bolts, noting the position of the spacer, and remove the engine steady rod*
b) *Undo the bolts and remove the flywheel or torque converter cover plate from the bellhousing*
c) *Drain the engine oil*
d) *Where fitted, disconnect the two wires at the oil level sensor on the front face of the sump*

2 Undo and remove the bolts securing the sump to the crankcase (photo). Tap the sump with a hide or plastic mallet to break the seal between sump flange and crankcase, and remove the sump. Note that on some models a gasket is not used, only a sealing compound. On Turbo models it is necessary to remove the right-hand engine mounting first, and to do this the engine must be lined approximately 10.0 cm (4.0 in) using a hoist and chain (Fig. 1.8) and having removed the air filter.

15 Oil pump - removal

1 If the oil pump is to be removed with the engine in the car, first remove the sump as described in the previous Section.

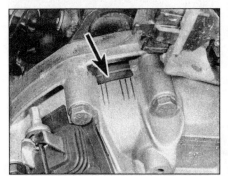

16.2 Flywheel notch (arrowed) aligned with TDC mark on the bellhousing timing scale

15.2 Undo the retaining bolts and withdraw the oil pump

2 Undo the retaining bolts (photo) and withdraw the oil pump from the crankcase and drivegear.

16 Timing cover, gears and chain - removal

1 If the engine is in the car, first carry out the following operations:
a) *Remove the alternator drivebelt*
b) *Remove the sump*

2 If the engine is in the car, rotate the crankshaft until the notch in the flywheel or torque converter is aligned with the TDC mark on the bellhousing timing scale (photo), and the distributor rotor is pointing towards the No 1 cylinder HT lead segment in the cap.
3 Using a socket or spanner, undo the crankshaft pulley retaining bolt. If the engine is in the car lock the starter ring gear to prevent the engine turning using a wide-bladed screwdriver between the ring gear teeth and the crankcase or apply the handbrake and engage top gear. If the engine is out of the car the ring gear can be locked using a strip of angle iron engaged with the dowel bolt (photo).
4 With the bolt removed, lift off the pulley and withdraw the pulley hub. If the hub is tight, carefully lever it off using two screwdrivers or use a two- or three-legged puller (photo).
5 Undo the nuts and bolts securing the timing

16.3 Lock the starter ring gear using a strip of angle iron

Fig. 1.8 Chain position for lifting the Turbo engine for sump removal (Sec 14)

A Right-hand engine mounting

cover to the cylinder block and carefully prise the timing cover off using a screwdriver to release the sealant. Note that a gasket is not used on all models.
6 If the engine is out of the car, rotate the crankshaft by means of the flywheel or torque converter driveplate until No 1 piston is returned to TDC, and the timing marks on the crankshaft and camshaft sprockets are towards each other. If the cylinder head has been removed, make sure that the cylinder liners are retained with bolts and washers, as described in Section 35, otherwise the liners will be displaced when the crankshaft is rotated.
7 Observe the components of the timing chain tensioner, noting that one of three types may be fitted. These are; a mechanical tensioner, identifiable by its coil tensioning spring; a hydraulic tensioner with manual presetting, identifiable by the small bolt on the side of the tensioner body; a hydraulic tensioner with automatic presetting identifiable by the absence of a small bolt on the side of the tensioner body.
8 To remove the mechanical tensioner, undo the retaining bolt using an Allen key, hold the tensioner slipper and spring end together and

16.4 A puller may be needed to remove the crankshaft pulley hub

Fig. 1.9 Mechanical timing chain tensioner components (Sec 16)

5 *Washer*	8 *Collar*
6 *Spring*	9 *Washer*
7 *Slipper arm*	10 *Retaining bolt*

withdraw the assembly from the cylinder block.

9 If an hydraulic tensioner with manual presetting is fitted, bend up the locktab and unscrew the small bolt on the side of the tensioner body. Insert a suitable Allen key into the bolt hole and engage the Allen key with the end of the slipper piston. Turn the key clockwise to retract the tensioner slipper. Now undo the two retaining bolts, lift off the tensioner and recover the spacer plate located behind the tensioner body. Removal of the tensioner with automatic presetting follows the same procedure, except that the piston cannot be retracted manually and must be held in compression by hand as the tensioner is removed.

10 Bend back the locktab then undo and remove the camshaft sprocket retaining bolt.

11 Withdraw the camshaft and crankshaft sprockets, complete with chain, using two screwdrivers to lever the sprockets off if they are tight (photo).

12 With the sprockets and chain removed, check that the Woodruff key in the end of the crankshaft is a tight fit in its groove, but if not, remove it now and store it safely to avoid the risk of it dropping out and getting lost.

Fig. 1.10 Hydraulic timing chain tensioner with manual presetting (Sec 16)

Remove bolt (b) and turn slipper piston clockwise using an Allen key to retract the tensioner slipper

17 Camshaft and followers - removal

1 Using a suitable bolt screwed into the distributor drivegear, or a length of tapered dowel rod, extract the drivegear from the distributor aperture.

2 Withdraw the camshaft followers from the top of the cylinder block, keeping them in strict order of removal (photo).

3 Undo and remove the two bolts securing the camshaft retaining plate to the cylinder block and carefully withdraw the camshaft from its location (photo).

18 Liners, pistons and connecting rods - removal

1 If the engine is in the car, first carry out the following operations:
a) *Remove the sump*
b) *For easier access, remove the oil pump*
c) *Remove the cylinder head (not necessary*

16.11 Removing the timing chain and sprockets

if only the big-end bearings are to be removed)

2 Rotate the crankshaft so that No 1 big-end cap (nearest the flywheel) is at the lowest point of its travel. If the big-end cap and rod are not already numbered, mark them with a centre punch on the side opposite the camshaft (rear facing side of engine when in the car). Mark both the cap and rod in relation to the cylinder liner they operate in, noting that No 1 is nearest the flywheel end of the engine.

3 Undo and remove the big-end bearing cap nuts and withdraw the cap, complete with shell bearing from the connecting rod. If only the bearing shells are being attended to, push the connecting rod up and off the crankpin and remove the upper bearing shell. Keep the bearing shells and cap together in their correct sequence if they are to be refitted.

4 Remove the liner clamps and withdraw the liner together with piston and connecting rod, from the top of the cylinder block.

> **HAYNES HiNT** *Mark the liners using masking tape, so that they may be refitted in their original locations.*

5 Push the connecting rod up and remove the piston and rod from the liner.

6 Now repeat these operations on the remaining three liner, piston and connecting rod assemblies.

17.2 Withdraw the cam followers and keep them in order

17.3 Undo the bolts (arrowed) and withdraw the camshaft

Fig. 1.11 Mark the big-end bearing caps and connecting rods before removal (Sec 18)

20.1 Identification number on main bearing cap

20.2 The oil dipstick tube is secured to No 2 main bearing cap

20.3 Crankshaft removal

19 Flywheel or torque converter driveplate - removal

1 Lock the crankshaft using a strip of angle iron between the ring gear teeth and the engine dowel bolt, or a block of wood between one of the crankshaft counter-weights and the crankcase.

2 Mark the flywheel or driveplate in relation to the crankshaft, undo the retaining bolts and withdraw the unit.

20 Crankshaft and main bearings - removal

1 Identification numbers should be cast onto the base of each main bearing cap (photo), but if not, number the cap and crankcase using a centre punch, as was done for the connecting rods and caps.

2 Undo and remove the main bearing cap retaining bolts and withdraw the caps, complete with bearing shells. Withdraw the oil dipstick tube first after undoing the bolts at No 2 bearing cap (photo).

3 Carefully lift the crankshaft from the crankcase (photo).

4 Remove the thrust washers at each side of the centre main bearing, then remove the bearing shell upper halves from the

crankcase. Place each shell with its respective bearing cap.

21 Crankshaft rear oil seal - renewal

1 With the engine removed from the car and separated from the gearbox or automatic transmission (if these units were removed with it), remove the flywheel or torque converter driveplate.

2 Clean the area around the crankshaft rear oil seal, then use a screwdriver to prise it from the block and bearing cap.

3 Wipe clean the oil seal recess. Dip the new oil seal in clean engine oil and carefully install it over the crankshaft rear journal. Take great care not to damage the delicate lip of the seal and make sure that the seal open face is towards the engine.

4 Using a tube of suitable diameter, a block of wood or the old seal, install the new seal squarely into its location until the outer face is flush with the block and bearing cap.

 HAYNES HiNT *If the original seal has worn a groove in the journal, drive the seal in a further 3 mm (0.12 in).*

5 Refit the flywheel and the engine, as described in the applicable Sections of this Chapter.

22 Engine mountings - renewal

Front mountings

1 Place a jack and an interposed block of wood under the sump if the right-hand mounting is to be removed, or under the gearbox or transmission if the left-hand mounting is to be removed. Raise the jack to just take the weight of the engine and gearbox or automatic transmission.

2 Undo the nut securing the rubber mounting to the subframe from below, and remove the flat washer (photo).

Fig. 1.12 Engine/gearbox mounting and brackets (Sec 22)

22.2 Engine rubber mounting-to-subframe retaining nut

22.3A Front right-hand engine mounting bracket

22.3B Front left-hand engine/gearbox mounting

22.3C Front left-hand engine/gearbox mounting with bracket removed

3 Undo the two nuts and bolts securing the rubber mounting to the engine/gearbox or automatic transmission mounting brackets. Undo the bolts securing the bracket to the engine, gearbox or transmission, lift off the bracket and withdraw the rubber mounting (photos).

4 Refitting is the reverse sequence to removal.

Rear mounting

5 Disconnect the battery negative terminal and remove the air cleaner, as described in Chapter 3.

6 Place a jack beneath the gearbox or transmission with an interposed block of wood and just take the weight of the unit.

7 Undo the nut and remove the washer securing the rubber mounting to the gearbox or automatic transmission mounting bracket.

Fig. 1.3 Crankcase ventilation hose layout for C1C, C1E and non-Turbo C1J engines (Sec 23)

8 Undo the two bolts securing the mounting rear support bracket to the subframe, slide out the bracket and withdraw the rubber mounting.

9 Refitting is the reverse sequence to removal.

23 Crankcase ventilation system - description

The layout of the crankcase ventilation system according to engine type is shown in the accompanying illustrations.

When the engine is idling, or under partial load conditions, the high depression in the inlet manifold draws the crankcase fumes (diluted by air from the air cleaner) through the calibrated restrictor and into the combustion chambers.

The system ensures that there is always a partial vacuum in the crankcase, and so prevents pressure which could cause oil contamination, fume emission and oil leakage past seals.

On C1J Turbo engines a one-way valve is fitted on the inlet manifold to prevent the crankcase being pressurised when the turbocharger is in operation, however the system still operates in a reduced capacity by feeding fumes into the inlet system upstream of the turbocharger.

Fig. 1.14 Crankcase ventilation hose layout for C1J Turbo engines (Sec 23)

Fig. 1.15 Crankcase ventilation hose layout for C2J engines (Sec 23)

Fig. 1.16 Exploded view of the oil pump components (Sec 25)

25.1 Lift off the oil pump cover

25.2A Remove the pressure relief valve ball seat and ball . . .

25.2B . . . followed by the spring and spring seat

25.5 Check the gear-to-body clearance using feeler gauges

24 Examination and renovation - general

With the engine completely stripped, clean all components and examine them for wear. Each part should be checked and, where necessary, renewed or renovated as described in the following Sections. Renew main and big-end shell bearings as a matter of course, unless you know that they have had little wear and are in perfect condition.

25 Oil pump - examination and renovation

1 Undo the four retaining bolts and lift off the pump cover (photo), taking care not to lose the oil pressure relief valve components which may be ejected under the action of the spring.
2 Remove the pressure relief valve ball seat, ball, spring and spring seat from the pump body (photos).
3 Lift out the idler gear, and the drivegear and shaft.
4 Clean the components and carefully examine the gears, pump body and relief valve ball and seat for any signs of scoring or wear. Renew the pump if these conditions are apparent.
5 If the components appear serviceable, measure the clearance between the pump body and the gears using a feeler blade (photo). If the clearance exceeds the specified amount, the pump must be renewed.
6 If the pump is satisfactory, reassemble the components in the order of removal, fill the pump with oil and refit the cover.

26 Crankshaft and main bearings - examination and renovation

1 Examine the bearing surfaces of the crankshaft for scratches or scoring and, using a micrometer, check each journal and crankpin for ovality. Where this is found to be in excess of 0.0254 mm, the crankshaft will have to be reground and undersize bearings fitted.
2 Crankshaft regrinding should be carried out by a suitable engineering works, who will normally supply the matching undersize main and big-end shell bearings.
3 If the crankshaft endfloat is more than the maximum specified amount, new thrust washers should be fitted to the centre main bearing, these are usually supplied together with the main and big-end bearings on a reground crankshaft.

27 Cylinder liners and crankcase - examination and renovation

1 Examine the liners for taper, ovality, scoring and scratches. If a ridge is found at the top of the bore on the thrust side, the bores are worn. The owner will have a good indication of the bore wear prior to dismantling the engine or on removing the cylinder head. Excessive oil consumption accompanied by blue smoke from the exhaust is a sure sign of worn bores and piston rings.
2 Measure the bore diameter just under the ridge with an internal micrometer and compare it with the diameter at the bottom of the bore, which is not subject to wear. If the difference between the two measurements exceeds 0.20 mm then it will be necessary to fit oversize pistons and rings or obtain new piston and liner assemblies. Contrary to popular belief the liners can be rebored if necessary and fitted with oversize pistons.
3 The liners should also be checked for cracking.
4 If the bores are only slightly worn, special oil control rings can be fitted which will restore compression and stop the engine burning oil. Several different types are available and the manufacturer's instructions concerning their fitting must be followed closely.
5 If new pistons only are being fitted and the bores have not been reground, it is essential to slightly roughen the hard glaze on the sides

27.11 Measuring the cylinder liner protrusion

Fig. 1.17 Sectional view of engine showing liner base seal details (Sec 27)

Upper inset - seal type fitted to 1397 cc engines

Lower inset - seal type fitted to 1108 cc engines

1 and all the others are stepped down in order so that the one with the least protrusion becomes No 4. This is checked in the same way as for liner protrusion described previously. The base seals must be in position for this check on 956 cc and 1108 cc engines, but not on 1397 cc engines. Recheck that liner protrusion remains within tolerance. Also make sure when moving a liner from one position to another that its matched piston stays with it.

13 Having finally selected the correct location for each liner, identify the liner and its piston with a number 1 to 4 to identify the assembly to be fitted to each location on reassembly.

28 Piston and connecting rod assemblies - examination and renovation

1 Examine the pistons for ovality, scoring and scratches, and for wear of the piston ring grooves.

2 If the pistons or connecting rods are to be renewed it is necessary to have this work carried out by a Renault dealer or suitable engineering works who will have the necessary tooling to remove the gudgeon pins.

3 If new rings are to be fitted to the original pistons, expand the old rings over the top of the pistons (photo). The use of two or three old feeler blades will be helpful in preventing the rings dropping into empty grooves.

of the bores with fine glasspaper to enable the new piston rings to bed in properly.

6 Examine the crankcase for cracks and leaks, then clean the oil galleries and waterways using a piece of wire.

7 Note that if new piston and liner assemblies have been obtained, each piston is matched to its respective liner and they must not be interchanged.

8 Whether new liners or the original components are being refitted, new liner base seals will be required. On the 1397 cc engine the base seals are in the form of a rubber O-ring. On the 956 cc and 1108 cc engines the seals are a flat ring type gasket of special material and are available in three sizes colour-coded blue, red or green. The three sizes are necessary so that the liner protrusion can be accurately set.

9 To check the liner protrusion, first ensure that the sealing area at the base of the liner and in the cylinder block is perfectly clean.

10 Place a blue seal on each liner (956 cc and 1108 cc engines only, liners on 1397 cc engines should have no seal for this check) and place the liner firmly in position in the cylinder block. If previously used liners are being checked, place them in their correct locations. If new liners are being fitted they may initially be placed in any location, but keep their respective matched pistons together with them. With the liners in place,

the flats on liners 1 and 2 must be towards each other and the flats on liners 3 and 4 must be towards each other also.

11 Lay a straight-edge across the top of the liner and measure the gap between the straight-edge and the top of the cylinder block (photo). This is the liner protrusion and must be within the tolerance given in the Specifications. If not, try a red seal or green seal.

12 On 956 cc, 1108 cc and 1397 cc engines the liner height variation must be checked, but only if new liners are being fitted. The liner height variation is the difference in cylinder liner protrusion between one liner and the next. The liner must be arranged so that the one with the greatest protrusion becomes No

28.3 Remove the piston rings from the top of the pistons

Fig. 1.18 Piston ring fitting and groove spacing details (Sec 28)

28.5 The word TOP (arrowed) indicates the second compression ring upper face

4 Before fitting the new rings, ensure that the ring grooves in the piston are free of carbon by cleaning them using an old ring. Break the ring in half to do this.
5 Install the new rings by fitting them over the top of the piston, starting with the oil control scraper ring. Note that the second compression ring is tapered and must be fitted with the word TOP uppermost (photo).
6 With all the rings in position, space the ring gaps at 120° to each other.
7 Note that, if new piston and liner assemblies have been obtained, each piston is matched to its respective liner and they must not be interchanged.

29 Camshaft and followers - examination and renovation

1 Examine the camshaft bearing surfaces, cam lobes and skew gear for wear ridges, pitting, scoring or chipping of the gear teeth. Renew the camshaft if any of these conditions are apparent.
2 If the camshaft is serviceable, temporarily refit the sprocket and secure with the retaining bolt. Using a feeler gauge measure the clearance between the camshaft retaining plate and the outer face of the bearing journal. If the clearance exceeds the specified dimension, renew the retaining plate. To do this, remove the sprocket and draw off the

Fig. 1.19 Check the camshaft endfloat using feeler gauges (Sec 29)

B *Camshaft retaining plate*
J *Specified endfloat*

plate and retaining collar using a suitable puller. Fit the new plate and a new collar using a hammer and tube to drive the collar into position.
3 Examine the condition of the camshaft bearings, and if renewal is necessary have this work carried out by a Renault dealer or engineering works.
4 Inspect the cam followers for wear ridges and pitting of their camshaft lobe contact faces, and for scoring on the sides of the follower body. Light scuff marks and side discolouration are normal, but there should be no signs of scoring or ridges. If the followers show signs of wear, renew them. Note that they must all be renewed if a new camshaft is being fitted.

30 Timing cover, gears and chain - examination and renovation

1 Examine all the teeth on the camshaft and crankshaft sprockets. If these are "hooked" in appearance, renew the sprockets.
2 If a mechanical chain tensioner is fitted, examine the chain contact pad and renew the tensioner assembly if the pad is heavily scored.
3 If a hydraulic tensioner is fitted, dismantle the components by taking them apart on the automatic presetting type (photo), or by releasing the slipper piston (turn it

Fig. 1.20 Hydraulic timing chain tensioner components (Sec 30)

1 *Piston with tensioner slipper*
2 *Spring*
3 *Sleeve*
4 *Tensioner body*

Fig. 1.21 Using an Allen key to lock the sleeve in the hydraulic tensioner with automatic presetting (Sec 30)

anti-clockwise with an Allen key) on the manual presetting type. Examine the piston, spring, sleeve and tensioner body bore for signs of scoring and renew if evident. Also renew the tensioner if the chain contact pad is heavily scored.
4 If the hydraulic tensioner is serviceable, lubricate the components and reassemble. On the manual presetting type, retain the slipper piston in the retracted position by turning it clockwise with an Allen key. On the automatic presetting type, lock the sleeve in the slipper piston first by turning it clockwise with an Allen key, then slide this assembly into the tensioner body (photo). Avoid pressing the slipper now or the sleeve will be released and the whole assembly will fly apart.
5 Renew the oil seal in the timing cover by driving out the old seal using a suitable drift and then install the new seal using a large socket or block of wood (photo).

30.3 Hydraulic timing chain tensioner with automatic presetting

30.4 Refitting the locked sleeve and slipper piston assembly on the automatic presetting hydraulic tensioner

30.5 Use a socket or tube to renew the timing cover oil seal

Fig. 1.22 Valve guide fitted height dimensions (Sec 32)

A Inlet   B Exhaust

31 Flywheel or torque converter driveplate - examination and renovation

1 Examine the flywheel for scoring of the clutch face and for wear or chipping of the ring gear teeth. If the clutch face is scored, the flywheel may be machined until flat, but renewal is preferable. If the ring gear is worn or damaged it may be renewed separately, but this job is best left to a Renault dealer or engineering works. The temperature to which the new ring gear must be heated for installation is critical and, if not done accurately, the hardness of the teeth will be destroyed.
2 Check the torque converter driveplate carefully for signs of distortion or any hairline cracks around the bolt holes or radiating outwards from the centre.

32 Cylinder head and pistons - decarbonizing, valve grinding and renovation

1 The operation will normally only be required at comparatively high mileages. However, if persistent pinking occurs and performance has deteriorated, even though the engine adjustments are correct, decarbonizing and valve grinding may be required.
2 With the cylinder head removed, use a scraper to remove the carbon from the combustion chambers and ports. Remove all traces of gasket from the cylinder head surface, then wash it thoroughly with paraffin.
3 Use a straight-edge and feeler blade to check that the cylinder head surface is not distorted. If it is, it must be resurfaced by a suitably equipped engineering works.
4 If the engine is still in the car, clean the piston crowns and cylinder bore upper edges, but make sure that no carbon drops between the pistons and bores. To do this, locate two of the pistons at the top of their bores and seal off the remaining bores with paper and masking tape. Press a little grease between the two pistons and their bores to collect any carbon dust; this can be wiped away when the piston is lowered.

 HAYNES HINT *To prevent carbon build-up, polish the piston crowns with metal polish, but remove all traces of polish afterwards.*

5 Examine the heads of the valves for pitting and burning, especially the exhaust valve heads. Renew any valve which is badly burnt. Examine the valve seats at the same time. If the pitting is very slight, it can be removed by grinding the valve heads and seats together with coarse, then fine grinding paste.
6 Where excessive pitting has occurred, the valve seats must be recut or renewed by a suitably equipped engineering works.
7 Valve grinding is carried out as follows: Place the cylinder head upside down on a bench with a block of wood at each end to give clearance for the valve stems.
8 Smear a trace of coarse carborundum paste on the seat face and press a suction grinding tool onto the valve heads. With a semi-rotary action, grind the valve head to its seat, lifting the valve occasionally to redistribute the grinding paste. When a dull matt even surface is produced on both the valve seat and the valve, wipe off the paste and repeat the process with fine carborundum paste. A light spring placed under the valve head will greatly ease this operation. When a smooth unbroken ring of light grey matt finish is produced on both the valve and seat, the grinding operation is complete.
9 Scrape away all carbon from the valve head and stem, and clean away all traces of grinding compound. Clean the valves and seats with a paraffin-soaked rag, then wipe with a clean rag.
10 If the valve guides are worn, indicated by a side-to-side motion of the valve, new guides must be fitted. To do this, use a suitable mandrel to press the worn guides downwards and out through the combustion chamber. Press the new guides into the cylinder head in the same direction until they are at the specified fitted height.
11 Examine the pushrods and rocker shaft assembly for wear, and renew them as necessary.

33 Engine reassembly - general

1 To ensure maximum life with minimum trouble from a rebuilt engine, not only must everything be correctly assembled, but it must also be spotlessly clean. All oilways must be clear, and locking washers and spring washers must be fitted where indicated. Oil all bearings and their working surfaces thoroughly with engine oil during assembly.
2 Before assembly begins, renew any bolts or studs with damaged threads and have all new components at hand ready for assembly.
3 Gather together a torque wrench, oil can,

clean rags and a set of engine gaskets, together with a new oil filter. A tube of RTV sealing compound will also be required for the joint faces that are fitted without gaskets. It is recommended that CAF 4/60 THIXO paste, obtainable from Renault dealers is used, as it is specially formulated for this purpose.

34 Crankshaft and main bearings - refitting

1 Clean the backs of the bearing shells and the bearing recesses in both the cylinder block and main bearing caps.
2 Press the bearing shells without oil holes into the caps, ensuring that the tag on the shell engages in the notch in the cap.
3 Press the bearing shells with the oil holes into the recesses in the cylinder block. If all five shells have two oil holes they may be fitted onto any location. If two of the shells only have one oil hole, these must be fitted to journals No 1 and 3 (No 1 journal being nearest the flywheel). Fit the remaining shells to any of the three remaining locations.
4 If the original main bearing shells are being re-used these must be refitted to their original locations in the block and caps.
5 Using a little grease, stick the thrust washers to each side of the centre main bearing journal in the block (photo). Ensure that the oilway grooves on each thrust washer face outwards.

34.5 Fit the thrust washers with their oilway grooves (arrowed) facing outwards

34.7 Lubricate the bearing shells, then lower the crankshaft into place

34.8 Fit the bearing caps and retaining bolts . . .

34.11 . . . and tighten the bolts to the specified torque

34.12 Measure the crankshaft endfloat using feeler gauges when installed . . .

6 Lubricate the lips of a new crankshaft oil seal and carefully slip it over the end of the crankshaft. Do this carefully as the seal lips are very delicate. Ensure that the open side of the seal faces the engine.

7 Liberally lubricate each bearing shell in the cylinder block and lower the crankshaft into position (photo).

8 Fit the bearing caps in their numbered, or, previously noted locations, so that the bearing shell locating notches in the cap and block are both on the same side (photo).

9 Fit the main bearing cap retaining bolts and make sure that the dipstick tube is in position with its bracket located under the No 2 bearing cap retaining bolt.

10 Tighten the bolts until they are moderately

35.5A Check that the arrow on the piston crown will face the flywheel when installed . . .

35.5B . . . then fit the piston-connecting rod assembly to the liner

tight, but before tightening No 1 bearing cap position the oil seal so that its face is 3.0 mm (0.12 in) inset from the outer face of the block and bearing cap. This will ensure that its sealing lip does not bear on the worn section of the journal.

11 Check that the crankshaft is free to turn and then tighten the main bearing retaining bolts to the specified torque (photo).

12 Check the crankshaft endfloat using feeler gauges inserted between the thrust washers and the side of the bearing journal (photo). If new thrust washers have been fitted the endfloat should be in accordance with the dimension given in the Specifications. If the original washers have been refitted and the endfloat is excessive, new thrust washers must be fitted. These are obtainable in a number of oversizes.

13 Finally check that the crankshaft turns reasonably freely without any tight spots.

35 Liners, pistons and connecting rods - refitting

1 If the liner protrusion and liner height variation have not already been checked, do this now using the procedure described in Section 27, before proceeding further.

2 Lay the four liners face down in a row on the bench, in their correct order. Turn them as necessary so that the flats on the edges of

liners 1 and 2 are towards each other, and the flats on liners 3 and 4 are towards each other also.

3 Lubricate the pistons and piston rings then lay each piston and connecting rod assembly with its respective liner.

4 Starting with assembly No 1, make sure that the piston rings are still spaced out at 120° to each other and clamp the piston rings using a piston ring compressor.

5 Insert the piston and connecting rod assembly into the bottom of the liner ensuring that the arrow on the piston crown faces the flywheel end of the engine (photos). In other words, if the liners are laid out as described, the arrow should face away from the other liners. Using a block of wood or hammer handle against the end of the connecting rod, tap the piston into the liner until the top of the piston is approximately 25 mm (1.0 in) away from the top of the liner.

6 Repeat this procedure for the remaining three piston and liner assemblies.

7 Turn the crankshaft so that No 1 crankpin is at the bottom of its travel.

8 Press the upper half of the big-end shell in the connecting rod and press the lower half into the cap (photo). Ensure that the tags on the shells engage with the notches on the cap and rod.

9 With the liner base seal in position, place No 1 liner, piston and connecting rod assembly into its location in the cylinder block (photo). Ensure that the arrow on the piston

35.8 Fit the bearing shells with their tags (arrowed) engaged with the cap and rod notches

35.9 Fit the liner, piston and connecting rod assemblies

35.10A Fit the bearing caps to their respective connecting rods . . .

35.10B . . . and tighten the retaining nuts to the specified torque

35.11 Retain the liners using washers, nuts and bolts

crown faces the flywheel end of the engine and the flat on the liner is positioned as described previously.

10 Liberally lubricate the crankpin journal, pull the connecting rod down and engage it with the crankpin. Check that the marks made on the cap and rod during removal are opposite the camshaft side of the engine then refit the cap and retaining nuts. The notches for the bearing shell tags in the cap and rod must be together. Tighten the connecting rod cap retaining nut to the specified torque (photos).

11 With the liner piston and connecting rod assembly installed, retain the liner using a bolt and washer screwed into the cylinder head bolt holes. This will prevent damage to the base seal due to displacement of the liner as the engine is turned (photo).

12 Repeat the foregoing procedures for the remaining piston and liner assemblies, turning the crankshaft each time to make sure it is free.

13 If the engine is in the car, refit the oil pump, sump and cylinder head.

36 Camshaft and followers - refitting

1 Lubricate the camshaft bearings and carefully insert the camshaft from the timing gear end of the engine (photo).

37.2 Use a thread locking compound on the flywheel bolts

2 Refit the retaining plate bolts and tighten them. Check that the camshaft rotates smoothly.

3 Lubricate the cam followers and insert them into their original bores in the cylinder block.

37 Flywheel or torque converter driveplate - refitting

1 Clean the flywheel and crankshaft faces, then fit the flywheel or driveplate making sure that any previously made marks are aligned.

2 Apply a few drops of thread locking compound to the retaining bolt threads, fit the bolts and tighten them in a diagonal sequence to the specified torque (photo).

38 Timing cover, gears and chain - refitting

1 Refit the Woodruff key to the crankshaft groove and then tap the crankshaft sprocket into position. Ensure that the timing mark on the sprocket is on the side facing away from the engine.

2 If the engine is in the car, turn the crankshaft until the timing notch on the

Fig. 1.23 Correct alignment of crankshaft and camshaft sprocket timing marks (Sec 38)

flywheel or torque converter is in line with the TDC mark on the bellhousing timing scale (photo 16.2). If the engine is out of the car, turn the crankshaft until Nos 1 and 4 pistons are at the very top of their travel.

3 Temporarily place the camshaft sprocket in position and turn the camshaft so that the timing marks on the sprocket faces are facing each other, and coincide with an imaginary line joining the crankshaft and camshaft centres, then remove the camshaft sprocket.

4 Fit the timing chain to the camshaft sprocket, position the sprocket in its approximate fitted position and locate the chain over the crankshaft sprocket. Position the camshaft sprocket on the camshaft and check that the marks are still aligned when there is an equal amount of slack on both sides of the chain.

36.1 Refitting the camshaft

38.7 Fit the hydraulic tensioner spacer . . .

1

38.8 . . . followed by the tensioner

Fig. 1.24 Secure the hydraulic tensioner with the bolts (arrowed), then, if the tensioner has manual presetting, release the piston using an Allen key inserted in hole B (Sec 38)

Fig. 1.25 Apply a bead of sealant paste to the timing cover and sump before fitting (Secs 38 and 40)

5 Refit the camshaft sprocket retaining bolt using a new locktab and tighten the bolt to the specified torque. Bend up the locktabs to retain the bolt.

6 If a mechanical tensioner is fitted, place it in position and locate the spring ends in the block and over the slipper arm. Refit the retaining bolt and tighten it securely with an Allen key.

7 If a hydraulic tensioner is fitted, first position the spacer on the cylinder block and retain it in place using a little grease (photo).

8 Locate the tensioner body over the plate then refit and tighten the retaining bolts (photo). If the tensioner is of the manual presetting type, release the slipper piston by turning it anti-clockwise using an Allen key inserted in the end of the tensioner body. With

the piston released, refit the small bolt to the tensioner body and secure with a new locktab. If the tensioner is of the automatic presetting type, push the slipper piston in and then release it. The piston should spring out automatically under spring pressure.

9 Ensure that the mating faces of the timing cover are clean and dry with all traces of old sealant removed and a new oil seal in place in the timing cover.

10 If there are no locating dowels for the timing cover, a gasket must be fitted. Locate the gasket on the cylinder block then fit the

timing cover inserting the bolts loosely. Oil the pulley hub and temporarily fit it on the end of the crankshaft so that the timing cover is positioned correctly then tighten the cover bolts.

11 Where locating dowels are fitted, apply a bead of CAF 4/60 THIXO paste to the timing cover joint face then position the cover over the dowels and the two studs. Refit the nuts and retaining bolts then progressively tighten them in a diagonal sequence (photo).

12 Lubricate the crankshaft pulley hub and carefully slide it onto the end of the crankshaft (photo).

13 Place the pulley in position, refit the retaining bolt and washer and tighten the bolt to the specified torque (photos).

14 If the engine is in the car, refit the sump and alternator drivebelt.

39 Oil pump - refitting

1 Enter the oil pump shaft into its location in the cylinder block and, if the engine is in the car, engage the shaft with the distributor drivegear (photo).

2 Push the pump up into contact with the block, then refit and tighten the three retaining bolts. Note that a gasket is not used.

3 If the engine is in the car, refit the sump.

38.11 Applying CAF 4/60 THIXO paste to the timing cover

38.12 Refit the crankshaft pulley hub . . .

38.13A . . . followed by the pulley . . .

38.13B . . . and retaining bolt

39.1 Refitting the oil pump

Fig. 1.26 Do not apply sealant to the shaded area if rubber seals are fitted to the end main bearing caps (Sec 40)

Note: *some models have a rubber seal at the timing chain end*

40 Sump - refitting

1 Check that the mating faces of the sump and cylinder block are perfectly clean and dry.
2 Check if rubber seals are fitted between the sump and Nos 1 and 5 main bearing caps. This is the case on Turbo models and certain other models.
3 Apply a uniform bead of CAF 4/60 THIXO paste to the sump in accordance with Fig. 1.25 or 1.26, ensuring that a liberal quantity of the paste is used at the corners. Where rubber seals are fitted leave the areas shown in Fig. 1.26 clear of paste.
4 Where applicable fit the rubber seals to Nos 1 and 5 main bearing caps.
5 Place the sump in position then refit the retaining bolts (photo). Tighten the bolts progressively and in a diagonal sequence.
6 If the engine is in the car, refit the engine steady rod, the flywheel or torque converter cover plate and, where fitted, the two wires to the engine oil level sensor. Refill the engine with the specified grade of oil. On Turbo models refit the right-hand engine mounting and air filter. Finally refit the splash shield and lower the car to the ground.

41.3A Compress the valve spring and locate the split collets . . .

40.5 Place the sump in position and secure with the retaining bolts

41 Cylinder head - reassembly and refitting

1 Lubricate the stems of the valves and insert them into their original locations. If new valves are being fitted, insert them into the locations to which they have been ground (photo).
2 Working on the first valve, fit the thrust washer to the cylinder head, followed by the valve spring and retainer. Note that the spring should be fitted with the end where the coils are closest towards the cylinder head (photos).
3 Compress the valve spring and locate the split collets in the recess in the valve stem.

41.2A Fit the thrust washer . . .

41.3B . . . noting that those for the exhaust valves (arrowed) have two curved collars

41.1 Insert the valves into their guides

Note that the collets are different for the inlet and exhaust valves (photos), the latter type having two curved collars. Release the compressor, then repeat the procedure on the remaining valves.
4 With all the valves installed, place the cylinder head flat on the bench and, using a hammer and interposed block of wood, tap the end of each valve stem to settle the components.
5 Oil the rocker shaft, then reassemble the springs, rocker arms and pedestals in the reverse order to removal, and finally fit the circlip. Check that the bolt holes in the pedestals are aligned with the recesses in the rocker shaft, and that the pedestal with the oilway (where applicable) is fitted at the flywheel end.

41.2B . . . followed by the spring and retainer

Fig. 1.27 Sectional view of the rocker pedestal (C) with oil hole (B) which must be fitted at the flywheel end of the shaft assembly (Sec 41)

Fig. 1.28 Cylinder head tightening sequence (Sec 41)

41.6 Place the gasket in position

41.7A Lower the cylinder head onto the gasket and . . .

6 Remove the cylinder liner clamps, if fitted, and make sure that the faces of the cylinder head and the cylinder block are perfectly clean. Lay a new gasket on the cylinder block with the words "Haut-Top" uppermost (photo). Do not use any kind of jointing compound.
7 Lower the cylinder head into position, insert the cylinder head bolts, and tighten them to the specified torque in the sequence shown in Fig. 1.28 (photos).
8 Install the pushrods in their original locations (photo).
9 Lower the rocker shaft assembly onto the cylinder head, making sure that the adjusting ball-ends locate in the pushrods. Install the

spring washer (convex side uppermost), nuts and bolts, and tighten them to the specified torque (photo).
10 Adjust the valve clearances, as described in Section 47 to the cold setting (see Specifi-cations).
11 If the engine is in the car refit the controls, cables and services using the reverse of the removal procedure described in Section 11, but bearing in mind the following points:
a) Tighten the exhaust front section to manifold retaining bolts so that the tension springs are coil-bound, then loosen them 1 1/2 turns each
b) Adjust the choke and accelerator cables, as described in Chapter 3

c) Adjust the drivebelt tension, as described in Chapter 2
d) Refill the cooling system, as described in Chapter 2

42 Distributor drivegear - refitting

1 Using a ring spanner on the crankshaft pulley bolt, turn the crankshaft until No 1 piston (flywheel end) is at the top of its compression stroke. This position can be established by placing a finger over No 1 plug hole and rotating the crankshaft until compression can be felt; continue turning the crankshaft until the piston reaches the top of its stroke. Use a screwdriver through the plug hole to feel the movement of the piston, but be careful not to damage the piston crown or plug threads in the cylinder head.
2 Without moving the crankshaft, position the drivegear so that its slots are at the 2 o'clock and 8 o'clock positions with the larger offset side facing away from the engine (photo).
3 Now lower the drivegear into mesh with the camshaft and oil pump driveshaft. As the gear meshes with the camshaft it will rotate anti-clockwise and should end up with its slot at right angles to the crankshaft centreline and

41.7B . . . fit the retaining bolts and tighten in the correct sequence to the specified torque

41.8 Install the pushrods in their original locations

41.9 Refit the rocker shaft assembly

42.2 Fit the distributor drivegear . . .

42.3 . . . so that the slot is at right-angles to the crankshaft centreline with its larger offset side facing the flywheel when fitted

Fig. 1.29 Fitted position of distributor drivegear (Sec 42)

D = Larger offset side

with the larger offset towards the flywheel. It will probably be a tooth out on the first attempt and will take two or three attempts to get it just right (Fig. 1.29 and photo).

43 Ancillary components - refitting

Refer to Section 10 and refit the listed components with reference to the Chapters indicated.

44 Engine - attachment to manual gearbox or automatic transmission

Refer to Section 8 and attach the engine using the reverse of the removal procedure. Apply a trace of molybdenum disulphide grease to the end of the gearbox input shaft or torque converter locator before fitting.

45 Engine - refitting

Refitting the engine, either on its own or complete with manual gearbox or automatic transmission, is a reverse of the removal

procedures contained in Sections 6 and 7. In addition bear in mind the following points:
a) *Tighten the exhaust front section-to-manifold retaining bolts so that the tension springs are coil-bound, then loosen them 1 1/2 turns each*
b) *Refill the cooling system with reference to Chapter 2*
c) *Adjust the choke and accelerator cables with reference to Chapter 3*
d) *If the drivebelt was removed, adjust its tension with reference to Chapter 2*
e) *Where applicable, refill the gearbox or automatic transmission with oil, as described in Chapter 6, and the engine, as described in Section 2 of this Chapter*

46 Engine - adjustments after major overhaul

1 With the engine and gearbox refitted to the car, make a final check to ensure that everything has been reconnected and that no rags or tools have been left in the engine compartment.
2 Make sure that the oil and water levels are topped up and then start the engine; this may take a little longer than usual as the fuel pump and carburettor float chamber may be empty.
3 As soon as the engine starts, watch for the oil pressure light to go out and check for any oil, fuel or water leaks. Don't be alarmed if there are some odd smells and smoke from parts getting hot and burning off oil deposits.
4 Allow the engine to run for approximately 20 minutes then switch it off and allow it to cool for at least 2 1/2 hours. Remove the rocker cover and re-torque the cylinder head bolts in the sequence shown in Fig. 1.28. Slacken each bolt in turn, half a turn then retighten it to the specified torque before moving on to the next bolt. After retightening, adjust the valve clearances again, as described in Section 47.
5 If new pistons, rings or crankshaft bearings have been fitted the engine must be run-in for

the first 500 miles (800 km). Do not exceed 45 mph (72 kph), operate the engine at full throttle or allow it to labour in any gear.

47 Valve clearances - adjustment

1 If the engine is in the car, remove the air cleaner or inlet duct as applicable as described in Chapter 3.
2 Detach the crankcase ventilation hose at the rocker cover and disconnect the throttle linkage return spring (photo).
3 Mark the spark plug HT lead locations and withdraw them from the spark plugs. Remove the distributor cap retaining screws or clips, and move the cap and leads to one side.
4 Undo the nuts securing the rocker cover in place, tap the cover lightly to free it then manipulate it off the studs.
5 Number the valves 1 to 8 from the flywheel end of the engine then, using a ring spanner on the crankshaft pulley bolt, turn the engine in a clockwise direction until No 8 valve is fully open (ie spring compressed).
6 Insert a feeler blade of the correct thickness for an exhaust valve (see Specifications) between the end of No 1 valve stem and the rocker arm, then adjust the rocker arm ball-end (after loosening the locknut) until the feeler blade is a firm sliding fit (photo). Tighten the locknut and recheck the adjustment, then repeat the procedure on the remaining seven valves in the following sequence.

Valve open	Valve to adjust
No 8 ex	No 1 ex
No 6 in	No 3 in
No 4 ex	No 5 ex
No 7 in	No 2 in
No 1 ex	No 8 ex
No 3 in	No 6 in
No 5 ex	No 4 ex
No 2 in	No 7 in

7 On completion, refit the rocker cover using a new gasket (photo). If the engine is in the car refit the disconnected components using the reverse of the removal sequence.

1

47.2 Throttle linkage return spring attachment on rocker cover

47.6 Adjusting the valve clearances

47.7 Refit the rocker cover using a new gasket

Fault finding - engine

Engine fails to start
☐ Discharged battery
☐ Loose battery connection
☐ Loose or broken ignition leads
☐ Moisture on spark plugs, distributor cap, or HT leads
☐ Incorrect spark plug gaps
☐ Cracked distributor cap or rotor
☐ Other ignition system fault
☐ Dirt or water in carburettor
☐ Empty fuel tank
☐ Faulty fuel pump
☐ Other fuel system fault
☐ Faulty starter motor
☐ Low cylinder compressions

Engine idles erratically
☐ Inlet manifold air leak
☐ Leaking system head gasket.
☐ Worn rocker arms, timing chain or sprockets
☐ Worn camshaft lobes
☐ Faulty fuel pump
☐ Incorrect valve clearances
☐ Loose crankcase ventilation hoses
☐ Carburettor adjustment incorrect
☐ Uneven cylinder compressions

Engine misfires
☐ Spark plugs worn or incorrectly gapped
☐ Dirt or water in carburettor
☐ Carburettor adjustment incorrect
☐ Burnt out valve
☐ Leaking cylinder head gasket
☐ Distributor cap cracked
☐ Incorrect valve clearances
☐ Uneven cylinder compressions
☐ Worn carburettor

Engine stalls
☐ Carburettor adjustment incorrect
☐ Inlet manifold air leak
☐ Ignition timing incorrect

Excessive oil consumption
☐ Worn pistons, cylinder bores or piston rings
☐ Valve guides and valve stems worn
☐ Oil leaking from rocker cover, timing cover, engine gaskets or oil seals

Engine backfires
☐ Carburettor adjustment incorrect
☐ Ignition timing incorrect
☐ Incorrect valve clearances
☐ Inlet manifold air leak
☐ Sticking valve

Chapter 2 Cooling system

For modifications, and information applicable to later models, see Supplement at end of manual

Contents

Degrees of difficulty

Easy, suitable for novice with little experience	**Fairly easy,** suitable for beginner with some experience	**Fairly difficult,** suitable for competent DIY mechanic	**Difficult,** suitable for experienced DIY mechanic	**Very difficult,** suitable for expert DIY or professional

2

Specifications

System type	Pressurised with belt-driven pump, front-mounted crossflow radiator with expansion tank, electric cooling fan, and thermostat
Thermostat opening temperature	83°C or 86°C (181°F or 187°F) depending on model
Water pump/alternator drivebelt tension	4 mm (0.16 in)
Coolant type	Ethylene glycol based antifreeze
System capacity (total)	5.5 litre (9.7 Imp pint)

1 General description

The cooling system is of the pressurised type consisting of a belt-driven pump, aluminium crossflow radiator, expansion tank, electric cooling fan and a thermostat located in the radiator top hose.

The system functions as follows: Cold coolant in the bottom of the radiator right-hand tank passes through the bottom hose to the water pump where it is pumped around the cylinder block and head passages. After cooling the cylinder bores, combustion surfaces and valve seats, the coolant reaches the underside of the thermostat, which is initially closed, and is diverted through passages in the water pump to the heater and carburettor hose outlets. After passing through the heater matrix and through passages in the carburettor body, the coolant is returned to the water pump. When the engine is cold the thermostat remains closed and the coolant circulates only through the engine, heater and carburettor. When the coolant reaches a predetermined temperature, the thermostat opens and the coolant passes through the top hose and back to the radiator. As the coolant circulates through the radiator it is cooled by the inrush of air when the car is in forward motion. Airflow is supplemented by the action of the electric cooling fan when necessary. Upon reaching the bottom right-hand side of the radiator, the coolant is now cooled and the cycle is repeated.

When the engine is at normal operating temperature the coolant expands and some of it is displaced into the expansion tank. This coolant collects in the tank and is returned to the radiator when the system cools.

The electric cooling fan mounted behind the radiator is controlled by a thermostatic switch located in the radiator side tank. At a predetermined coolant temperature the switch contacts close, thus actuating the fan.

2 Routine maintenance

At the intervals specified in the "Routine maintenance" section in the front of the manual carry out the following procedures.

1 With the engine and coolant cold, check the level in the system and if necessary top up to the maximum mark on the expansion tank

Fig. 2.1 Diagram of cooling system on Turbo models (Sec 1)

1 Engine
2 Radiator
3 Expansion tank (constant flow type on Turbo models only)
4 Heater matrix

8 Inlet manifold
11 Carburettor base
14 3.5 mm jet
T = Thermostat in top hose

(photo). With a sealed type cooling system, topping-up should only be necessary at very infrequent intervals. If this is not the case and frequent topping-up is required, it is likely there is a leak in the system. Check all hoses and joint faces for any straining or actual wetness, and rectify if necessary. If no leaks can be found it is advisable to have the system pressure tested as the leak could possibly be internal. It is a good idea to keep a check on the engine oil level as a serious internal leak can often cause the level in the sump to rise, thus confirming suspicions.

2 Carefully inspect all the hoses, hose clips and visible joint gaskets of the system for cracks, corrosion, deterioration or leakage. Renew any hoses and clips that are suspect

2.1 Topping-up coolant level

and also renew any gaskets, if necessary.
3 Carefully inspect the condition of the drivebelt and renew it if there is any sign of cracking or fraying, using the procedure described in Section 12. Check and adjust tension of the belt, as described in the same Section.
4 Drain, flush and refill the cooling system with a new antifreeze mixture as described in Sections 3, 4 and 5.

3 Cooling system - draining

Note: *The hose clips fitted in manufacture are not intended to be re-used. They are released by prising up their tabs (ratchet type) or by unwinding the tensioning key ("sardine can" type). As a last resort they may be cut off, at risk of damaging the hose. Obtain new worm drive hose clips before draining the cooling system.*

1 It is preferable to drain the cooling system when the engine is cold. If the engine is hot the pressure in the system must be released before attempting to drain the system. Place a cloth over the pressure cap of the expansion tank and slowly unscrew the cap. Wait until the pressure has escaped and then remove the cap.

2 Raise and support the front of the vehicle. Remove the engine splash shield for access to the bottom of the radiator.
3 Place a suitable container beneath the right-hand side of the radiator. Slacken the hose clip and carefully ease the bottom hose off the radiator outlet. Allow the coolant to drain into the container.
4 Now position the container beneath the cylinder block drain plug located on the crankshaft pulley end of the engine, below the water pump. Unscrew the plug and drain the coolant into the container. (The drain plug may be seen in Chapter 1, photo 6.12.)
5 If the system needs to be flushed after draining, refer to the next Section, otherwise refit the drain plug and secure the bottom hose to the radiator. Use a new hose clip if necessary.

4 Cooling system - flushing

1 With time the cooling system may gradually lose its efficiency as the radiator core becomes choked with rust, scale deposits from the water and other sediment.
2 To flush the system, first drain the coolant, as described in the previous Section.
3 Remove the radiator filler cap, insert a hose through the filler neck and allow water to circulate through the radiator until it runs clear from the bottom outlet. If, after a reasonable period, the water still does not run clear, the radiator should be flushed with a good proprietary cleaning system.
4 To flush the engine and the remainder of the system, disconnect the top hose at the water pump, place a hose in the outlet and allow water to circulate until it runs clear from the bottom hose. Also flush the expansion tank and hoses.
5 In severe cases of contamination the radiator should be reverse flushed. To do this, first remove it from the car, as described in Section 7, invert it and insert a hose in the bottom outlet. Continue flushing until clear water runs from the top hose outlet.
6 The use of chemical cleaners should only be necessary as a last resort. The regular renewal of corrosion inhibiting antifreeze should prevent severe contamination of the system. Note that as the radiator is of aluminium it is important not to use caustic soda or alkaline compounds to clean it.

5 Cooling system - filling

1 Refit the cylinder block drain plug, radiator bottom hose and any other hoses removed if the system has just been flushed.
2 Unclip the expansion tank from its location and tie it up, as high as the hose will allow, on the open bonnet.

5.3A Bleed screw located in the top hose

5.3B Bleed screws located in the heater hoses

7.4 Wiring on the radiator thermostatic switch

3 Open the bleed screws located on the top hose, heater hose(s) and where applicable the hose to the carburettor (photos).

4 Remove the plug and gasket from the top left-hand side of the radiator then fill the radiator with the appropriate mixture of water and antifreeze (see Section 6). Refit the gasket and tighten the plug.

5 Fill the rest of the cooling system by pouring the coolant in the expansion tank. Close each bleed screw in turn as soon as a continuous flow of coolant can be seen flowing from it. Fill the expansion tank to the maximum mark (MAXI) then fit the pressure cap.

6 Refit the expansion tank in its correct location.

7 Run the engine at 1500 rpm (ie a fast idle speed) until it reaches the normal operating temperature, then switch it off and allow it to cool.

8 With the engine cold check the level in the expansion tank and if necessary top it up to the MAXI mark.

6 Antifreeze mixture

1 The antifreeze should be renewed at regular intervals. This is necessary not only to maintain the antifreeze properties, but also to

7.5 Cooling fan wiring connector

prevent corrosion which would otherwise occur as the corrosion inhibitors become progressively less effective.

2 Always use a good quality ethylene glycol based antifreeze which is suitable for use in mixed cooling systems.

3 Before adding fresh antifreeze the cooling system should be completely drained, preferably flushed, and all hoses checked for security and condition.

4 Follow the antifreeze manufacturer's recommendations as to concentration, but generally a 50% solution of antifreeze will give protection down to -37°C (-34°F) and a 33% solution will give protection down to -20°C (-4°F). Do not allow the concentration of antifreeze in the system to fall below 25% regardless of the temperature or time of year.

5 After filling with antifreeze, a label should be attached to the radiator stating the type and concentration of antifreeze used and the date installed. Any subsequent topping-up should be made with the same type and concentration of antifreeze.

6 Do not use engine antifreeze in the screen washer system as it will cause damage to the vehicle paintwork. Screen washer antifreeze is available from most accessory shops.

7 Radiator - removal, inspection, cleaning and refitting

1 Disconnect the battery negative terminal and then drain the cooling system, as described in Section 3.

2 Slacken the hose clip and detach the top hose from the radiator.

3 Release the retaining clip and detach the expansion tank hose from the outlet beneath the filler cap.

4 Disconnect the two wires from the thermostatic switch on the right-hand side of the radiator (photo).

5 Disconnect the cooling fan wires at the two-pin connector (photo). Where fitted, unscrew the transmission oil cooler unions.

2

Fig. 2.2 Radiator components (Sec 7)

1 Cowling
2 Radiator
3 Mounting rubber (upper)
4 Plug and gasket
5 Retaining clip
6 Mounting rubber (lower)

7.6A Radiator top retaining clip

7.6B Removing the radiator

7.6C Radiator lower retaining peg

6 Lift up the large wire retaining clip at the top, move the radiator towards the engine and lift it upwards to disengage the two lower retaining pegs (photos). Withdraw the radiator, complete with cooling fan assembly, from the engine compartment.

7 Extensive damage should be repaired by a specialist or the unit exchanged for a new or reconditioned radiator. Clear the radiator matrix of flies and small leaves with a soft brush, or by hosing.

8 If the radiator is to be left out of the car for more than 48 hours, special precautions must be taken to prevent the brazing flux used during manufacture from reacting with the chloride elements remaining from the coolant. This reaction could cause the aluminium core to oxidize causing leakage. To prevent this,

either flush the radiator thoroughly with clean water, dry with compressed air and seal all outlets, or refill the radiator with coolant and temporarily plug all outlets.

9 Refitting the radiator is the reverse sequence to removal. Fill the cooling system, as described in Section 5, and on automatic transmission models top up the fluid, as described in Chapter 6.

8 Cooling fan assembly - removal and refitting

1 Remove the radiator as described in Section 7.

2 According to model the fan assembly bracket is either bolted or riveted to the radiator (photo). In the latter case the rivets must be drilled out to remove the bracket.

3 Unscrew the nut and slide the fan off the motor shaft noting which way round it is fitted.

4 Separate the motor from the bracket by drilling out the rivets.

5 If the motor is faulty it must be renewed as it is not possible to obtain spare parts.

6 Refitting is a reversal of removal using new rivets where required.

9 Cooling fan thermostatic switch - testing, removal and refitting

1 If the thermostatic switch, located on the right-hand side of the radiator, develops a fault it is most likely to fail open circuit. This will result in the fan motor remaining stationary even though the coolant may reach boiling point.

2 To test for a faulty thermostatic switch,

7.6D Location grommet for the radiator lower retaining peg

8.2 Cooling fan assembly mounting bolts on the radiator

Fig. 2.3 Cooling fan components (Sec 8)

1 Thermostatic switch and washer
2 Fan

3 Mounting bracket (alternative types)
4 Motor (alternative types)

9.4 Cooling fan thermostatic switch

10.1 Thermostat retaining clip

10.4 View of the thermostat in the top hose

disconnect the two switch wires and join them together with a suitable length of wire. If the fan now operates with the ignition switched on, the thermostatic switch is proved faulty and must be renewed.

3 To remove the switch, disconnect the battery negative terminal and drain the cooling system, as described in Section 3.

4 Disconnect the two wires and then unscrew the switch from the radiator. Remove the washer (photo).

5 Refitting is the reverse sequence to removal. Refill the cooling system, as described in Section 5, after refitting the switch.

10 Thermostat -
removal, testing and refitting

1 The thermostat is located in the end of the radiator top hose at the water pump and is retained by a hose clip (photo).

2 To remove the thermostat, first unscrew the expansion tank filler cap. If the engine is hot, place a cloth over the cap and unscrew it slowly allowing all the pressure to escape before removing the cap completely.

3 Place a suitable container beneath the radiator bottom hose outlet. Disconnect the bottom hose and drain approximately 1 litre (1.76 pints) of the coolant. Reconnect the bottom hose and tighten the clip.

4 Slacken the two clips on the radiator top hose adjacent to the water pump. Detach the hose from the pump outlet and withdraw the thermostat from the hose (photo).

5 To test whether the unit is serviceable, suspend it on a string in a saucepan of cold water together with a thermometer. Heat the water and note the temperature at which the thermostat begins to open. Continue heating the water until the thermostat is fully open and then remove it from the water.

6 The temperature at which the thermostat should start to open is stamped on the unit. If the thermostat does not start to open at the specified temperature, does not fully open in boiling water or does not fully close when removed from the water, then it must be discarded and a new one fitted.

7 Refitting the thermostat is the reverse sequence to removal, but make sure that the thermostat bleed hole is in the slot on the end of the water pump outlet. After fitting, fill the cooling system, with reference to Section 5.

11 Water pump -
removal and refitting

Note: *Water pump failure is indicated by water leaking from the gland at the front of the pump, or by rough and noisy operation. This is usually accompanied by excessive play of the pump spindle which can be checked by*

Fig. 2.4 Align the thermostat bleed hole with the pump outlet slot (arrowed) (Sec 10)

moving the pulley from side to side. Repair or overhaul of a faulty pump is not possible, as internal parts are not available separately. In the event of failure a replacement pump must be obtained. However if the gasket between the two halves of the water pump is the cause of a leak, it can be renewed.

1 Disconnect the battery negative terminal and then refer to Section 3 and drain the cooling system.

2 Refer to Section 12 and remove the drivebelt.

3 Undo the bolt securing the alternator adjusting arm to the pump body, remove the bolt and swing the arm clear (photo).

4 Slacken the hose clips and disconnect the hoses from the pump (photos).

11.3 Removing the alternator adjusting arm from the water pump

11.4A Disconnecting the top hose

11.4B Disconnecting the bottom hose

11.4C Heater hoses (1) and carburettor base return hose (2) on the water pump

11.4D Carburettor base feed hose on the water pump

11.5 Disconnecting the lead from the coolant temperature switch

5 Disconnect the lead from the coolant temperature switch on top of the pump body (photo).

6 Undo and remove the bolts securing the water pump to the cylinder head. Access to the bolt behind the pulley can be gained by inserting a socket bar through a hole in the pulley (photo).

7 With all the bolts removed, withdraw the pump from the cylinder head (photos). If it is stuck, strike it sharply with a plastic or hide mallet.

8 If necessary unbolt the water pump halves and prise them apart taking care not to damage the mating surfaces (photos).

9 Remove all traces of gasket from the surfaces of the water pump and cylinder head.

10 Refitting is a reversal of removal, but use new gaskets. Adjust the drivebelt tension as described in Section 12, and refill the cooling system as described in Section 5.

12 Drivebelt -
renewal and adjustment

1 The drivebelt should be checked and if necessary re-tensioned at regular intervals (see "*Routine maintenance*"). It should be renewed if it shows any signs of fraying or deterioration.

2 To remove the drivebelt, slacken the nuts at the alternator pivot mounting and at the adjustment arm.

3 Move the alternator towards the engine and slip the drivebelt off the three pulleys.

4 Fit the new drivebelt over the pulleys then lever the alternator away from the engine until it is just possible to deflect the belt using moderate finger pressure by 4 mm (0.16 in) at a point midway between the water pump and crankshaft pulleys (photo). The alternator must only be levered at the drive end bracket.

5 Hold the alternator in this position and tighten the adjusting arm bolt and nut followed by the pivot mounting nut.

6 Run the engine for approximately ten minutes and then recheck the tension.

11.6 One of the water pump mounting bolts is located behind the pulley

11.7A Removing the water pump from the cylinder head

11.7B Water pump removed from the engine

11.8A Water pump half securing bolts on the rear of the pump

11.8B The two halves of the water pump separated

12.4 Checking the drivebelt tension

13 Temperature gauge sensor - removal and refitting

1 Unscrew the expansion tank filler cap. If the engine is hot, place a cloth over the cap and unscrew it slowly allowing all the pressure to escape before removing the cap completely.

2 Place a suitable container beneath the radiator bottom hose outlet. Disconnect the bottom hose and drain approximately 1 litre (1.76 pints) of the coolant. Reconnect the hose and tighten the clip.

3 Disconnect the lead at the sensor, located on top of the water pump. Unscrew the sensor from its location.

4 Refitting is the reverse sequence to removal. Fill the cooling system, as described in Section 5, on completion.

Fault finding - cooling system

Overheating

☐ Low coolant level (this may be the result of overheating for other reasons)
☐ Drivebelt slipping or broken
☐ Radiator blockage (internal or external), or grille restricted
☐ Thermostat defective
☐ Ignition timing incorrect
☐ Carburettor maladjustment
☐ Faulty cooling fan thermostatic switch
☐ Faulty cooling fan
☐ Blown cylinder head gasket (combustion gases in coolant)
☐ Water pump defective
☐ Expansion tank pressure cap faulty
☐ Brakes binding

Overcooling

☐ Thermostat missing, defective or wrong heat range

Water loss - external

☐ Loose hose clips
☐ Perished or cracked hoses
☐ Radiator core leaking
☐ Heater matrix leaking
☐ Expansion tank pressure cap leaking
☐ Boiling due to overheating
☐ Water pump leaking
☐ Core plug leaking

Water loss internal

☐ Cylinder head gasket blown
☐ Cylinder head cracked or warped
☐ Cylinder block cracked

Corrosion

☐ Infrequent draining and flushing
☐ Incorrect antifreeze mixture or inappropriate type
☐ Combustion gases contaminating coolant

2

Notes

Chapter 3 Fuel and exhaust systems

For modifications, and information applicable to later models, see Supplement at end of manual

Contents

Degrees of difficulty

Easy, suitable for novice with little experience	**Fairly easy,** suitable for beginner with some experience	**Fairly difficult,** suitable for competent DIY mechanic	**Difficult,** suitable for experienced DIY mechanic	**Very difficult,** suitable for expert DIY or professional

Specifications

Part 1: Non-Turbo models

Air cleaner

Type . . . . Automatic or manual air temperature control with renewable paper element

Application:
956 cc and 1108 cc . . . . Champion W191
1397 cc . . . . Champion W145

Fuel filter . . . . Champion L101

Fuel pump . . . . Mechanical, driven by camshaft

Fuel tank capacity . . . . 43.0 litre (9.5 Imp gal)

Carburettor

Type . . . . Single or dual throat downdraught
Application:
C1C, 956 cc engine . . . . Zenith 32 IF 2*
C1E, 1108 cc engine . . . . Solex 32 BIS* or Zenith 32 IF 2**
C1J, 1397 cc engine . . . . Solex 32 BIS** or Zenith 32 IF 2***
C2J, 1397 cc engine . . . . Weber 32 DRT

3

Carburettor data

Zenith 32 IF 2:

	V10508*	V10509**	V10511***
Type identification number	**V10508***	**V10509****	**V10511*****
Venturi	21	23	24
Main jet	100	122	124
Idling jet	52	54	55
Air compensating jet	90 x 160	80 x 180	90 x 160
Pneumatic enrichment jet	50	80	80
Accelerator pump stroke	27.8 mm (1.1 0 in)	28.3 mm (1.11 in)	28.3 mm (1.11 in)
Accelerator pump jet	45	45	50
Accelerator pump delivery tube setting	58.0 mm (2.284 in)	6.0 mm (2.362 in)	58.0 mm (2.284 in)
Needle valve	1.25	1.25	1.25
Float height dimension	1 3.65 mm (0.537 in)	1 3.65 mm (0.537 in)	1 3.65 mm (0.537 in)
Auxiliary jet	60	70	11 0
Auxiliary jet tube setting	6.0 mm (0.236 in)	6.0 mm (0.236 in)	6.0 mm (0.236 in)
Defuming valve setting	2.0 mm (0.079 in)	2.0 mm (0.079 in)	2.0 mm (0.079 in)
Initial throttle opening (fast idle)	0.9 mm (0.035 in)	0.8 mm (0.032 in)	0.85 mm (0.034 in)
Idling speed	700 ± 25 rpm	625 ± 50 rpm	650 ± 25 rpm
CO mixture	1 ± 0.5%	1 ± 0.5%	1 ± 0.5%

Solex 32 BIS:

	836*	849**
Type identification number	**836***	**849****
Venturi	23	24
Main jet	110	112.5
Air compensating jet	145	155
Idling jet	42	40
Enrichener	50	60
Needle valve	1.3	1.6
Accelerator pump jet	40	40
Initial throttle opening (fast idle)	0.7 mm (0.028 in)	0.75 mm (0.030 in)
Defuming valve setting	3.0 ± 0.5 mm (0.118 ± 0.02 in)	3.0 ± 0.5 mm (0.118 ± 0.02 in)
Idling speed	625 ± 50 rpm	650 ± 25 rpm
CO mixture	1 ± 0.5%	1 ± 0.5%

Weber 32 DRT:

	Primary	Secondary
Venturi	23	24
Main jet	107	105
Air compensating jet	220	135
Idling jet	47	70
Emulsifier	F58	F56
Needle valve	1.75	
Float height dimension	8.0 mm (0.315 in)	
Float travel dimension	13.0 mm (0.512 in)	
Accelerator pump jet	50	
Initial throttle opening (fast idle)	0.75 mm (0.030 in)	
Choke flap pneumatic part opening setting.	3.5 mm (0.138 in)	
Defuming valve throttle opening	0.3 mm (0.012 in)	
Idling speed	700 ± 25 rpm	
CO mixture	1.5 ± 0.5%	

Torque wrench settings

	Nm	lbf ft
Exhaust pipe section clamp	40	30
Manifold retaining nuts	30	22
Fuel gauge sender unit ring nut	30	22

Part 2: Turbo models

Air cleaner

Type	Automatic air temperature control with renewable paper element
Application	Champion W109

Fuel filter

Champion L203

Fuel pump

Type	Electric, roller cell
Delivery	60 litre per hour at pressure of 2.5 bar

Fuel tank capacity

Main	43.0 litre (9.5 Imp gal)
Auxiliary	7.0 litre (1.54 Imp gal)

| Fuel pressure regulator pressure at idling | 275 ± 25 mbar |

Anti-percolation thermostatic switch temperature range . . . . 95 to 89°C (203 to 192°F)

Turbocharger

Type	Garret T2
Boost pressure	680 ± 30 mbar at 3500 rpm or 700 ± 30 mbar at 5500 rpm
Safety switch operating pressure	1100 ± 50 mbar

Carburettor

Type	Single throat downdraught, sealed
Application:	
C1J (suffix 782), 1397 cc engine	Solex 32 DIS

Carburettor data

Solex 32 DIS:

	854	931
Type identification number	854	931
Venturi	25	115
Main jet	120	115
Air compensating jet	125	135
Idling jet	45	46
Enrichener	100	80
Needle valve	1.7	1.7
Accelerator pump jet	40	40
Accelerator pump stroke	5 mm (0.20 in)	5 mm (0.20 in)
Initial throttle opening (fast idle)	0.75 mm (0.03 in) or 20°	0.75 mm (0.03 in) or 20°
Pneumatic part-opening setting	6.4 mm (0.25 in)	2.7 mm (0.11 in)
Idling speed	650 ± 50 rpm	700 ± 50 rpm
CO mixture	1.0 + 0.5 % − 0	1.5 ± 0.5%

| Torque wrench settings | As non-Turbo models |

3

Part 1: Non-Turbo models

1 General description

The fuel system consists of a fuel tank mounted under the rear of the car, mechanical fuel pump and a single or dual throat downdraught carburettor.

The mechanical fuel pump is separated by an eccentric on the camshaft and is mounted on the forward facing side of the cylinder block. The air cleaner contains a disposable paper filter element and incorporates a flap valve air temperature control system. This system allows cold air from the air cleaner main intake spout, or warm air from the exhaust manifold stove, to enter the air cleaner via a secondary intake according to the position of the flap valve. Depending on model, the flap valve may be either manually-controlled by a two position selector on the side of the air cleaner body, or automatically-controlled by a temperature sensitive wax capsule located in the intake spout.

Carburettors may be of Zenith, Solex or Weber manufacture according to model. All types incorporate a water-heated lower body

to improve fuel atomization, particularly when the engine is cold. Mixture enrichment for cold starting is by a manually-operated choke control on all models.

The exhaust system consists of three push-fit sections secured with circular clamps and a cast iron exhaust manifold. A spring-loaded semi ball and socket joint is used to connect the exhaust front pipe section to the manifold and to provide a certain degree of flexibility, thus catering for engine and exhaust system movement. A silencer is fitted to the tailpipe section of all models, with an additional silencer incorporated in the intermediate section of certain versions. The system is suspended throughout its length on rubber block type mountings.

> ⚠ **Warning: Many of the procedures in this Chapter entail the removal of fuel pipes and connections which may result in some fuel spillage. Before carrying out any operation on the fuel system, refer to the precautions given in "Safety first!" at the beginning of this manual and follow them implicitly. Petrol is a highly dangerous and volatile liquid, and the precautions necessary when handling it cannot be overstressed.**

2 Routine maintenance

At the intervals specified in the "Routine maintenance" section in the front of the manual carry out the following procedures.

1 With the car over a pit, raised on a vehicle lift or securely supported on axle stands, carefully inspect the underbody fuel pipes, hoses and unions for chafing, leaks and corrosion. Renew any pipes that are severely pitted with corrosion or in any way damaged. Renew any hoses that show signs of cracking or other deterioration.
2 Check the fuel tank for leaks, for any signs of damage, and the security of the mountings.
3 Check the exhaust system condition, as described in Section 20.
4 From within the engine compartment, check the security of all fuel hose attachments and inspect them for chafing, kinks, leaks or deterioration.
5 Clean the fuel filter in the fuel pump, as described in Section 4, and where fitted, renew the additional filter in the pump outlet

2.5 In-line fuel filter in the fuel pump outlet pipe

pipe (photo). Ensure that this filter is fitted with the arrows stamped on the filter body pointing in the direction of fuel flow.

6 Renew the air cleaner paper filter element, as described in Section 3. On models with a manually-operated air temperature control, set the control or inlet tube to the summer or winter position according to season. On models with automatically-operated air cleaner air temperature control, check the operation of the flap valve, as described in Section 3.

7 Check the operation of the accelerator and choke control linkage and lubricate the linkage, cables and accelerator pedal pivot with a few drops of engine oil.

8 Check the carburettor idle speed and mixture settings and adjust, if necessary, as described in Section 15.

Fig. 3.1 Throw-away type air cleaner and inlet duct (Sec 3)

A Summer position   B Winter position

3 Air cleaner and filter element - removal and refitting

1 If a "throw-away" type air cleaner is fitted (Fig. 3.1), disconnect the inlet duct then release the straps and lift the air cleaner from the carburettor.

2 If a conventional air cleaner is fitted, unscrew the wing nut and where applicable release the clips securing the cover. Lift off

Fig. 3.2 Cross-section of the automatic air temperature control device (Sec 3)

A Cold air inlet   D Mixed air flow
B Warm air inlet   E Wax thermostatic
C Flap   element

the cover and remove the filter element (photos).

3 Clean the inside of the air cleaner body and fit a new filter if the old one is dirty or has exceeded its service life (see Routine maintenance). Refit the top cover and secure with the wing nut.

4 To remove the air cleaner body from the engine proceed as follows:

Zenith or Solex carburettor

5 Undo the two nuts securing the air cleaner to the rocker cover and the bolt securing the air cleaner to the left-hand rear support bracket (photos). Note the arrangement of rubber spacer, washers and sleeve under each front mounting nut.

3.2A Unscrew the wing nut . . .

3.2B . . . release the clips . . .

3.2C . . . then lift off the cover and remove the filter element

3.5A Air cleaner mounting on the rocker cover

3.5B Unscrew the bolt from the left-hand rear support bracket

3.6 Removing the air cleaner assembly

3.15 Manually-operated air temperature control on the air cleaner inlet

4.4A Removing the fuel pump cover . . .

4.4B . . . and dome filter

6 Detach the hot air duct from the stove on the exhaust manifold and lift the air cleaner assembly off the engine (photo).

Weber carburettor

7 Remove the air cleaner top cover and filter element, as previously described.
8 Undo the nut securing the air cleaner body to the rocker cover, noting the arrangement of rubber spacer, washers and sleeve under the nut.
9 Undo the three nuts securing the air cleaner body to the top of the carburettor. Detach the hot air duct from the stove on the exhaust manifold, detach the peg on the side of the body from the support bracket and lift up the air cleaner. Disconnect the crankcase ventilation hose and remove the air cleaner from the car. Recover the gasket.

All models

10 If the air cleaner is equipped with an automatic air temperature control device, this may be tested as follows:
11 First remove the air filter element, if still in place, and the hot air duct.
12 Immerse the air cleaner body in water at 26°C (79°F) or less, ensuring that the wax capsule in the intake spout is completely submerged. After 5 minutes observe the position of the flap valve which should be blanking off the cold air intake.
13 Now repeat the test in water at 36°C (97°F) and after 5 minutes check that the flap is blanking off the hot air intake. If the flap valve

does not operate as described at the specified temperatures, the wax capsule control assembly is faulty and must be renewed.
14 After completing the tests, dry off the air cleaner body and refit the hot air duct.
15 Refitting the air cleaner and element is the reverse sequence of removal. On models with a manually-operated air temperature control, set the flap valve to the summer or winter setting (photo), as applicable, after refitting.

4 Fuel pump - testing and cleaning

1 To test the fuel pump on the engine temporarily disconnect the outlet pipe which leads to the carburettor, and hold a wad of rag over the pump outlet while an assistant spins the engine on the starter. *Keep the hands away from the electric cooling fan.* Regular spurts of fuel should be ejected as the engine turns.
2 The pump can also be tested by removing it, but leaving the inlet and return pipes connected. Hold the wad of rag by the pump outlet. Operate the pump lever by hand and if the pump is in a satisfactory condition a strong jet of fuel should be ejected from the pump outlet as the lever is released. If this is not the case, check that fuel will flow from the inlet pipe when it is held below tank level, if so the pump is faulty or the filter blocked.

3 To clean the pump filter, first disconnect the fuel return pipe from the cover.
4 Remove the screws, lift off the cover and withdraw the flat and dome filters (photos). Clean the filters and brush or wipe out any dirt and sediment from the pump interior.
5 Reassemble the components in the reverse order of dismantling, but make sure that the retaining screws are not overtightened. If crimp type retaining clips were used to secure the fuel pipes, these should be replaced by screw type clips when reassembling.

5 Fuel pump - removal and refitting

1 Disconnect the battery negative terminal.
2 Note the location of the fuel inlet, outlet and return pipes then disconnect them from the pump (photo).
3 Unscrew the nut and bolt together with washers and withdraw the fuel pump from the cylinder block (photos).
4 Unscrew the bottom bolt and withdraw the insulating block over the stud (photo).
5 Thoroughly clean the mating faces of the pump and cylinder block then fit a new insulating block and tighten the bottom bolt.
6 Refit the fuel pump and tighten the nut and bolt. Depending on the position of the camshaft some initial pressure may be required to depress the operating lever as the pump is being fitted.

3

5.2 Pipe connections on the fuel pump showing flow direction arrows

5.3A Unscrewing the fuel pump mounting nut

5.3B Removing the fuel pump

5.4 Removing the fuel pump insulating block

7 Reconnect the fuel pipes to their original positions, as noted during removal. If crimp type retaining clips were used to secure the fuel pipes, these should be replaced by screw type clips.

8 Reconnect the battery negative terminal.

6 Fuel tank - removal, servicing and refitting

1 A drain plug is not provided on the fuel tank and it is therefore preferable to carry out the removal operation when the tank is nearly empty. Before proceeding, disconnect the battery negative terminal and then syphon or hand pump the remaining fuel from the tank.

2 Jack up the rear of the car and securely support it on axle stands. Chock the front wheels.

3 Lift the rear seat cushion and fold it forward then prise out the plastic cover for access to the fuel gauge sender unit.

4 Disconnect the electrical multi-plug and tape it to the rear seat floor.

5 Disconnect the fuel feed and return pipes leaving the vent pipe still attached.

6 Disconnect the handbrake cable from the primary rod adjusting yoke with reference to Chapter 8 and tie the cable to the rear of the car.

7 Unbolt the exhaust downpipe from the

Fig. 3.3 Fuel tank and filler neck components (Secs 6 and 7)

The vent pipe dimension E must be 5.0 mm (0.2 in)

manifold with reference to Section 19 then tie it as far forward as it will go on its mountings without damaging them.

8 Disconnect the short length of hose connecting the filler neck to the rear of the fuel tank.

9 Disconnect the tank vent pipes.

10 Take the weight of the tank on a suitable jack with a block of wood interposed. The plastic tank is not heavy so alternatively an assistant could support it.

11 Unscrew the mounting bolts and lower the tank from the underbody (photo).

12 If the tank is contaminated with sediment or water, remove the sender unit, as described in Section 8, and swill the tank out with clean fuel. If the tank is damaged, or leaks, it should be repaired by a specialist or, alternatively, renewed.

13 Refitting the tank is the reverse sequence to removal.

7 Fuel tank filler neck - removal and refitting

1 Carry out the procedure described in Section 6 paragraphs 1 and 2. Remove the right-hand rear wheel, the spare wheel and the spare wheel carrier.

2 Disconnect the short length of hose connecting the filler neck to the rear of the fuel tank.

3 Disconnect the tank vent pipes.

4 Open the filler lid and remove the filler cap.

5 Undo the screws and remove the plastic filler head (photo). Disconnect the vent pipes.

6 Remove the mounting bolts and withdraw the filler neck from the car.

7 Refitting is a reversal of removal, but when fitting the vent pipe to the filler head ensure that there is a gap as shown in Fig. 3.3.

8 Fuel gauge sender unit - removal and refitting

1 Disconnect the battery negative terminal.

2 Lift the rear seat cushion and fold it forward then prise out the plastic cover for access to the sender unit (photo).

3 Disconnect the electrical multi-plug and tape it to the rear seat floor.

4 Disconnect the fuel feed, return and vent pipes.

5 Unscrew the plastic ring nut. To do this it is recommended that a removal tool is made to the dimensions shown in Fig. 3.4. Do not use a screwdriver and hammer to loosen the nut otherwise there is a risk of damage to both the nut and the fuel tank.

6.11 Fuel tank mounting bolt

7.5 Plastic filler head

8.2 Fuel gauge sender unit viewed through the access hole

Fig. 3.4 Fuel gauge sender unit removal tool dimensions - in millimetres (Sec 8)

6 Withdraw the sender unit from the tank followed by the special gasket.
7 Refitting is a reversal of removal, but use a new gasket if the old one is damaged or shows signs of deterioration.

9 Accelerator cable - removal and refitting

1 Remove the air cleaner assembly, as described in Section 3, then disconnect the throttle/cable return spring (photo).
2 From inside the car release the cable end fitting, which is a push fit in the accelerator pedal rod.
3 At the carburettor, for Zenith and Solex types slacken the clamp bolt and remove the outer cable from the bracket then release the inner cable end fitting from the throttle lever. For the Weber type remove the spring clip from the ferrule (noting its location groove), remove the ferrule from the bracket then release the inner cable end fitting from the bellcrank.
4 According to model, the cable may be secured to a bracket attached to the brake master cylinder or engine compartment bulkhead, or it may be retained by a circlip adjacent to its bulkhead grommet. Disconnect the cable, depending on its method of retention and withdraw it from the car.
5 Refitting the cable is the reverse sequence

Fig. 3.5 Fuel gauge sender unit components (Sec 8)

A Ring nut   B Sender unit   C Gasket

to removal. Before finally securing the outer cable to the support bracket on the manifold, adjust its position so that there is a small amount of slack in the cable when the throttle is closed.

10 Accelerator pedal - removal and refitting

1 Working inside the car, release the accelerator cable end fitting, which is a push fit in the pedal rod (photo).
2 Undo the bolt securing the pedal assembly to the bulkhead and withdraw it from inside the car.
3 Refitting is the reverse sequence of removal.

9.1 Throttle/cable return spring

10.1 Accelerator pedal and cable end fitting (arrowed)

11 Choke cable - removal and refitting

1 Disconnect the battery negative terminal.
2 Remove the air cleaner assembly as described in Section 3.
3 Prise out and remove the spring clip securing the outer cable to the bracket on the carburettor (photo).
4 Release the inner cable spring loop from the choke operating linkage.
5 Remove the screw securing the choke control knob assembly to the facia and withdraw the assembly (photos).
6 Disconnect the warning lamp lead, the inner and outer cable and remove the assembly.
7 Prise out the bulkhead grommet then

11.3 Choke cable attachment to the carburettor

11.5A Remove the screw . . .

11.5B . . . and withdraw the choke control knob assembly

Fig. 3.6 Temporary limit stop (1) fitted to new choke knob assemblies (Sec 11)

12.1 Left-hand side view of the Zenith 32 IF 2 carburettor

12.2 Front view of the Zenith 32 IF 2 carburettor

withdraw the cable into the engine compartment and remove it.

8 Refitting is a reversal of removal, but initially place the control knob in the position shown in Fig. 3.6 then adjust the outer cable at the carburettor end so that the choke valve is fully open. New choke knob assemblies in fact incorporate a temporary limit stop at this position, and, after the cable adjustment, the knob must be pushed right down to break the stop.

12 Zenith carburettor - description and identification

The Zenith 321F2 carburettor is a single throat downdraught type and is fitted to the C1 C 956 cc engine, the C1 E 1108 cc engine and the C1J 1397 cc engine (photos). The type identification number is stamped on the float chamber body and reference should be made to this number before consulting the Specifications for repair or adjustment data.

The carburettor functions as follows: Fuel, maintained at a constant level in the float chamber by the float and needle valve, passes through the main jet where it reaches the emulsion tube.

Air is drawn through the air calibration jet to mix with the fuel in the emulsion tube. The vacuum created in the main and secondary venturis, according to engine speed and load, causes this emulsified mixture to be discharged into the airstream through the carburettor.

The calibration of the main and air jets and the shape of the venturi ensures that this emulsified mixture is in the right proportions at all engine speeds.

Under conditions of high engine speed, high engine load or acceleration, additional enrichment is provided by a pneumatic enrichment device and by an accelerator pump. The pneumatic enrichment device

senses high manifold vacuum below the throttle valve and opens an additional fuel circuit calibrated by a jet. A tube immersed in the float chamber and also fitted with a jet supplies fuel through the auxiliary jet tube when the vacuum rises above the throttle valve. Movement of the throttle linkage actuates the accelerator pump assembly through a series of levers. The pump, consisting of two pistons, springs and two valves, pumps fuel to the delivery tube where it is injected into the airstream.

When the engine is idling, the high manifold vacuum below the throttle valve draws fuel from the float chamber to the idling jet. The fuel is emulsified with air drawn through a calibrated jet and atomized as it is discharged into the airstream below the throttle valve. As the throttle is opened during the progression stage, the mixture is discharged through additional holes. The strength of the mixture is controlled by the mixture adjusting screw.

A manually-operated cold start (choke) control is used to provide the necessary rich mixture from starting. When the choke knob is pulled out the choke flap is closed by the action of the linkage. When the engine is cranking, high vacuum is created below the choke flap and a very rich mixture is discharged. The linkage also opens the throttle valve by a predetermined amount so that the engine will run at a fast idle speed.

13 Solex carburettor - description and identification

The solex 32BIS carburettor is a single throat downdraught type and is fitted to the C1E 1108 cc engine and the C1J 1397 cc engine. The carburettor type identification number is stamped to a plate attached to one of the float chamber retaining screws.

The function of the unit is as follows: Fuel, maintained at a constant level in the float chamber by the float and needle valve, passes through the main jet to the emulsion tube. The fuel is emulsified with air drawn in through the air compensating jet. The vacuum created in the carburettor venturi causes the emulsified

mixture to be discharged and atomized by the air passing through the venturi. The calibration of the main and air jets and the shape of the venturi ensures that this emulsified mixture is in the right proportions at all engine speeds.

Under condition of high engine speed, high engine load or acceleration, additional enrichment is provided by a full throttle enrichment device and an accelerator pump. The diaphragm of the full throttle enrichment device moves under the influence of manifold vacuum and spring pressure to open an additional fuel circuit calibrated by a jet. This provides an additional fuel mixture at high engine speed. The accelerator pump is operated by a cam and rod connected to the throttle valve spindle. The necessary rich mixture needed for acceleration is provided by the accelerator pump diaphragm which ejects a stream of neat fuel through the discharge nozzle whenever the throttle is operated.

When the engine is idling, the high manifold vacuum below the throttle valve draws fuel from the float chamber to the idling jet. The fuel is emulsified with air drawn through a calibrated orifice and atomized as it is discharged into the airstream below the throttle valve. The strength of this mixture is controlled by the mixture adjusting screw. An additional idling circuit is also used, whereby an emulsified mixture of fuel from the auxiliary jet and air from a calibrated orifice are mixed with air from a drilling in the venturi wall. This mixture is regulated by the volume control screw before being discharged below the throttle plate. This circuit allows a fine degree of engine idling speed adjustment via the volume control screw without upsetting the mixture strength to any degree.

A slotted bypass machined in line with the higher edge of the throttle valve is supplied with an emulsified mixture in the same way as the main idling circuit. This provides the correct mixture strength during progression from the idling phase to the main jet phase.

A manually-operated cold start (choke) control is used to provide the necessary rich mixture from starting. When the choke knob is pulled out the choke flap is closed by the

Fig. 3.7 Idle speed screw (A) and mixture adjustment screw (B) on the Zenith 32 IF 2 carburettor (Sec 15)

Fig. 3.8 Idle speed screw (A) and mixture adjustment screw (B) on the Solex 32 BIS carburettor (Sec 15)

Fig. 3.9 Idle speed screw (A) and mixture adjustment screw (B) on the Weber 32 DRT carburettor (Sec 15)

action of the linkage. When the engine is cranking, high vacuum is created below the choke flap and a very rich mixture is discharged. The linkage also opens the throttle valve by a predetermined amount so that the engine will run at a fast idle speed.

14 Weber carburettor - description and identification

The Weber 32 DRT carburettor is a dual throat downdraught type and is fitted to the C2J 1397 cc engine. The type identification number is stamped on the carburettor lower flange and reference should be made to this number before consulting the Specifications for repair or adjustment data.

The carburettor functions as follows: During normal running, fuel maintained at a constant level in the float chamber by the float and needle valve passes through the main jet to the emulsion tubes.

Air is drawn through the air calibration jets to mix with the fuel in the emulsion tubes. The vacuum created in the main and secondary venturis, according to engine speed and load causes this emulsified mixture to be discharged into the airstream through the carburettor. The calibration of the main and air jets and the shape of the venturi ensures that this emulsified mixture is in the right proportions at all engine speeds.

Under conditions of high engine speed, high engine load or acceleration, additional enrichment is provided by a pneumatic enrichment device and by an accelerator pump. Under the action of manifold vacuum and spring pressure a diaphragm in the pneumatic enrichment device opens a valve to allow fuel, calibrated by a jet, to enter the main jet circuit to the primary throat. Under full load and at high engine speed, the vacuum created in the venturi of the secondary throat draws an emulsified mixture of fuel and air from the secondary enrichment

jets and discharges it into the airstream above the secondary venturi. The accelerator pump is actuated by movement of the throttle valve to inject fuel into the primary throat via a discharge nozzle.

When the engine is idling the high manifold vacuum below the throttle valve draws fuel from the float chamber to the idling jet. The fuel is emulsified with air drawn through a calibrated jet and atomized as it is discharged into the airstream below the throttle valve. As the throttle is opened during the progression stage, the mixture is discharged through additional holes. The strength of the mixture is controlled by the mixture adjusting screw.

A manually-operated cold start (choke) control is used, operating on the primary throat only, to provide the necessary rich mixture for starting. When the choke knob is pulled out, the choke flap is closed by the action of the linkage. With the engine cranking, high vacuum is created below the choke flap and a very rich mixture is discharged. The linkage also opens the primary throat throttle valve by a predetermined amount so that the engine will run at a fast idle, but holds the secondary

Fig. 3.10 A long screwdriver is required to reach the idle speed screw (A) on the Weber 32 DT carburettor (Sec 15)

throat throttle valve closed while the choke is in operation. A pneumatically-controlled cold start device allows manifold vacuum to act on a diaphragm connected to the choke flap. Under certain conditions this "override" device alters the position of the choke flap on demand, thus altering the strength of the cold start mixture.

15 Carburettor - idle speed and mixture adjustment

1 The procedure for idle speed and mixture adjustment is the same on each of the three carburettor types that may be fitted. Refer to the accompanying illustrations and identify the carburettor type fitted and the adjustment screw locations. Note that on the Weber carburettor, the mixture adjustment screw is contained in an extension housing attached to the side of the carburettor body and a 200 to 250 mm (7.87 to 9.84 in) long screwdriver will be required to adjust the idle speed screw.
2 Before carrying out the following adjustments, ensure that the spark plugs are in good condition and correctly gapped and that, where applicable, the contact breaker points and ignition timing settings are correct.
3 Connect a tachometer to the engine in accordance with the manufacturer's instructions if one is not already fitted to the car. The use of an exhaust gas analyser (CO

Fig. 3.11 Extension housing on the Weber 32 DRT carburettor for the mixture adjustment screw (B) (Sec 15)

1 Tamperproof cap

3

15.6 Idle speed screw location on the Zenith 32 IF 2 carburettor

16.6 Disconnect the fuel inlet pipe

16.7 Crankcase ventilation hose attachment to the Zenith 32 IF 2 carburettor

meter) is also preferable, although not essential. If a CO meter is available this should also be connected in accordance with the maker's recommendations.

4 Before proceeding with the adjustments, remove the tamperproof cap (if fitted) over the mixture adjustment screw by hooking it out with a scriber or small screwdriver.

5 Run the engine until it reaches normal operating temperature. Increase the engine speed to 2000 rpm for 30 seconds and repeat this at three minute intervals during the adjustment procedure. This will ensure that any excess fuel is cleared from the inlet manifold.

6 With the engine idling, turn the idle speed screw until the engine is idling at the specified speed (photo).

7 Turn the mixture adjustment screw clockwise to weaken the mixture until the engine screw just starts to drop or the tickover becomes lumpy. Now turn the screw slowly anti-clockwise to richen the mixture until the maximum engine speed is obtained consistent with even running. If a CO meter is being used, turn the mixture adjustment screw as necessary to obtain the specified CO content.

8 Return the engine idling speed to the specified setting by means of the idle speed screw.

9 Repeat the above procedure a second time and then switch off the engine and disconnect the instruments.

16 Carburettor - removal and refitting

1 Unscrew the filler cap on the cooling system expansion tank. If the engine is hot, place a rag over the cap and unscrew it slowly, allowing all the pressure in the system to be released before completely removing the cap.

2 Place a suitable container beneath the radiator bottom hose outlet. Disconnect the hose and drain approximately 1 litre (1.76 pint) of the coolant. Refit the hose and tighten the clip.

3 Refer to Section 3, and remove the air cleaner assembly.

4 On Zenith and Solex carburettors disconnect the accelerator cable with reference to Section 9. On the Weber carburettor prise the accelerator bellcrank rod ball socket off the stud on the carburettor throttle linkage.

5 Disconnect the choke cable from the carburettor with reference to Section 11.

6 Disconnect the fuel inlet pipe from the carburettor and plug the pipe end after removal (photo).

7 Disconnect the crankcase ventilation hose(s) and vacuum pipe(s) (photo).

8 Slacken the clips and remove the coolant hoses from their outlets on the base of the carburettor.

9 Unscrew the mounting nuts, remove the washers and withdraw the carburettor from the inlet manifold. Recover the set of gaskets and where applicable the heat shield from the manifold studs (photos).

10 Refitting is a reversal of removal, bearing in mind the following points:
a) Ensure that the mating faces of the carburettor and heat shield are clean and use a new gasket set
b) If crimp type clips were used to secure the coolant or fuel hoses these should be replaced by the screw type clips
c) Adjust the position of the choke and accelerator cables in their support bracket clips to give a small amount of free play at rest, consistent with full travel of the relevant linkage
d) Refill the cooling system, with reference to Chapter 2

17 Carburettor - overhaul

1 Under normal circumstances, overhaul means removing the fixing screws and separating the main bodies of the carburettor so that the float chamber can be cleaned out and the jets and other passages cleaned with compressed air.

2 If the carburettor has been in service for a high mileage or the throttle spindles and their

16.9A Unscrew the mounting nuts and remove the carburettor . . .

16.9B . . . followed by the set of gaskets . . .

16.9C . . . and heat shield

Fig. 3.12 Zenith carburettor overhaul (Sec 17)

E Pneumatic enrichment device
Gg Main jet   i Accelerator pump jet
g Idling jet   k Venturi

bushes have become worn, it is recommended that a new carburettor is obtained. It is unlikely that the individual parts will be available to recondition the carburettor yourself, and the cost involved in purchasing a new unit will soon be offset by the increase in fuel economy.
3 When reassembling the carburettor, carry out the following adjustments as work proceeds and use all the new gaskets, seals and other items supplied in the special repair kit for each carburettor.
4 It is necessary to remove the carburettor from the engine to carry out the following adjustments.

Zenith carburettors

Initial throttle opening (fast idle) adjustment

5 Turn the choke operating cam on the side of the carburettor by hand as far as it will go, so that the choke flap is fully closed.
6 A twist drill or suitable rod having a diameter equal to the initial throttle opening setting given

Fig. 3.15 Auxiliary jet tube setting - Zenith carburettor (Sec 17)

W Specified auxiliary jet tube setting dimension

Fig. 3.13 Initial throttle opening adjustment - Zenith carburettor (Sec 17)

M.S. 787 Gauge rod equal to specified initial throttle opening setting
23 Choke operating cam fully open
24 Fast idle adjusting screw

in the Specifications, should just slide between the throttle valve and the venturi wall (Fig. 3.13).
7 If adjustment is necessary, slacken the locknut and turn the fast idle adjusting screw to obtain the special setting. Tighten the locknut when adjustment is complete (photo).

Float height adjustment

8 Turn the carburettor top cover upside down.
9 Measure the distance between the upper face of the needle valve body washer and the end of the needle valve (Fig. 3.14). If the measured dimension is greater than specified, tighten the needle valve body to compress the washer until the dimension is correct. If the measured dimension is less than specified, renew the washer and tighten the needle valve body until the correct dimension is obtained.

Auxiliary jet tube (Econostat) setting

10 Measure the distance between the top of the carburettor venturi and the top of the tube (Fig. 3.15).

Fig. 3.16 Accelerator pump delivery tube setting - Zenith carburettor (Sec 17)

Y Specified delivery tube height setting
Fuel should strike diffuser (K) in the zone indicated (L)

17.7 Fast idle adjusting screw location on the Zenith 32 IF 2 carburettor

Fig. 3.14 Float height adjustment - Zenith carburettor (Sec 17)

V Specified float height dimension

11 If necessary bend the tube up or down slightly to obtain the specified dimension.

Accelerator pump delivery tube setting

12 Measure the distance between the end of the tube and the bottom of the carburettor mounting flange. If necessary bend the tube slightly to achieve the specified setting.
13 Also make sure that the jet of fuel that flows from the tube strikes the diffuser in the position shown in Fig. 3.16. Again bend the tube slightly as required.

Fig. 3.17 Accelerator pump stroke - Zenith carburettor (Sec 17)

2 Pump operating rod adjusting nut
9 Fuel delivery valve
Z Specified accelerator pump stroke dimension

3

Fig. 3.18 Defuming valve adjustment - Zenith carburettor (Sec 17)

X Specified defuming valve setting
Lower illustration indicates desired free play between blade and lifting peg with choke flap closed

Accelerator pump stroke

14 With the carburettor top cover removed, withdraw the fuel delivery valve.

15 With the choke flap open and the throttle valve fully closed, measure the depth between the delivery valve locating face and the bottom of the piston (Fig. 3.17).

16 Turn the nut on the pump operating rod as necessary to obtain the specified dimension.

Defuming valve adjustment

17 With the throttle valve open in the idling position the defuming valve on the float chamber should also be open by the amount shown in Fig. 3.18. With the choke flap closed, the valve should also be closed and a small amount of free play should exist between the spring blade and the lifting peg. Bend the spring blade as necessary to achieve these conditions.

Fig. 3.21 Defuming valve adjustment - Solex carburettor (Sec 17)

X Specified defuming valve setting

Fig. 3.19 Pneumatic cold start device choke flap opening - Zenith carburettor (Sec 17)

1 Operating rod
2 Mounting bracket
3 Specified choke flap opening

Pneumatically-controlled cold start device adjustment

18 On certain Zenith carburettors a vacuum diaphragm is used to control the opening of the choke flap when the choke is in operation. Adjustment of the unit is as follows:

19 Move the choke linkage by hand to the fully closed position. A twist drill or suitable rod having a diameter equal to the specified choke flap opening dimension should just fit between the edge of the flap and the venturi wall (Fig. 3.19). Bend the vacuum diaphragm mounting bracket as necessary to achieve the specified dimension.

Fig. 3.22 Weber carburettor overhaul (Sec 17)

a Air compensating jets
Gg Main jet
g Idling jet
i Accelerator pump jet
k Venturis

Fig. 3.20 Solex carburettor overhaul (Sec 17)

A Idle speed screw
a Air compensating jet
B Mixture adjustment screw
Gg Main jet
g Idling jet
K Venturi
i Accelerator pump jet

Solex carburettors

Initial throttle opening (fast idle) adjustment

20 Turn the carburettor upside down and turn the choke linkage by hand as far as it will go, so that the choke flap is fully closed.

21 A twist drill or suitable rod having a diameter equal to the specified initial throttle opening should just slide between the throttle valve and the venturi wall.

22 If adjustment is necessary, remove the tamperproof cap (where fitted) and turn the fast idle adjusting screw as necessary to obtain the specified setting.

Defuming valve adjustment

23 With the choke flap fully open and the throttle valve against the idling stop, the defuming valve should be open by an amount equal to the specified defuming valve stroke. If adjustment is required, bend the defuming valve lever as necessary (Fig. 3.21)

Weber carburettors

Float level adjustment

24 With the float chamber cover held vertically so that the float just closes the fuel needle valve without causing the valve ball to enter the housing, the dimension A in Fig. 3.23 should be as specified. Note that the cover gasket should be in position. Bend the tag of the float arm that contacts the needle valve if adjustment is necessary.

25 Allow the float to hang under its own weight and measure dimension B in Fig. 3.23. Bend the float stop tag as necessary to achieve the specified dimension.

Fig. 3.23 Float level adjustment - Weber carburettor (Sec 17)

1 Needle valve
2 Needle valve ball
3 Float arm tag
4 Float arm tag end must remain at right-angles to the valve ball
5 Float stop tag
A Specified float height dimension
B Specified float travel dimension

Initial throttle opening (fast idle) adjustment

26 Turn the carburettor upside down and turn the choke linkage by hand as far as it will go, so that the choke flap is fully closed.

27 A twist drill or suitable rod having a

Fig. 3.26 Choke flap pneumatic part opening setting - Weber carburettor (Sec 17)

1 Operating rod
2 Adjuster screw
3 Twist drill equal to the specified choke flap pneumatic part opening setting dimension

Fig. 3.24 Initial throttle opening adjustment - Weber carburettor (Sec 17)

M.S. 787 Gauge rod equal to specified initial throttle opening
1 Fast idle adjusting screw

diameter equal to the specified initial throttle opening should just slide between the throttle valve and the venturi wall (Fig. 3.24).

28 If adjustment is required, slacken the locknut and turn the fast idle adjusting screw on the linkage as necessary. Tighten the locknut after adjustment.

Defuming valve adjustment

29 With the carburettor upside down and the choke flap open, press the defuming valve rod down as far as it will go (Fig. 3.25).

30 In this position a twist drill or suitable rod have a diameter equal to the specified defuming valve throttle opening should just fit between the throttle valve and venturi wall.

31 Alter the position of the nuts of the defuming valve rod as necessary to achieve the correct setting.

Choke flap pneumatic part open setting

32 Move the choke linkage by hand to the fully closed position and push the operating rod as far as it will go into the vacuum diaphragm unit (Fig. 3.26). In this position a twist drill or suitable rod having a diameter

18.2A Swivel the choke control angled lever clear . . .

Fig. 3.25 Defuming valve adjustment - Weber carburettor (Sec 17)

M.S. 787 Gauge rod equal to the specified defuming valve throttle opening dimension
1 Defuming valve rod
E Defuming valve rod nut

equal to the choke flap pneumatic part open setting should just fit between the choke flap and venturi wall.

33 If adjustment is necessary, turn the small screw in the vacuum unit cover as required.

18 Carburettor - cleaning

3

Note: This Section describes dismantling the Zenith carburettor for cleaning of the float chamber and jets. The procedure is basically the same for Solex and Weber carburettors although different components are involved.

1 Remove the carburettor as described in Section 16 then clean the exterior with paraffin.

2 Using a screwdriver depress the defuming valve rod and swivel the angled lever (from the choke control) away from the top cover. Turn the plastic cap through 90° and remove it from the tip of the defuming valve rod (photos).

3 Undo the top cover retaining screws then

18.2B . . . and remove the plastic cap

18.3A Undo the retaining screws . . .

18.3B . . . and lift off the cover

18.4 Extract the plastic spacer and float

lift the cover from the main body (photos). Remove the gasket.

4 Extract the plastic spacer and lift out the float and pivot (photo).

5 Unscrew the plug from the bottom outside of the float chamber then insert a screwdriver and unscrew the main jet (photo).

6 Unscrew the idling jet from the throttle lever side of the carburettor (photo).

7 Unscrew the needle valve from the top cover (photo).

8 Using paraffin or preferably clean fuel, clean all sediment from the float chamber. Clean the main body and top cover then use low air pressure from a tyre pump or air line to clear all internal passages (photo).

9 Reassembly is a reversal of the dismantling procedure using a new gasket, but make all the necessary adjustments as described in Section 17. Refit the carburettor with reference to Section 16.

19 Inlet and exhaust manifolds - removal and refitting

1 Remove the carburettor as described in Section 16.

2 Disconnect the brake servo vacuum hose and the crankcase ventilation hose from the inlet manifold (photos).

3 Remove the starter motor protective shield with reference to Chapter 11.

4 Remove the hot air ducting then unbolt the metal tube and air cleaner support bracket (photo).

5 Unscrew the nut and withdraw the heat shield from the exhaust manifold (photo).

6 Unscrew the two nuts, washers and tension springs securing the exhaust front pipe to the manifold (photo). Slide the flange plate off the manifold studs to separate the joint.

7 Progressively unscrew the nuts securing the manifold assembly to the cylinder head and remove the washers (photos).

8 Withdraw the manifold assembly from the studs on the cylinder head (photo). Remove the gasket.

9 Refitting the manifold assembly is the reverse sequence of removal. Ensure that the cylinder head and manifold mating faces are clean and use a new gasket. Tighten the

18.5 Removing the main jet

18.6 Idling jet location

18.7 Needle valve location in the top cover

18.8 Top view of the main body with cover removed

19.2A Brake servo vacuum hose connection to the inlet manifold

19.2B Crankcase ventilation hose connection to the inlet manifold

19.4 Hot air tube and air cleaner support bracket

19.5 Removing the heat shield

19.6 Exhaust front pipe to manifold flange plate and tension springs

manifold nuts to the specified torque and tighten the front pipe flange nuts so that the springs are coil-bound then loosen them by 1½ turns. Refit the carburettor with reference to Section 16.

20 Exhaust system - checking

1 The exhaust system should be examined for leaks, damage and security at regular intervals (see Routine maintenance). To do this, apply the handbrake and allow the engine to idle. Lie down on each side of the car in turn and check the full length of the exhaust system for leaks while an assistant

temporarily places a wad of cloth over the end of the tailpipe. If a leak is evident, stop the engine and use a proprietary repair kit to seal it. If the leak is excessive, or damage is evident, renew the section. Check the rubber mountings for deterioration, and renew them if necessary.

21 Exhaust system - removal and refitting

1 To remove the system, jack up the front and/or the rear of the car and support it securely on axle stands. Alternatively drive the front or rear wheels up on ramps.
2 The system consists of three sections

which can be individually removed. If the intermediate section is to be removed it will, however, be necessary to remove the front or rear section also.
3 To remove the rear or intermediate sections of the system, unscrew the retaining clamp nut and bolt and tap the clamp clear of the joint (photos).
4 Release the mounting hooks from the rubber mounting blocks and twist the section clear (photos). If the joint is stubborn, liberally apply penetrating oil and leave it to soak. Tap the joint with a hammer and it should now be possible to twist it free. If necessary, carefully heat the joint with a blowlamp to assist removal, but shield the fuel tank, fuel pipes and underbody adequately from heat.
5 To remove the front section, undo the nuts

3

19.7A Manifold upper mounting nuts

19.7B Manifold centre lower mounting nuts

19.8 Removing the manifold assembly

21.3A Exhaust intermediate section to front pipe joint

21.3B Exhaust intermediate section to rear pipe joint

21.4A Exhaust intermediate section mounting

21.4B Exhaust rear section mounting

and tension springs securing the front pipe flange to the exhaust manifold. Slide the flange off the manifold studs and separate the joint. Undo the retaining clamp nut and bolt and withdraw the front section forwards, as previously described.

6 Refitting is the reverse sequence to removal. Position the joints so that there is adequate clearance between all parts of the system and the underbody, and ensure that there is equal load on all mounting blocks.

Fig. 3.27 Exhaust system components (Sec 21)

Part 2: Turbo models

22 General description and precautions

The fuel system consists of a main and auxiliary fuel tank mounted under the rear of the car, electric fuel pump and canister type fuel filter also mounted at the rear, fuel pressure regulator and sealed carburettor.

The inlet system consists of a thermostatically controlled air cleaner, turbocharger and an air-to-air intercooler.

The turbocharger consists of two turbines mounted on a single shaft. One turbine is driven by the flow of exhaust gases from the exhaust manifold and this turns the turbine in the inlet system forcing air into the engine under pressure. The system is controlled by a vacuum capsule operating a bypass (or wastegate) for the exhaust turbine.

The intake air is maintained at constant temperature by the intercooler which functions like a conventional radiator, but with the intake air passing through it instead of water.

Since the intake air pressure varies according to the speed of the turbocharger turbines, the fuel pressure within the carburettor must also be varied. This requirement is controlled by the pressure regulator located in the carburettor supply

Fig. 3.28 Diagram of Turbocharging system (Sec 22)

1 Air filter with 26°-32°C thermostatic flap
2 Compressor
3 Pressure regulator capsule
4 Exhaust gas bypass valve (wastegate)
5 Turbine
6 Safety pressure switch
7 Air-cooler with 43°-47°C thermostatic flap
8 Fuel pressure regulator
9 Blown carburettor
10 Anti-percolation system temperature switch
11 Anti-percolation fan motor
12 Pressure gauge on instrument panel
13 Electronic ignition system module
14 Pinking detector
15 Radiator and cooling fan
16 Oil filter
17 Oil-water cooler
18 Non-return valve
19 T-piece unions

Fig. 3.29 Air intake system (Sec 22)

1 Air cleaner
2 Cold and hot air supplies to air cleaner
4 Intercooler
5 Turbocharger-to-intercooler hose
6 Intercooler-to-carburettor hose
7 Carburettor inlet elbow

line. The unit incorporates a spring tensioned diaphragm subject to intake air pressure on one side and fuel pressure on the other. Under full load conditions the boost pressure forces the diaphragm valve against the fuel return outlet which effectively causes the fuel pressure to rise.

The turbocharger turbines rotate at very high speeds and, in order to prevent damage to the bearings through lack of oil, the engine should always be allowed to idle for approximately 30 seconds before switching it off.

If a fault develops in the turbocharger wastegate control system it should be checked by a Renault dealer since special calibration equipment is required which is not normally available to the home mechanic.

A four section exhaust system is fitted with rubber block type mountings.

Observe the warning given in Part 1, Section 1.

23 Routine maintenance

At the intervals specified in the "Routine maintenance" section in the front of the manual carry out the following procedures.
1 Check the condition and security of all intake hoses, turbocharger control hoses, crankcase ventilation hoses, vacuum/pressure hoses and fuel hoses.
2 Renew the fuel filter as described in Section 28.

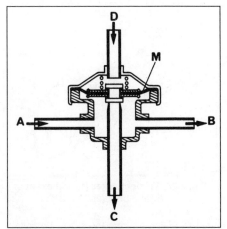

Fig. 3.30 Cross-section of the pressure regulator (Sec 22)

A Fuel inlet from pump
B Fuel outlet to carburettor
C Fuel return to tank
D Air inlet pressure
M Diaphragm

24 Air cleaner and filter element
- removal and refitting

1 Release the strap securing the air cleaner to the left-hand side of the engine compartment and lift out leaving the hoses still connected.
2 Release the clips and separate the cover from the main body then remove the filter element.
3 Clean the inside of the air cleaner body and fit a new filter element if the old one is dirty or has exceeded its service life.
4 Refit the cover then secure the unit to the bracket with the strap, making sure that the location peg on the bottom engages the grommet.
5 To remove the main body first remove the filter element as previously described then disconnect the three ducts for the cold air inlet, hot air shroud and turbocharger.
6 The automatic air temperature control device within the air cleaner cover may be checked using the procedure given in Part 1, Section 3 paragraphs 12 and 13 however the operating temperatures are 26°C (79°F) and 32°C (90°F).
7 Refitting of the air cleaner main body is a reversal of removal.

25 Intercooler -
removal, testing and refitting

1 Disconnect the inlet and outlet hoses from the intercooler, then release the strap and lift the unit from its location at the front left-hand side of the engine compartment.

Fig. 3.31 Air cleaner components (Sec 24)

1 Element
2 Bracket
3 Strap
4 Air cleaner body
5 Grommet
6 Bracket

2 Clean any debris from the matrix by hosing or using an air line.
3 A thermostatic capsule is fitted in the intercooler outlet its purpose being to prevent further cooling of incoming air which is less than 43 ± 2°C (109 ± 4°F). It does this by activating an internal flap between the unit inlet and outlet. To check the operation of the capsule immerse it in water at 43 ± 2°C (109 ± 4°F). After five minutes the internal flap should open the direct passage between the inlet and outlet.
4 Repeat the test in water at 47 ± 2°C (117 ± 2°F). After five minutes the flap should close the direct passage between the inlet and outlet so that the flow of air is through the intercooler matrix. If the flap does not operate correctly renew the intercooler complete.
5 Refitting is a reversal of removal, but make sure that the hoses are fitted correctly as they form part of the boost pressure circuit. The hoses must be clean and dry before refitting.

Fig. 3.32 Intercooler header tank (Sec 25)

1 Thermostatic capsule
2 Flap
A Inlet
B Outlet

3

Fig. 3.33 Anti-percolation system cooling fan and hose (Sec 26)

Cut-away section shows fuel supply pipe located within the hose

26 Anti-percolation system - description

The anti-percolation system is provided to maintain the carburettor and fuel pressure regulator together with associated hoses at a constant specified temperature. It comprises a fresh air electric cooling fan on the right-hand side of the engine compartment and a hose directing the air to the base of the carburettor. The fan is controlled by a thermostatic switch located on the right-hand side of the inlet manifold just below the carburettor mounting flange.

The anti-percolation system is energised at all times regardless of whether the ignition is switched on or off, therefore it is important to disconnect the battery negative terminal when working on or near the components. The cooling fan will normally operate approximately 10 minutes after the engine is switched off.

27 Turbocharger - removal and refitting

1 Disconnect the battery negative terminal.
2 Remove the air cleaner as described in Section 24.
3 Disconnect the inlet and outlet hoses from the turbocharger and the air cleaner cold air supply from the intake at the front of the engine compartment.
4 Disconnect the wiring from the engine safety pressure switch located in the turbocharger outlet.hose, then disconnect the hose from the intercooler and remove it.
5 Remove the electronic ignition computer module from the bulkhead as described in Chapter 4.
6 Remove the non-return valve and bracket and disconnect the hoses.
7 Unscrew the mounting bolts and withdraw

Fig. 3.34 Turbocharger (1) and exhaust outlet elbow (2) (Sec 27)

the hot air shroud from the exhaust manifold. Recover the washers, spacer and mounting components.
8 Unscrew the two bolts from the flange securing the angled exhaust pipe to the turbocharger outlet.
9 Unscrew the union nut and disconnect the oil inlet pipe from the top of the turbocharger. Loosen the clip and disconnect the oil return pipe from the bottom of the unit. Plug the pipes and holes to prevent entry of dirt.
10 Identify the location of the pipes on the wastegate regulator capsule then disconnect them.
11 Unscrew the nuts securing the turbocharger to the end of the exhaust manifold then withdraw it from the car. Do not however lift it by the wastegate operating rod. As some of the mounting nuts are difficult to reach a thin spanner is required.
12 Clean the mating faces of the turbocharger and exhaust manifold before refitting the unit using a reversal of the removal procedure. However before starting the engine it is most important to prime the oil circuit, otherwise the turbine bearings may be damaged. To do this, temporarily disconnect the centre plug from the top of the electronic ignition computer module (Fig. 3.35) and spin the engine on the starter motor until the oil pressure light is extinguished. Reconnect the plug then start the engine and let it idle for several minutes.

28 Fuel filter - renewal

1 Chock the front wheels then jack up the rear of the car and support on axle stands.
2 The filter is located on the right-hand rear crossmember in front of the fuel pump. First clamp the inlet and outlet hoses.
3 Loosen the clips and disconnect the hoses then pull the filter from its spring clip mounting.
4 Fit the new filter using a reversal of the removal procedure, but make sure that the arrow on the unit faces the hose which leads to the fuel pressure regulator and carburettor.

Fig. 3.35 Disconnect plug (A) on the electronic ignition computer module when priming the turbocharger (Sec 27)

29 Fuel pump - removal and refitting

1 Chock the front wheels then jack up the rear of the car and support on axle stands.
2 The fuel pump is located on the right-hand rear crossmember. First clamp the inlet and outlet hoses.
3 Disconnect the battery negative terminal.
4 Disconnect the wiring from the fuel pump.
5 Disconnect the hoses then unscrew the clamp bolt, lift and unhook the clamp, and withdraw the fuel pump.
6 Refitting is a reversal of removal.

30 Auxiliary fuel pump - removal and refitting

1 Chock the front wheels then jack up the rear of the car and support on axle stands.
2 The auxiliary fuel pump is located on the front of the auxiliary fuel tank. First clamp the inlet and outlet hoses.
3 Disconnect the battery negative terminal.
4 Disconnect the wiring from the fuel pump.

Fig. 3.36 Fuel filter (1) and fuel pump (2) (Sec 28)

Fig. 3.37 Fuel pressure regulator location (Sec 31)

A *Fuel inlet from pump*
B *Fuel return to tank*
C *Fuel outlet to carburettor*
D *Air inlet pressure*

5 Disconnect the hoses then detach the pump from the mounting clip.
6 Refitting is a reversal of removal, but ensure that the pump is located correctly in the notch.

31 Fuel pressure regulator - removal and refitting

1 Apply the handbrake then jack up the front of the car and support on axle stands.
2 The fuel pressure regulator is located on the right-hand front sidemember above the steering gear. First clamp the fuel inlet, outlet and return hoses.
3 Disconnect the fuel hoses and the boost pressure hose then detach the regulator from the bracket by unscrewing the nut.
4 Refitting is a reversal of removal.

32 Fuel tanks - removal, servicing and refitting

Note: *The removal, servicing and refitting of the main and auxiliary fuel tanks follows closely the procedure for the fuel tank and filler neck given in Part 1, Sections 6 and 7. This Section therefore only outlines the additional work necessary.*

Main fuel tank

1 Remove the fuel filter (Section 28) and the fuel pump (Section 29), then unbolt and remove the fuel pump mounting bracket.

Fig. 3.38 Fuel tank and filler neck components (Sec 32)

1 *Auxiliary pump connector*	4 *Transfer pipe*	6 *Non-return flap*
2 *Filler neck*	5 *Intermediate hose*	7, 8 and 9 *Vent pipes*
3 *Vent pipe*		

2 Disconnect the fuel transfer pipe from the front of the tank.
3 Refitting is a reversal of removal with reference also to Sections 28 and 29.

Auxiliary tank and filler neck

4 Disconnect the wiring from the auxiliary fuel pump.
5 Disconnect the short length of hose connecting the filler neck to the fuel tank.
6 Disconnect the additional vent pipe and the fuel transfer pipe.
7 Unscrew the nut from the mounting strap then pull open the strap sufficiently to withdraw the auxiliary fuel tank.
8 Refitting is a reversal of removal, but if the non-return flap is removed from the front of the tank make sure it is refitted with the notch uppermost. When refitting the vent pipe to the filler head ensure that there is a gap as shown in Fig. 3.38.

33 Fuel gauge sender unit - removal and refitting

Refer to Part 1, Section 8.

34 Accelerator cable - removal and refitting

The procedure is similar to that described in Part 1, Section 9, however there is no need to remove the air cleaner. A ball and socket arrangement is used to connect the cable to the throttle lever on the carburettor.

35 Accelerator pedal - removal and refitting

Refer to Part 1, Section 10.

36 Choke cable - removal and refitting

The procedure is similar to that described in Part 1, Section 11, however there is no need to remove the air cleaner. The inner cable is attached to the linkage on the carburettor by a pivoting clamp bolt

37 Solex carburettor - description

The Solex 32 DIS carburettor is a single throat downdraught type. It is located downstream of the turbocharger and therefore all its internal circuits are subject to boost pressure when the turbocharger is in operation. As the carburettor operation depends on a fine balance of air pressure and fuel pressure the entire unit must be completely sealed at every joint. To this end the carburettor incorporates a magnesium cover and float chamber, a reinforced cover gasket, strengthened accelerator pump and enrichener diaphragms, and seals for the throttle shaft, idling jet and mixture screw.
Apart from the differences described the carburettor operates conventionally.

38 Carburettor - idle speed and mixture adjustment

The procedure is as described in Part 1, Section 15, but prior to commencing work check that all intake hoses, turbocharger central hoses, crankcase ventilation hoses, vacuum hoses and fuel hoses are secure and in good condition.

3

Fig. 3.39 Idle speed screw (A) and mixture adjustment screw (B) on the Solex 32 DIS carburettor (Sec 38)

Fig. 3.40 Solex 32 DIS carburettor overhaul (Sec 40)

A Air compensating jet
K Venturi
g Idling jet
Gg Main jet
i Accelerator pump jet

39 Carburettor - removal and refitting

The procedure is as described in Part 1, Section 16, but instead of removing the air filter unbolt the intake elbow from the top of the carburettor and remove the O-ring. Refer also to Sections 34 and 36. The anti-percolation duct must be removed when disconnecting the fuel inlet hose.

40 Carburettor - overhaul

Refer to Part 1, Section 17 and also Part 2 Specifications. Although there are differences, the procedures are the same.

Fig. 3.41 Manifold components (Sec 41)

1 Hot air shroud   2 Inlet manifold   3 Exhaust manifold   4 Gasket

Fig. 3.42 Exhaust system components (Sec 42)

41 Inlet and exhaust manifolds - removal and refitting

1 Refer to Part 1, Section 19, however the inlet and exhaust manifolds can be removed separately although a one-piece gasket is fitted.
2 Before removing the exhaust manifold remove the turbocharger as described in Section 27.

42 Exhaust system - checking, removal and refitting

1 The procedure is as described in Part 1, Sections 20 and 21, but additionally an angled length of pipe is fitted between the turbocharger outlet and the exhaust downpipe.
2 When refitting the downpipe flange bolts and tension springs, maintain the dimension shown in Fig. 3.43.

Fig. 3.43 Exhaust downpipe flange tension spring adjustment dimension (Sec 42)

Fault finding - fuel and exhaust systems

Unsatisfactory engine performance and excessive fuel consumption are not necessarily the fault of the fuel system or carburettor. In fact they more commonly occur as a result of ignition and timing faults, particularly on models equipped with conventional contact breaker point ignition systems. Before acting on the following it is necessary to check the ignition system first. Even though a fault may lie in the fuel system it will be difficult to trace unless the ignition system is correct. The faults below, therefore, assume that this has been attended to first (where appropriate).

Engine difficult to start when cold

- ☐ Choke cable incorrectly adjusted
- ☐ Choke flap not closing
- ☐ Insufficient fuel in float chamber

Engine difficult to start when hot

- ☐ Choke cable incorrectly adjusted
- ☐ Air cleaner element dirty or choked
- ☐ Insufficient fuel in float chamber
- ☐ Float chamber flooding
- ☐ Anti-percolation cooling fan not working or thermostatic switch faulty (Turbo models)

Fuel consumption excessive

- ☐ Choke cable incorrectly adjusted or linkage sticking
- ☐ Air cleaner dirty or choked
- ☐ Fuel leaking from carburettor, fuel pump, fuel tank or fuel pipes
- ☐ Float chamber flooding

Engine will not idle or idles erratically

- ☐ Air cleaner dirty or choked
- ☐ Choke cable incorrectly adjusted
- ☐ Carburettor idling adjustments incorrectly set
- ☐ Blocked carburettor jets or internal passages
- ☐ Disconnected, perished or leaking crankcase ventilation hoses
- ☐ Air leaks at carburettor or manifold joint faces
- ☐ Generally worn carburettor
- ☐ Engine internal defect

Engine performance poor

- ☐ Blocked carburettor jets or internal passages
- ☐ Accelerator pump faulty or diaphragm punctured
- ☐ Float level low
- ☐ Fuel filter choked
- ☐ Fuel pump faulty or delivery pressure low
- ☐ Fuel tank vent blocked
- ☐ Fuel pipes restricted
- ☐ Air leaks at carburettor or manifold joint faces
- ☐ Engine internal components worn or out of adjustment
- ☐ Turbocharger wastegate system not functioning correctly

Excessive noise or fumes from exhaust system

- ☐ Leaking pipe or manifold joints
- ☐ Leaking, corroded or damaged silencers or pipe
- ☐ System in contact with body or suspension due to broken mounting

Excessive noise

- ☐ Turbocharger bearings worn

3

Notes

Chapter 4 Ignition system

For modifications, and information applicable to later models, see Supplement at end of manual

Contents

Degrees of difficulty

Easy, suitable for novice with little experience	**Fairly easy,** suitable for beginner with some experience	**Fairly difficult,** suitable for competent DIY mechanic	**Difficult,** suitable for experienced DIY mechanic	**Very difficult,** suitable for expert DIY or professional

Specifications

Part 1: Conventional ignition system

System type . . . . Coil, and distributor with contact breaker points and condenser

Application . . . . 956 cc (C1C) engine

Distributor
Rotor arm rotation . . . . Clockwise
Firing order . . . . 1 - 3 - 4 - 2 (No 1 cylinder nearest flywheel)
Contact breaker points gap . . . . 0.4 mm (0.016 in)
Dwell angle . . . . 57° ± 3°
Dwell percentage . . . . 63% ± 3%

Ignition timing
Static, or dynamic with vacuum pipe disconnected . . . . 10° ± 1° BTDC

Spark plugs*
Type . . . . Champion N9YCC or N281YC
Electrode gap . . . . 0.8 mm (0.032 in)

HT leads . . . . Champion LS-07 (boxed set)

Torque wrench setting	**Nm**	**Ibf ft**
Spark plugs	15 to 20	11 to 15

Part 2: Transistorized ignition system

System type . . . . As conventional system but with transistor assistance unit in low tension circuit

Application . . . . 1108 cc (C1E) engine

Distributor . . . . As conventional system

Ignition timing
Static, or dynamic with vacuum pipe disconnected . . . . 8° ± 1° BTDC

Spark plugs* . . . . As conventional system

HT leads . . . . As conventional system

Part 3: Full electronic ignition system

System type .... Computer module incorporating a coil and vacuum advance unit, basic distributor for HT circuit, and a flywheel angular position sensor

Application .... 1397 cc (C1J and C2J) engine

Distributor

Rotor arm rotation .... Clockwise

Firing order .... 1 - 3 - 4 - 2 (No 1 cylinder nearest flywheel)

Ignition timing (not adjustable)

At idle, with vacuum pipe disconnected:

Turbo models .... 8° BTDC

Non-Turbo models (manual gearbox) .... 10° BTDC (C1J) or 8° BTDC (C2J)

Non-turbo models (automatic transmission) .... 6° BTDC

Spark plugs*

Type:

Turbo models .... Champion N3G or N6YCC

Non-Turbo models .... Champion N9YCC or N281YC

Gap:

Champion N3G .... 0.6 mm (0.024 in)

Champion N6YCC, N9YCC or N281YC .... 0.8 mm (0.032 in)

HT leads .... Champion LS-40 (boxed set)

Torque wrench settings .... As conventional system

Information on spark plug types and electrode gaps is as recommended by Champion Spark Plug. Where alternative types are used, refer to the manufacturer's recommendations

Part 1: Conventional ignition system

1 General description

In order that the engine may run correctly it is necessary for an electrical spark to ignite the fuel/air mixture in the combustion chamber at exactly the right moment in relation to engine speed and load.

Basically the ignition system functions as follows: Low tension voltage from the battery is fed to the ignition coil where it is converted into high tension voltage. The high tension voltage is powerful enough to jump the spark plug gap in the cylinder many times a second under high compression pressure, providing that the ignition system is in good working order and that all adjustments are correct.

The ignition system consists of two individual circuits known as the low tension (LT) circuit and high tension (HT) circuit.

The low tension circuit (sometimes known as the primary circuit) consists of the battery, lead to ignition switch, lead to the low tension or primary coil windings and the lead from the low tension coil windings to the contact breaker points and condenser in the distributor.

The high tension circuit (sometimes known as the secondary circuit) consists of the high tension or secondary coil winding, the heavily insulated ignition lead from the centre of the coil to the centre of the distributor cap, the rotor arm, the spark plug leads and the spark plugs.

The complete ignition system operation is as follows: Low tension voltage from the battery is changed within the ignition coil to high tension voltage by the opening and closing of the contact breaker points in the low tension circuit. High tension voltage is then fed, via a contact in the centre of the distributor cap, to the rotor arm of the distributor. The rotor arm revolves inside the distributor cap, and each time it comes in line with one of the four metal segments in the cap, the opening and closing of the contact breaker points causes the high tension voltage to build up, jump the gap from the rotor arm to the appropriate metal segment and so, via the spark plug lead, to the spark plug where it finally jumps the gap between the two spark plug electrodes, one being earthed.

The ignition timing is advanced and retarded automatically to ensure the spark occurs at just the right instant for the particular load at the prevailing engine speed.

The ignition advance is controlled both mechanically and by a vacuum-operated system. The mechanical governor mechanism consists of two weights which move out under centrifugal force from the central distributor shaft as the engine speed rises. As they move outwards they rotate the cam relative to the distributor shaft, and so advance the spark. The weights are held in position by two light springs, and it is the tension of these springs which is largely responsible for correct spark advancement.

The vacuum control consists of a diaphragm, one side of which is connected,

Fig. 4.1 Diagrammatic representation of the ignition circuit (Sec 1)

Fig. 4.2 Location of the ballast resistor (A) on the ignition coil (Sec 1)

via a small bore tube, to the carburettor and the other side to the contact breaker plate. Depression in the induction manifold and carburettor, which varies with engine speed and throttle opening, causes the diaphragm to move so rotating the contact breaker plate and advancing or retarding the spark.

The LT circuit incorporates a ballast resistor located on the ignition coil bracket which is in circuit all the time that the engine is running. When the starter motor is operated, the resistance is bypassed to provide increased voltage at the spark plugs.

2 Routine maintenance

At the intervals specified in the "Routine maintenance" section in the front of the manual carry out the following procedures.
1 Check the condition of the distributor cap and contact breaker points, as described in Section 3. Renew the points if necessary using the procedure contained in Section 4.
2 With the distributor cap removed, lift off the rotor arm and the plastic shield. Carefully apply two drops of engine oil to the felt pad in the centre of the cam spindle. Also lubricate the centrifugal advance mechanism by applying two or three drops of oil through one of the holes in the distributor baseplate. Wipe away any excess oil and refit the plastic shield, rotor arm and distributor cap.
3 Renew the spark plugs as described in Section 10. Preferably using a stroboscopic timing light, check and, if necessary, reset the ignition timing, as described in Section 8. Finally wipe off all traces of dirt, oil and grease from the HT and LT leads and all wiring and also check the security of all cables and connectors.

3 Contact breaker points - adjustment

1 Release the two spring clips and lift off the distributor cap. Pull the rotor arm off the shaft and remove the plastic shield (photo).
2 Clean the distributor cap on the inside and outside with a clean dry cloth and examine the four HT lead segments inside the cap. Scrape away any deposits that may have built up on the segments, using a knife or small screwdriver. If the segments appear badly burned or pitted, renew the cap.
3 Push in the carbon brush located in the centre of the cap, and ensure that it moves freely and stands proud by at least 3 mm (0.1 in). Renew the cap if the brush is worn or if there are signs of burning on the brush holder.
4 Gently prise the contact breaker points open to examine the condition of their faces. If they are rough and pitted, or dirty, they should be renewed, as described in Section 4.
5 Assuming that the points are in a

3.1 With the distributor cap removed, lift off the rotor arm and plastic shield to gain access to the contact breaker points

satisfactory condition, or that they have been renewed, the gap between the two faces should be measured using feeler gauges. To do this turn the engine over using a socket or spanner on the crankshaft pulley bolt, until the heel of the contact breaker arm is on the peak of one of the four cam lobes.
6 With the points fully open, a feeler gauge equal to the contact breaker points gap, as given in the Specifications, should now just fit between the contact faces (photo).
7 If the gap is too large or too small turn the adjusting nut on the side of the distributor body using a small spanner until the specified gap is obtained.
8 With the points correctly adjusted, refit the plastic shield, rotor arm and distributor cap.
9 If a dwell meter is available, a far more accurate method of setting the contact breaker points is by measuring and setting the distributor dwell angle.
10 The dwell angle is the number of degrees of distributor shaft rotation during which the contact breaker points are closed, ie the period from when the points close after being opened by one cam lobe until they are opened again by the next cam lobe. The advantages of setting the points by this method are that any wear of the distributor shaft or cam lobes is taken into account, and also the inaccuracies of using a feeler gauge are eliminated.

Fig. 4.3 Conventional ignition distributor components (Secs 3 and 4)

A *Contact breaker points adjusting nut*
B *Baseplate retaining screws*
D *Adjustment rod and spring*
E *Fixed contact retaining screw*

3.6 Measure the points gap with a feeler gauge and adjust if necessary by turning nut (A)

11 To check and adjust the dwell angle connect one lead of the meter to the ignition coil + terminal and the other lead to the coil - terminal, or in accordance with the maker's instructions.
12 Start the engine, allow it to idle and observe the reading on the dwell meter scale. If the dwell angle is not as specified, turn the adjusting nut on the side of the distributor body as necessary to obtain the correct setting. Note: Owing to machining tolerances, or wear in the distributor shaft or bushes, it is not uncommon for a contact breaker points gap correctly set with feeler gauges, to give a dwell angle outside the specified tolerances. If this is the case the dwell angle should be regarded as the preferred setting.
13 After completing the adjustment, switch off the engine and disconnect the dwell meter.

4 Contact breaker points - removal and refitting

1 Release the two spring clips and lift off the distributor cap. Pull the rotor arm off the shaft and remove the plastic shield.
2 Undo the contact breaker adjusting nut on the side of the distributor body and then unscrew the two baseplate retaining screws (photo). Lift off the support bracket.
3 Disengage the end of the adjustment rod

4.2 To remove the contact breaker points, undo the adjusting nut (A), the two screws (B) and lift off the support bracket

4.3 Disengage the adjustment rod from the fixed contact and withdraw the rod and spring

4.4A Prise out the small plastic plug . . .

4.4B . . . to gain access to the retaining clip (arrowed) . . .

from the fixed contact and slide the rod and spring out of the distributor body (photo).

4 Prise out the small plug and then remove the retaining clip, noting that the hole in the clip is uppermost (photos).

5 Slacken the LT terminal nut and detach the lead (photo).

6 Remove the spring retaining clip from the top of the moving contact pivot post and take off the fibre insulating washer (photo).

7 Ease the spring blade away from its nylon support and lift the moving contact upwards and off the pivot post (photo).

8 Undo the retaining screw and remove the fixed contact from the baseplate (photo).

9 Examine the faces of the breaker points and if they are rough, pitted or dirty they should be renewed.

10 Refitting the contact breaker points is the reverse sequence to removal, but clean the point faces with methylated spirit, to ensure complete freedom from greasy deposits.

11 After refitting adjust the contact breaker points gap, as described in Section 3.

5 Condenser - testing, removal and refitting

1 The purpose of the condenser, which is located externally on the side of the distributor body, is to ensure that, when the contact breaker points open, there is no sparking across them, which would cause wear of their faces and prevent the rapid

collapse of the magnetic field in the coil. This would cause a reduction in coil HT voltage and ultimately lead to engine misfire.

2 If the engine becomes very difficult to start, or begins to miss after several miles of running, and the contact breaker points show signs of excessive burning, the condition of the condenser must be suspect. A further test can be made by separating the points by hand with the ignition switched on. If this is accompanied by a strong bright flash, it is indicative that the condenser has failed.

3 Without special test equipment, the only sure way to diagnose condenser trouble is to substitute a suspect unit with a new one and note if there is any improvement.

4 To remove the condenser, unscrew the nut at the LT terminal post and slip off the lead. Undo the condenser retaining screw and remove the component from the side of the distributor body.

5 Refitting is the reverse sequence to removal.

6 Distributor - removal and refitting

1 Mark the spark plug HT leads to aid refitting and pull them off the ends of the plugs. Release the distributor cap retaining clips and place the cap and leads to one side.

4.4C . . . which can then be removed using pliers. Note the fitted position of the clip

4.5 Slacken the LT terminal nut (A) and detach the lead (B) from the connector

4.6 Remove the spring retaining clip and fibre washer from the pivot post

4.7 Ease the spring blade off its support and withdraw the moving contact from the pivot post

4.8 Undo the retaining screw and remove the fixed contact

6.4 With Nos 1 and 4 cylinders at TDC the mark on the flywheel (A) will be aligned with the notch (B) in the bellhousing

2 Remove No 1 spark plug (nearest the flywheel end of the engine).
3 Place a finger over the plug hole and turn the engine in the normal direction of rotation (clockwise from the crankshaft pulley end) until pressure is felt in No 1 cylinder. This indicates that the piston is commencing its compression stroke. The engine can be turned with a socket or spanner on the crankshaft pulley bolt.
4 Continue turning the engine until the mark on the flywheel is aligned with the TDC notch on the clutch bellhousing (photo).
5 Using a dab of paint or a small file, make a reference mark between the distributor base and the cylinder block.
6 Detach the vacuum advance pipe and disconnect the LT lead at the wiring connector. Release the wiring loom from the support clip on the distributor body.
7 Unscrew the distributor clamp retaining nut and lift off the clamp. Withdraw the distributor from the engine and recover the seal.
8 To refit the distributor, first check that the engine is still at the TDC position with No 1 cylinder on compression. If the engine has been turned while the distributor was removed return it to the correct position, as previously described.
9 With the rotor arm pointing directly away from the engine and the vacuum unit at approximately the 5 o'clock position, slide the distributor into the cylinder block and turn the rotor arm slightly until the offset peg on the distributor drive dog positively engages with the drivegear.
10 Align the previously made reference marks, if a new distributor is being fitted, position the distributor body so that the rotor arm points toward the No 1 spark plug HT lead segment in the cap. Hold the distributor in this position, refit the clamp and secure with the retaining nut.
11 Reconnect the LT lead at the connector, refit the vacuum advance pipe and secure the wiring loom in the support clip.
12 Before refitting the distributor cap, leads and spark plug, refer to Section 8 and adjust the ignition timing as necessary.

7.1 Distributor vacuum unit serrated cam adjuster (arrowed)

7 Distributor - overhaul

1 Renewal of the contact breaker assembly, condenser, rotor and distributor cap should be regarded as the limit of overhaul on these units, as few other spares are available separately. It is possible to renew the vacuum unit, but this must then be set up to suit the advance curve of the engine, by adjustment of the serrated cam on the baseplate (photo), and is best left to a dealer or automotive electrician.
2 When the distributor has seen extended service and the shaft, bushes and centrifugal mechanism become worn it is advisable to purchase a new distributor.

8 Ignition timing - adjustment

1 In order that the engine can run efficiently, it is necessary for a spark to occur at the spark plug and ignite the fuel/air mixture at the instant just before the piston on the compression stroke reaches the top of its travel. The precise instant at which the spark occurs is determined by the ignition timing, and this is quoted in degrees before top-dead-centre (BTDC).
2 The timing may be checked and adjusted in one of two ways; either by using a test bulb to obtain a static setting with the engine stationary or by using a stroboscopic timing light to obtain a dynamic setting with the engine running.
3 Before checking or adjusting the ignition timing, make sure that the contact breaker points are in good condition and correctly adjusted, as described in Section 3.

Static setting

4 Refer to the Specifications at the beginning of this Chapter and note the specified setting for static ignition timing. This value will also be

8.4 Ignition timing static setting is stamped on a clip fastened to one of the HT leads

found stamped on a clip fastened to one of the HT leads (photo).
5 Pull off the HT lead and remove No 1 spark plug (nearest the flywheel end of the engine).
6 Place a finger over the plug hole and turn the engine in the normal direction of rotation (clockwise from the crankshaft pulley end) until pressure is felt in No 1 cylinder. This indicates that the piston is commencing its compression stroke. The engine can be turned using a socket or spanner on the crankshaft pulley bolt.
7 Continue turning the engine until the mark on the flywheel is aligned with the appropriate notch on the clutch bellhousing (Fig. 4.4).
8 Remove the distributor cap and check that the rotor arm is pointing towards the No 1 spark plug HT lead segment in the cap.
9 Connect a 12 volt test lamp and leads between a good earth and the LT terminal nut on the side of the distributor body.
10 Slacken the distributor clamp retaining nut and then switch on the ignition.
11 If the test lamp is on, turn the distributor slightly clockwise until the lamp goes out.
12 Now turn the distributor anti-clockwise until the test lamp just lights up, hold the distributor in this position and tighten the clamp retaining nut.
13 Test the setting by turning the engine two

Fig. 4.4 Timing mark positions on clutch bellhousing (Sec 8)

Fig. 4.5 Diagnostic socket with cap lifted (Sec 9)

complete revolutions and observing when the lamp lights up in relation to the timing marks.
14 Switch off the ignition and remove the test lamp. Refit No 1 spark plug, the distributor cap and HT lead.

Dynamic setting

15 Refer to the Specifications at the beginning of this Chapter and note the specified setting for dynamic ignition timing. This initial value will also be found stamped on a clip fastened to one of the HT leads. To make subsequent operations easier it is advisable to highlight the mark on the flywheel and the appropriate notch on the clutch bellhousing with white paint or chalk (Fig. 4.4).
16 Connect the timing light in accordance with the manufacturer's instructions (usually interposed between the end of No 1 spark plug HT lead and No 1 spark plug terminal).
17 Disconnect the vacuum advance pipe

Fig. 4.6 Diagnostic socket terminals (Sec 9)

1 TDC sensor (supply)   4 TDC sensor (return)
2 Distributor earth   5 TDC sensor (screen)
3 Coil earth   6 Coil +

X and Y Location studs

from the distributor vacuum unit and plug its end.
18 Start the engine and leave it idling at the specified idling speed (refer to Specifications, Chapter 3).
19 Point the timing light at the timing marks and they should appear to be stationary with the mark on the flywheel aligned with the appropriate notch on the clutch bellhousing.
20 If adjustment is necessary (ie the flywheel mark does not line up with the appropriate notch) slacken the distributor clamp retaining nut and turn the distributor body anti-clockwise to advance the timing, and clockwise to retard it. Tighten the clamp nut when the setting is correct.
21 Gradually increase the engine speed while still pointing the timing light at the marks. The mark on the flywheel should appear to advance further, indicating that the distributor centrifugal advance mechanism is functioning. If the mark remains stationary or moves in a jerky, erratic fashion, the advance mechanism must be suspect.
22 Reconnect the vacuum pipe to the distributor and check that the advance alters when the pipe is connected. If not, the vacuum unit on the distributor may be faulty.
23 After completing the checks and adjustments, switch off the engine and disconnect the timing light.

9 Diagnostic socket and TDC sensor - general

1 A diagnostic socket, used in conjunction with special test equipment to check the function of the complete ignition system, is mounted on the left-hand side of the engine, adjacent to the TDC sensor. Although the related test equipment is not normally available to the home mechanic it is useful to know of the existence and purpose of these components.
2 When connected to the appropriate equipment the socket enables the following checks to be carried out:

LT circuit voltage
Ignition timing
Centrifugal and vacuum advance curves
Dwell angle
Engine rpm

3 The six pins in the socket are connected to various engine earthing points, to the supply voltage terminal of the ignition coil and to the

Fig. 4.7 TDC sensor and shouldered mounting bolt (Sec 9)

TDC sensor. The sensor itself is mounted on a bracket attached to the clutch bellhousing. The probe of the sensor is positioned directly in line with the periphery of the flywheel and is used to check the ignition timing and advance curves.

10 Spark plugs and HT leads - general

1 The correct functioning of the spark plugs is vital for the correct running and efficiency of the engine. It is essential that the plugs fitted are appropriate for the engine; the suitable type is specified at the beginning of this chapter. If this type is used and the engine is in good condition, the spark plugs should not need attention between scheduled replacement intervals. Spark plug cleaning is rarely necessary, and should not be attempted unless specialised equipment is available, as damage can easily be caused to the firing ends.
2 To remove the plugs, first mark the LT leads to ensure correct refitment, and then pull them off the plugs. Using a spark plug spanner, or suitable deep socket and extension bar, unscrew the plugs and remove them from the engine.
3 The condition of the spark plugs will also tell much about the overall condition of the engine.
4 If the insulator nose of the spark plug is clean and white, with no deposits, this is indicative of a weak mixture, or too hot a plug. (A hot plug transfers heat away from the electrode slowly - a cold plug transfers it away quickly.)
5 If the tip and insulator nose are covered with hard black-looking deposits, then this is indicative that the mixture is too rich. Should the plug be black and oily, then it is likely that the engine is fairly worn, as well as the mixture being too rich.
6 If the insulator nose is covered with light tan to greyish brown deposits, then the mixture is correct and it is likely that the engine is in good condition.
7 The spark plugs should be renewed at the interval specified in *"Routine maintenance"*, regardless of their apparent condition. Note that the spark plugs should always be renewed as a complete set. Prior to installing the new plugs check their gaps as follows.
8 The spark plug gap is of considerable importance as, if it is too large or too small, the size of spark and its efficiency will be seriously impaired. The spark plug gap should be set to the figure given in the Specifications at the beginning of this Chapter.
9 To set it, measure the gap with a feeler gauge, and then bend open, or close, the outer plug electrode until the correct gap is achieved. The centre electrode should never be bent as this may crack the insulation and cause plug failure, if nothing worse.

10 To refit the plugs, screw them in by hand initially and then fully tighten to the specified torque. If a torque wrench is not available, tighten the plugs until initial resistance is felt as the sealing washer contacts its seat and then tighten by a further eighth of a turn. Refit the HT leads in the correct order, ensuring that they are a tight fit over the plug ends. Periodically wipe the leads clean to reduce the risk of HT leakage by arcing.

It is very often difficult to insert spark plugs into their holes without cross-threading them. To avoid this possibility, fit a short length of 5/16 inch internal diameter rubber hose over the end of the spark plug. The flexible hose acts as a universal joint to help align the plug with the plug hole. Should the plug begin to cross-thread, the hose will slip on the spark plug, preventing thread damage to the cylinder head.

11 Fault finding - conventional ignition system

By far the majority of breakdown and running troubles are caused by faults in the ignition system, either in the low tension or high tension circuits.

There are two main symptoms indicating faults. Either the engine will not start or fire, or the engine is difficult to start and misfires. If it is a regular misfire, ie the engine is running on only two or three cylinders, the fault is almost sure to be in the secondary or high tension circuit. If the misfiring is intermittent, the fault could be in either the high or low tension circuits. If the car stops suddenly, or will not start at all, it is likely that the fault is in the low tension circuit. Loss of power and overheating, apart from faulty carburation settings, are normally due to faults in the distributor or to incorrect ignition timing.

Engine fails to start

1 If the engine fails to start and the car was running normally when it was last used, first check that there is fuel in the petrol tank. If the engine turns over normally on the starter motor and the battery is evidently well charged, then the fault may be in either the high or low tension circuits. First check the HT circuit. If the battery is known to be fully charged, the ignition light comes on, and the starter motor fails to turn the engine, check the tightness of the leads on the battery terminals and also the secureness of the earth lead to its connection to the body. It is quite common for the leads to have worked loose, even if they look and feel secure. If one of the battery terminal posts gets very hot when trying to work the starter motor this is a sure indication of a faulty connection to that terminal.

2 One of the most common reasons for bad starting is wet or damp spark plug leads and distributor. Remove the distributor cap. If condensation is visible a moisture dispersant can be very effective. Refit the cap.

3 If the engine still fails to start, check that the current is reaching the plugs, by disconnecting each plug lead in turn at the spark plug end, and holding the end of the cable about 5 mm (0.2 in) away from the cylinder block. Spin the engine on the starter motor.

4 Sparking between the end of the cable and the block should be fairly strong with a good, regular blue spark. (Hold the lead with rubber to avoid electric shocks.) If current is reaching the spark plugs, then they are confirmed faulty. Renew or re-gap the plugs as described in Section 10, the engine should now start.

5 If there is no spark at the plug leads, take off the HT lead from the centre of the distributor cap and hold it to the block as before. Spin the engine on the starter once more. A rapid succession of blue sparks between the end of the lead and the block indicates that the coil is in order and that the distributor cap is cracked, the rotor arm faulty, or the carbon brush in the top of the distributor cap is not making good contact with the rotor arm.

6 If there are no sparks from the end of the lead from the coil check the connections at the coil end of the lead. If it is in order start checking the low tension circuit.

7 Use a 12V voltmeter or a 12V bulb and two lengths of wire. With the ignition switched on and the points open, test between the low tension wire to the coil positive (+) terminal and earth. No reading indicates a break in the supply from the ignition switch. Check the connections at the switch to see if any are loose. Refit them and the engine should run. A reading shows a faulty coil or condenser, or broken lead between the coil and the distributor.

8 Take the condenser wire off the points assembly, and with the points open test between the moving point and earth. If there is now a reading then the fault is in the condenser. Fit a new one, as described in this Chapter, Section 5, and the fault should clear.

9 With no reading from the moving point to earth, take a reading between earth and the coil negative (-) terminal. A reading here shows a broken wire which will need to be renewed between the coil and distributor. No reading confirms that the coil has failed and must be renewed, after which the engine will run once more. Remember to refit the condenser wire to the points assembly. For these tests it is sufficient to separate the points with a piece of paper while testing with the points open.

Engine misfires

10 If the engine misfires regularly, run it at a fast idling speed. Pull off each of the plug caps in turn and listen to the note of the engine. Hold the plug cap in a dry cloth or with a rubber glove as additional protection against a shock from the HT supply.

11 No difference in engine running will be noticed when the lead from the defective circuit is removed. Removing the lead from one of the good cylinders will accentuate the misfire.

12 Remove the plug lead from the end of the defective plug and hold it about 5 mm (0.2 in) away from the block. Restart the engine. If the sparking is fairly strong and regular the fault must lie in the spark plug.

13 The plug may be loose, the insulation may be cracked, or the electrodes may have burnt away, giving too wide a gap for the spark to jump. Worse still, one of the electrodes may have broken off.

14 If there is no spark at the end of the plug lead, or if it is too weak and intermittent, check the ignition lead from the distributor to the plug. If the insulation is cracked or perished, renew the lead. Check the connections at the distributor cap.

15 If there is still no spark, examine the distributor cap carefully for tracking. This can be recognised by a very thin black line running between two or more electrodes, or between an electrode and some other part of the distributor. These lines are paths which now conduct electricity across the cap, thus letting it run to earth. The only answer is a new distributor cap.

16 Apart from the ignition timing being incorrect, other causes of misfiring have already been dealt with under the section dealing with the failure of the engine to start. To recap - these are that:

a) *The coil may be faulty giving an intermittent misfire*
b) *There may be a damaged wire or loose connection in the low tension circuit*
c) *The condenser may be short circuiting*
d) *There may be a mechanical fault in the distributor (broken driving spindle or contact breaker spring)*

17 If the ignition timing is too far retarded, it should be noted that the engine will tend to overheat, and there will be quite a noticeable drop in power. If the engine is overheating and the power is down, and the ignition timing is correct, then the carburettor should be checked, as it is likely that this is where the fault lies.

Part 2: Transistorized ignition system

12 General description

This type of ignition system is fitted to some 1108 cc engines. It consists of the basic conventional ignition system as described in Part 1, but with the addition of a transistor assistance unit (see Fig. 4.8).

The system functions as described in Section 1, but the action of the contact breaker points is used to switch a transistor on and off thus relieving the points carrying the full primary current.

The transistor operates as follows. With the points open the base (B) and emitter (E) are of the same potential and therefore no current flows. When the points close, the base (B) becomes negative due to the voltage drop at point (A) (Fig. 4.9) and current then flows through the transistor collector (C). The resistances R1 and R2 are fitted in the circuit to provide a low control voltage, and this also

greatly increases the life of the contact points as they only carry a small current. When the points open again the voltage increases at point (A) and the base (B), and the transistor is switched off.

The transistorized ignition system does not incorporate a ballast resistor.

13 Transistorized ignition system - servicing

1 The transistorized ignition system is serviced using the same procedures described in Part 1, however before checking the dwell angle, checking the condenser, or setting the ignition timing *statically*, the transistorized circuit should be bypassed by pulling the connector from the top of the transistor assistance unit (Fig. 4.10) then fitting it in the lower socket. Refit the connector in the upper socket after completing the work.

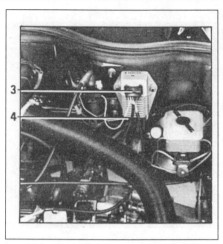

Fig. 4.8 Transistor assistance unit showing normal plug locations (3) and emergency socket (4) (Sec 12)

2 If a fault occurs in the ignition system first transfer the connector as described in paragraph 1. If the fault then disappears the transistor assistance unit is proved unserviceable and it should be checked for damage such as broken or corroded terminals. If the fault persists check the system as for the conventional type in Section 11. Where the transistor assistance unit is faulty the engine can be run smoothly with the connector in the lower socket, but if it is left in this position the contact points will deteriorate quicker and there may be a slight loss of performance.

Fig. 4.9 Diagram of the transistorized ignition system (Sec 12)

A Battery
B Ignition coil
C Distributor body and contact points
D Distributor cap
E Spark plugs
F Transistor and resistances

Fig. 4.10 Transistor assistance unit socket terminals (Sec 13)

A Normal socket using transistor assistance
B Socket by-passing transistor assistance
1 Coil -
2 Transistor circuit + supply
3 Contact breaker points
4 Earth
5 Transistor circuit to contact breaker points

Part 3: Full electronic ignition system

14 General description

The electronic ignition system operates on an advanced principle whereby the main functions of the distributor are replaced by a computer module.

The system consists of three main components, namely the computer module which incorporates an ignition coil and a vacuum advance unit, the distributor which directs the HT voltage received from the coil to the appropriate spark plug, and an angular position sensor which determines the position and speed of the crankshaft by sensing special segments in the flywheel.

The computer module receives information on crankshaft position relative to TDC and BDC and also engine speed from the angular position sensor, and receives information on engine load from the vacuum advance unit. From these constantly changing variables, the computer calculates the precise instant at which HT voltage should be supplied and triggers the coil accordingly. The voltage then passes from the coil to the appropriate spark plug, via the distributor in the conventional way. The function of the centrifugal and vacuum advance mechanisms as well as the contact breaker points normally associated with a distributor, are all catered for by the computer module, so that the sole purpose of the distributor is to direct the HT voltage from the coil to the appropriate spark plug.

On Turbo models a "pinking" detector is fitted to the cylinder head in order to retard the ignition by 6° in the event of "pinking" (detonation in the combustion chambers).

15 Electronic ignition system - precautions

Due to the sophisticated nature of the electronic ignition system the following precautions must be observed to prevent damage to the components and reduce the risk of personal injury.

1 Ensure that the ignition is switched off before disconnecting any of the ignition wiring.
2 Ensure that the ignition is switched off before connecting or disconnecting any ignition test equipment such as a timing light.
3 Do not connect a suppression condenser or test lamp to the ignition coil negative terminal.
4 Do not connect any test appliance or stroboscopic timing light requiring a 12 volt supply to the ignition coil positive terminal.
5 Do not allow an HT lead to short out or spark against the computer module body.
6 Do not earth the coil primary or secondary circuits.

16 Routine maintenance

1 The only components of the electronic ignition system which require periodic maintenance are the distributor cap, HT leads and spark plugs. These should be treated in the same way as on a conventional system and reference should be made to Section 2 and other applicable Sections of Part 1.
2 On this system dwell angle and ignition timing are a function of the computer module and there is no provision for adjustment. It is possible to check the ignition timing using a stroboscopic timing light, but this should only be necessary as part of a fault finding procedure, as any deviation from the specified setting would indicate a possible fault in the computer module.

17 Distributor - removal and refitting

1 Undo the two screws securing the distributor cap to the distributor body, lift off the cap and move it to one side (photo).
2 Undo the bolt securing the distributor to the cylinder block, withdraw the distributor from its location and recover the seal (photo).
3 To refit the distributor, place it in position in the cylinder block and turn the rotor arm until the drive dog at the base of the distributor shaft positively engages with the driveshaft.
4 Align the hole at the base of the distributor with that in the block and refit the retaining bolt.
5 Refit the distributor cap and tighten the two screws.

Fig. 4.11 Full Electronic ignition system components (Sec 14)

1 Positive (+) supply	8 Coil positive (+) contact (joined internally to 11)	41 and 51 TDC sensor
2 Earth (-)		A Supply connector
3 Tachometer	9 Coil negative (-) contact	B TDC sensor connector
4 and 5 TDC sensor	10 Rotor arm	C Vacuum capsule
6 Coil positive (+) terminal and interference suppression capacitor terminal	11 Positive (+) supply (joined internally to 8)	E Computer module
	12 Coil HT terminal	HT Ignition coil
	21 Earth (-)	M Distributor cap
7 Coil negative (-) terminal	31 Tachometer	P Angular position sensor
		V Flywheel

17.1 Undo the two screws and lift off the distributor cap

18.3 Vacuum pipe location on the computer module (arrowed)

18.4 Pull the multi-plugs from the computer module

18 Computer module - removal and refitting

1 Disconnect the battery negative terminal.

2 Disconnect the HT lead from the ignition coil on the side of the module.

3 Detach the vacuum pipe from the vacuum advance unit (photo).

4 Disconnect the two multi-plug wiring connectors from the module (photo).

5 Unscrew the two nuts securing the unit to the bulkhead and withdraw it from the car. Note the location of the interference suppression capacitor beneath the upper nut (photo).

6 If required, the ignition coil may be removed after disconnecting the wires and undoing the four retaining screws. Do not, however, attempt to remove the vacuum unit, as it is attached internally by a very fine wire which will break if the unit is removed.

7 Refitting the ignition coil to the module, and the module to the car is the reverse sequence of removal.

18.5 The interference suppression capacitor is located beneath the upper mounting nut

19 Angular position sensor - removal and refitting

1 Disconnect the battery negative terminal.
2 Disconnect the smaller of the two wiring multi-plugs from the computer module.
3 Undo and remove the two bolts securing the sensor to the top of the clutch bellhousing and lift off the unit (photo). Note that the two

19.3 The angular position sensor

retaining bolts are of the shouldered type and must not be replaced with ordinary bolts.
4 Refitting is the reverse sequence to removal.

20 Spark plugs and HT leads

Refer to Section 10.

Fault finding - electronic ignition system

Problems associated with the electronic ignition system can usually be grouped into one of two areas, those caused by the more conventional HT side of the system, such as the spark plugs, HT leads, rotor arm and distributor cap, and those caused by the LT circuitry including the computer module and its related components.

It is recommended that the checks described in Section 11 paragraphs 1 to 6 under the heading "Engine fails to start" or paragraphs 10 to 15 under the heading "Engine misfires" should be carried out first, according to the symptoms, paying careful attention to Section 15. If the fault still exists, the following step by step test procedure should be used. For these tests a good quality 0 to 12 volt voltmeter and an ohmmeter will be required.

Engine fails to start

Note: *The figures and numbers shown in brackets refer to the multi-plug connectors and terminal locations shown in Fig. 4.11*

Test conditions	Test	Remedy
1 Connector (A) disconnected, ignition switched on, starter cranking	Is the voltage between pin (1) in connector (A) and earth at least 9.5 volts?	Yes: Proceed to next test No: Check battery condition, check feed wire to connector (A)
2 Connector (A) disconnected, ignition switched off	Is the resistance between pin (2) in connector (A) and earth 0 ohms?	Yes: Proceed to next test No: Check module earth wire to connector (A)

3 Connector (A) disconnected, ignition switched off	Is the resistance between module pin (11) and coil terminal (6) 0 ohms?	Yes: Proceed to next test No: Renew the computer module
4 Connector (A) plugged in, ignition switched on	Is the voltage between coil terminal (6) and earth at least 9.5 volts?	Yes: Proceed to next test No: Move connector (A) in and out, and check coil terminal connections. Renew connector (A) if necessary
5 Connector (B) disconnected, ignition switched off	Is the resistance between pins (4) and (5) in connector (B) 200 ± 50 ohms?	Yes: Proceed to next test No: Renew the angular position sensor
6 Connector (B) disconnected, ignition switched off	Is the distance between the angular position sensor and the flywheel 1.0 ± 0.5 mm (0.04 ± 0.02 in)?	Yes: Proceed to next test No: Renew the angular position sensor
7 Connectors (A) and (B) plugged in, coil removed, starter cranking	Does a test bulb connected between terminal (8) and (9) flash at starter motor speed?	Yes: Proceed to next test No: Renew the computer module
8 Coil removed, ignition switched off	Is the resistance between coil terminals (7) and (12) 2000 to 12000 ohms?	Yes: Proceed to next test No: Renew the ignition coil
9 Coil removed, ignition switched off	Is the resistance between coil terminals (6) and (7) 0.4 to 0.8 ohms?	Yes: Proceed to next test No: Renew the ignition coil
10 Connector (A) disconnected, ignition switched off	Is the resistance between pins (2) and (3) of connector (A) greater than 20 000 ohms?	Yes: Renew computer module if no HT No: Repair wiring or renew tachometer

Engine is difficult to start, but performs satisfactorily once running

Test conditions	Test	Remedy
1 Disconnect HT lead from centre of distributor cap, hold lead 5 to 20 mm away from the cylinder block	Is there a rapid succession of blue sparks between the end of the lead and the cylinder block with the engine cranking?	Yes: Proceed to next test No: Carry out the test procedure under "Engine fails to start" earlier in this Section
2 Stroboscopic timing light connected to No 1 cylinder, engine idling, vacuum pipe disconnected	Is the ignition timing in accordance with the specified setting?	Yes: Check carburation and engine mechanical condition No: Renew the computer module

Engine performance unsatisfactory

Test conditions	Test	Remedy
1 Run engine at a steady 3000 rpm, disconnect vacuum pipe at computer module	Does the engine speed drop as the vacuum pipe is disconnected?	Yes: Carry out the previous tests under "Engine difficult to start" No: Renew the computer module after checking that the vacuum pipe is in good condition and correctly fitted

Engine "pinking" (pinging noise under load)

Test conditions	Test	Remedy
1 Stroboscopic timing light connected to No. 1 cylinder, engine idling	Does the ignition timing retard by 6° when the cylinder head is tapped gently with a bronze drift near the "pinking" detector?	Yes: Check ignition timing, carburettor settings and carbon build-up in engine No: Renew the "pinking" detector

4

Notes

Chapter 5 Clutch

For modifications, and information applicable to later models, see Supplement at end of manual

Contents

Degrees of difficulty

Easy, suitable for novice with little experience	**Fairly easy,** suitable for beginner with some experience	**Fairly difficult,** suitable for competent DIY mechanic	**Difficult,** suitable for experienced DIY mechanic	**Very difficult,** suitable for expert DIY or professional

Specifications

Type .... Single dry plate, self-adjusting cable operation

Clutch disc diameter
Non-Turbo models .... 181.5 mm (7.146 in)
Turbo models .... 200.0 mm (7.874 in)

Disc lining thickness (total) .... 7.7 mm (0.303 in)

Torque wrench setting | **Nm** | **lbf ft**
Clutch cover bolts .... 25 | 18

1 General description

All manual transmission models are equipped with a cable-operated, single dry plate diaphragm spring clutch assembly. The unit consists of a steel cover which is dowelled and bolted to the rear face of the flywheel, and contains the pressure plate and diaphragm spring.

The clutch disc is free to slide along the splined gearbox input shaft and is held in position between the flywheel and the pressure plate by the pressure of the diaphragm spring. Friction lining material is riveted to the clutch disc which has a spring cushioned hub to absorb transmission shocks and help ensure a smooth take-up of the drive.

The clutch is actuated by a cable controlled by the clutch pedal. The clutch release mechanism consists of a release arm and bearing which are in permanent contact with the fingers of the diaphragm spring.

Depressing the clutch pedal actuates the release arm by means of the cable. The arm pushes the release bearing against the diaphragm fingers, so moving the centre of the diaphragm spring inwards. As the centre of the spring is pushed in, the outside of the spring pivots out, so moving the pressure plate backwards and disengaging its grip on the clutch disc.

When the pedal is released, the diaphragm spring forces the pressure plate into contact with the friction linings on the clutch disc. The disc is now firmly sandwiched between the

1.1 Self-adjusting quadrant (1) and tension spring (2) on the clutch pedal

Fig. 5.1 Clutch components (Sec 1)
1 Disc
2 Cover (including pressure plate and diaphragm spring)
3 Release bearing
4 Cable
5 Automatic adjuster
6 Pad
7 Pedal

Fig. 5.2 Cross-section of clutch components (Sec 1)

pressure plate and the flywheel, thus transmitting engine power to the gearbox.

Wear of the friction material on the clutch disc is automatically compensated by a self-adjusting mechanism attached to the clutch pedal. The mechanism consists of a serrated quadrant, a notched cam and a tension spring. One end of the clutch cable is attached to the quadrant which is free to pivot on the pedal, but is kept in tension by the spring (photo). As the pedal is depressed the notched cam contacts the quadrant thus locking it and allowing the pedal to pull the cable and operate the clutch. As the pedal is released the tension spring causes the quadrant to move free of the notched cam and rotate slightly, thus taking up any free play that may exist in the cable.

There are no Routine maintenance procedures for the clutch components as attention is only necessary when a component is worn out.

2 Clutch assembly - removal and refitting

Note: *For Turbo and 1721 cc models, see Chapter 12.*

1 Access to the clutch is gained by separating the gearbox from the engine, and there is a choice of three ways to achieve this. The engine and gearbox can be removed as

2.2 Removing the clutch cover retaining bolts

one unit then separated on the bench, the engine can be removed leaving the gearbox in situ, or the gearbox can be removed leaving the engine in situ. If no other work is necessary it is suggested that the latter method is used as described in Chapter 6.

2 Having separated the gearbox from the engine, undo and remove the clutch cover retaining bolts, working in a diagonal sequence and slackening the bolts only a few turns at a time (photo).

3 Ease the clutch cover off its locating dowels and be prepared to catch the clutch disc which will drop out as the cover is removed. Note which way round the disc is fitted.

4 It is important that no oil or grease is allowed to come into contact with the friction material of the clutch disc or the pressure plate and flywheel faces. It is advisable to refit the clutch assembly with clean hands and to wipe down the pressure plate and flywheel faces with a clean dry rag before assembly begins.

5 Begin reassembly by placing the clutch disc against the flywheel with the side having the larger offset facing away from the flywheel.

6 Place the clutch cover over the dowels, refit the retaining bolts and tighten them finger tight so that the clutch disc is gripped, but can still be moved.

7 The clutch disc must now be centralised so that, when the engine and gearbox are mated, the splines of the gearbox input shaft will pass through the splines in the centre of the clutch disc hub.

8 Centralisation can be carried out quite easily by inserting a round bar or long screwdriver through the hole in the centre of the clutch disc so that the end of the bar rests in the hole in the end of the crankshaft containing the input shaft support bearing.

9 Using the support bearing as a fulcrum, moving the bar sideways or up and down will move the clutch disc in whichever direction is necessary to achieve centralisation.

10 Centralisation is easily judged by removing the bar and viewing the clutch disc hub in relation to the support bearing. When the support bearing appears exactly in the centre of the clutch disc hub, all is correct.

TOOL TiP

An accurate method of clutch disc centralisation is to use a commercially available clutch aligning tool obtainable from most accessory shops.

11 Once the clutch is centralised, progressively tighten the cover bolts in a diagonal sequence to the torque setting given in the Specifications. If necessary prevent the flywheel from turning by inserting a screwdriver in the teeth of the starter ring gear by one of the gearbox location studs.

12 Assemble the gearbox to the engine in reverse order. Check that the self-adjusting mechanism on the clutch pedal is correctly positioned with the quadrant teeth opposite the notched cam. The mechanism will automatically set itself to the correct position.

3 Clutch assembly - inspection

1 With the clutch assembly removed, clean off all traces of asbestos dust using a dry cloth. This is best done outside or in a well-ventilated area; *asbestos dust is harmful, and must not be inhaled.*

2 Examine the linings of the clutch disc for wear and loose rivets, and the disc rim for distortion, cracks, broken torsion springs and worn splines. The surface of the friction linings may be highly glazed, but, as long as the friction material pattern can be clearly seen, this is satisfactory. If there is any sign of oil contamination, indicated by a continuous, or patchy, shiny black discolouration, the disc must be renewed and the source of the contamination traced and rectified. This will be either a leaking crankshaft oil seal or gearbox input shaft oil seal - or both. Renewal procedures are given in Chapter 1 and Chapter 6 respectively. The disc must also be renewed if the lining thickness has worn down to, or just above, the level of the rivet heads.

3 Check the machined faces of the flywheel and pressure plate. If either is grooved, or heavily scored, renewal is necessary. The pressure plate must also be renewed if any cracks are apparent, or if the diaphragm spring is damaged or its pressure suspect.

4 With the gearbox removed it is advisable to check the condition of the release bearing, as described in the following Section.

4.2 Showing attachment of release bearing to release fork

4.5A Release fork rubber cover

4.5B Pull the release fork from the ball pivot stub (arrowed)

4 Clutch release bearing - removal, inspection and refitting

1 To gain access to the release bearing it is necessary to separate the engine and gearbox either by removing the engine or gearbox individually, or by removing both units as an assembly and separating them after removal. Depending on the method chosen, the appropriate procedures will be found in Chapter 1 or Chapter 6.

2 With the gearbox removed from the engine, tilt the release fork and slide the bearing assembly off the gearbox input shaft guide tube (photo).

3 To remove the bearing from its holder (where applicable), release the four tags of the spring retainer, lift off the retainer and remove the bearing.

4 Check the bearing for smoothness of operation and renew it if there is any roughness or harshness as the bearing is spun.

5 To remove the release fork, disengage the rubber cover and then pull the fork upwards to release it from its ball pivot stud (photos).

6 Refitting the release fork and release bearing is the reverse sequence to removal, but note the following points:
a) Lubricate the release fork pivot ball stud and the release bearing-to-diaphragm spring contact areas sparingly with molybdenum disulphide grease.
b) Ensure that the release fork spring retainer locates behind the flat shoulder of the ball pivot stud.

5 Clutch cable - removal and refitting

1 Working in the engine compartment pull the inner cable and remove it from the end of the release fork (photo), then disengage the outer cable from the bracket on the bellhousing.

2 Working inside the car release the inner cable from the quadrant and cam on the pedal.

3 Using a screwdriver push the outer cable from its location in the bulkhead.

4 Pull the cable through into the engine compartment, detach it from the support clips and remove it from the car.

5 Refitting is a reversal of removal. When the inner cable is attached to the end of the release fork, the quadrant on the pedal will be repositioned in relation to the cam automatically. Depress the pedal several times to settle the cable ends so that the self-adjusting mechanism obtains its final working position which provides 2.0 mm (0.079 in) free play on the inner cable.

Fig. 5.4 Cross-section of ball pivot stud showing correct location of release fork spring (1) on pivot stud (2) (Sec 4)

Fig. 5.3 Showing correct location of the release fork in the release bearing (Sec 4)

A Retaining shoulder

5.1 Detach the inner cable from the release fork

6 Clutch pedal -
removal and refitting

1 Working in the engine compartment pull the inner cable and remove it from the end of the release fork.

2 Working inside the car release the inner cable from the quadrant and cam on the pedal self-adjusting mechanism. Remove the steering column lower shroud if necessary.

3 Prise the spring clip from the clutch pedal end of the pivot shaft and remove the washer.

4 Slide the pivot shaft to the right until the clutch pedal and quadrant arms can be withdrawn.

5 With the pedal removed inspect the two bushes and the self-adjusting mechanism for wear and damage. Renew the components as necessary.

6 Refitting is a reversal of removal, but lubricate the pivot shaft and self-adjusting mechanism components with molybdenum disulphide grease. After re-connecting the cable depress the pedal several times.

Fig. 5.5 Diagram of cable self-adjusting mechanism on the pedal (Sec 6)

A Quadrant arms (free to pivot on shaft)
B Quadrant (free to pivot on arms)
C Toothed cam (fixed to pedal)
D Tension spring

Fault finding - clutch

Judder when taking up drive

☐ Loose or worn engine mountings
☐ Clutch disc contaminated with oil, or linings worn
☐ Clutch cable sticking or frayed
☐ Faulty pressure plate assembly

Clutch fails to disengage

☐ Clutch self-adjusting mechanism faulty or inoperative
☐ Clutch disc sticking on input shaft splines
☐ Faulty pressure plate assembly
☐ Cable broken

Clutch slips

☐ Clutch self-adjusting mechanism faulty or inoperative
☐ Clutch disc contaminated with oil or linings worn
☐ Faulty pressure plate assembly
☐ Diaphragm spring broken

Noise when depressing clutch pedal

☐ Worn release bearing
☐ Faulty pressure plate assembly
☐ Diaphragm spring broken
☐ Worn or dry cable or pedal bushes

Noise when releasing clutch pedal

☐ Faulty pressure plate assembly
☐ Broken clutch disc cushioning springs
☐ Gearbox internal wear

Chapter 6
Manual gearbox and automatic transmission

For modifications, and information applicable to later models, see Supplement at end of manual

Contents

Degrees of difficulty

Easy, suitable for novice with little experience		**Fairly easy,** suitable for beginner with some experience		**Fairly difficult,** suitable for competent DIY mechanic	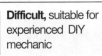	**Difficult,** suitable for experienced DIY mechanic		**Very difficult,** suitable for expert DIY or professional	

Specifications

Part 1: Manual gearbox

Type . . . . Four or five forward speeds (all synchromesh) and reverse. Final drive differential integral with main gearbox

Designation
Four-speed units JB4
Five-speed units . . . . JB3 or JB5

Ratios
JB4:
  1st . . . . 3.727 : 1
  2nd . . . . 2.053 : 1
  3rd . . . . 1.320 : 1
  4th . . . . 0.903 : 1
  Reverse . . . . 3.545 : 1
  Final drive . . . . 3.867 : 1 (58/15) or 3.294 : 1 (56/17)
JB3 . . . . See Chapter 12
JB5:
  1st . . . . 3.727 : 1 or 3.091 : 1
  2nd . . . . 2.053 : 1 or 1.842 : 1
  3rd . . . . 1.320 : 1
  4th . . . . 0.967 : 1
  5th . . . . 0.794 : 1 or 0.758 : 1
  Reverse . . . . 3.545 : 1
  Final drive . . . . 4.067 : 1 (61/15), 3.428 : 1 (55/16), or 3.294 : 1 (56/17)

Lubricant
Type/specification:
  Non-Turbo models . . . . Gear oil, viscosity SAE 80W
  Turbo models . . . . Gear oil, viscosity SAE 75W/90S

Capacity:	Steel filler plug	Plastic filler plug
JB4	3.25 litre (5.72 Imp pt)	2.75 litre (4.34 Imp pt)
JB3 and JB5	3.40 litre (5.98 Imp pt)	2.90 litre (5.10 Imp pt)

6

Torque wrench settings

	Nm	lbf ft
Gearbox mounting nuts	40	30
Bellhousing-to-engine nuts and bolts	25	18
Mechanism casing to clutch and differential housing	25	18
Input shaft nut (five-speed)	135	100
Mainshaft bolt (five-speed)	80	59

Part 2: Automatic transmission

Type . . . . Three forward speeds and reverse, final drive differential integral with transmission

Designation MB1

Ratios

1st	2.50 : 1
2nd	1.50 : 1
3rd	1.00 : 1
Reverse	2.00 : 1
Final drive	3.294 : 1 (56/17)

Lubricant

Type/specification . . . . Dexron type ATF
Capacity:
    Total - dry unit . . . . 4.5 litre (7.92 Imp pt)
    Refill after fluid change - approximate . . . . 2.0 litre (3.52 Imp pt)

Torque wrench settings

	Nm	lbf ft
Transmission mounting nuts	40	30
Bellhousing-to-engine nuts and bolts	25	18
Torque converter to driveplate:		
Bolts	30	22
Nuts	19	14
Fluid cooler union nuts	20	15
Fluid cooler mounting bolts	40	30

Fig. 6.1 Cut-away view of the four-speed (JB4) and five-speed (JB5) manual gearboxes (Sec 1)

Note: *JB3 five-speed gearbox similar to JB5*

Fig. 6.2 Cross-section view of the four-speed gearbox and final drive assembly (Sec 1)

3.3 Disconnecting the gearbox breather tube (shown with gearbox removed)

3.4 Drain plug location

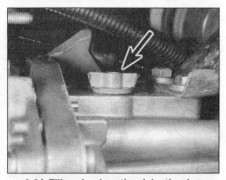

3.6A Filler plug location (plastic plug shown)

1 General description - manual gearbox

The gearbox is equipped with either four forward and one reverse gear or five forward and one reverse gear, according to model. Baulk ring synchromesh gear engagement is used on all forward gears.

The final drive (differential) unit is integral with the main gearbox and is located between the mechanism casing and clutch and differential housing. The gearbox and differential both share the same lubricating oil.

Gearshift is by means of a floor-mounted lever connected by a remote control housing and gearchange rod to the gearbox fork control shaft.

If gearbox overhaul is necessary, due consideration should be given to the costs involved, since it is often more economical to obtain a service exchange or good secondhand gearbox rather than fit new parts to the existing unit.

2 Routine maintenance - manual gearbox

At the intervals specified in the "Routine maintenance" section in the front of the manual carry out the following procedures.

1 Unscrew the filler plug from the front-facing side of the gearbox with the car positioned on a level surface. Check and if necessary top up the level with reference to Section 3.
2 Drain and refill the gearbox with fresh oil as described in Section 3.
3 Visually inspect the gearbox joint faces and oil seals for signs of oil leakage or damage.

3 Manual gearbox - draining and refilling

1 Position the car over an inspection pit, on car ramps, or jack it up but make sure that it is level.
2 Place a suitable container beneath the gearbox.
3 Where applicable remove the splash shield from the underbody. Disconnect the gearbox breather tube (photo).
4 Unscrew the drain plug and allow the oil to drain into the container (photo).
5 With all the oil drained wipe clean the drain plug then refit and tighten it.
6 Unscrew the filler plug from the side of the gearbox then pour in the specified grade and quantity of oil (photos).
7 Where a steel filler plug is fitted the oil level should be up to the lower edge of the filler hole. Insert a finger to check the level.

8 Where a plastic filler plug is fitted check the level by inserting the shouldered end of the plug through the hole without engaging the threads, then positioning the plug so that the outer arrow is pointing upwards. On removal of the plug the level should be at the top of the black section (Fig. 6.3). The bottom of the black indicates the minimum level (photo).
9 After filling refit and tighten the filler plug and re-connect the breather tube.

4 Manual gearbox - removal and refitting

Note: *For Turbo and 1721 cc models, see Chapter 12.*

1 Apply the handbrake then jack up the front of the car and support on axle stands.
2 Remove the bonnet as described in Chapter 10.
3 Drain the gearbox as described in Section 3.
4 Remove both driveshafts as described in Chapter 7.

6

3.6B Filling the gearbox with oil

3.8 Showing the plastic filler plug and level extension

Fig. 6.3 Method of using plastic filler plug to check the gearbox oil level (Sec 3)

A Maximum level   C Locating shoulder
B Minimum level   D Point of arrow

4.5A Slide back the gearchange rod rubber cover . . .

4.5B . . . undo the retaining nut and bolt . . .

4.5C . . . then slide off the rod and recover the distance sleeve (arrowed)

5 Disconnect the gearchange rod from the gearbox with reference to Section 6 (photos).
6 Unbolt the tie-rod from the clutch bellhousing and engine cylinder block.
7 Unbolt the cover plate from the clutch bellhousing.
8 Disconnect the battery negative lead, then disconnect the wiring from the reversing switch (photo).
9 Unbolt the starter cover plate.
10 Remove the splash shield from under the left-hand wheel arch.
11 Unscrew the nuts from the gearbox front and rear mountings and loosen only the engine mountings. Using a socket and universal joint bar unscrew the bolt from the gearbox rear mounting.
12 Remove the air cleaner as described in Chapter 3.
13 Place a piece of thick cardboard on the engine large enough to take the radiator. Unclip the expansion bottle/tank and disconnect the wiring from the electric cooling fan and thermostatic switch. Lift the radiator from its mountings and place it on the cardboard together with the expansion tank. Do not disconnect the top and bottom hoses.
14 Remove the ignition transistor assistance unit or computer module and the angular position sensor (photo) as described in Chapter 4.
15 Disconnect the clutch cable (Chapter 5) and the speedometer cable (Chapter 11).
16 Unbolt the earthing braid from the body.
17 Disconnect the exhaust downpipe from

the exhaust manifold with reference to Chapter 3.
18 Using a trolley jack and block of wood raise the engine until the gearbox mountings are free.
19 Unscrew the starter mounting bolts leaving the starter attached to the bracket on the cylinder block.
20 Support the weight of the gearbox using a suitable hoist. Alternatively a trolley jack can be used, but in this case an assistant will be required to help lift out the gearbox by hand.
21 Unscrew and remove the nuts and bolts securing the gearbox to the engine. On models where there is limited working room it will also be necessary to unscrew the two location studs from the engine using two nuts tightened together then turning the innermost nut.
22 Unbolt the front mounting bracket from the gearbox (photo).
23 Lower the engine a little then pull away the gearbox keeping it level with the engine and guiding it between the left-hand side members. Now raise the engine again and lift the gearbox from the engine compartment taking care not to damage the surrounding bodywork.
24 Refitting is a reversal of removal, but tighten all nuts and bolts to the specified torque. Refill the gearbox with oil as described in Section 3. Refer to Chapter 3 for the special method of tightening the exhaust downpipe nuts.

5 Manual gearbox overhaul - general

Complete dismantling and overhaul of the gearbox, particularly with respect to the differential and the bearings in the clutch and differential housing, entails the use of a hydraulic press and a number of special tools. For this reason it is not recommended that a complete overhaul be attempted by the home mechanic unless he has access to the tools required and feels reasonably confident after studying the procedure.

Before starting any repair work on the gearbox, thoroughly clean the exterior of the casings using paraffin or a suitable solvent. Dry the unit with a lint-free rag. Make sure that an uncluttered working area is available with some small containers and trays handy to store the various parts. Label everything as it is removed.

Before starting reassembly all the components must be spotlessly clean and should be liberally lubricated with the recommended grade of gear oil during assembly.

Apart from the additional 5th gear and slight differences in the selector mechanism, the four- and five-speed gearboxes are virtually identical.

After dismantling, all roll pins, circlips and snap-rings must be renewed, regardless of their condition, before reassembling.

4.8 Reverse lamp switch location

4.14 Angular position sensor location

4.22 Front mounting bracket

Fig. 6.4 Exploded view of the differential assembly (Sec 5)

38 O-ring
39 Oil seal
40 Circlip
41 Speedometer drivegear
42 Differential inner bearing
43 Plain thrust washer
44 Dished thrust washer
45 Differential crownwheel assembly
46 Snap-ring
47 Shim
48 Spider sun wheel
49 Planet wheel shaft
50 Planet wheels
51 Planet wheel thrust washers
52 Planet wheel and stub shaft

Fig. 6.5 Exploded view of the mainshaft and input shaft (Sec 5)

1 Roller bearing
2 Mainshaft
3 Roller
4 Spring plate
5 Snap-ring
6 2nd speed gear
7 3rd speed gear
8 Baulk ring
9 3rd/4th synchroniser unit
10 4th speed gear
11 Thrust washer
12 5th speed driven gear
13 Collar
14 Bolt
15 1st speed gear
16 1st/2nd synchroniser unit
17 Input shaft
18 Thrust washers
18 Ball bearing
20 Circlip
21 Thrust washer
22 Bush
23 Needle roller bearing
24 5th speed driving gear
25 Spring
26 5th synchroniser unit
27 Nut
32 Reverse selector shaft and gear

6

6.2 Gearchange tension spring on the underbody

6.4 Gear lever with rubber gaiter removed

1 Gearchange rod
2 Tension spring
3 Remote control housing
4 Gear lever knob
5 Rubber gaiter
6 Roll pin
7 Reverse stop release
8 Circlip
9 Gear lever
10 O-ring
11 Roll pin
12 Reverse stop release holder
13 Spring
14 Top cup
15 Half cup
16 Support
17 Bottom cup
18 Half cup holder
19 Protector
20 Spring washer
21 Roll pin
22 Stop

Fig. 6.6 Exploded view of the gear lever and remote control housing components (Sec 6)

6 Gear lever and remote control housing - removal, refitting and adjustment

1 To remove the gear lever and remote control housing first jack up the front of the car and support it on axle stands.
2 From underneath, unhook the tension spring fitted between the gearchange rod and the stud on the vehicle floor (photo).

Fig. 6.7 Gear lever O-ring (10) and remote control housing (3) (Sec 6)

3 Slacken the clamp bolt securing the gearchange rod to the gear lever yoke and withdraw the yoke from the rod.
4 Refer to Chapter 10 and remove the centre console where fitted, or on models without a centre console remove the rubber gaiter and slide it up the gear lever (photo).
5 Undo the four bolts securing the remote control housing to the floor and withdraw the assembly from the car. Recover the sealing gasket.
6 If necessary the gear lever assembly may be dismantled by referring to the component locations shown in Fig. 6.6. Note that the gear lever knob is bonded with adhesive to the lever.
7 Reassembly and refitting are the reverse of the above procedures. Adjust the gear lever as follows before tightening the yoke clamp bolt.
8 Select 2nd gear at the gearbox by moving the fork control shaft.
9 Move the gear lever so that the O-ring on the gear lever rests against the rear left face of the housing (Fig. 6.7) and at the same time insert the yoke in the gearchange rod. There should be a space of 5.0 mm (0.2 in) between the end of the rod and the yoke end nearest the lever. Hold the components in this position and tighten the clamp bolt. Refit the tension spring.
10 Check that all the gears can be selected then refit the rubber gaiter or centre console as applicable. Lower the car to the ground.

7 General description - automatic transmission

The automatic transmission is of three-speed type incorporating a torque converter, an epicyclic geartrain, hydraulically-operated clutches and brakes, and an electronic control unit.

The torque converter provides a fluid coupling between engine and transmission which acts as an automatic clutch, and also provides a degree of torque multiplication when accelerating.

The epicyclic geartrain provides either of the three forward or one reverse gear ratios according to which of its component parts are held stationary or allowed to turn. The components of the geartrain are held or released by brakes and clutches which are activated by a hydraulic control unit. An oil pump within the transmission provides the necessary hydraulic pressure to operate the brakes and clutches.

Impulses from switches and sensors connected to the transmission, throttle and selector linkage are directed to a computer module which determines the ratio to be selected from the information received. The computer activates solenoid valves which in turn open or close ducts within the hydraulic control unit. This causes the clutches and brakes to hold or release the various components of the geartrain and provide the correct ratio for the particular engine speed or

Fig. 6.8 Cut-away view of the automatic transmission (Sec 7)

Note: *MJ type automatic transmission shown but MB1 type uses the same components*

Fig. 6.9 Automatic transmission electronic control layout (Sec 7)

1 Fuse - reversing lamp (5 amp)	6 Starter	BE Computer module
2 Fuse (1.5 amp)	7 Automatic transmission warning lamp	CM Multi-function switch
3 Ignition switch	8 Automatic transmission earth	CV Speed sensor
4 Starter relay		EL Solenoid valve
5 Reversing lamps	22 Vacuum capsule	RC Kick-down switch
		P Load potentiometer

load. The information from the computer module can be overriden by use of the selector lever and a particular gear can be held if required, regardless of engine speed.

Due to the complexity of the automatic transmission any repair or overhaul work must be left to a Renault dealer with the necessary special equipment for fault diagnosis and repair. The contents of the following Sections are therefore confined to supplying general information and any service information and instruction that can be used by the owner.

8 Routine maintenance - automatic transmission

At the intervals specified in the "Routine maintenance" section in the front of the manual carry out the following procedures.
1 Check and if necessary top up the automatic transmission fluid level as described in Section 9.
2 Drain and refill the automatic transmission with fresh fluid as described in Section 10.
3 Visually inspect the automatic transmission joint faces and oil seals for signs of fluid leakage or damage.

9 Automatic transmission fluid - level checking

1 Check the fluid level when the car has been standing for some time and the fluid is cold.
2 With the car standing on level ground, start the engine and allow it to run for a few minutes.
3 Move the selector lever to P if not already in this position.
4 With the engine still idling withdraw the dipstick from the front of the transmission, wipe it on a clean cloth, insert it again then withdraw it once more and read off the level. Ideally the level should be in the centre of the mark on the dipstick. The fluid must never be allowed to fall below the bottom of the mark

6

Fig. 6.10 Transmission fluid dipstick location (arrowed) (Sec 9)

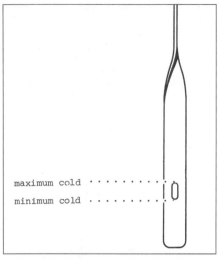

Fig. 6.11 Dipstick fluid level markings (Sec 9)

and the transmission must never be overfilled so that the level is above the top of the mark.

5 If topping-up is necessary, switch off the engine and add a quantity of the specified fluid to the transmission through the dipstick tube.

> *When topping-up the automatic transmission fluid use a funnel with a fine mesh screen to avoid spillage and to ensure that any foreign matter is trapped.*

6 After topping-up recheck the level again, as described above, refit the dipstick and switch off the engine.

10 Automatic transmission fluid - draining and refilling

1 The fluid must only be drained when cold.
2 Position the car on level ground and place a suitable container beneath the drain plug on the transmission fluid pan and at the base of the transmission housing (Fig. 6.12).
3 Remove the dipstick to speed up the draining operation, undo the two drain plugs and allow the fluid to drain.
4 When all the fluid has drained (this may take quite some time) refit the drain plugs.
5 Place a funnel with fine mesh screen in the dipstick tube and fill the transmission with the specified type of fluid. Depending on the extent to which the fluid was allowed to drain, refilling will only require approximately 2 litre (3.5 Imp pint). Add about half this amount and then check the level on the dipstick. When the level approaches the mark, place the selector lever in P, start the engine and allow it to run for approximately 2 minutes. Now check the level and complete the final topping up, as described in Section 9.

Fig. 6.12 Transmission drain plug locations (arrowed) (Sec 10)

11 Automatic transmission - removal and refitting

Note: *This Section describes removal of the automatic transmission leaving the engine in the car, however as from 1986 models the transmission must be removed together with the engine as described in Chapter 1 then separated using the procedure described in paragraphs 6,10,14,16 to 18,20,23 and 25 of this Section. This is because a larger torque converter is fitted to these models. Refit with reference to paragraph 28 of this Section.*

1 After disconnecting all the relevant attachments, controls and services, the automatic transmission is removed upwards and out of the engine compartment. Due to the weight of the unit, it will be necessary to have some form of lighting equipment available, such as an engine crane or suitable hoist to enable the unit to be removed in this way.
2 Begin by disconnecting the battery negative terminal and then refer to Section 10 and drain the transmission fluid.
3 Jack up the front of the car and support it on axle stands. Remove both front roadwheels.
4 Refer to Chapter 7 and remove the left-hand driveshaft completely, then disconnect the right-hand driveshaft inner joint yoke.
5 Working in the engine compartment, remove the air cleaner, as described in Chapter 3.
6 Undo the two shouldered bolts and remove the angular position sensor from the bellhousing.
7 Extract the speedometer cable wire retaining clip from its locating holes in the rear engine mounting bracket and transmission housing. Note the fitted direction of the clip. Withdraw the speedometer cable from the transmission.
8 Undo the two bolts and remove the tension

Fig. 6.13 Transmission selector control rod disconnection points (A and B) (Sec 11)

springs securing the exhaust front section flange to the exhaust manifold.
9 Note the locations of the wires at the starter solenoid and disconnect them.
10 Undo the starter motor support bracket bolt and the three bolts securing the starter to the bellhousing, then remove the starter. Note the locating dowel in the upper rear bolt location.
11 Disconnect the wiring to the radiator fan motor and thermostatic switch on the right-hand side of the radiator. Release the radiator upper spring retaining clamp, lift the radiator up and lay it over the engine with the hoses still attached. Protect the matrix with a sheet of card.
12 Disconnect the transmission selector control rod from the bracket and bellcrank, as shown in Fig. 6.13.
13 Disconnect the vacuum hose from the vacuum capsule on the front of the transmission.
14 Remove the multi-function switch from the left-hand side of the transmission.
15 Detach any clips and remaining cables as necessary and position all the disconnected wiring, harness and cables to one side so that

Fig. 6.14 Fluid cooler union nuts (A and B) at the transmission (Sec 11)

Fig. 6.15 The Renault tool shown or a suitable strip of metal may be used to retain the torque converter (Sec 11)

there is clear access to the transmission from above.

16 From under the car, undo the bolts securing the lower cover plate to the bellhousing and remove the plate.

17 Mark the driveplate in relation to the torque converter then turn the driveplate as necessary and undo the bolts or nuts securing it to the torque converter.

18 Undo the bolts securing the steady rod to the engine and transmission, then remove the rod.

19 Undo the fluid cooler union nuts and remove the pipes from the transmission. Plug the unions to prevent dirt entry.

20 Bolt a suitable strip of metal, using one of the coverplate bolt holes, so that the torque converter will remain in place on the transmission as it is removed.

21 Position a jack under the engine sump with an interposed block of wood, and attach a crane or hoist to the transmission using chain slings. Depending on the type of lifting equipment being used, it may be beneficial to remove the bonnet, as described in Chapter 10.

22 Raise the jack and crane and just take the weight of the engine and transmission.

23 Undo all the bolts around the periphery of the bellhousing securing the transmission to the engine. In addition to the bolts there are two nuts or studs, one each side of the bellhousing. After undoing the nuts, the studs must be removed and this can be done by locking two nuts tightly together on the stud then unscrewing it using the innermost nut.

24 Undo the bolts and nuts securing the transmission mounting brackets to the rubber mountings. Raise the engine and transmission slightly to free the mountings then remove the transmission mounting brackets. Also slacken the engine mountings.

25 Move the engine and transmission as necessary and withdraw the transmission sideways off the engine.

26 Temporarily lower the transmission onto blocks and reposition the chain, as shown in Fig. 6.16. The transmission must be tipped up

Fig. 6.16 After separating the transmission from the engine, attach the lifting chains as shown and position the crane (H) at point (E) on the chain (Sec 11)

vertically to provide clearance for removal.

27 Lift the transmission using the crane, move the engine within its limits and allow the transmission to adopt the position shown in Fig. 6.17. Continue carefully lifting the transmission until it can swing over the wing or front panel, then lower the unit to the ground.

28 Refitting the automatic transmission is the reverse sequence to removal, but bear in mind the following points:

a) *Lubricate the torque converter location in the crankshaft with molybdenum grease.*

b) *Fit the two studs to either side of the bellhousing before refitting the remainder of the transmission-to-engine retaining bolts.*

c) *Refer to Chapter 3 for the special method of tightening the exhaust downpipe nuts.*

d) *Refit the driveshafts, as described in Chapter 7.*

e) *Refill the transmission with fluid, as described in Section 10 of this Chapter.*

Fig. 6.18 Selector rod clamp plate location under the car (D) (Sec 12)

Fig. 6.17 The transmission must be tipped up vertically to allow removal from the engine compartment (Sec 11)

12 Automatic transmission selector mechanism - adjustment

1 Jack up the front of the car and support it on axle stands.

2 Move the selector lever inside the car to the P position.

3 Slacken the selector rod clamp plate nuts under the car so that the rod is free to move within the clamp plate.

4 Check that the selector lever on the transmission is also in the P position by turning it anti-clockwise as far as it will go if not already in this position.

5 Now tighten the selector rod clamp plate nuts.

6 Lower the car to the ground and check that all the selector positions can be engaged and that the starter only operates in the P and neutral positions.

6

Fig. 6.19 Move the transmission selector lever (L) as shown to select P (Sec 12)

13 Automatic transmission selector mechanism - removal and refitting

1 Jack up the front of the car and support it on axle stands.

2 Remove the centre console, as described in Chapter 11.

3 From under the car, extract the retaining clip, washer and clevis pin securing the gear selector lever to the selector rod.

4 Undo the nuts and bolts securing the gear selector housing to the floor, disconnect the illumination bulb wiring and remove the housing from the car.

5 If necessary the housing can be dismantled by referring to the component locations shown in Fig. 6.20.

6 Reassembling and refitting are the reverse of the above procedures. Adjust the mechanism, as described in Section 12, after refitting.

Fig. 6.20 Exploded view of the selector mechanism components (Sec 13)

Fault finding - manual gearbox

Gearbox noisy in neutral
☐ Input shaft bearings worn

Gearbox noisy only when moving (in all gears)
☐ Mainshaft bearings worn
☐ Differential bearings worn

Difficulty in engaging gears
☐ Clutch fault
☐ Gear lever out of adjustment

Gearbox noisy in only one gear
☐ Worn, damaged or chipped gear teeth

Ineffective synchromesh
☐ Worn baulk rings or synchroniser units

Jumping out of gear
☐ Worn synchroniser units
☐ Worn selector shaft detent grooves or broken plunger or ball spring
☐ Worn selector forks
☐ Gear or synchroniser unit loose on shaft (5th gear only)

Fault finding - automatic transmission

In the event of a fault occurring on the transmission, it is first necessary to determine whether it is of an electrical, mechanical or hydraulic nature and to do this special test equipment is required. It is therefore essential to have this work carried out by a Renault dealer if a transmission fault is suspected or if the transmission warning lamp on the instrument panel illuminates.

Do not remove the transmission from the car for possible repair before professional fault diagnosis has been carried out, since most tests require the transmission to be in the vehicle.

Chapter 7 Driveshafts

For modifications, and information applicable to later models, see Supplement at end of manual

Contents

Degrees of difficulty

Easy, suitable for novice with little experience	Fairly easy, suitable for beginner with some experience	Fairly difficult, suitable for competent DIY mechanic	Difficult, suitable for experienced DIY mechanic	Very difficult, suitable for expert DIY or professional

Specifications

Type .... Unequal length tubular driveshafts with sliding tripod constant velocity joints

Lubrication
Outer CV joints and right-hand inner CV joint .... Elf S747
Left-hand inner CV joint .... Lubricated by gearbox oil or automatic transmission fluid

Grease quantities
Outer CV joints .... 196 g (6.91 oz)
Left-hand inner CV joint .... 140 g (4.94 oz)

Torque wrench settings	Nm	lbf ft
Driveshaft retaining nut	250	184
Left-hand inner bellows retaining plate	25	18
Stub axle carrier to strut bolts	80	59
Steering tie-rod end	40	30

1 General description

Drive is transmitted from the differential to the front wheels by means of two, unequal length, tubular steel driveshafts.

Both driveshafts are fitted with a constant velocity joint of the sliding tripod type at their outer ends. The constant velocity joint consists of the stub axle member which is splined to engage with the front wheel hub, and a spider containing needle bearings and rollers which engage with the driveshaft yoke. The complete assembly is protected by a rubber bellows secured to the driveshaft and stub axle member.

At the driveshaft inner ends a different arrangement is used each side. On the right-hand side the driveshaft is splined to engage

with a spider also containing needle bearings and rollers. The spider is free to slide within the joint yoke which is splined and retained by a roll pin to the differential sun wheel stub shaft. As on the outer joints a rubber bellows secured to the driveshaft and yoke protects the complete assembly.

On the left-hand side the driveshaft also engages with a spider, but the yoke in which the spider is free to slide is an integral part of the differential sun wheel. On this side the rubber bellows is secured to the transmission casing with a retaining plate and to a ball-bearing on the driveshaft with a retaining clip. The bearing allows the driveshaft to turn within the bellows which does not revolve.

The design and construction of the driveshaft components is such that the only repairs possible are renewal of the rubber bellows and renewal of the inner joint spiders. Wear or damage to the outer constant velocity

joints or the driveshaft splines can only be rectified by fitting a complete new driveshaft assembly.

2 Routine maintenance

1 A thorough inspection of the driveshafts and driveshaft joints should be carried out at the intervals given in *"Routine maintenance"*, using the following procedure:
2 Jack up the front of the car and support it securely on axle stands.
3 Slowly rotate the roadwheel and inspect the condition of the outer constant velocity joint rubber bellows. Check for signs of cracking, splits or deterioration of the rubber which may allow the grease to escape and lead to water and grit entry into the joint. Also check the

Fig. 7.1 Tool made from metal bar for holding the front hub stationary (Sec 3)

security and condition of the retaining clips and then repeat these checks on the inner joint bellows. If any damage or deterioration is evident, renew the bellows.

4 Continue rotating the roadwheel and check for any distortion or damage to the driveshaft. Check for any free play in the outer joints by holding the driveshaft firmly and attempting to turn the wheel. Any noticeable movement indicates wear in the joints, wear in the constant velocity joint or wheel hub splines, a loose driveshaft retaining nut or loose wheel bolts.

3 Driveshaft - removal and refitting

1 Jack up the front of the car and support securely on axle stands. Apply the handbrake and remove the appropriate roadwheel.
2 Remove the front brake caliper with reference to Chapter 8, but leaving the hydraulic hose connected. Tie the caliper to one side with wire or string taking care not to damage the hose.
3 Hold the front hub stationary by using two roadwheel bolts to attach a length of metal bar, then unscrew the driveshaft nut (photo).
4 Disconnect the steering tie-rod end from the stub axle carrier with reference to Chapter 9.
5 Unscrew the two nuts and withdraw the bolts securing the stub axle carrier to the suspension strut. Note that the nuts are on the brake caliper side.

Left-hand driveshaft

6 Drain the gearbox oil or automatic transmission fluid with reference to Chapter 6.
7 Unscrew the three bolts securing the rubber bellows retaining plate to the side of the gearbox/transmission (photos).

Right-hand driveshaft

8 Using a parallel pin punch drive out the roll pin securing the inner joint yoke to the differential stub shaft. The roll pin is in fact two roll pins, one inside the other.

Both driveshafts

9 Pull the top of the stub axle carrier outwards until the inner end of the driveshaft is released from the yoke (left-hand) (photo) or shaft (right-hand).
10 Withdraw the outer joint stub axle from the hub, if necessary using a soft metal drift or suitable extractor to release the stub axle from the splines.
11 When refitting, insert the driveshaft in the gearbox/transmission first then locate the outer joint stub axle in the hub splines. Lubricate the splines with molybdenum disulphide grease and make sure that the roll pin holes on the right-hand side inner joint yoke are correctly aligned. Drive in the roll pins with their slots 90° apart (Fig. 7.2) then seal the holes with sealing compound (photos).
12 Insert the stub axle carrier bolts and reconnect the steering tie-rod end. Tighten the nuts to the specified torque.
13 Fit the driveshaft nut and tighten it to the specified torque using the metal bar (paragraph 3).
14 Before locating the left-hand side inner joint bellows clean the contact area of the gearbox/transmission. Position the bellows evenly before fitting the retaining plate and tightening the bolts (photo). Fill the gearbox/transmission with oil/fluid with reference to Chapter 6.

3.3 Driveshaft nut

3.7A Rubber bellows and retaining plate on the left-hand driveshaft inner joint

3.7B Removing the left-hand driveshaft retaining plate bolts

3.9 Withdraw the left-hand driveshaft spider from the differential yoke

Fig. 7.2 Double roll pin location on the right-hand driveshaft inner joint yoke (Sec 3)

Fig. 7.3 Removing the left-hand driveshaft (Sec 3)

3.11A The roll pin holes must be aligned when refitting the right-hand driveshaft

3.11B Secure the right-hand driveshaft to the differential stub shaft by driving in the large roll pin . . .

3.11C . . . followed by the small roll pin . . .

15 Refit the front brake caliper (Chapter 8) and roadwheel, then lower the car to the ground. Depress the brake pedal several times to re-set the disc pads.

4 Outer constant velocity joint rubber bellows - renewal

1 Remove the driveshaft as described in Section 3.
2 Cut through the metal bands with snips without damaging the groove in the stub axle casing or the driveshaft itself.
3 Slide the bellows away from the constant velocity joint and scoop out as much grease as possible from the joint.
4 Mount the stub axle in a soft jawed vice then pull the driveshaft from it while prising up the starplate retainer arms with a screwdriver. Prising up one arm should be sufficient to release the driveshaft. Do not twist the arms.
5 Recover the thrust plunger, shim and spring from the stub axle. The original shim must be refitted to maintain the correct end play.
6 Cut the old bellows from the driveshaft. Clean the driveshaft yoke and remove as much of the remaining grease as possible from the spider and stub axle member. Do this using a wooden spatula or old rags; *do not use any cleaning solvent, petrol or paraffin.*

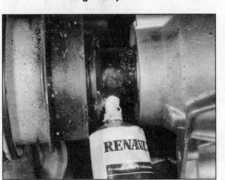

3.11D . . . then seal the holes with sealing compound

7 Obtain a new rubber bellows, retaining clips and a small quantity of the special lubricating grease. All these parts are available in the form of a repair kit obtainable through Renault parts stockists.
8 In order to fit the new bellows a special tool is required to expand the small end of the bellows and allow it to slide over the driveshaft yoke. The manufacturer's tool is shown in the accompanying illustrations, but a suitable alternative can be made by bending a sheet of tin in conical fashion and then bonding the seams using superglue or pop rivets. An old 5 litre oil container is quite useful for this purpose. Make sure that the seam is well protected with tape to prevent it cutting the new bellows.
9 Before fitting the new bellows generously

3.14 Showing the left-hand driveshaft spider located in the differential yoke prior to fitting the rubber bellows and retaining plate

lubricate the expander tool and the inside of the bellows with clean engine oil.
10 Position the small end of the bellows over the small end of the tool and move it up and down the expander two or three times to make the rubber more pliable.
11 Mount the driveshaft in a soft jawed vice with the yoke angled upwards.
12 Position the large end of the expander against the driveshaft yoke and pull the bellows up the expander and onto the yoke. Make sure that the end of the bellows does not tuck under as it is being fitted, and use plenty of lubricant.
13 When the small end of the bellows is in

Fig. 7.4 Cut-away view of the outer constant velocity joint (Sec 4)

1 Stub axle member
2 Starplate
3 Spider and rollers
4 Driveshaft yoke
5 Metal band clip
6 Rubber bellows
7 Metal band clip

Fig. 7.5 Using a screwdriver to prise up the starplate retainer arms (Sec 4)

7

Fig. 7.6 Showing shim location beneath the thrust plunger (Sec 4)

place over the yoke, remove the tool and slide the bellows up the driveshaft.

14 Insert the spring and thrust plunger in the stub axle and make sure that the spider rollers are fully on the trunnions.

15 Fit the starplate retainer with the arms between the rollers.

16 With the stub axle mounted in the vice offer the driveshaft and yoke to it. Move the driveshaft from side to side until one of the retainer arms can be engaged in its cut-out, then press the driveshaft firmly over the spider

Fig. 7.9 Using a slotted screwdriver to fit the starplate retainer arms (Sec 4)

5.2 Right-hand driveshaft inner joint and rubber bellows

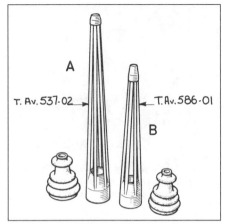

Fig. 7.7 Tools for fitting the outer joint bellows (Sec 4)

A For 1397 cc models
B For 956 cc and 1108 cc models

and insert the remaining arms. A slotted screwdriver will facilitate lifting the arms in position (Fig. 7.9).

17 Move the driveshaft in the direction of one of the spider trunnions. This will cause the thrust plunger to lift, and the shim can then be inserted beneath the plunger head.

18 Remove the driveshaft from the vice then articulate the joint through all angles and check that it moves freely.

19 Distribute the grease supplied in the repair kit evenly around the spider and the grooves in the driveshaft yoke.

20 Position the large end of the bellows on the stub axle casing making sure that the two lips are correctly located in the two grooves. Position the small end so that the bellows convolutions are neither stretched nor compressed.

21 With the stub axle and driveshaft aligned, lift the small end of the bellows temporarily to equalise the air pressure.

22 Fit the metal band clips on the ends of the bellows and secure by squeezing the raised portion. Ideally a crimping tool should be used, but alternatively pincers or pliers may be used.

23 Wipe away any external grease then refit the driveshaft as described in Section 3.

Fig. 7.8 Fit the starplate retainer (1) with the spider rollers pressed inwards (Sec 4)

5 Right-hand driveshaft inner rubber bellows - renewal

1 Remove the driveshaft from the car, as described in Section 3.

2 Using a screwdriver, slip off the retaining spring securing the bellows to the yoke (photo).

3 Release the rubber retaining collar securing the bellows to the driveshaft and slide the bellows down the shaft.

4 Using pliers, carefully bend back the anti-separation plate tags and then slide the yoke off the spider. Be prepared to hold the rollers in place otherwise they will fall off the spider trunnions as the yoke is withdrawn. Secure the rollers in place using tape after removal of the yoke. The rollers are matched to their trunnions and it is most important that they are not interchanged.

5 Extract the circlip securing the spider to the driveshaft using circlip pliers. Using a dab of paint or a small file mark, identify the position of the spider in relation to the driveshaft, as a guide to refitting.

6 The spider can now be removed in one of the following ways. Preferably using a press or by improvisation with a hydraulic puller, support the spider under the rollers and press out the driveshaft. If a press is not available support the spider under its central boss, using suitable half-round packing pieces, and

Fig. 7.10 Cut-away view of the right-hand constant velocity joint (Sec 5)

1 Yoke
2 Spider and rollers
3 Metal casing
4 Retaining spring
5 Rubber bellows
6 Retaining collar
7 Driveshaft

Fig. 7.11 Form plate dimensions (Sec 5)
Thickness = 2.5 mm (0.1 in)

Fig. 7.12 Using the form plate (1) to reshape the anti-separation plate tags (Sec 5)

Fig. 7.13 Bellows setting dimension (Sec 5)
A = 153.5 ± 1.0 mm (6.043 ± 0.04 in)

drive the shaft out using a hammer and brass drift. It is important, if this method is used, that only the central boss of the spider is supported and not the rollers. The shock loads imposed could easily damage the inner faces of the rollers and spider and also the small needle roller bearings.

7 With the spider removed the rubber bellows can now be slid off the driveshaft.

8 Clean the driveshaft and remove as much of the grease as possible from the spider and yoke using a wooden spatula or old rags. *Do not use any cleaning solvent, petrol or paraffin.*

9 Examine the spider, rollers and yoke for any signs of scoring or wear and for smoothness of movement of the rollers on the spider trunnions. If wear is evident the spider and rollers can be renewed, but it is not possible to obtain a replacement yoke. Obtain a new rubber bellows, retaining clips and a quantity of the special lubricating grease. These parts are available in the form of a repair kit available from Renault parts stockists.

10 Begin reassembly by lubricating the driveshaft and the inside of the bellows generously with engine oil.

11 Place the rubber retaining collar over the driveshaft and then fit the bellows.

12 Place the spider on the driveshaft splines in the same position as noted prior to removal.

13 Drive the spider fully onto the driveshaft using a hammer and tubular drift, then refit the retaining circlip.

14 Evenly distribute the special grease contained in the repair kit around the spider and inside the yoke.

15 Slide the yoke into position over the spider.

16 Using a piece of 2.5 mm (0.1 in) thick steel or similar material, make up a form plate to the dimensions shown in Fig. 7.11.

17 Position the form plate under each anti-separation plate tag in the yoke in turn, and tap the tag down onto the form plate. Remove the plate when all the tags have been returned to their original shape.

18 Slide the bellows up the driveshaft and locate the bellows in its respective grooves in the driveshaft and in the yoke.

19 Slip the rubber retaining collar into place over the bellows.

20 Insert a thin blunt instrument, such as a knitting needle, under the lip of the bellows to allow all trapped air to escape. With the instrument in position, compress the joint until the dimension from the small end of the bellows to the flat end face of the yoke is as shown in Fig. 7.13. Hold the yoke in this position and withdraw the instrument.

21 Slip a new retaining spring into place to secure the bellows and then refit the driveshaft, as described in Section 3.

6 Left-hand driveshaft inner rubber bellows - renewal

1 Remove the driveshaft, as described in Section 3.

2 Using circlip pliers, extract the circlip securing the spider to the driveshaft. Using a dab of paint or a small file mark, identify the position of the spider in relation to the driveshaft, as a guide to refitting (photo).

3 The spider can now be removed in one of the following ways. Preferably using a press or by improvisation with a hydraulic puller, support the spider under the rollers and press out the driveshaft. Alternatively support the spider under its central boss, using suitable half-round packing pieces, and drive the shaft out using a hammer and brass drift. It is important, if this method is used, that only the central boss of the spider is supported and not the rollers. The

6.2 Left-hand driveshaft inner joint spider, rubber bellows and retaining plate

shock loads imposed could easily damage the inner faces of the rollers and spider and also the small needle roller bearings.

4 Now support the bearing at the small end of the bellows and press or drive the shaft out of the bellows and bearing assembly.

5 Carefully inspect the spider and rollers for signs of wear or deterioration. The rollers should be free from any signs of scoring and they should turn smoothly on the spider trunnions. Renew the spider assembly if necessary. Obtain a new bellows which is supplied complete with the small bearing.

6 Owing to the lip type seal used in the bearing, the bearing and bellows must be refitted using a press or by improvising using a hydraulic puller. There is a very great risk of damaging the seal by distortion if a hammer and tubular drift are used to drive the assembly onto the driveshaft.

7 Fig. 7.14 shows the arrangement for fitting the bellows and bearing if a press is being

Fig. 7.14 Arrangement of hydraulic press and manufacturer's tool for refitting bellows bearing (Sec 6)

G Machined groove in driveshaft

7

used. The bellows and bearing must be positioned so that the distance from the end of the driveshaft to the flat face at the small diameter end of the bellows is 148.5 mm (5.85 in) - see Fig. 7.15.

8 Now place the spider on the driveshaft in the same position as noted during removal. Drive or press the spider onto the shaft and refit the circlip.

9 Refit the driveshaft to the car, as described in Section 3.

7 Driveshaft inner joint spiders - removal and refitting

Removal and refitting of the spiders is an integral part of the rubber bellows renewal procedure and reference should be made to Section 5 or Section 6, as appropriate.

Fig. 7.15 Bellows bearing setting dimension (Sec 6)

G Machined groove in driveshaft

Manufacturer's tool shown on driveshaft

Fault finding - driveshafts

Vibration

☐ Worn joints
☐ Worn wheel or differential bearings

Noise on taking up drive

☐ Worn driveshaft splines
☐ Worn joints
☐ Loose driveshaft nut

Chapter 8 Braking system

For modifications, and information applicable to later models, see Supplement at end of manual

Contents

Degrees of difficulty

Easy, suitable for novice with little experience	Fairly easy, suitable for beginner with some experience	Fairly difficult, suitable for competent DIY mechanic	Difficult, suitable for experienced DIY mechanic	Very difficult, suitable for expert DIY or professional

Specifications

System type . . . . Dual hydraulic circuit split diagonally with pressure regulating valve to rear brakes. Disc front brakes, and drum rear brakes on non-Turbo models, disc rear brakes on Turbo models. Servo assistance on some models. Cable-operated handbrake on rear brakes

Brake fluid type/specification . . . . Hydraulic fluid to SAE J1073F, DOT 3, or DOT 4

Front brakes

Type . . . . Disc with Bendix or Girling single piston sliding calipers
Disc diameter . . . . 238.0 mm (9.37 in)
Disc thickness (new):
  Except 1397 cc models . . . . 8.0 mm (0.315 in)
  1397 cc models (except Turbo) . . . . 12.0 mm (0.472 in)
  Turbo models . . . . 20.0 mm (0.787 in)
Minimum disc thickness:
  Except 1397 cc models . . . . 7.0 mm (0.276 in)
  1397 cc models (except Turbo) . . . . 10.5 mm (0.413 in)
  Turbo models . . . . 18.0 mm (0.709 in)
Maximum disc run-out . . . . 0.07 mm (0.003 in)
Minimum disc pad thickness (including backplate) . . . . 6.0 mm (0.236 in)

Rear brakes (drum)

Type . . . . Self-adjusting Bendix or Girling type
Drum diameter (new) . . . . 180.25 mm (7.097 in)
Maximum drum diameter . . . . 181.25 mm (7.136 in)
Minimum lining thickness (including shoe) . . . . 2.5 mm (0.098 in)

Rear brakes (disc)

Type . . . . Bendix single piston sliding calipers incorporating self-adjusting handbrake mechanism
Disc diameter . . . . 238.0 mm (9.37 in)
Disc thickness (new) . . . . 8.0 mm (0.315 in)
Minimum disc thickness . . . . 7.0 mm (0.276 in)
Maximum disc run-out . . . . 0.07 mm (0.003 in)
Minimum disc pad thickness (including backplate) . . . . 5.0 mm (0.197 in)

8

Servo unit
Diameter . . . . 178.0 mm (7.0 in)

Handbrake
Lever minimum travel . . . . 12 notches

Torque wrench settings	Nm	lbf ft
Bleed screws	6 to 8	4 to 6
Hose or pipe unions	13	10
Master cylinder	13	10
Servo unit	20	15
Brake caliper	100	74
Brake caliper reaction frame (Bendix)	60	44
Brake caliper guide bolts (Girling)	35	26
Rear hub nut	160	118

1 General description

The braking system is of dual hydraulic circuit type employing a tandem master cylinder. The circuit is split diagonally with the primary and secondary circuits each supplying one front brake and one diagonally opposite rear brake. Under normal conditions both circuits operate in unison, however in the event of failure of one circuit the remaining circuit will provide adequate braking to stop the car in an emergency. A dual circuit pressure regulating valve controls the braking pressure to the rear wheels in order to prevent rear wheel locking; on some models the valve is load sensitive.

Disc brakes are fitted to the front wheels. On non-Turbo models the rear brakes are drum type and on Turbo models disc type.

The cable operated handbrake operates independently on the rear wheels. A vacuum servo is fitted to some models to provide additional braking effort when the brake pedal is depressed.

2 Routine maintenance

At the intervals specified in the "Routine maintenance" section in the front of the manual carry out the following procedures.

1 Check that the brake fluid level in the reservoir is at or near the maximum mark (photo). The reservoir is located on the master cylinder on the right-hand side of the bulkhead in the engine compartment. Slight variations of level will occur according to the wear of the brake linings, however if the level drops towards the minimum mark the complete hydraulic system should be checked for leaks.

2 With the car raised on a hoist, over an inspection pit or supported on ramps or axle stands, carefully inspect all the hydraulic pipes, hoses and unions for chafing, cracks, leaks and corrosion. Details will be found in Section 17.

3 Remove the plugs over the inspection holes in the rear brake backplates and check the thickness of the brake linings. Renew the brake shoes if the linings have worn to the specified minimum thickness. Note that it is only possible to check the thickness of the brake shoe linings in one position when viewing through the inspection holes. To check the lining condition and the operation of the wheel cylinders, it is recommended that the rear brake drums be removed so that a thorough inspection can be carried out, as described in Section 6.

4 Check the operation of the handbrake on each rear wheel and lubricate the exposed cables and linkages under the car.

5 Remove the front wheels and check the thickness of the front brake pads. Renew the pads, as described in Section 3, if they are worn to the specified minimum thickness.

6 At less frequent intervals (see "Routine maintenance") the brake servo air filter and non-return valve should also be renewed, using the procedure described in Section 25. Also renew the brake fluid by bleeding it completely as described in Section 18 and allowing for all old fluid to be removed.

3 Front disc pads - inspection and renewal

1 Jack up the front of the car and support it on axle stands. Remove the front roadwheels.

2 View the brake pads end on and measure their thickness. If any of the pads is less than the specified minimum thickness, all four pads must be renewed as follows, according to brake caliper type.

Bendix calipers

3 Remove the brake fluid reservoir cap. Disconnect the brake pad wear warning light wire at the connector.

4 Extract the small spring clip and then withdraw the retaining key (photos).

5 Using a screwdriver, carefully lever between the disc and caliper so that the piston is pushed back sufficiently to allow removal of the pads.

6 Using pliers, if necessary, withdraw the

2.1 Topping-up brake fluid level

3.4A Extract the small spring . . .

34.4B . . . and withdraw the retaining key

Fig. 8.1 Correct fitting of the anti-rattle
spring (1) to the Bendix disc pad (Sec 3)

3.6A Removing the outer disc pad . . .

3.6B . . . and inner disc pad

pads from the caliper, and remove the
anti-rattle spring from each pad (photos).

7 With the pads removed, check that the
caliper is free to slide on the guide sleeves
and that the rubber dust excluders around the
piston and guide sleeves are undamaged. If
attention to these components is necessary
refer to Section 4.

8 To refit the pads, move the caliper
sideways as far as possible towards the
centre of the car. Fit the anti-rattle spring to
the innermost pad making sure that this pad is
the one with the wear warning light wire, then
locate the pad in position, with the backing
plate against the piston.

9 Note that the pads are symmetrical for
non-1397 cc models or offset for 1397 cc
models (photo). The offset type must be fitted
as shown in Fig. 8.2.

10 Move the caliper outwards then fit the
anti-rattle spring to the outer pad and locate
the pad in the caliper.

11 Slide the retaining key into place and refit
the small spring clip at the inner end (photo). It
may be necessary to file an entry chamfer on
the edge of the retaining key to enable it to be
fitted without difficulty.

12 Reconnect the brake pad wear warning
light wire, refit the roadwheel and repeat the
renewal procedures on the other front brake.
On completion check the hydraulic fluid level
in the reservoir then depress the footbrake

two or three times to bring the pads into
contact with the disc, refit the roadwheels and
lower the car to the ground.

Girling calipers

13 Grasp the caliper body and pull it
outwards by hand away from the centre of the
car. This will push the piston back into its bore
to facilitate removal and refitting of the pads.

14 Disconnect the brake pad wear warning
light at the connector (photo).

15 Undo the upper and lower guide pin bolts
using a suitable spanner while holding the
guide pins with a second spanner (photo).

16 With the guide pin bolts removed, lift the
caliper off the brake pads and carrier bracket

3.9 Showing offset disc pads fitted to
1397 cc models

Fig. 8.2 Correct fitting of Bendix off-set
disc pads viewed from the front (Sec 3)

Fig. 8.3 Bendix disc pad retaining key (2)
and spring (1) showing filed chamfer (A)
(Sec 3)

8

3.11 Showing retaining key correctly fitted

3.14 Disconnect the brake pad wear
warning light wire

3.15 Using two spanners, undo the guide
pin bolts

3.16 Lift the caliper off the carrier bracket . . .

3.17 . . . and withdraw the brake pads

3.19 Refit the pads as shown so that the pad with the warning light is on the inside

(photo), and tie it up in a convenient place under the wheel arch. Do not allow the caliper to hang unsupported on the flexible brake hose.

17 Withdraw the two brake pads from the carrier bracket (photo).

18 Before refitting the pads, check that the guide pins are free to slide in the carrier bracket and check that the rubber dust excluders around the guide pins are undamaged. Brush the dust and dirt from the caliper and piston but do not *inhale as it is injurious to health*. Inspect the dust excluder around the piston for damage and the piston for evidence of fluid leaks, corrosion or damage. If attention to any of these components is necessary, refer to Section 4.

19 To refit the pads, place them in position on the carrier bracket noting that the pad with the warning light must be nearest to the centre of the car (photo). The anti-rattle springs must be located as shown in Fig. 8.4.

20 Make sure that the caliper piston is fully retracted in its bore. If not, carefully push it in using a flat bar or screwdriver as a lever or preferably use a G-clamp.

21 Position the caliper over the pads then fit the lower guide pin bolt having first coated its threads with locking fluid. Apply the fluid to the upper guide pin bolt, press the caliper into position, and fit the bolt. Tighten the bolts to the specified torque starting with the lower bolt.

22 Reconnect the brake pad wear warning, light wire and repeat the renewal procedures on the other front brake. On completion check the hydraulic fluid level in the reservoir, depress the footbrake two or three times to bring the pads into contact with the disc, then refit the roadwheels and lower the car to the ground.

4 **Front brake caliper** - removal, overhaul and refitting

Bendix calipers

1 Jack up the front of the car and support it on axle stands. Remove the appropriate front roadwheel.

2 Remove the brake pads, as described in the previous Section.

3 Undo the two bolts securing the caliper assembly to the stub axle carrier and withdraw the caliper.

4 With the flexible brake hose still attached to the caliper, have an assistant very slowly depress the brake pedal until the piston has been ejected just over halfway out of its bore.

5 Using a brake hose clamp, or self-locking wrench with protected jaws, clamp the brake hose. This will minimise brake fluid loss during subsequent operations.

Fig. 8.4 Girling caliper showing guide pin bolts (1) and anti-rattle spring location on the disc pad (Sec 3)

Fig. 8.5 Bendix type brake caliper components (Sec 4)

1 Retaining strip
2 Guide sleeve inner dust excluders
3 Guide sleeves
4 Guide sleeve seals
5 Caliper body
6 Guide sleeve outer dust excluders
7 Reaction frame retaining bolts
8 Reaction frame
9 Piston
10 Piston seal
11 Piston dust excluder

Fig. 8.6 Using a feeler blade to remove the piston seal from the Bendix type caliper (Sec 4)

4.18 Tightening the caliper guide bolts

Fig. 8.7 Girling type brake caliper components (Sec 4)

1 Piston   2 Piston seal   3 Dust cover

6 Slacken the brake hose-to-caliper body union, and then, while holding the hose, rotate the caliper to unscrew it from the hose. Lift away the caliper and plug or tape over the end of the hose to prevent dirt entry.

7 With the caliper on the bench wipe away all traces of dust and dirt, but *avoid inhaling the dust as it is injurious to health.*

8 Undo the two bolts securing the caliper body to the reaction frame and lift off the body.

9 Withdraw the partially ejected piston from the caliper body and remove the dust cover.

10 Using a suitable blunt instrument such as a knitting needle or a thick feeler blade, carefully extract the piston seal from the caliper bore.

11 Clean all the parts in methylated spirit or clean brake fluid and wipe dry using a lint-free cloth. Inspect the piston and caliper bore for signs of damage, scuffing or corrosion, and if these conditions are evident renew the caliper body assembly. Inspect the condition of the dust excluders over the guide sleeves and renew these too if there is any sign of damage or deterioration.

12 If the components are in a satisfactory condition, a repair kit consisting of new seals and dust excluders should be obtained.

13 Thoroughly lubricate the components and piston seal with clean brake fluid and carefully fit the seal to the caliper bore.

14 Insert the piston into its bore, fit the new dust cover and then push the piston fully into its bore.

15 Place the caliper in position on the reaction frame and secure with the two bolts, tightened to the specified torque.

16 Where necessary fit the new seals and dust excluders to the caliper guide sleeves.

17 Hold the flexible brake hose and screw the caliper body back onto the hose.

18 Refit the two bolts securing the caliper assembly to the stub axle carrier and tighten the bolts to the specified torque (photo).

19 Fully tighten the brake hose-to-caliper body union and remove the brake hose clamp.

20 Refit the brake pads, as described in Section 3, and bleed the hydraulic system, as described in Section 18. Note that providing

the precautions described were taken to minimise brake fluid loss, it should only be necessary to bleed the relevant front brake.

21 Refit the roadwheel and lower the car to the ground.

Girling calipers

22 Jack up the front of the car and support it on axle stands. Remove the appropriate front roadwheel.

23 Using a suitable spanner, unscrew the guide pin bolts while holding the guide pins with a second spanner.

24 Disconnect the pad wear indicator wiring and lift away the caliper body, leaving the disc pads and carrier bracket still in position. It is not necessary to remove the carrier bracket unless it requires renewal because of accident damage or severe corrosion.

25 With the flexible brake hose still attached to the caliper body, very slowly depress the brake pedal until the piston has been ejected just over halfway out of its bore.

26 Using a brake hose clamp or self-locking wrench with protected jaws, clamp the flexible brake hose. This will minimise brake fluid loss during subsequent operations.

27 Slacken the brake hose-to-caliper body union, and then, while holding the hose, rotate the caliper to unscrew it from the hose. Lift away the caliper and plug or tape over the end of the hose to prevent dirt entry.

28 With the caliper on the bench wipe away all traces of dust and dirt, but *avoid inhaling the dust as it is injurious to health.*

29 Withdraw the partially ejected piston from the caliper body and remove the dust cover and clip.

30 Using a suitable blunt instrument, such as a knitting needle, carefully extract the piston seal from the caliper bore.

31 Clean all the parts in methylated spirit, or clean brake fluid, and wipe dry using a lint-free cloth. Inspect the piston and caliper bore for signs of damage, scuffing or corrosion and if these conditions are evident renew the caliper body assembly. Also renew the guide pins if bent or damaged.

32 If the components are in a satisfactory condition, a repair kit consisting of new seals and dust cover should be obtained.

33 Thoroughly lubricate the components and new seals with clean brake fluid and carefully fit the seal to the caliper bore.

34 Position the dust cover over the innermost end of the piston so that the caliper bore sealing lip protrudes beyond the base of the piston. Using a blunt instrument, if necessary, engage the sealing lip of the dust cover with the groove in the caliper. Now push the piston into the bore until the other sealing lip of the dust cover can be engaged with the groove in the piston. Having done this, push the piston fully into its bore. Ease the piston out again slightly, and make sure that the cover lip is correctly seating in the piston groove. Fit the clip.

35 Remove the guide pins from the carrier bracket and smear them with high melting-point brake grease. Fit new dust covers to the guide pins and refit them to the carrier bracket.

36 Hold the flexible brake hose and screw the caliper body back onto the hose.

37 With the piston pushed fully into its bore, refit the caliper and secure it with the guide pin bolts. Tighten the bolts to the specified torque.

38 Fully tighten the brake hose union and remove the clamp. Reconnect the pad warning light wiring.

39 Refer to Section 18 and bleed the brake hydraulic system, noting that if precautions were taken to minimise fluid loss, it should only be necessary to bleed the relevant front brake.

40 Refit the roadwheel and lower the car to the ground.

5 Front brake disc - inspection, removal and refitting

1 Jack up the front of the car and support it on axle stands. Remove the appropriate front roadwheel.

2 Rotate the disc by hand and examine it for deep scoring, grooving or cracks. Light scoring is normal, but, if excessive, the disc must be renewed. Any loose rust and scale around the outer edge of the disc can be

5.2 Checking the disc thickness with a micrometer

5.4 Torx type disc securing screw

Fig. 8.8 Bendix type rear brake components (Sec 6)

A *Return spring*
B *Link*
C *Adjusting arm*
D *Quadrant*
E *Spring for link*
F *Spring for quadrant*
G *Clearance slow*

removed by lightly tapping it with a small hammer while rotating the disc. Measure the disc thickness with a micrometer if available (photo).

3 To remove the disc, undo the two bolts securing the brake caliper assembly to the stub axle carrier. Withdraw the caliper, complete with pads, off the disc and support it to one side. Avoid straining the flexible brake hose. An alternative method on models with Bendix brakes is to unbolt the reaction frame from the caliper body.

4 Using a Torx type socket bit or driver, undo

the two screws securing the disc to the hub and withdraw the disc (photo). If it is tight, lightly tap its rear face with a hide or plastic mallet.

5 Refitting the disc is the reverse sequence to removal. Ensure complete cleanliness of the hub and disc mating faces and tighten all bolts to the specified torque. Coat the threads of the caliper or reaction frame bolts with locking fluid before fitting and tightening them.

6 Rear brake shoes - inspection and renewal

1 Jack up the rear of the car and support it on axle stands. Remove the rear roadwheels. Release the handbrake.

2 By judicious tapping and levering, remove the hub cap from the centre of the brake drum.

3 Using a socket and long bar, undo the hub nut and remove the thrust washer.

4 It should now be possible to withdraw the brake drum and hub bearing assembly from the stub axle by hand. It may be difficult to remove the drum due to the tightness of the hub bearing on the stub axle, or due to the brake shoes binding on the inner circumference of the drum.

> **HAYNES HiNT** *If the bearing is tight, tap the periphery of the drum using a hide or plastic mallet, or use a universal puller, secured to the drum with the wheel bolts, to pull it off.*

5 If the brake shoes are binding, proceed as follows.First ensure that the handbrake is fully off. From under the car slacken the locknut then back off the knurled adjuster on the primary rod.

6 Refer to Fig. 8.9 and insert a screwdriver through one of the wheel bolt holes in the brake drum so that it contacts the handbrake operating lever on the trailing brake shoe. Push the lever until the peg slips behind the brake shoe web allowing the brake shoes to

retract. The brake drum can now be withdrawn.

7 With the brake drum assembly removed, brush or wipe the dust from the drum, brake shoes, wheel cylinder and backplate. *Take great care not to inhale the dust as it is injurious to health.*

8 Measure the thickness of the friction material, including the shoe. If any of the brake shoes have worn down to the specified minimum thickness, all four brake shoes must be renewed. The shoes must also be renewed if any are contaminated with brake fluid or grease, or show signs of cracking or scoring. If contamination is evident, the cause must be traced and rectified before fitting new brake shoes. Contamination will be caused either by leaking fluid seals in the wheel cylinder or by a faulty hub bearing oil seal in the brake drum assembly.

9 Examine the internal surface of the brake drum for signs of scoring or cracks. If any deterioration of the surface finish is evident the drum may be skimmed to a maximum of 1.0 mm (0.04 in) on the internal diameter, otherwise renewal is necessary. If the drum is

Fig. 8.9 Using a screwdriver inserted through the brake drum to release the handbrake operating lever (Sec 6)

E *Handbrake operating lever peg (Bendix type brake shown)*

6.11 Bendix rear brake layout

6.13 Removing the brake shoe steady springs and cups

6.16 Disconnecting the handbrake cable from the trailing shoe lever

6.17A Fit the spring . . .

6.17B . . . and operating link to the trailing shoe

to be skimmed it will be necessary to have the work carried out on both drums to maintain a consistent internal diameter on both sides.

10 If the brake shoes and drum are in a satisfactory condition, proceed to paragraph 26. If the brake shoes are to be removed proceed as follows, according to type:

Bendix brake assemblies

11 Before proceeding, make a note of the position and fitted direction of the brake shoe return springs and components as a guide to reassembly (photo).

12 Using pliers, detach the upper shoe return spring from both brake shoes.

13 Again using pliers, depress the brake shoe steady spring cups while supporting the steady spring pin from the rear of the backplate with your finger. Turn each spring cup through 90º and withdraw it, together with the spring, from the pin (photo). Withdraw the trailing shoe steady spring pin from the backplate, but note that it is not possible to withdraw the leading shoe pin due to the close proximity of the suspension trailing arm. Note also that there is a hole in the hollow suspension arm directly in line with the steady pin, and, if care is not taken, the pin will drop into the arm. Place a wooden wedge or other suitable packing between the backplate and suspension arm to stop this happening.

14 Move the serrated adjusting arms on the leading shoe as far as possible towards the stub axle then release the shoe and arm from

the operating link while twisting the shoe outwards.

15 Return the serrated adjusting arm beneath the shoe web then pull the lower end of the leading shoe from the anchor and disconnect the return spring. Remove the shoe.

16 Disconnect the handbrake cable from the operating lever on the trailing brake shoe and lift off the shoe complete with operating link (photo).

17 Extract the spring clips and pivot pins and transfer the self-adjusting mechanism and handbrake lever to the new brake shoes (photos). Also fit the operating link and spring to the new trailing shoe.

18 Before refitting the new brake shoes, clean off the backplate with a rag and apply a trace of silicone grease to the shoe contact areas and pivots on the backplate.

19 Engage the handbrake cable with the operating lever on the trailing shoe and position the shoe complete with operating link on the backplate.

20 Hook one end of the lower return spring into the hole in the trailing shoe and attach the other end to the leading shoe (photo). Place the leading shoe in position on the backplate.

21 Move the leading shoe adjusting arm in towards the stub axle as far as possible and engage the notch on the operating link with the slot on the adjusting arm (photo).

22 Move the serrated quadrant towards the stub axle and allow the adjusting arm to move back to the fully retracted position.

23 Refit the upper return spring.

24 Refit the steady pins, springs and cups to both brake shoes.

25 Ensure that the adjusting arm is fully retracted and that the brake shoes are centrally positioned on the backplate.

26 Slide the brake drum onto the stub axle and refit the thrust washer and hub nut. Tighten the hub nut to the specified torque and then tap the hub cap into place.

27 Depress the footbrake several times to operate the self-adjusting mechanism.

28 The handbrake should now be adjusted, as described in Section 16, or after attending to the brake shoes on the other rear brake if this is being done.

29 On completion, refit the roadwheels and lower the car to the ground.

8

6.17C Fit the serrated adjusting arm mechanism to the leading shoe

6.20 Lower return spring position

6.21 Showing operating link attachment to the adjusting arm on the leading shoe

6.30 Girling rear brake layout

6.34 Correct fitting of the leading brake shoe adjusting lever and return spring

Fig. 8.10 Girling type rear brake components (Sec 6)

1 Threaded rod	5 Adjusting lever tension	C Adjusting lever
2 Link	spring	J Ideal clearance between
3 Serrated nut	A Shoe steady springs	linings and drum
4 Pivot	B Link	

Girling brake assemblies

30 Before proceeding, make a note of the position and fitted direction of the brake shoe return springs and components as a guide to reassembly (photo).

31 Using pliers, detach the upper and lower brake shoe return springs from both brake shoes.

32 Again using pliers, depress the brake shoe steady spring cups while supporting the steady spring from the rear of the backplate with your finger. Turn each spring cup through 90° and withdraw it, together with the spring, from the pin. Withdraw the trailing shoe steady spring pin from the backplate, but note that it is not possible to withdraw the leading shoe pin due to the close proximity of the suspension trailing arm. Note also that there is a hole in the hollow suspension arm directly in line with the steady pin, and, if care is not taken, the pin will drop into the arm. Place a wooden wedge or other suitable packing between the backplate and suspension arm to stop this happening.

33 Lift off the leading shoe and the adjusting link, detach the handbrake cable from the trailing shoe operating lever and lift off the trailing shoe.

34 Detach the return spring and adjusting lever from the leading shoe and fit these components to the new leading shoe. Make sure that the spring is fitted correctly (photo).

Fig. 8.11 Detach the operating link (B) from the adjusting arm after moving the arm toward the stub axle - Bendix brake assemblies (Sec 6)

Fig. 8.12 Turn the brake shoe at right-angles to the backplate. Detach the handbrake cable and remove both shoes - Bendix brake assemblies (Sec 6)

Fig. 8.13 Position the operating link and spring (E) as shown before refitting the brake shoes - Bendix brake assemblies (Sec 6)

35 Before fitting the new brake shoes, clean off the backplate with a rag and apply a trace of silicone grease to the shoe contact areas and pivots on the backplate (photo).

36 Engage the handbrake cable with the operating lever on the trailing shoe, position the shoe on the backplate and retain it in place with the steady pin, spring and cup (photos).

37 Lubricate the threads in the adjusting link and make sure it is free to turn. Note that the links are not interchangeable from side to side and are colour coded for identification. The link fitted to the left-hand side of the car has a silver coloured end, while the link fitted to the right-hand side has a gold coloured end.

38 Engage the adjusting link ends with both brake shoes (photo) ensuring that the notch on the threaded end locates against the adjusting lever on the leading shoe (photo).

39 Position the leading shoe on the backplate and retain it in place with the steady pin, spring and cup (photo).

40 Refit the upper and lower brake shoe return springs (photos).

41 Hold the adjusting lever clear and turn the toothed wheel on the adjusting link as necessary so that the overall diameter of the brake shoes is between 178.7 and 179.2 mm (7.04 to 7.06 in).

42 Refit the brake drum and complete the remainder of the reassembly, as described in paragraphs 26 to 29 inclusive.

Fig. 8.14 Adjusting link notch (A) must locate against the adjusting lever on the leading brake shoe - Girling brake assemblies (Sec 6)

Fig. 8.15 Before refitting the brake drum, turn the toothed wheel on the adjusting link (B) to give a brake shoe diameter of between 178.7 and 179.2 mm (7.04 and 7.06 in) - Girling brake assemblies (Sec 6)

6.35 Apply a trace of silicone grease to the areas arrowed before refitting the brake shoes

6.36A Engage the handbrake cable with the trailing shoe operating lever . . .

6.36B . . . then secure the shoe in place with the steady pin, spring and cup (arrowed)

6.38A Engage the adjusting link ends with both brake shoes . . .

6.38B . . . ensuring that the notch on the adjusting link locates against the adjusting lever (arrowed)

6.39 Secure the leading shoe in place with the steady pin, spring and cup (arrowed)

6.40A Refit the upper return spring in the holes (arrowed) . . .

6.40B . . . followed by the lower return spring in the elongated slots (arrowed)

8

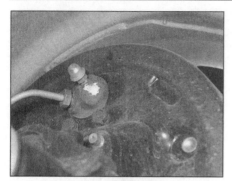

7.4 Rear wheel cylinder viewed from behind the backplate

Fig. 8.16 Exploded view of the two types of rear wheel cylinder (Sec 8)

1 Dust covers	2 Pistons	3 Seals	4 Body	5 Spring

7 Rear wheel cylinder - removal and refitting

1 Begin by removing the brake drum assembly, as described in Section 6, paragraphs 1 to 6 inclusive.

2 Using pliers, detach the brake shoe upper return spring from both brake shoes.

3 Using a brake hose clamp or self-locking wrench with protected jaws, clamp the flexible brake hose just in front of the rear suspension transverse member. This will minimise brake fluid loss during subsequent operations.

4 Wipe away all traces of dirt around the brake pipe union at the rear of the wheel cylinder (photo).

5 Unscrew the union nut securing the brake pipe to the wheel cylinder. Carefully ease out the pipe and plug or tape over its end to prevent dirt entry.

6 Undo the two bolts securing the wheel cylinder to the backplate. Move the brake shoes apart at the top and withdraw the cylinder from between the two shoes.

7 To refit the wheel cylinder, spread the brake shoes and place the cylinder in position on the backplate.

8 Engage the brake pipe and screw in the union nut two or three turns to ensure that the thread has started.

9 Refit the two retaining bolts and tighten them to the specified torque. Now fully tighten the brake pipe union nut.

10 On models equipped with Bendix brakes, move the serrated quadrant of the self-adjusting mechanism towards the stub axle so that the adjusting arm moves back to the fully retracted position. Refit the upper brake shoe return spring. On models equipped with Girling brakes, refit the upper brake shoe return spring and turn the toothed wheel on the adjusting link as necessary so that the overall diameter of the brake shoes is between 178.7 and 179.2 mm (7.04 and 7.06 in).

11 Slide the brake drum over the stub axle, refit the thrust washer and hub nut then tighten the hub nut to the specified torque. Tap the hub cap into place.

12 Remove the clamp from the brake hose and bleed the brake hydraulic system, as described in Section 18. Providing suitable precautions were taken to minimise loss of fluid, it should only be necessary to bleed the relevant rear brake.

13 After bleeding the system, depress the brake pedal several times to operate the self-adjusting mechanism. If it was necessary to slacken the handbrake linkage to remove the brake drum, adjust the handbrake, as described in Section 19.

14 Refit the roadwheel and lower the car to the ground.

8 Rear wheel cylinder - overhaul

1 Remove the wheel cylinder from the car, as described in the previous Section.

2 With the wheel cylinder on the bench, remove the dust covers, the two pistons, cup seals and spring. If necessary tap the end of the cylinder on a block of wood to eject the pistons. Unscrew the bleed screw from the cylinder body.

3 Thoroughly clean all the components in methylated spirits or clean brake fluid, and dry with a lint-free rag.

4 Carefully examine the surfaces of the pistons and cylinder bore for wear, score marks or corrosion and, if evident, renew the complete wheel cylinder. If the components are in a satisfactory condition, obtain a repair kit consisting of new seals and dust covers.

5 Dip the new seals and pistons in clean brake fluid and assemble them wet, as follows:

6 Insert one of the seals into one end of the cylinder with the flat face of the seal facing outwards. Insert the piston and fit the new dust cover.

7 From the other end of the cylinder, slide in the spring followed by the second seal, flat face outwards, then the piston and finally the dust cover.

8 Screw the bleed screw into the cylinder body and then refit the wheel cylinder to the car, as described in Section 7.

9 Rear brake backplate - removal and refitting

1 Begin by removing the rear brake shoes, as described in Section 6, and the wheel cylinder, as described in Section 7.

2 Slide the hub bearing inner spacer off the stub axle, undo the four retaining bolts and withdraw the backplate (photo).

3 To refit the backplate, place it in position over the stub axle and refit the four bolts. Tighten the bolts to the specified torque.

4 Place the spacer over the stub axle and refit the wheel cylinder and brake shoes, as described in Sections 7 and 6 respectively.

5 Bleed the hydraulic system after the brake shoes and brake drum have been refitted using the procedure described in Section 18.

9.2 Rear brake backplate retaining bolts (arrowed)

1 Hub bearing inner spacer

Fig. 8.17 Showing correct alignment of piston marks (A) with bleed screw (B) (Sec 10)

1 Frame retaining bolts

10 Rear disc pads - inspection and renewal

1 Chock the front wheels then jack up the rear of the car and support on axle stands. Remove the rear roadwheels and release the handbrake.
2 View the disc pads end on and measure their thickness including the backplates. If any of the pads is less than the specified minimum thickness, renew all four pads as follows.
3 Extract the small spring clip then withdraw the retaining key.
4 Using pliers if necessary, withdraw the pads from the caliper and remove the anti-rattle springs from each pad.
5 Brush away the accumulated dust and dirt *taking care not to inhale it as it is injurious to health.* Check the condition of the piston and guide sleeve dust covers and if necessary renew them with reference to Section 11.
6 Using a suitable tool, turn the piston until it is screwed in as far as possible and further rotation will not make it enter any deeper. Align the piston so that the two lines on the rim point to the bleed screw.

Fig. 8.18 Rear disc brake caliper showing mounting bolts (A) (Sec 11)

7 Fit the anti-rattle springs to the new pads (see Fig. 8.1).
8 Insert the pads in the caliper with the anti-rattle springs toward the bottom, then tap in the retaining key and fit the spring clip at the inner end of the key next to the frame bolt.
9 Depress the brake pedal several times to reset the disc pads.
10 Repeat the procedure on the remaining side then refit the roadwheels and lower the car to the ground.

11 Rear brake caliper - removal, overhaul and refitting

1 Remove the disc pads as described in Section 10.
2 Remove the brake fluid reservoir filler cap and retighten it onto a piece of polythene in order to reduce the loss of fluid when the caliper is removed. Alternatively, use a hose clamp on the relevant rear flexible hose.
3 Unscrew the union nut securing the hydraulic pipe to the caliper.
4 Disconnect the handbrake cable from the lever on the caliper.

Fig. 8.19 Rear disc brake caliper dust covers (arrowed) (Sec 11)

5 Unbolt the caliper from the trailing arm. If necessary unbolt the frame from the caliper.
6 Clean away external dirt then grip the caliper in a soft-jawed vice.
7 Prise off the piston dust cover.
8 Using a suitable tool unscrew the piston and at the same time apply air pressure from a tyre pump to the part of the caliper to eject the piston.
9 Examine the piston and cylinder bore for scoring and excessive wear. If evident renew the caliper complete, however if they are in good condition remove the seal from the bore using a blunt instrument and obtain a repair kit including a new seal and dust covers.

Fig. 8.21 Using the Renault tools to compress the Belleville spring washers (Sec 11)

6 *Belleville spring washers*   12 *Sleeve*
7 *Lever and spindle*   13 *O-ring*

Fig. 8.20 Exploded view of the rear disc brake caliper (Sec 11)

1 *Dust cover*
2 *Piston*
3 *Clip*
4 *Dust cover*
5 *Circlip*
6 *Belleville spring washers*
7 *Lever and spindle*
8 *Control cam*
9 *Return spring*
10 *Threaded adjustment screw*
11 *Plain washer*

8

Fig. 8.22 The sleeve must be flush with face A (Sec 11)

12 Sleeve   13 O-ring

10 If required the handbrake operating lever components can be dismantled. To do this first remove the clip and release the dust seal cover from the caliper.

11 Extract the circlip from the end of the spindle.

12 The spring washers on the adjustment screw must now be compressed. The Renault tools for this operation are shown in Fig. 8.21 however it should be possible to use a universal puller and a locally made adaptor.

13 Remove the lever and spindle together with the dust cover, followed by the plunger cam and spring clip.

14 Remove the tool and pull out the adjustment screw together with the spring and plain washers.

15 Using a soft metal drift, drive the guide sleeve from the caliper and extract the O-ring seal.

16 Clean all the components using only hydraulic fluid or methylated spirit.

Fig. 8.23 Thrust/pushrod dimensions on models with a servo unit (Sec 13)

P Adjustable extension
E Clip
C Clevis
X = 22.3 mm (0.878 in)
L = 137.5 mm (5.413 in) for RHD models
 or 121.0 mm (4.764 in) for LHD models

17 Commence reassembly by locating the O-ring seal in the caliper, then drive in the guide sleeve until flush with the face of the caliper as shown in Fig. 8.22.

18 Fit the spring washers on the adjacent screw as shown in Fig. 8.22, then locate the plain washer in its recess and insert the adjustment screw in the caliper.

19 Fit the dust cover to the lever and spindle.

20 Compress the adjustment screw spring washers and fit the plunger cam, spring clip, lever and spindle. Retain the spindle with the circlip.

21 Position the dust cover on the caliper and fit the clip.

22 Fit the new piston seal, manipulating it into its groove using the fingers only.

23 Apply clean hydraulic fluid to the piston and cylinder bore and insert the piston squarely using hand pressure.

24 Using a suitable tool turn the piston until it is screwed in as far as possible and further rotation will not make it enter any deeper. Align the piston so that the two lines on the rim point to the bleed screw.

25 Apply a little brake grease to the outer surface of the piston which contacts the bore, then fit the new dust cover.

12 Rear brake disc - inspection, removal and refitting

1 Remove the rear disc pads as described in Section 10.

2 Inspect the disc with reference to Section 5.

3 To remove the disc unbolt the caliper frame then remove the disc and hub assembly as described in Chapter 9.

4 Refitting is as described in Chapter 9. Apply locking fluid to the caliper frame bolt threads before inserting and tightening them. Refit the rear disc pads with reference to Section 10.

13 Master cylinder - removal and refitting

1 The master cylinder is located on the bulkhead behind the right-hand side of the engine (photo). For better access on non-Turbo models remove the air cleaner as described in Chapter 3.

2 Syphon the brake fluid from the reservoir or

Fig. 8.24 Pushrod dimension on models without a servo unit (Sec 13)

L = 110.0 mm (4.331 in)

alternatively place a container beneath the master cylinder and cover the surrounding components with rags.

3 Pull the reservoir direct from the top of the master cylinder.

4 Identify the brake pipes for position then unscrew the union nuts and disconnect them. Tape over the pipe ends to prevent entry of dust and dirt.

5 Unscrew the mounting nuts and withdraw the master cylinder from the servo unit or bulkhead (as applicable). On servo-equipped models, recover the sealing ring. Use a new seal on reassembly.

6 Before refitting the master cylinder, clean the mounting faces. On models with a servo unit, check that the thrust rod protrusion is as shown in Fig. 8.23. Adjust the thrust rod extension if necessary.

7 Refitting is a reversal of removal, but tighten the nuts to the specified torque. Working inside the car check the length of the pedal pushrod with reference to Fig. 8.23 or 8.24 and adjust it if necessary. Finally bleed the hydraulic system as described in Section 18.

14 Master cylinder - overhaul

1 Remove the master cylinder as described in Section 13.

Teves type

2 Mount the master cylinder in a soft-jawed vice.

3 Prise out the reservoir seals.

4 Depress the primary piston extension then extract the circlip from the mouth of the cylinder using circlip pliers. Remove the stop washer.

5 Extract the primary piston and spring followed by the secondary piston and spring. If the latter is tight remove the master cylinder from the vice and tap it on a block of wood.

Early Bendix type

6 To dismantle the master cylinder it will be necessary to make up a piston retaining tool

13.1 Master cylinder on a model fitted with a vacuum servo unit (1)

Fig. 8.25 Cross-section of the Teves master cylinder (Sec 14)

1 Spring
2 Secondary piston
3 Primary piston
4 Circlip
5 Stop washer

from 6 mm diameter steel rod, as shown in Fig. 8.26.

7 Locate the retaining tool over the cylinder so that it holds the primary piston in place.

8 Place a 3.5 mm diameter twist drill in a vice and place the master cylinder over it so that the drill engages with the secondary piston retaining roll pin through the reservoir port. Turn the master cylinder round the drill and then pull it to extract the roll pin.

9 Extract the primary piston roll pin in the same way.

10 Release the retaining tool and withdraw the two piston assemblies by tapping the cylinder on a block of wood. Prise out the reservoir seals.

Fig. 8.26 Piston retaining tool for early Bendix master cylinder (Sec 14)

Note: all dimensions are in mm

Late Bendix type

11 Mount the master cylinder in a soft-jawed vice.

12 Prise out the reservoir seals.

13 Depress the primary piston extension then extract the secondary piston stop pin from the secondary port.

14 Using circlip pliers extract the circlip from the mouth of the cylinder.

15 Extract the primary piston and spring followed by the secondary piston and spring. If necessary tap the cylinder on a block of wood to remove the components.

All types

16 Clean the two piston assemblies and the cylinder body in methylated spirit or clean brake fluid and dry with a lint-free cloth.

17 Carefully examine the cylinder bore and the two piston assemblies for signs of wear

Fig. 8.27 Using the retaining tool to compress the pistons on the early Bendix master cylinder (Sec 14)

ridges, scoring or corrosion. If these conditions are evident on the cylinder bore, a new master cylinder must be obtained. If the cylinder bore is serviceable it will be necessary to obtain a new primary and secondary piston assembly, as the rubber seals and piston components are not available separately. The assembly includes new reservoir seals.

18 Before reassembling, liberally lubricate all the parts in clean brake fluid and assemble them wet.

19 Reassembly is a reversal of dismantling, but on the early Bendix type fit the pistons with their slots aligned with the reservoir ports, and fit the roll pins with their slots facing the master cylinder mounting flange. Refit the master cylinder with reference to Section 13.

15 Pressure regulating valve - description and testing

1 The pressure regulating valve is located beneath the rear of the car (photo) and it effectively limits the braking force available at the rear wheels in order to prevent locking especially during heavy braking. On some models the unit is load sensitive to vary the pressure according to the load being carried, and this unit is identified by having a spring connection to the rear axle.

Fig. 8.28 Using a twist drill to extract the piston roll pins on the early Bendix master cylinder (Sec 14)

Fig. 8.29 Cross-section of the later Bendix master cylinder (Sec 14)

1 Secondary piston stop pin   2 Circlip

Fig. 8.30 On the early Bendix master cylinder fit the roll pins with their slots facing the flange (Sec 14)

15.1 Pressure regulating valve

8

Fig. 8.31 Load sensitive pressure regulating valve fitted to non-Turbo models (Sec 15)

A Adjusting nut   *B Locknut*

2 In the event of continual rear wheel locking the rear brake shoes should first be checked for correct operation before checking the pressure regulating valve.

3 To check the unit, pressure gauges must be fitted to the front and rear hydraulic circuits and this work is therefore best left to a Renault dealer. On the load sensitive type one person must be sitting in the driver's seat and a load according to model placed in the rear luggage compartment, then the spring tension adjusted as required. No adjustment is possible on the non-load sensitive type.

16 Pressure regulating valve - removal and refitting

1 Check the front wheels then jack up the rear of the car and support it on axle stands.
2 Working in the engine compartment unscrew the brake fluid reservoir cap then tighten it down onto a piece of polythene sheeting. This will minimise brake fluid loss during subsequent operations.
3 Clean the regulating valve then identify the hydraulic pipes for position.
4 Unscrew the union nuts and disconnect the pipes. Plug the pipe ends to prevent loss of fluid.

17.6A Front brake flexible hose to rigid pipe connection

Fig. 8.32 Load sensitive pressure regulating valve fitted to Turbo models (Sec 15)

A Adjusting sleeve   *B Locking screw*

5 Unscrew the mounting bolts or nuts and withdraw the unit from the underbody. On the load sensitive type unhook the spring from the rear axle.
6 Refitting is a reversal of removal. On completion bleed the hydraulic system as described in Section 18 and where applicable have the unit adjusted by a Renault dealer. On the non-load sensitive type the inlet hydraulic pipes must be fitted to the end with unequal height unions (Fig. 8.33).

17 Hydraulic pipes and hoses - inspection, removal and refitting

1 At the specified service intervals, carefully examine all brake pipes, hoses, hose connections and pipe unions.
2 First check for signs of leakage at the pipe unions. Then examine the flexible hoses for signs of cracking, chafing and fraying.
3 The brake pipes must be examined carefully and methodically. They must be cleaned off and checked for signs of dents, corrosion or other damage. Corrosion should be scraped off, and, if the depth of pitting is significant, the pipes renewed. This is particularly likely in those areas underneath

17.6B Rear brake flexible hose to rigid pipe connection

Fig. 8.33 Inlet pipe locations on the non-load sensitive type pressure regulating valve (Sec 15)

the vehicle body where the pipes are exposed and unprotected.
4 If any section of the pipe or hose is to be removed, first unscrew the master cylinder reservoir filler cap and place a piece of polythene over the filler neck. Refit and tighten the cap. This will minimise brake fluid loss when the pipe or hose is removed.
5 Brake pipe removal is usually quite straight-forward. The union nuts at each end are undone, the pipe and union pulled out and the centre section of the pipe removed from the body clips. Where the union nuts are exposed to the full force of the weather they can sometimes be quite tight. As only an open-ended spanner can be used, burring of the flats on the nuts is not uncommon when attempting to undo them. For this reason a self-locking wrench is often the only way to separate a stubborn union.
6 To remove a flexible hose, wipe the unions and bracket free of dirt and undo the union nut from the brake hose end(s) (photos).
7 Next lift off the hose retaining spring clip and withdraw the end of the hose out of its serrated mounting. If a front brake hose is being removed, it can now be unscrewed from the brake caliper.
8 Brake pipes with flared ends and union nuts in place can be obtained individually or in sets from Renault dealers or accessory shops. The pipe is then bent to shape, using the old pipe as a guide, and is ready for fitting to the car.
9 Refitting the pipes and hoses is a reversal of the removal sequence. Make sure that the brake pipes are securely supported in their clips and ensure that the hoses are not kinked. Check also that the hoses are clear of all suspension components and underbody fittings and will remain clear during movement of the suspension or steering. Reposition one of the hose ends in its serrated mounting if necessary. After refitting, remove the polythene from the reservoir and bleed the brake hydraulic system, as described in Section 18.

18.13 Bleed tube fitted to a rear wheel cylinder

18.14 Bleed tube fitted to a front brake caliper

19.2 Handbrake primary rod and adjusting yoke

18 Hydraulic system - bleeding

1 The correct functioning of the brake hydraulic system is only possible after removal of all air from the components and circuit; this is achieved by bleeding the system. Note that only clean unused brake fluid, which has remained unshaken for at least 24 hours, must be used.
2 If there is any possibility of incorrect fluid being used in the system, the brake lines and components must be completely flushed with uncontaminated fluid and new seals fitted to the components.
3 Never reuse brake fluid which has been bled from the system.
4 During the procedure, do not allow the level of brake fluid to drop more than halfway down the reservoir.
5 Before starting work, check that all pipes and hoses are secure, unions tight and bleed screws closed. Take great care not to allow brake fluid to come into contact with the car paintwork, otherwise the finish will be seriously damaged. Wash off any spilled fluid immediately with cold water.
6 If the brake fluid has been lost from the master cylinder due to a leak in the system, ensure that the cause is traced and rectified before proceeding further.
7 If the hydraulic system has only been partially disconnected and suitable precautions were taken to prevent further loss of fluid, then it should only be necessary to bleed the brake concerned, or that part of the circuit "downstream" from where the work took place.
8 If possible, one of the DIY brake bleeding kits available from accessory shops should be used, particularly the type which pressurise the system, as they greatly simplify the task and reduce the risk of expelled air and fluid being drawn back into the system. Where one of these kits is being used, follow the manufacturer's instructions concerning their operation.
9 If a brake bleeding kit is not being used, the

system may be bled in the conventional way as follows:
10 Obtain a clean glass jar, a suitable length of plastic or rubber tubing which is a tight fit over the bleed screws, a tin of the specified brake fluid and the help of an assistant.
11 On models fitted with a servo unit depress the footbrake pedal several times so that the vacuum is dissipated.
12 Clean the area around the bleed screw and remove the rubber dust cap. If the complete system is to be bled, start at the left-hand rear brake first.
13 Fit the tube to the bleed screw (photo), immerse the free end of the tube in the jar and pour in sufficient brake fluid to keep the end of the tube submerged. Open the bleed screw half a turn and have your assistant depress the brake pedal to the floor and then release it. Tighten the bleed screw at the end of each downstroke to prevent the expelled air and fluid from being drawn back into the system. Repeat the procedure until clean brake fluid, free from air bubbles, can be seen emerging from the tube then finally tighten the bleedscrew, remove the tube and refit the dust cap. Remember to check the brake fluid level in the reservoir periodically and keep it topped up.
14 Repeat the procedure on the right-hand front brake (photo) followed by the right-hand rear brake and left-hand front brake. When completed, recheck the fluid level in the

reservoir, top up if necessary and refit the cap. Depress the brake pedal several times; it should feel firm and free from "sponginess" which would indicate air is still present in the system.

19 Handbrake - adjustment

1 Jack up the rear of the car and support on axle stands. Chock the front wheels and fully release the handbrake.
2 Working under the car loosen the locknut on the handbrake primary rod in front of the adjusting yoke and unscrew the locknut several turns (photo).

Non-Turbo models (rear drum brakes)

3 Make sure that the rear brake self-adjusting mechanism is set correctly by depressing the footbrake pedal several times.
4 Tighten the nut inside the adjusting yoke until the rear wheels begin to bind, then loosen it until the wheels just turn freely.
5 Tighten the locknut then check that from fully released, the handbrake lever moves a minimum of 12 notches to the fully applied position. If necessary make final adjustments to the adjusting yoke.
6 Lower the car to the ground.

Fig. 8.34 Handbrake primary rod components (Sec 19)

1 Clevis pin
2 Support/guide block
3 Primary rod
4 Adjustment locknut

8

Fig. 8.35 On Turbo models loosen the cable adjustment until dimension J is 5.0 mm (0.2 in) (Sec 19)

Turbo models (rear disc brakes)

7 Loosen the nut inside the adjusting yoke until the cable ends can be pulled approximately 5.0 mm (0.2 in) clear of the levers on the rear calipers (Fig. 8.35).

8 Depress the footbrake pedal several times.

9 Operate the levers on the calipers several times and check that they return fully by themselves. If not, the caliper(s) will need to be overhauled or renewed as described in Section 11.

10 Tighten the nut inside the adjusting yoke until the cable end stops just touch the levers, then tighten the locknut.

11 Check that from fully released, the handbrake lever moves at least 11 or 12 notches to the fully applied position. If necessary make final adjustments to the adjusting yoke.

12 Lower the car to the ground.

20 Handbrake lever - removal and refitting

1 Chock the front wheels then jack up the rear of the car and support on axle stands. Fully release the handbrake lever.

2 Working under the car remove the split pin,

22.2 Footbrake pedal and bracket

21.4 Handbrake cable support bracket on the rear suspension trailing arm

washer and clevis pin securing the primary rod adjusting yoke to the cable compensator.

3 Release the primary rod from the support/guide block.

4 Undo the retaining bolts and remove the two seat belt flexible stalk anchorages.

5 Make a slit in the carpet just to the rear of the lever assembly to provide access to the lever mountings.

6 Spread the carpet and disconnect the warning light switch wires.

7 Undo the two bolts securing the lever to the floor and remove the assembly from inside the car.

8 Refitting is the reverse sequence to removal, but finally adjust the handbrake as described in Section 19.

21 Handbrake cable - removal and refitting

1 Chock the front wheels then jack up the rear of the car and support on axle stands. Fully release the handbrake lever and remove the rear wheels.

2 Remove the rear brake shoes on all models except the GT Turbo (fitted with rear disc brakes). Refer to Section 6.

3 Working under the car remove the split pin, washer and clevis pin securing the primary rod adjusting yoke to the cable compensator.

23.2 Disconnecting the stoplamp switch wiring plug

21.5 Handbrake outer cable entry in rear brake backplate, also showing brake lining inspection hole plug (arrowed)

4 Release the cables from the rear suspension trailing arms by unscrewing the rear bolt and opening up the bracket (photo).

5 Tap the outer cables from the brake backplates (photo) or disconnect the inner cables from the handbrake levers on the rear calipers as applicable, then withdraw the cable assembly from under the car.

6 Refitting is a reversal of removal. On completion adjust the handbrake as described in Section 19.

22 Footbrake pedal - removal and refitting

1 Remove the steering column lower shroud with reference to Chapter 9.

2 Extract the split pin, washer and clevis pin securing the master cylinder or servo pushrod to the pedal (photo).

3 Prise the spring clip from the brake pedal end of the pivot shaft and remove the washer.

4 Slide the pivot shaft to the left until the footbrake pedal can be withdrawn.

5 Inspect the bushes for wear and damage. Also inspect the return spring where fitted. Renew the components as necessary.

6 Refitting is a reversal of removal, but lubricate the bushes and pivot shaft with molybdenum disulphide grease.

23 Stoplamp switch - removal, refitting and adjustment

1 The stoplamp switch is located on the pedal bracket beneath the facia.

2 To remove the switch, pull off the wiring plug then unscrew it from the bracket (photo).

3 Refitting is a reversal of removal, but adjust the position of the switch so that the stop lights operate after approximately 6.0 mm (0.24 in) of pedal travel.

Fig. 8.36 Servo unit air filter renewal
(Sec 25)

A Cut in filter to facilitate fitting
F Filter location in servo end

Fig. 8.37 Servo unit non-return valve and
grommet (Sec 25)

26.6 Vacuum servo unit mounting nuts

24 Vacuum servo unit - description

On some models a vacuum servo unit is fitted into the brake hydraulic circuit in series with the master cylinder, to provide assistance to the driver when the brake pedal is depressed. This reduces the effort required by the driver to operate the brakes under all braking conditions.

The unit operates by vacuum obtained from the inlet manifold and comprises basically a booster diaphragm, control valve and a non-return valve.

The servo unit and hydraulic master cylinder are connected together so that the servo unit piston rod acts as the master cylinder pushrod. The driver's braking effort is transmitted through another pushrod to the servo unit piston and its built-in control system. The servo unit piston does not fit tightly into the cylinder, but has a strong diaphragm to keep its edges in constant contact with the cylinder wall, so assuring an airtight seal between the two parts. The forward chamber is held under vacuum conditions created in the inlet manifold of the engine and, during periods when the brake pedal is not in use, the controls open a passage to the rear chamber so placing it under vacuum conditions as well. When the brake pedal is depressed, the vacuum passage to the rear chamber is cut off and the chamber opened to atmospheric pressure. The consequent rush of air pushes the servo piston forward in the vacuum chamber and operates the main pushrod to the master cylinder.

The controls are designed so that assistance is given under all conditions and, when the brakes are not required, vacuum in the rear chamber is established when the

brake pedal is released. All air from the atmosphere entering the rear chamber is passed through a small air filter.

25 Vacuum servo unit - servicing and testing

1 At the specified service intervals the servo unit air filter and non-return valve should be renewed, as follows:

Air filter

2 Working inside the car remove the steering column lower shroud with reference to Chapter 9.
3 Ease the convoluted rubber cover off the servo end and move it up the pushrod.
4 Using a screwdriver or scriber, hook out the old air filter and remove it from the servo.
5 Make a cut in the new filter, as shown in Fig. 8.36 and place it over the pushrod and into position in the servo end.
6 Refit the rubber cover and moulded plastic cover.

Non-return valve

7 Slacken the clip and disconnect the vacuum pipe from the non-return valve on the front face of the servo.
8 Withdraw the valve from its rubber sealing grommet by pulling and twisting.
9 Refit the new valve using the reverse of the removal sequence.

Testing

10 If the operation of the servo is suspect, the following test can be carried out to determine whether the unit is functioning correctly.
11 Depress the footbrake several times then hold it down and start the engine. As the engine starts there should be a noticeable "give" in the brake pedal. Allow the engine to run for at least two minutes and then switch it off. If the brake pedal is now depressed again it should be possible to detect a hiss from the

unit as the pedal is depressed. After about four or five applications no further hissing will be heard and the pedal will feel noticeably firmer.
12 If the servo does not work as described, check the vacuum pipe condition and ensure that it is not kinked. Run the engine with the pipe disconnected at the servo and check that there is vacuum at the pipe end. If the servo air filter and non-return valve are in a satisfactory condition then the servo is faulty and renewal will be necessary.

26 Vacuum servo unit - removal and refitting

1 Disconnect the battery negative terminal.
2 Refer to Section 13 and remove the master cylinder.
3 Slacken the clip and disconnect the vacuum pipe at the servo non-return valve.
4 Working inside the car remove the steering column lower shroud with reference to Chapter 9.
5 Extract the split pin, washer and clevis pin securing the servo unit pushrod to the brake pedal.
6 Undo the four nuts and remove the washers securing the servo to the bulkhead and withdraw the unit into the engine compartment (photo).
7 Note that the servo cannot be dismantled for repair or overhaul and, if faulty, must be renewed.
8 Before refitting the servo, measure the length of the servo pushrod and output rod, ensuring that they are set to the specified length, as shown in Fig. 8.23. If necessary, slacken the locknuts and adjust the rod lengths. Tighten the locknuts after adjustment.
9 Refitting the servo unit is the reverse sequence to removal. Bleed the brake hydraulic system, as described in Section 18 after refitting the master cylinder.

8

Fault finding - braking system

Excessive pedal travel

☐ Rear brake self-adjusting mechanism faulty (except GT Turbo)
☐ Air in hydraulic system

Brakes pull to one side

☐ Worn or contaminated linings
☐ Seized caliper or wheel cylinder
☐ Incorrect tyre pressures

Rear wheels locking under normal braking

☐ Faulty pressure regulating valve

Brake judder

☐ Excessive run-out or distortion of discs or drums
☐ Worn or contaminated linings
☐ Brake backplate or disc caliper loose
☐ Worn suspension balljoints

Excessive effort to stop car

☐ Servo unit faulty
☐ Worn or contaminated linings

x

Chapter 9 Suspension and steering

For modifications, and information applicable to later models, see Supplement at end of manual

Contents

Degrees of difficulty

Easy, suitable for novice with little experience	Fairly easy, suitable for beginner with some experience	Fairly difficult, suitable for competent DIY mechanic	Difficult, suitable for experienced DIY mechanic	Very difficult, suitable for expert DIY or professional

Specifications

Front suspension
Type . . . . Independent by MacPherson struts with inclined coil springs, integral telescopic shock absorbers and anti-roll bar (except C and TC models)

Anti-roll bar diameter
Except Turbo models . . . . 22.0 mm (0.866 in)
Turbo models . . . . 21.0 mm (0.827 in)

Front underbody height
H1 - H2 (see Section 18):
  956 cc models . . . . 79 mm (3.11 in)
  1108 cc models . . . . 66 mm (2.60 in)
  1237 cc, 1397 cc (except Turbo) and 1721 cc models . . . . 72 mm (2.84 in)
  Turbo models up to 1988 . . . . 97 mm (3.82 in)
  Turbo models from 1988 . . . . 101 mm (3.98 in)
  Tolerance . . . . + 10 - 5 mm (+ 0.39 - 0.20 in)

Rear suspension
Type . . . . Independent by trailing arms with transverse torsion bars (enclosed on non-Turbo models, open on Turbo models), inclined telescopic shock absorbers and anti-roll bar

Anti-roll bar diameter
TC models . . . . 13.5 mm (0.532 in)
Other non -Turbo models . . . . 15.5 mm (0.610 in)
Turbo models . . . . 23.4 mm (0.921 in)

9

Torsion bar diameter
Except Turbo models .... 18.0 mm (0.709 in)
Turbo models .... 20.8 mm (0.819 in)

Rear underbody height
H4 - H5 (see Section 18):
    All except Turbo models .... -10 mm (- 0.39 in)
    Turbo models up to 1988 .... + 20 mm (+ 0.79 in)
    Turbo models from 1988 .... + 23 mm (+ 0.91 in)
    Tolerance:
        Except Turbo models .... -10 +5 mm (-0.39 +0.20 in)
        Turbo models .... + 10 - 5 mm (+ 0.39 -0.30 in)

Rear wheel camber angle (unladen) .... - 50' ± 30'

Rear wheel toe setting
Except Turbo models .... 0° to 30' toe-in (equivalent to 0 to 3.0 mm/0.118 in toe-in)
Turbo models .... 20' to 50' toe-in (equivalent to 2.0 to 5.0 mm/0.079 to 0.197 in toe-in)

Steering
Type .... Rack and pinion

Camber angle
Except Turbo models .... 30' ± 30'
Turbo models .... -1° ± 30'

Maximum camber angle difference side-to-side ..... 1°

Castor angle at specified underbody heights

H5 - H2 (see Section 18):	Castor angle
50.0 mm (1.969 in)	3° 30'
70.0 mm (2.756 in)	3° 0'
90.0 mm (3.543 in)	2° 30'
110.0 mm (4.331 in)	2° 0'
130.0 mm (5.118 in)	1° 30'

Maximum castor angle difference side-to-side .... 1°

Steering axis inclination
Except Turbo models .... 12° 10' ± 30'
Turbo models .... 13° 10' ± 30'

Front wheel toe setting .... 0° 10' toe-out (equivalent to 1.0 ± 1.0 mm/0.039 ± 0.039 in toe-out)

Roadwheels
Type .... Pressed steel or aluminium alloy according to model

Size .... 4.5 B 13, 5J 13, 5.5 J 13 or 5B 13 according to model

Maximum wheel run-out (measured at rim) .... 1.2 mm (0.047 in)

Tyres
Tyre size .... 145/70 R 13, 155/70 R 13, 165/65 SR 13, 175/60 HR 13 or 195/55 HR 13 according to model

Tyre pressures (cold) - bar/lbf/in²

	Front	Rear
Except Turbo models	2.0/29	2.2/32
Turbo models	1.8/26	1.8/26

Suspension and steering

Torque wrench settings	Nm	lbf ft
Front suspension		
Driveshaft nut	250	184
Lower balljoint to stub axle carrier	60	44
Lower balljoint to arm	75	55
Lower suspension arm pivot	80	59
Strut to stub axle carrier	80	59
Strut upper mounting	25	18
Shock absorber piston rod nut	60	44
Anti-roll bar mountings	30	22

Torque wrench settings

	Nm	lbf ft
Rear suspension		
Bearing bracket	85	63
Hub bearing	160	118
Anti-roll bar (enclosed bar rear axle)	50	37
Shock absorber mountings	60	44
Steering		
Steering gear mounting	60	44
Track rod to stub axle carrier	40	30
Track rod locknut	40	30
Track rod inner balljoint	50	37
Steering wheel	40	30
Column intermediate shaft joints	25	18
Damper plunger adjusting nut	10	8
Roadwheels		
Wheel bolts	80	59

1 General description

The independent front suspension is of the MacPherson strut type incorporating inclined coil springs, integral telescopic shock absorbers and on some models an anti-roll bar. The struts are attached to stub axle carriers at their lower ends, and the carriers are in turn attached to the lower suspension arm by balljoints. Where an anti-roll bar is fitted it is attached to the subframe and lower suspension arms by rubber bushes.

The independent rear suspension is of the trailing arm type incorporating torsion bars. On non-Turbo models the torsion bars are enclosed within tubes which are themselves part of the trailing arms, and the one-piece anti-roll bar is mounted externally between the arms. On Turbo models the trailing arms are connected by a length of flexible metal section with open torsion bars and anti-roll bars mounted beneath.

Rack and pinion steering is fitted together with a conventional column and "safety" intermediate shaft.

2 Routine maintenance

At the intervals specified in the "Routine maintenance" section in the front of the manual carry out the following procedures.

1 Check each tyre for excessive or uneven wear and for damage or tread separation. For better access to the inner sides of the tyres use car ramps or jack up the car.

2 Jack up the front of the car and support on axle stands. Grip the top and bottom of the roadwheel and attempt to rock it. If excessive play is evident check if this is in the lower suspension balljoint or hub bearing and repair as necessary.

3 Check the track rod ends for wear by pushing the socket against the ball. Excessive

Fig. 9.1 Front suspension layout (Sec 1)

Fig. 9.2 Cross-section of the front suspension and steering components (Sec 1)

9

Fig. 9.3 Rear suspension layout (enclosed bar rear axle) (Sec 1)

Fig. 9.4 Cross-section of the rear suspension components (enclosed bar rear axle) (Sec 1)

Fig. 9.5 Rear suspension components (open bar rear axle (Sec 1)

1 Bearing brackets
2 Rear axle complete with trailing arms
3 Bearing bracket mounting bolts
4 Bump stop

movement will require renewal of the track rod end.

4 Although not specified by Renault it is worthwhile checking the operation of the shock absorbers annually. To do this press down on one corner of the car and release it quickly. The body should rise then find its level on the next downward movement. If it oscillates a number of times the relevant shock absorber should be renewed. Repeat the check at the three remaining corners of the car.

3 Front stub axle carrier - removal and refitting

1 Jack up the front of the car and support on axle stands. Apply the handbrake and remove the appropriate roadwheel.
2 Remove the front brake caliper with reference to Chapter 8, but leaving the hydraulic hose connected. Tie the caliper to one side with wire or string taking care not to damage the hose.
3 Hold the front hub stationary by using two roadwheel bolts to attach a length of metal bar, then unscrew the driveshaft nut. Remove the washer.
4 Disconnect the steering track rod end from the stub axle carrier with reference to Section 22.
5 Unscrew the two nuts and withdraw the bolts securing the stub axle carrier to the suspension strut (photo). Note that the nuts are on the side of the brake caliper.
6 Unscrew the nut and withdraw the clamp bolt securing the lower suspension arm balljoint to the base of the stub axle carrier (photo).
7 Release the stub axle carrier from the strut and then lift it, while pushing down on the suspension arm, to disengage the lower balljoint. Withdraw the stub axle carrier from the driveshaft and remove it from the car (photo). If the driveshaft is a tight fit in the hub bearings, tap it out using a plastic mallet, or use a suitable puller.

3.5 Removing the bolts securing the stub axle carrier to the suspension strut

3.6 Clamp bolt securing the balljoint to the stub axle carrier

3.7 Disengage the stub axle carrier from the balljoint then withdraw the assembly from the driveshaft

3.8A Undo the two Torx type screws securing the disc to the hub flange using a splined key . . .

3.8B . . . then lift off the disc

3.8C If the disc is tight, support it on blocks and drive out the hub

8 If the stub axle carrier is being removed for attention to the hub bearings. undo the two Torx type screws securing the disc to the hub flange using a splined key (photo). The disc can now be withdrawn from the hub. If it is tight, lay the disc over two blocks of wood and tap the hub out (photos).

9 Refitting is the reverse sequence to removal, bearing in mind the following points:

a) *Ensure that the mating faces of the disc and hub flange are clean and flat before refitting the disc*

b) *Lubricate the hub splines with molybdenum disulphide grease*

c) *Tighten all nuts and bolts to the specified torque (photo)*

d) *Depress the brake pedal several times to reset the disc pads*

4 Front hub bearings - renewal

Note 1: *The following procedure is given as a guide for those people wishing to do the work themselves, and will prove difficult in the best of circumstances mainly due to the very high press loads required to remove and refit the bearing outer race. It is strongly recommended that the stub axle is removed from the car, and the entire bearing renewal*

procedure is entrusted to a Renault dealer.

Note 2: *Do not attempt to remove the bearing unless it is to be renewed as the removal procedure renders it unserviceable.*

1 Remove the stub axle carrier from the car, as described in the previous Section.

2 Support the stub axle carrier securely on blocks or in a vice. Using a tube of suitable diameter in contact with the inner end of the hub flange (photo), drive the hub flange out of the bearing.

3 The bearing will come apart as the hub flange is removed and one of the bearing inner races will remain on the hub flange. To remove it, support the flange in a vice and use a two- or three-legged puller. Recover the thrust washer from the hub flange after removal of the inner race.

4 Extract the bearing retaining circlip from the inner end of the stub axle carrier.

5 Support the stub axle carrier on blocks or in a vice so that the side nearest the roadwheel is uppermost.

6 Place the previously removed inner race back in position over the ball cage. Using a tube of suitable diameter in contact with the inner race, drive the complete bearing assembly out of the stub axle carrier.

7 Before fitting the new bearing, remove the plastic covers protecting the seals at each end, but leave the inner plastic sleeve in position to hold the inner races together.

3.9 Tightening the stub axle carrier-to-strut bolts

8 Support the stub axle carrier so that the side away from the roadwheel is uppermost, and place the new bearing squarely in position.

9 Using a tube of suitable diameter in contact with the bearing outer race, drive the bearing into the stub axle carrier. Ensure that the bearing does not tip slightly and bind as it is being fitted. If this happens the outer race may be damaged so take great care to keep it square.

10 With the bearing in position, lubricate the lips of the two seals with multi-purpose grease. Remove the plastic retaining sleeve.

11 Place the thrust washer over the hub flange and lay it on the bench, flat face down.

12 Locate the stub axle carrier and bearing inner race over the hub flange and drive the

Fig. 9.6 Exploded view of front stub axle carrier showing hub bearings (Sec 4)

1 *Spacer/thrust washer*
2 *Circlip*
3 *Bearing*
4 *Stub axle carrier*
5 *Splash guard*
6 *Hub flange*
7 *Disc*
8 *Cup*
9 *Driveshaft nut*
10 *Screw*
11 *Washer*
12 *Bolt*
13 *Bearing kit*

4.2 Hub flange inner end (A) and bearing retaining circlip (B) in the stub axle carrier

9

5.3A Unscrew the strut upper mounting bolts . . .

5.3B . . . and remove them

5.4 Front suspension strut removed from the car

bearing onto the flange using a tube in contact with the bearing inner race.

13 Fit a new bearing retaining circlip to the stub axle carrier and then refit the assembly to the car, as described in the previous Section.

5 Front suspension strut - removal and refitting

1 Jack up the front of the car and support it on axle stands. Remove the appropriate front roadwheel.

2 Undo the nuts and remove the two bolts and washers securing the suspension strut to the upper part of the stub axle carrier.

3 From within the engine compartment undo the two bolts securing the strut upper mounting to the turret (photos).

4 Release the strut from the stub axle carrier and withdraw it from under the wheel arch while pressing on the lower suspension arm to prevent damage to the driveshaft bellows (photo).

5 Refitting the strut is the reverse sequence to removal. Ensure that the strut-to-stub axle carrier bolts are fitted with the nuts facing the rear of the car and tighten all the retaining bolts to the specified torque.

Fig. 9.7 Removing the nut from the front shock absorber piston rod (Sec 6)

6 Front suspension strut - dismantling and reassembly

Note: *Before attempting to dismantle the front suspension strut a tool to hold the coil spring in compression must be obtained. The Renault tool is shown in Fig. 9.7 and consists of upper and lower plates, four through-bolts, locating studs and two bolts to hold the upper mounting, however, careful use of conventional coil spring compressors should prove satisfactory.*

1 With the strut removed from the car clean

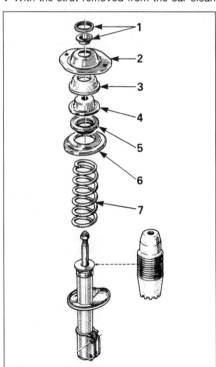

Fig. 9.8 Front suspension strut components (Sec 6)

1 Washer and cup
2 Mounting plate
3 Rubber
4 Bearing
5 Collar
6 Spring seat
7 Coil spring

away all external dirt then mount it upright in a vice.

2 Fit the spring compressor tool and compress the coil spring until all tension is relieved on the upper mounting (photo).

3 Withdraw the plastic cap over the strut upper mounting nut, hold the strut piston with an Allen key and undo the nut with a ring spanner (photo).

4 Lift off the washer and cup, the mounting and rubber, and the bearing assembly followed by the spring and compressor tool. Leave the tool or the spring unless the latter is to be renewed. Finally remove the bump stop.

5 With the strut assembly now completely dismantled, examine all the components for

6.2 Spring compressor tool fitted to the front suspension coil spring

6.3 Strut upper mounting showing nut on piston rod

wear, damage or deformation and check the bearing for smoothness of operation. Renew any of the components as necessary.

6 Examine the strut for signs of fluid leakage. Check the strut piston for signs of wear or pitting along its entire length and check the strut body for signs of damage or elongation of the mounting bolt holes. Test the operation of the strut, while holding it in an upright position, by moving the piston through a full stroke and then through short strokes of 50 to 100 mm (2 to 4 in). In both cases the resistance felt should be smooth and continuous. If the resistance is jerky, or uneven, or if there is any visible sign of wear or damage to the strut, renewal is necessary.

7 Reassembly is a reversal of dismantling. The spring must be compressed to less than 300.0 mm (11.8 in) to allow the mounting nut to be fitted to the piston rod. Tighten the nut to the specified torque. Make sure that the spring ends are correctly located in the upper and lower seats when releasing the compressor tool.

7 Front anti-roll bar - removal and refitting

1 Apply the handbrake then jack up the front of the car and support on axle stands.
2 Remove the exhaust downpipe with reference to Chapter 3.
3 Disconnect the gearchange linkage from the gearbox with reference to Chapter 6.
4 Unscrew the nuts and remove the clamp bolts holding the ends of the anti-roll bar to the lower suspension arms. Pull down the clamps.
5 Unscrew the nuts and remove the clamp bolts from the mountings on the subframe (photo). Pull down the clamps and remove them.

Fig. 9.9 Front lower suspension arm pivot bush renewal (Sec 8)

Use a 30.0 mm (1.18 in) diameter tube to remove and refit the bushes. Dimension A must be 146.5 to 147.5 mm (5.77 to 5.81 in)

7.5 Front anti-roll bar mounting on the subframe

6 Lower the anti-roll bar from the rear of the subframe.
7 Check the bar for damage and the rubber bushes for wear and deterioration. If the bushes are in need of renewal slide them off the bar and fit new ones after lubricating them with rubber grease.
8 Refitting is a reversal of removal, but delay tightening the clamp bolts until the unladen weight of the car is on the suspension.

8 Front lower suspension arm - removal and refitting

1 Remove the front anti-roll bar as described in Section 7. Remove the roadwheel.
2 Unscrew the nut and remove the clamp bolt securing the lower suspension balljoint to the stub axle carrier.
3 Unscrew the nuts and remove the spacers and pivot bolts from the inner end of the suspension arm then withdraw the arm from the subframe and stub axle carrier (photo). If the balljoint stub is seized in the stub axle carrier, lever or drive it out with a mallet. Recover the protector from the balljoint boot.
4 If the inner pivot bushes are to be renewed this can be done using suitable lengths of tube and a press or wide-opening vice. Renew the bushes one at a time so that the distance between the bush inner edges is maintained at 146.5 to 147.5 mm (5.77 to 5.81 in).
5 Refitting is a reversal of removal. Make sure that the plastic protector is positioned over the balljoint boot. Tighten the pivot and clamp

9.3 Front lower suspension balljoint

8.3 Front lower suspension arm inner mounting

bolts to the specified torque, and refit the anti-roll bar with reference to Section 7.

9 Front lower suspension balljoint - renewal

1 Apply the handbrake then jack up the front of the car and support on axle stands. Remove the roadwheel.
2 Unscrew the nut and remove the clamp bolt securing the lower suspension balljoint to the stub axle carrier.
3 Unscrew the two nuts and bolts securing the balljoint to the lower suspension arm and withdraw the balljoint (photo). Recover the plastic protector from the balljoint boot.
4 Fit the new balljoint using a reversal of the removal procedure, but tighten the nuts to the specified torque.

10 Rear hub bearings - renewal

Note: *Removal of the bearing will make it unsuitable for further use.*

1 Jack up the rear of the car and support on axle stands. Remove the appropriate rear roadwheel.

Fig. 9.10 Exploded view of the rear hub (Sec 10)

1 Hub/drum (disc on some models)
2 Spacer/thrust washer
3 Bearing
4 Thrust washer
5 Circlip
6 Hub nut
7 Grease cap

9

10.3 Removing the rear hub grease cap

10.4 Removing the rear hub nut and washer

10.6 Extracting the rear hub bearing circlip

2 On models with rear disc brakes remove the disc pads and caliper frame with reference to Chapter 8.

3 Lever or tap off the grease cap from the centre of the brake drum or disc (photo).

4 Using a socket unscrew the hub nut then remove the thrust washer (photo).

5 Pull the brake drum or disc assembly from the stub axle, if necessary using a soft-head mallet to help release the bearing inner race from the stub axle. On rear brake drum models make sure that the handbrake is fully released, however if the shoes still bind on the drum use the procedures described in Chapter 8, Section 6 to further release the shoes.

6 With the brake drum or disc assembly removed extract the circlip and drive out the bearing using a tube of suitable diameter inserted through the inside of the hub and in contact with the bearing race (photo).

7 Place the new bearing in the hub and drive it fully home, again using a tube in contact with the bearing outer race. Take great care to keep the bearing square as it is installed, otherwise it may jam in the hub bore.

8 With the bearing in position, refit the retaining circlip.

9 Check that the bearing inner spacer/thrust washer is located on the stub axle. On rear brake drum models set the handbrake lever on the shoe to its normal position if moved and shorten the automatic adjuster as required.

10 Refit the brake drum or disc followed by the thrust washer and a new hub nut.

11 Tighten the hub nut to the specified torque then tap the grease cap back into place (photo).

12 On rear disc brake models refit the disc pads and caliper frame with reference to Chapter 8.

13 Refit the roadwheel then depress the footbrake pedal several times to reset the shoes or disc pads.

14 On rear brake drum models adjust the handbrake cable if necessary as described in Chapter 8.

15 Lower the car to the ground.

11 Rear shock absorber - removal and refitting

1 Jack up the rear of the car and support on axle stands. Chock the front wheels. Remove the appropriate rear wheel.

2 Using a trolley jack lift the trailing arm until the shock absorber is compressed slightly then unscrew and remove the lower mounting bolt (photo).

3 Unscrew and remove the upper mounting nut and bolt and withdraw the shock absorber from the underframe (photo).

4 Mount the shock absorber upright in a vice and test it as described in Section 6 for the front suspension strut. Also check the mounting rubbers for damage and deterioration. Renew the complete unit if any damage or excessive wear is apparent.

5 Before fitting the shock absorber mount it upright in the vice and operate it fully through several strokes in order to prime it.

6 Coat the threads of the mounting bolts with locking fluid then position the shock absorber, insert the bolts and screw on the upper nut finger tight.

7 Raise the trolley jack until the full weight of the car is on the suspension then tighten the mounting bolts to the specified torque.

8 Refit the roadwheel and lower the car to the ground.

12 Rear anti-roll bar (enclosed bar rear axle) - removal and refitting

Note: *The procedure for the open bar rear axle is given in Section 17.*

1 Chock the front wheels then jack up the rear of the car and support it on axle stands.

2 From each end of the anti-roll bar unscrew the through-bolts securing the brackets to the rear suspension trailing arms. Note the location of the handbrake cable brackets. Recover the plates with the trapped nuts.

3 Withdraw the anti-roll bar from under the car. If the bar is to be refitted identify it for position to ensure correct positioning when refitting.

4 Refitting is a reversal of removal, but tighten the through-bolts to the specified torque. Note that the cut-away sides of the brackets must be towards the front of the car.

10.11 Tightening the rear hub nut

11.2 Rear shock absorber lower mounting

11.3 Rear shock absorber upper mounting

Fig. 9.11 Using the Renault slide hammer to remove a rear torsion bar (Sec 13)

Fig. 9.12 Rear torsion bar identification (Sec 13)

A Left-hand bar - 2 marks   B Right-hand bar - 3 marks

13 Rear torsion bar - removal and refitting

1 Chock the front wheels then jack up the rear of the car and support on axle stands. Remove the appropriate rear roadwheel.
2 On models with the enclosed-bar rear axle remove the anti-roll bar as described in Section 12.
3 Remove the rear shock absorber as described in Section 11.
4 Lower the trailing arm until all the tension in the torsion bar is released.
5 Prise the cap from the trailing arm bearing bracket.
6 Mark the position of the torsion bar in relation to the bearing bracket, and on the open-bar rear axle in relation to the centre link block.
7 The torsion bar can now be withdrawn outwards using a slide hammer such as Renault tool Emb.880 or a suitable alternative. It is possible to improvise by screwing a long bolt with a flat washer into the torsion bar and placing the jaws of a spanner against the washer. Striking the spanner sharply with a hammer should free the torsion bar.
8 Once the splines of the torsion bar are free, the bar can be withdrawn completely from its location. Note that the torsion bars are not interchangeable from side to side and are marked with symbols on their ends for identification as shown in Fig. 9.12.
9 If the original torsion bar is being refitted insert it so that the marks made in paragraph 6 are aligned. However if a new bar is being fitted, the trailing arm must be positioned to provide the dimension shown in Fig. 9.13. A tool similar to that shown will hold the trailing arm in position, or the arm can be positioned with the trolley jack.
10 With the trailing arm supported in this position lubricate the torsion bar splines with molybdenum disulphide grease and insert the bar into the bracket. The number of splines at

each end of the bar is different so it will be necessary to turn it to find the point where both sets of splines enter freely. Having found this, tap the bar fully home using a hammer and soft metal drift.
11 Refit the cap to the bearing bracket.
12 Refit the rear shock absorber (Section 11), if applicable the anti-roll bar (Section 12), and the rear roadwheel. Lower the car to the ground.
13 It is now necessary to check the rear underbody height. The fuel tank should be full or an equivalent weight placed in the luggage compartment and the tyres correctly inflated. Refer to Section 18 for further information.

14 Rear suspension trailing arm (enclosed bar rear axle) - removal and refitting

1 Jack up the rear of the car and support it on axle stands. Remove the appropriate rear roadwheel.
2 Remove the anti-roll bar and the shock absorber, as described in Sections 12 and 11 respectively. Remove the torsion bar on the side concerned, as described in Section 13.

Fig. 9.13 Rear trailing arm setting for fitting torsion bar (Sec 13)

X = 405.0 mm (15.945 in) for non-Turbo models
X = 385.0 mm (15.158 in) for Turbo models

3 Refer to Chapter 8 and remove the brake drum and hub assembly.
4 With the drum removed, detach the handbrake cable from the operating lever on the trailing brake shoe and withdraw the cable from the brake backplate.
5 Using a brake hose clamp or self-locking wrench with protected jaws, clamp the appropriate flexible brake hose just in front of the rear axle. This will minimise brake fluid loss during subsequent operations. Clean the union on the trailing arm then unscrew the union nut and withdraw the hose from the bracket. Recover the clip then tape over the ends of the hose and pipe to prevent entry of dirt.
6 Where applicable disconnect the brake pressure regulating control valve spring with reference to Chapter 8.
7 Support the weight of the trailing arm with a trolley jack.
8 Working inside the rear of the car remove the rear seat cushion and cut away the plastic to reveal the plates and bolt heads of the bearing bracket mounting bolts.
9 Unscrew the nuts from beneath the car then tap the bolts through the bearing bracket with a suitable drift (photo).
10 Lower the jack as necessary to allow the trailing arm to clear the sill.
11 Pull the trailing arm from the remaining arm. If it is tight Renault recommend using a hydraulic ram between the two arms, however a similar arrangement is possible using a length of wood and a screw or bottle jack.

14.9 Rear suspension bearing bracket

Fig. 9.14 Renault tool for removing the rear suspension trailing arm bushes (Sec 15)

12 With the arm removed the brake backplate can be unbolted if required and the spacer removed from the stub axle.

13 To refit the arm push it onto the other arm having first lubricated the inner bushes with grease. If it is tight use a rope as a tourniquet between the two arms. Temporarily position the anti-roll bar over the mounting holes to determine how far the bars should be interlocked.

14 Raise the trolley jack to lift the arm, and insert the mounting bolts, tightening the nuts to the specified torque.

15 Refit the rear seat cushion.

16 Refit the brake backplate and stub axle spacer.

17 Where applicable reconnect the brake pressure regulating control valve spring.

18 Refit the flexible brake hose and rigid pipe together with the clip and tighten the union nut.

19 Refit the handbrake cable and drum with reference to Chapter 8.

20 Refit the torsion bar (Section 13), shock absorber (Section 11), and anti-roll bar (Section 12).

21 Bleed the brake hydraulic system as

Fig. 9.16 Using a puller to remove the rear suspension bearing bracket (Sec 16)

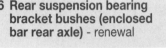

Fig. 9.15 Showing trailing arm bush removal and bush fitting dimensions (Sec 15)

L = 140.0 + 2 (5.512 + 0.079
        - 0 mm   - 0 in)
Y = 15.0 + 2 (0.591 + 0.079
        - 0 mm   - 0 in)

described in Chapter 8, noting that it should only be necessary to bleed the relevant rear brake providing the hose was clamped as described.

22 Finally refit the roadwheel and lower the car to the ground.

15 Rear suspension trailing arm bushes (enclosed bar rear axle) - renewal

Note: *The rear suspension trailing arm bushes are located in the left-hand trailing arm.*

1 Remove the left-hand trailing arm as described in Section 14 and mount it in a vice. Prise out the oil seal.

2 To remove the bushes it will be necessary to obtain the Renault tool shown in Fig. 9.14 or make up a similar tool using the Renault tool as a pattern, as follows:

3 Obtain a threaded rod long enough to reach the inner bush, a tube of suitable diameter as shown, one thick washer of diameter equal to that of the bush, a washer of diameter greater than the tube and two nuts. Cut two sides off the smaller washer so that just a flat strip with a hole in the centre remains. This will form the swivelling end part shown on the Renault tool. Pass the threaded rod through the hole in the strip and screw on a nut. Feed the strip and rod through the bush so that the strip locates behind the bush. Place the tube over the rod and in contact with the edge of the arm. Place the large washer over the end of the tube and then screw on the remaining nut. Hold the rod with grips and tighten the nut to draw out the bush, then repeat this operation to remove the remaining bush.

Fig. 9.17 Trailing arm and bearing bracket positioning for assembly (Sec 16)

X = 80.0 ± 2.0 mm (3.150 ± 0.079 in)

4 Clean the inside of the arm then drive in the new bushes using suitable tubing. Position the bushes to the dimensions shown in Fig. 9.1 5.

5 Press in a new seal and smear a little grease on its lip.

6 Refit the left-hand trailing arm with reference to Section 14.

16 Rear suspension bearing bracket bushes (enclosed bar rear axle) - renewal

1 Remove the trailing arm as described in Section 14.

2 Apply brake fluid to the bush to soften the rubber.

3 Using a two- or three-legged puller draw the bearing bracket from the trailing arm. The rubber will tear during this process leaving the inner part of the bush on the arm.

4 Remove the remaining part of the bush by cutting with a hacksaw taking care not to damage the trailing arm tube. Also remove the outer remains of the bush from the bearing bracket. Clean the tube and bracket.

5 The fitted position of the new bush must be flush with the end of the trailing arm tube so mark the inner part of the tube to indicate the final position of the bush.

6 Press or drive the new bush fully into the bearing bracket.

7 Position the bracket as shown in Fig. 9.17 in relation to the trailing arm then press or drive the bracket on the tube until the bush reaches the mark made in paragraph 5.

8 Refit the trailing arm with reference to Section 14.

17 Rear axle (open bar type) - removal and refitting

1 Remove the rear shock absorbers as described in Section 11.

2 Remove both rear torsion bars with reference to Section 13.

3 Remove the brake components from the trailing arms with reference to Chapter 8.

4 Using a brake hose clamp compress both rear flexible hoses then disconnect them by unscrewing the union nuts. Recover the clips

Fig. 9.18 Showing correct fitted positions of rear bearing bracket bush (Sec 16)

Fig. 9.20 Place the link block and block of wood on the L-shaped sections (Sec 17)

Fig. 9.19 Open bar type rear axle components (Sec 17)

1 Integral trailing arms and flexible bar   2 Link block   3 Anti-roll bars   4 Torsion bars

and tape over the ends of the hoses and pipes to prevent entry of dirt.

5 Disconnect the brake pressure regulating control valve spring with reference to Chapter 8.

6 Support the weight of the rear axle with a trolley jack.

7 Working inside the rear of the car remove the rear seat cushion and cut away the mastic to reveal the plates and bolt heads of the bearing bracket mounting bolts.

8 Unscrew the nuts from beneath the car then tap the bolts through the bearing brackets.

9 Lower the rear axle from the underbody and remove it.

10 If required, remove the bearing brackets using the method described for the enclosed bar rear axle in Section 6.

11 Mark the anti-roll bars in relation to the trailing arms and link block, then extract them using a slide hammer such as Renault tool Emb.880 or a suitable alternative.

12 Examine all the components for damage and wear. Check the splines on the torsion

bars, anti-roll bars, link block and trailing arms. If the trailing arms or L-shaped section is damaged it will be necessary to obtain a new rear axle which is supplied with the bearing brackets already fitted, but requiring the torsion bars and anti-roll bars to be fitted. If the bearing bracket bushes require renewal use the procedure described in Section 16.

13 Commence re-assembly by placing the rear axle upside-down on blocks of wood positioned under the L-shaped section so that the bearing brackets are free.

Anti-roll bars with no marks

14 Make up a small block of wood 8.0 mm (0.315 in) thick and position it on the middle of the L-shaped section with the link block on top (Fig. 9.20).

15 Clean the anti-roll bar splines and grease them well.

16 Insert one anti-roll bar through the trailing arm and engage the splines with the link block. It will be necessary to try the bar in different positions to find the point where both sets of splines enter freely.

17 Fit the remaining anti-roll bar using the same procedure then mark each bar in relation to the trailing arms and link block. Remove the wooden block.

Anti-roll bars with special marks

18 Using a ruler as shown in Fig. 9.21 mark each trailing arm between the centres of the torsion bar and anti-roll bar holes.

19 Clean the anti-roll bar splines and grease them well.

20 Insert one anti-roll bar with the marked spline aligned with the mark made in paragraph 18.

21 Fit the link block with the centre section parallel to the L-shaped section.

22 Insert the remaining anti-roll bar from the opposite side with the marked spline aligned with the mark made in paragraph 18.

All types

23 The clearance between the centre of the link block and the L-shaped section must now be measured. If it is more than 2.0 mm (0.08 in) the block must be re-positioned bearing in mind that one spline is equal to 2.0 mm (0.08 in) clearance. If the clearance is incorrect the link block may touch the L-shaped section during movement of the suspension.

24 Clean the torsion bar splines and grease them well.

25 Insert the torsion bars on their correct sides until fully entered in the link block. Try them in different positions to find the point where both sets of splines enter freely.

9

Fig. 9.21 Using a ruler to mark the trailing arms (Sec 17)

Fig. 9.22 Rear torsion bar identification on some Turbo models (Sec 17)

A Left-hand bar   B Right-hand bar

Fig. 9.23 Underbody height checking points (Sec 18)

26 Place the rear axle on the trolley jack and lift it into position.

27 Tap the bolts through the bearing brackets then fit the nuts and tighten them to the specified torque. Refit the rear seat cushion.

28 Refit the brake components, flexible hoses and pressure control valve spring with reference to Chapter 8.

29 Check that with the weight of the trailing arms taken off the torsion bars the distance between the shock absorber upper and lower mounting centres is 385.0 mm (15.16 in). If not, remove the torsion bars and re-position them in the splines with reference to Section 13.

30 Refit the rear shock absorbers with reference to Section 11.

31 Check the rear underbody height and adjust if necessary with reference to Section 18.

18 Underbody height - checking and adjustment

1 Position the car on a level surface with the tyres correctly inflated and the fuel tank full.

2 Measure and record the dimensions H1, H2, H4, and H5 shown in Fig. 9.23. The results should be within the specified tolerances and should not vary side-to-side by more than 10.0 mm (0.40 in) except on Turbo models where the *rear* suspension height should not vary side-to-side by more than 5.0 mm (0.20 in).

3 It is not possible to adjust the front underbody height, however, if the rear height is outside the specified amount proceed as follows.

Fig. 9.24 The underbody height H5 is measured from the centre of the torsion bar (Sec 18)

4 *If the side-to-side height difference is excessive* on the open bar type rear axle, the anti-roll bar on the lower side must be re-positioned to raise that side. On the enclosed type rear axle, excessive side-to-side difference may be due to a distorted anti-roll bar in which case it should be removed and checked. To adjust the open bar type first remove both rear torsion bars and the anti-roll bar on the lower side after marking their positions. Determine the position of the trailing arm where the anti-roll bar can be refitted in its original location freely, then lower the arm by the side-to-side difference previously noted and insert the anti-roll bar again, this time turning it as required to find the position where both sets of splines enter freely. Finally refit the torsion bars.

5 If the height is incorrect remove the torsion bar from the appropriate side after marking its position. Determine the position of the trailing arm where the torsion bar can be refitted in its original formation freely, then adjust the arm up or down as necessary by the difference of height required, and insert the torsion bar again this time turning it as required to find the position where both sets of splines enter freely.

6 After adjusting the underbody height the load sensitive type brake pressure regulator spring tension should be checked and adjusted (Chapter 8) and the headlight beam alignment adjusted (Chapter 11).

19.3 Unscrew the retaining nut . . .

19 Steering wheel - removal and refitting

1 Set the front wheels in the straight-ahead position.

2 Ease off the steering wheel pad to provide access to the retaining nut.

3 Using a socket and knuckle bar undo and remove the retaining nut (photo).

4 Mark the steering wheel and steering column shaft in relation to each other and withdraw the wheel from the shaft splines (photo). If it is tight, tap it upwards near the centre, using the palm of your hand. Refit the steering wheel retaining nut two turns before doing this, for obvious reasons.

5 Refitting is the reverse of removal, but align the previously made marks and tighten the retaining nut to the specified torque.

20 Steering column assembly - removal, overhaul and refitting

1 Disconnect the battery negative lead.

2 Remove the steering wheel as described in Section 19.

3 Remove the screws and withdraw the lower shroud from the column (photos).

4 Unscrew the direction indicator switch mounting screws.

5 Extract the circlip from the top of the column.

19.4 . . . and remove the steering wheel

20.3A Remove the screws . . .

20.3B . . . and withdraw the steering column lower shroud

20.8 Steering column mounting bolts and nuts

Fig. 9.25 Cross-section of the steering column showing the bush location tabs (Sec 20)

6 At the base of the column unscrew and remove the clamp bolt securing the intermediate shaft to the inner column. Mark both components in relation to each other.

7 Check that the ignition switch is in the "Garage" position with the steering unlocked, then temporarily refit the steering wheel with the nut finger tight. Pull on the steering wheel to release the inner column from the intermediate shaft and also to release the upper bush.

8 Unscrew the facia-to-column bolts and also the steering column mounting bolts/nuts (photo).

9 Where applicable separate the centre console from the facia then release the facia panel lower mountings with reference to Chapter 10.

10 Disconnect the ignition switch wiring multi-plug.

11 Lift the facia panel as necessary and withdraw the steering column from the car.

12 Using a long metal tube of 35.0 mm (1.378 in) outside diameter drive the lower bush from the outer column. Also pull the upper bush from the inner column.

13 Clean the inner and outer columns. Renew the inner column if it is worn excessively. Obtain two new bushes.

14 Lubricate the bushes with grease then drive the lower bush into the outer column between the location tabs. Tap in the tabs using a punch in order to lock the bush.

15 Insert the inner column through the top of the outer column and through the lower bush.

16 Drive in the upper bush and refit the circlip. Tap in the location tabs to lock the bush.

17 Refitting is a reversal of removal, but when re-connecting the intermediate shaft to

Fig. 9.26 Inner steering column and intermediate shaft components (Sec 20)

the inner column, the flat on the column must be aligned with the clamp opening as shown in Fig. 9.27. Tighten all bolts and bolts to the specified torque. Refit the steering wheel with reference to Section 19.

21 Steering column intermediate shaft - removal and refitting

1 Jack up the front of the car and support on axle stands. Apply the handbrake.

2 Remove the screws and withdraw the lower shroud from the column.

3 At the base of the column unscrew and remove the clamp bolt securing the intermediate shaft to the inner column. Mark both components in relation to each other.

4 Working in the engine compartment or from beneath the car unscrew and remove the lower bolt from the flexible coupling, but leave

Fig. 9.27 The flat (A) on the inner column must be aligned with the clamp opening (Sec 20)

the clamp and clamp bolt on the steering gear. Mark the coupling and clamp in relation to each other.

5 Prise the rubber boot from the bulkhead, pull the intermediate shaft down to release it from the inner column then withdraw the shaft from inside the car.

6 Release the rubber boot from the bearing halves and pull it from the shaft.

7 Check the intermediate shaft for wear and damage. There should be no noticeable play between the yokes of the universal joint. The shaft incorporates a safety feature whereby the two tubes slide into each other in the event of accident impact, however the shaft must not be used after accidental damage and it is therefore important to check that its length is as given in Fig. 9.28 before refitting it. Check and if necessary renew the rubber boot and bearing halves.

8 To refit the shaft first locate the rubber boot and bearing halves on the small diameter end.

9 Insert the shaft through the bulkhead and connect it to the lower flexible coupling and inner column making sure that the flat on the column is aligned with the clamp opening (Fig. 9.27). Do not tighten the bolts at this stage.

10 Tighten each of the lower flexible coupling bolts only when the bolt head is facing vertically upwards. This will ensure the centre rubber block flexes equally in both directions.

11 Tighten the upper clamp bolt.

12 Refit the rubber boot and lower shroud then lower the car to the ground.

9

Fig. 9.28 Intermediate shaft checking dimension (Sec 21)

L = 378.5 ± 1.0 mm (14.902 ± 0.04 in) on LHD models
L = 401.0 ± 1.0 mm (15.787 ± 0.04 in) on RHD models

22.3A Unscrew the nut . . .

22.3B . . . and use a separator tool to remove the track rod end balljoint

22 Track rod end balljoint - renewal

1 Jack up the front of the car and support it on axle stands. Remove the appropriate front roadwheel.

2 Using a suitable spanner, slacken the balljoint locknut on the track rod by a quarter of a turn. Hold the track rod with a second spanner engaged with the flats at its inner end to prevent it from turning.

3 Undo and remove the locknut securing the balljoint to the stub axle carrier and then release the tapered shank using a balljoint separator tool (photos).

4 Count the number of exposed threads between the end of the balljoint and the locknut and record this figure.

5 Unscrew the balljoint from the track rod and unscrew the locknut from the balljoint.

6 Screw the locknut onto the new balljoint and position it so that the same number of exposed threads are visible as was noted during removal.

7 Screw the balljoint onto the track rod until the locknut just contacts the arm. Now tighten the locknut while holding the track rod as before.

8 Engage the shank of the balljoint with the stub axle carrier and refit the locknut. Tighten the locknut to the specified torque.

HAYNES HiNT *If the balljoint shank turns while the locknut is being tightened, place a jack under the balljoint and raise it sufficiently to push the tapered shank fully into the stub axle carrier. The tapered fit of the shank will lock it and prevent rotation as the nut is tightened.*

9 On completion, remove the jack, refit the roadwheel and lower the car to the ground.

10 Check the front wheel alignment, as described in Section 28.

23 Steering gear rubber bellows - renewal

1 Remove the track rod end balljoint as described in Section 22.

2 Release the retaining wire or unscrew the retaining clip screws and slide the bellows off the rack and pinion housing and track rod.

3 Lubricate the inner ends of the new bellows with rubber grease and position it over the housing and track rod.

4 Using new clips, or two or three turns of soft iron wire, secure the bellows in position.

5 Refit the outer balljoint, as described in the previous Section.

24 Track rod and inner balljoint - removal and refitting

1 Remove the outer balljoint and rubber bellows, as described in Sections 22 and 23 respectively.

2 Hold the thrust washer with grips to prevent the rack turning and unscrew the inner balljoint housing with a small stilson wrench. Remove the balljoint housing and track rod assembly from under the wheel arch.

3 Clean the components and inspect them for damage. Always renew the lockplate and thrust washer. Check the balljoint for excessive play and damage to the lockplate serrations, and renew it if necessary.

26.3 Intermediate shaft to steering gear coupling

4 Fit the thrust washer and lockplate to the rack ensuring that the two tabs on the lockplate are in line with the two flats on the end of the rack.

5 Apply a drop of locking compound to the threads of the balljoint and screw the balljoint housing and track rod assembly into position. Tighten the housing securely.

6 Refit the rubber bellows and outer balljoint, as described in Sections 23 and 22 respectively.

25 Steering rack support bearing - removal and refitting

Note: *The support bearing is located in the left-hand end of the steering gear on RHD models, and in the right-hand end on LHD models.*

1 Remove the appropriate track rod and inner balljoint as described in Section 24.

2 Turn the steering onto full lock so that the rack is clear of the bearing.

3 Working under the wheel arch, extract the bearing from the rack and pinion housing by prising it out with a screwdriver.

4 Clean the rack, and rack and pinion housing, and then lubricate both with molybdenum disulphide grease. Liberally lubricate the new bearing also.

5 Carefully insert the new bearing into the housing and position it so that each of the three bearing tags enter their slots in the housing.

6 Move the steering on the opposite lock to settle the bearing and distribute the grease.

7 Refit the track rod and inner balljoint with reference to Section 24.

26 Steering gear - removal and refitting

1 Jack up the front of the car and support on axle stands. Apply the handbrake. Remove both front roadwheels.

2 On each side unscrew the nuts securing the track rod end balljoints to the stub axle carrier and use a separator tool to release the balljoints.

3 Working in the engine compartment unscrew and remove the lower bolt from the flexible coupling on the intermediate shaft, but leave the clamp and clamp bolt on the steering gear (photo). Mark the coupling and clamp in relation to each other.

4 Unscrew and remove the mounting nuts and bolts, spacers and clamp, then withdraw the steering gear sideways at the same time releasing the clamp from the flexible coupling (photo).

5 If necessary remove the track rod end balljoints as described in Section 22.

6 Refitting is a reversal of removal, but tighten all nuts and bolts to the specified torque. The flexible coupling bolt should be tightened with the bolt head facing upwards to ensure correct flexing of the centre rubber block.

26.4 View of the steering gear, shown with engine and gearbox removed

When fitting a new steering gear it will be necessary to place both the steering wheel and steering rack in their central straight-ahead positions before connecting the flexible coupling clamp to the steering gear pinion. Finally check and adjust the front wheel alignment as described in Section 28.

27 Steering gear - overhaul

Note: *Overhaul of the steering gear is limited as only certain parts are available separately. Renewal of the track rod end balljoints, track rods, rack support bearing and the rubber bellows may be carried out with the steering gear either in or out of the car, and these operations are covered in previous Sections of this Chapter. The only other repair possible is renewal and/or adjustment of the rack damper plunger. To carry out this work the steering gear must be removed from the car and the procedure is then as follows:*

1 With the steering gear on the bench, unlock the damper adjusting nut by straightening the tabs around the periphery of the nut (photo).
2 Using a suitable Allen key or hexagon socket bit, unscrew the adjusting nut and remove it from the rack and pinion housing.
3 Lift out the washer, spring and damper plunger.
4 Inspect the damper plunger and renew it if there is any sign of excessive scoring or wear of its contact face.
5 Lubricate the plunger and housing with molybdenum disulphide grease, then refit the plunger, spring, washer and adjusting nut.
6 To adjust the plunger, tighten the adjusting nut using a hexagon socket bit and torque wrench to the specified torque. Now back off the nut by a quarter of a turn.
7 Move the rack from lock to lock by turning the pinion yoke and check for any tight spots. If any are felt, slacken the adjusting nut further by a small amount until the rack will turn smoothly from lock to lock. Note that the rack will feel tight, but as long as the tightness is uniform over the entire length of travel, all is well.
8 After adjustment, secure the adjusting nut by punching the tabs down into the recesses in the housing.

27.1 Steering gear rack damper adjusting nut, shown in position in the car

28 Front wheel alignment and steering angles

1 Accurate front wheel alignment is essential to provide positive steering and prevent excessive tyre wear. Before considering the steering/suspension geometry, check that the tyres are correctly inflated, the front wheels are not buckled and the steering linkage and suspension joints are in good order, without slackness or wear.
2 Wheel alignment consists of four factors: Camber is the angle at which the front wheels are set from the vertical when viewed from front of the car. "Positive camber" is the amount (in degrees) that the wheels are tilted outward at the top of the vertical. Castor is the angle between the steering axis and a vertical line when viewed from each side of the car. "Positive castor" is when the steering axis is inclined rearward at the top. Steering axis inclination is the angle (when viewed from front of the car) between the vertical and an imaginary line drawn between the suspension strut upper mounting and the lower suspension arm balljoint. Toe setting is the amount by which the distance between the front inside edges of the roadwheels (measured at hub height) differs from the diametrically opposite distance measured between the rear inside edges of the front roadwheels.
3 With the exception of the toe setting all other steering angles are set during manufacture and no adjustment is possible. It can be assumed,

Fig. 9.31 Track rod inner balljoint components (Sec 27)

1 Rack
2 Thrust washer
3 Lockplate
4 Inner balljoint
B Flats

Fig. 9.30 Steering gear components (Sec 27)

1 Rubber bellows
2 Rack damper plunger
3 Spring
4 Washer
5 Adjusting nut
6 Rack support bearing
7 Rubber bellows
8 Yoke

therefore, that unless the car has suffered accident damage all the preset steering angles will be correct. Should there be some doubt about their accuracy it will be necessary to seek the help of a Renault dealer, as special gauges are needed to check the steering angles.
4 Two methods are available to the home mechanic for checking the toe setting. One method is to use a gauge to measure the distance between the front and rear inside edges of the roadwheels. The other method is to use a scuff plate in which each front wheel is rolled across a movable plate which records any deviation, or scuff, of the tyre from the

Fig. 9.32 Rack damper adjustment/renewal (Sec 27)

A Adjusting nut retaining tabs
5 Adjusting nut

9

straight-ahead position as it moves across the plate. Relatively inexpensive equipment of both types is available from accessory outlets to enable these checks, and subsequent adjustments to be carried out at home.

5 If, after checking the toe setting using whichever method is preferable, it is found that adjustment is necessary, proceed as follows.

6 Turn the steering wheel onto full left lock and record the number of exposed threads on the right-hand track rod end. Now turn the steering onto full right lock and record the number of threads on the left-hand side. If there are the same number of threads visible on both sides then subsequent adjustments can be made equally on both sides. If there are more threads visible on one side than the other it will be necessary to compensate for this during adjustment. *After adjustment there must be the same number of threads visible on each track rod end. This is most important.*

7 To alter the toe-setting slacken the locknut on the track rod end and turn the track rod using a self-grip wrench to achieve the desired setting. When viewed from the side of the car, turning the rod clockwise will increase the toe-in, turning it anti-clockwise will increase the toe-out. Only turn the track rods by a quarter of a turn each time and then recheck the setting using the gauges, or scuff plate. Note that turning the track rod by one complete turn will alter the toe-in or toe-out by 30' or 3 mm (0.12 in).

8 After adjustment tighten the locknuts and reposition the steering gear rubber bellows, if necessary, to remove any twist caused by turning the track rods.

29 Wheels and tyres - general care and maintenance

Wheels and tyres should give no real problems in use provided that a close eye is kept on them with regard to excessive wear or damage. To this end, the following points should be noted.

Ensure that tyre pressures are checked regularly and maintained correctly. Checking should be carried out with the tyres cold and not immediately after the vehicle has been in use. If the pressures are checked with the tyres hot, an apparently high reading will be obtained owing to heat expansion. Under no circumstances should an attempt be made to reduce the pressures to the quoted cold reading in this instance, or effective underinflation will result.

Underinflation will cause overheating of the tyre owing to excessive flexing of the casing, and the tread will not sit correctly on the road surface. This will cause a consequent loss of adhesion and excessive wear, not to mention the danger of sudden tyre failure due to heat build-up.

Overinflation will cause rapid wear of the centre part of the tyre tread coupled with reduced adhesion, harsher ride, and the danger of shock damage occurring in the tyre casing.

Regularly check the tyres for damage in the form of cuts or bulges, especially in the sidewalls. Remove any nails or stones embedded in the tread before they penetrate the tyre to cause deflation. If removal of a nail *does* reveal that the tyre has been punctured, refit the nail so that its point of penetration is marked. Then immediately change the wheel and have the tyre repaired by a tyre dealer. Do *not* drive on a tyre in such a condition. If in any doubt about the possible consequences of any damage found, consult your local tyre dealer for advice.

Periodically remove the wheels and clean any dirt or mud from the inside and outside surfaces. Examine the wheel rims for signs of rusting, corrosion or other damage. Light alloy wheels are easily damaged by "kerbing" whilst parking, and similarly steel wheels may become dented or buckled. Renewal of the wheel is very often the only course of remedial action possible.

The balance of each wheel and tyre assembly should be maintained to avoid excessive wear, not only to the tyres but also to the steering and suspension components. Wheel imbalance is normally signified by vibration through the vehicle's bodyshell, although in many cases it is particularly noticeable through the steering wheel.

Conversely, it should be noted that wear or damage in suspension or steering components may cause excessive tyre wear. Out-of-round or out-of-true tyres, damaged wheels and wheel bearing wear/maladjustment also fall into this category. Balancing will not usually cure vibration caused by such wear.

Wheel balancing may be carried out with the wheel either on or off the vehicle. If balanced on the vehicle, ensure that the wheel-to-hub relationship is marked in some way prior to subsequent wheel removal so that it may be refitted in its original position.

General tyre wear is influenced to a large degree by driving style - harsh braking and acceleration or fast cornering will all produce more rapid tyre wear. Interchanging of tyres may result in more even wear, but this should only be carried out where there is no mix of tyre types on the vehicle. However, it is worth bearing in mind that if this is completely effective, the added expense of replacing a complete set of tyres simultaneously is incurred, which may prove financially restrictive for many owners.

Front tyres may wear unevenly as a result of wheel misalignment. The front wheels should always be correctly aligned according to the settings specified by the vehicle manufacturer.

Legal restrictions apply to the mixing of tyre types on a vehicle. Basically this means that a vehicle must not have tyres of differing construction on the same axle. Although it is not recommended to mix tyre types between front axle and rear axle, the only legally permissible combination is crossply at the front and radial at the rear. When mixing radial ply tyres, textile braced radials must always go on the front axle, with steel braced radials at the rear. An obvious disadvantage of such mixing is the necessity to carry two spare tyres to avoid contravening the law in the event of a puncture.

In the UK, the Motor Vehicles Construction and Use Regulations apply to many aspects of tyre fitting and usage. It is suggested that a copy of these regulations is obtained from your local police if in doubt as to the current legal requirements with regard to tyre condition, minimum tread depth, etc.

Fault finding - suspension and steering

Note: *Before diagnosing steering or suspension faults, be sure that the trouble is not due to incorrect tyre pressures, a mixture of tyre types or binding brakes.*

Vehicle pulls to one side or tyre wear uneven
- [ ] Incorrect wheel alignment
- [ ] Wear in suspension or steering components
- [ ] Faulty tyre
- [ ] Accident damage to steering or suspension components
- [ ] Wheels out of balance

Steering stiff or heavy
- [ ] Lack of steering gear lubricant
- [ ] Seized balljoint
- [ ] Wheel alignment incorrect
- [ ] Steering rack or column bent or damaged

Excessive play in steering
- [ ] Worn steering or suspension joints
- [ ] Wear in intermediate shaft universal joints
- [ ] Worn rack and pinion assembly
- [ ] Worn or incorrectly adjusted rack damper

Wheel wobble and vibration
- [ ] Roadwheels out of balance, buckled or distorted
- [ ] Faulty or damaged tyre
- [ ] Worn steering or suspension joints
- [ ] Wheel bolts loose
- [ ] Worn rack and pinion assembly

Chapter 10 Bodywork and fittings

For modifications, and information applicable to later models, see Supplement at end of manual

Contents

Degrees of difficulty

Easy, suitable for novice with little experience	Fairly easy, suitable for beginner with some experience	Fairly difficult, suitable for competent DIY mechanic	Difficult, suitable for experienced DIY mechanic	Very difficult, suitable for expert DIY or professional

Specifications

Torque wrench setting	Nm	lbf ft
Seat belt anchorage and mounting bolts	20	15

1 General description

The bodyshell and underframe is of all-steel welded construction, incorporating progressive crumple zones at the front and rear and a rigid centre safety cell. The assembly and welding of the main body unit is completed by computer-controlled robots, and is checked for dimensional accuracy using computer and laser technology.

The front and rear bumpers are of collapsible cellular construction to minimise minor accident damage and the front wings are bolted in position to facilitate accident damage repair. The plastic side panels below the waistline are also designed to absorb light impact without damage.

2 Maintenance - bodywork and underframe

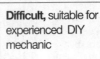

The general condition of a vehicle's bodywork is the one thing that significantly affects its value. Maintenance is easy, but needs to be regular. Neglect, particularly after minor damage, can lead quickly to further deterioration and costly repair bills. It is important also to keep watch on those parts of the vehicle not immediately visible, for instance the underside, inside all the wheel arches, and the lower part of the engine compartment.

The basic maintenance routine for the bodywork is washing - preferably with a lot of water, from a hose. This will remove all the loose solids which may have stuck to the vehicle. It is important to flush these off in such a way as to prevent grit from scratching the finish. The wheel arches and underframe need washing in the same way, to remove any accumulated mud, which will retain moisture and tend to encourage rust. Paradoxically enough, the best time to clean the underframe and wheel arches is in wet weather, when the mud is thoroughly wet and soft. In very wet weather, the underframe is usually cleaned of large accumulations automatically, and this is a good time for inspection.

Periodically, except on vehicles with a wax-based underbody protective coating, it is a good idea to have the whole of the underframe of the vehicle steam-cleaned, engine compartment included, so that a thorough inspection can be carried out to see what minor repairs and renovations are necessary. Steam-cleaning is available at

10

many garages, and is necessary for the removal of the accumulation of oily grime, which sometimes is allowed to become thick in certain areas. If steam-cleaning facilities are not available, there are some excellent grease solvents available which can be brush-applied; the dirt can then be simply hosed off. Note that these methods should not be used on vehicles with wax-based underbody protective coating, or the coating will be removed. Such vehicles should be inspected annually, preferably just prior to Winter, when the underbody should be washed down, and any damage to the wax coating repaired. Ideally, a completely fresh coat should be applied. It would also be worth considering the use of such wax-based protection for injection into door panels, sills, box sections, etc, as an additional safeguard against rust damage, where such protection is not provided by the vehicle manufacturer.

After washing paintwork, wipe off with a chamois leather to give an unspotted clear finish. A coat of clear protective wax polish will give added protection against chemical pollutants in the air. If the paintwork sheen has dulled or oxidised, use a cleaner/polisher combination to restore the brilliance of the shine. This requires a little effort, but such dulling is usually caused because regular washing has been neglected. Care needs to be taken with metallic paintwork, as special non-abrasive cleaner/polisher is required to avoid damage to the finish. Always check that the door and ventilator opening drain holes and pipes are completely clear, so that water can be drained out (photo). Brightwork should be treated in the same way as paintwork. Windscreens and windows can be kept clear of the smeary film which often appears, by the use of proprietary glass cleaner. Never use any form of wax or other body or chromium polish on glass.

3 Maintenance - upholstery and carpets

Mats and carpets should be brushed or vacuum-cleaned regularly, to keep them free of grit. If they are badly stained, remove them

2.4 Checking a door drain hole for obstruction

from the vehicle for scrubbing or sponging, and make quite sure they are dry before refitting. Seats and interior trim panels can be kept clean by wiping with a damp cloth. If they do become stained (which can be more apparent on light-coloured upholstery), use a little liquid detergent and a soft nail brush to scour the grime out of the grain of the material. Do not forget to keep the headlining clean in the same way as the upholstery. When using liquid cleaners inside the vehicle, do not over-wet the surfaces being cleaned. Excessive damp could get into the seams and padded interior, causing stains, offensive odours or even rot.

> **HAYNES HiNT** *If the inside of the vehicle gets wet accidentally, it is worthwhile taking some trouble to dry it out properly, particularly where carpets are involved. Do not leave oil or electric heaters inside the vehicle for this purpose.*

4 Minor body damage - repair

Note: *For more detailed information about bodywork repair, Haynes Publishing produce a book by Lindsay Porter called "The Car Bodywork Repair Manual". This incorporates information on such aspects as rust treatment, painting and glass-fibre repairs, as well as details on more ambitious repairs involving welding and panel beating.*

Repairs of minor scratches in bodywork

If the scratch is very superficial, and does not penetrate to the metal of the bodywork, repair is very simple. Lightly rub the area of the scratch with a paintwork renovator, or a very fine cutting paste, to remove loose paint from the scratch, and to clear the surrounding bodywork of wax polish. Rinse the area with clean water.

Apply touch-up paint to the scratch using a fine paint brush; continue to apply fine layers of paint until the surface of the paint in the scratch is level with the surrounding paintwork. Allow the new paint at least two weeks to harden, then blend it into the surrounding paintwork by rubbing the scratch area with a paintwork renovator or a very fine cutting paste. Finally, apply wax polish.

Where the scratch has penetrated right through to the metal of the bodywork, causing the metal to rust, a different repair technique is required. Remove any loose rust from the bottom of the scratch with a penknife, then apply rust-inhibiting paint to prevent the formation of rust in the future. Using a rubber or nylon applicator, fill the scratch with bodystopper paste. If required, this paste can be mixed with cellulose thinners to provide a

very thin paste which is ideal for filling narrow scratches. Before the stopper-paste in the scratch hardens, wrap a piece of smooth cotton rag around the top of a finger. Dip the finger in cellulose thinners, and quickly sweep it across the surface of the stopper-paste in the scratch; this will ensure that the surface of the stopper-paste is slightly hollowed. The scratch can now be painted over as described earlier in this Section.

Repairs of dents in bodywork

When deep denting of the vehicle's bodywork has taken place, the first task is to pull the dent out, until the affected bodywork almost attains its original shape. There is little point in trying to restore the original shape completely, as the metal in the damaged area will have stretched on impact, and cannot be reshaped fully to its original contour. It is better to bring the level of the dent up to a point which is about 3 mm below the level of the surrounding bodywork. In cases where the dent is very shallow anyway, it is not worth trying to pull it out at all. If the underside of the dent is accessible, it can be hammered out gently from behind, using a mallet with a wooden or plastic head. Whilst doing this, hold a suitable block of wood firmly against the outside of the panel, to absorb the impact from the hammer blows and thus prevent a large area of the bodywork from being "belled-out".

Should the dent be in a section of the bodywork which has a double skin, or some other factor making it inaccessible from behind, a different technique is called for. Drill several small holes through the metal inside the area - particularly in the deeper section. Then screw long self-tapping screws into the holes, just sufficiently for them to gain a good purchase in the metal. Now the dent can be pulled out by pulling on the protruding heads of the screws with a pair of pliers.

The next stage of the repair is the removal of the paint from the damaged area, and from an inch or so of the surrounding "sound" bodywork. This is accomplished most easily by using a wire brush or abrasive pad on a power drill, although it can be done just as effectively by hand, using sheets of abrasive paper. To complete the preparation for filling, score the surface of the bare metal with a screwdriver or the tang of a file, or alternatively, drill small holes in the affected area. This will provide a really good "key" for the filler paste.

To complete the repair, see the Section on filling and respraying.

Repairs of rust holes or gashes in bodywork

Remove all paint from the affected area, and from an inch or so of the surrounding "sound" bodywork, using an abrasive pad or a wire brush on a power drill. If these are not available, a few sheets of abrasive paper will do the job most effectively. With the paint removed, you will be able to judge the severity of the corrosion, and therefore decide whether to renew the whole panel (if this is possible) or to repair the affected area. New body panels are not as expensive as most people think, and it is often quicker and more satisfactory to fit a new panel than to attempt to repair large areas of corrosion.

Remove all fittings from the affected area, except those which will act as a guide to the original shape of the damaged bodywork (eg headlight shells etc). Then, using tin snips or a hacksaw blade, remove all loose metal and any other metal badly affected by corrosion. Hammer the edges of the hole inwards, in order to create a slight depression for the filler paste.

Wire-brush the affected area to remove the powdery rust from the
surface of the remaining metal. Paint the affected area with rust-inhibiting paint, if the back of the rusted area is accessible, treat this also.

Before filling can take place, it will be necessary to block the hole in some way. This can be achieved by the use of aluminium or plastic mesh, or aluminium tape.

Aluminium or plastic mesh, or glass-fibre matting, is probably the best material to use for a large hole. Cut a piece to the approximate size and shape of the hole to be filled, then position it in the hole so that its edges are below the level of the surrounding bodywork. It can be retained in position by several blobs of filler paste around its periphery.

Aluminium tape should be used for small or very narrow holes. Pull a piece off the roll, trim it to the approximate size and shape required, then pull off the backing paper (if used) and stick the tape over the hole; it can be overlapped if the thickness of one piece is insufficient. Burnish down the edges of the tape with the handle of a screwdriver or similar, to ensure that the tape is securely attached to the metal underneath.

Bodywork repairs - filling and respraying

Before using this Section, see the Sections on dent, deep scratch, rust holes and gash repairs.

Many types of bodyfiller are available, but generally speaking, those proprietary kits which contain a tin of filler paste and a tube of resin hardener are best for this type of repair. A wide, flexible plastic or nylon applicator will be found invaluable for imparting a smooth and well-contoured finish to the surface of the filler.

Mix up a little filler on a clean piece of card or board - measure the hardener carefully (follow the maker's instructions on the pack), otherwise the filler will set too rapidly or too slowly. Using the applicator, apply the filler paste to the prepared area; draw the applicator across the surface of the filler to achieve the correct contour and to level the

surface. As soon as a contour that approximates to the correct one is achieved, stop working the paste - if you carry on too long, the paste will become sticky and begin to "pick-up" on the applicator. Continue to add thin layers of filler paste at 20-minute intervals, until the level of the filler is just proud of the surrounding bodywork.

Once the filler has hardened, the excess can be removed using a metal plane or file. From then on, progressively-finer grades of abrasive paper should be used, starting with a 40-grade production paper, and finishing with a 400-grade wet-and-dry paper. Always wrap the abrasive paper around a flat rubber, cork, or wooden block - otherwise the surface of the filler will not be completely flat. During the smoothing of the filler surface, the wet-and-dry paper should be periodically rinsed in water. This will ensure that a very smooth finish is imparted to the filler at the final stage.

At this stage, the "dent" should be surrounded by a ring of bare metal, which in turn should be encircled by the finely "feathered" edge of the good paintwork. Rinse the repair area with clean water, until all of the dust produced by the rubbing-down operation has gone.

Spray the whole area with a light coat of primer - this will show up any imperfections in the surface of the filler. Repair these imperfections with fresh filler paste or bodystopper, and once more smooth the surface with abrasive paper. Repeat this spray-and-repair procedure until you are satisfied that the surface of the filler, and the feathered edge of the paintwork, are perfect. Clean the repair area with clean water, and allow to dry fully.

 If bodystopper is used, it can be mixed with cellulose thinners to form a really thin paste which is ideal for filling small holes

The repair area is now ready for final spraying. Paint spraying must be carried out in a warm, dry, windless and dust-free atmosphere. This condition can be created artificially if you have access to a large indoor working area, but if you are forced to work in the open, you will have to pick your day very carefully. If you are working indoors, dousing the floor in the work area with water will help to settle the dust which would otherwise be in the atmosphere. If the repair area is confined to one body panel, mask off the surrounding panels; this will help to minimise the effects of a slight mis-match in paint colours. Bodywork fittings (eg chrome strips, door handles etc) will also need to be masked off. Use genuine masking tape, and several thicknesses of newspaper, for the masking operations.

Before commencing to spray, agitate the aerosol can thoroughly, then spray a test area (an old tin, or similar) until the technique is mastered. Cover the repair area with a thick

coat of primer; the thickness should be built up using several thin layers of paint, rather than one thick one. Using 400-grade wet-and-dry paper, rub down the surface of the primer until it is really smooth. While doing this, the work area should be thoroughly doused with water, and the wet-and-dry paper periodically rinsed in water. Allow to dry before spraying on more paint.

Spray on the top coat, again building up the thickness by using several thin layers of paint. Start spraying at one edge of the repair area, and then, using a side-to-side motion, work until the whole repair area and about 2 inches of the surrounding original paintwork is covered. Remove all masking material 10 to 15 minutes after spraying on the final coat of paint.

Allow the new paint at least two weeks to harden, then, using a paintwork renovator, or a very fine cutting paste, blend the edges of the paint into the existing paintwork. Finally, apply wax polish.

Plastic components

With the use of more and more plastic body components by the vehicle manufacturers (eg bumpers. spoilers, and in some cases major body panels), rectification of more serious damage to such items has become a matter of either entrusting repair work to a specialist in this field, or renewing complete components. Repair of such damage by the DIY owner is not really feasible, owing to the cost of the equipment and materials required for effecting such repairs. The basic technique involves making a groove along the line of the crack in the plastic, using a rotary burr in a power drill. The damaged part is then welded back together, using a hot-air gun to heat up and fuse a plastic filler rod into the groove. Any excess plastic is then removed, and the area rubbed down to a smooth finish. It is important that a filler rod of the correct plastic is used, as body components can be made of a variety of different types (eg polycarbonate, ABS, polypropylene).

Damage of a less serious nature (abrasions, minor cracks etc) can be repaired by the DIY owner using a two-part epoxy filler repair material. Once mixed in equal proportions, this is used in similar fashion to the bodywork filler used on metal panels. The filler is usually cured in twenty to thirty minutes, ready for sanding and painting.

If the owner is renewing a complete component himself, or if he has repaired it with epoxy filler, he will be left with the problem of finding a suitable paint for finishing which is compatible with the type of plastic used. At one time, the use of a universal paint was not possible, owing to the complex range of plastics encountered in body component applications. Standard paints, generally speaking, will not bond to plastic or rubber satisfactorily. However, it is now possible to obtain a plastic body parts finishing kit which consists of a pre-primer treatment, a primer

10

and coloured top coat. Full instructions are normally supplied with a kit, but basically, the method of use is to first apply the pre-primer to the component concerned, and allow it to dry for up to 30 minutes. Then the primer is applied, and left to dry for about an hour before finally applying the special-coloured top coat. The result is a correctly-coloured component, where the paint will flex with the plastic or rubber, a property that standard paint does not normally possess.

5 Major body damage - repair

Where serious damage has occurred, or large areas need renewal due to neglect, it means that completely new sections or panels will need welding in, and this is best left to professionals. If the damage is due to impact, it will also be necessary to completely check the alignment of the bodyshell structure. Due to the principle of construction, the strength and shape of the whole car can be affected by damage to one part. In such instances the services of an accident repair specialist or Renault dealer with specialist checking jigs are essential. If a body is left misaligned, it is first of all dangerous, as the car will not handle properly, and secondly uneven stresses will be imposed on the steering, engine and transmission, causing abnormal wear or complete failure. Tyre wear may also be excessive.

6 Maintenance - hinges and locks

1 Oil the hinges of the bonnet, tailgate and doors with a drop or two of light oil at regular intervals (see "Routine maintenance").
2 At the same time, lightly oil the bonnet release mechanism and all door locks.
3 Do not attempt to lubricate the steering lock.

7 Door rattles - tracing and rectification

1 Check first that the door is not loose at the hinges, and that the latch is holding the door firmly in position. Check also that the door lines up with the aperture in the body. If the door is out of alignment, adjust it, as described in Sections 18 and 19 or 22 and 23.
2 If the latch is holding the door in the correct position, but the latch still rattles, the lock mechanism is worn and should be renewed.

8.2 Bonnet safety wire mounting rivet

3 Other rattles from the door could be caused by wear in the window operating mechanism, interior lock mechanism, or loose glass channels.

8 Bonnet - removal, refitting and adjustment

1 Open the bonnet and support it in the open position using the stay.
2 Using a suitable drill, drill the head off the rivet securing the safety wire to the front panel (photo). Tap out the remains of the rivet with a punch and remove the wire.
3 Disconnect the windscreen washer hose.
4 Mark the outline of the hinges with a soft pencil, then loosen the four retaining nuts (photo).
5 With the help of an assistant, remove the stay, unscrew the four nuts and lift the bonnet off the car.
6 Refitting is the reverse sequence of removal. Position the bonnet hinges within the outline marks made during removal, but alter its position as necessary to provide a uniform gap all round. Adjust the front height of the bonnet with shims beneath the hinges, and the rear height by re-positioning the lock up or down as necessary (refer to Section 9).

9.1 Bonnet lock

8.4 Loosening the bonnet hinge nuts

9 Bonnet lock and release cable - removal, refitting and adjustment

Bonnet lock

1 With the bonnet open remove the plastic cover, then disconnect the cable eye from the lock lever and withdraw the cable from the lock (photo).
2 Undo the two retaining bolts and remove the lock from the car.
3 Refitting is the reverse sequence of removal, but adjust the lock height so that the bonnet line is flush with the front wings and shuts securely without force. If necessary adjust the lock laterally so that the striker enters the lock recess correctly.

Release cable

4 With the bonnet open remove the plastic cover, then disconnect the cable eye from the lock lever and unclip the outer cable.
5 From inside the car unscrew the two bolts securing the release handle to the left-hand side panel under the facia. For better access remove the fusebox and surround panel (photo).
6 Unhook the cable from the handle and withdraw it through the bulkhead into the engine compartment (photo).
7 Refitting is a reversal of removal.

9.5 Bonnet release handle

Fig. 10.1 Bonnet lock components (Sec 9)

1 Lock   2 Cable   3 Clip   4 Release handle

10 Radiator grille -
removal and refitting

1 Open the bonnet then unscrew the centre top retaining bolt (photo).

10.1 Radiator grille centre top retaining bolt

10.2 Radiator grille upper clip and screw

2 Remove the screws from the two remaining upper clips and pull out the clips (photo).
3 From inside the car release the two clips either side of the radiator and withdraw the radiator grille (photo).
4 Refitting is a reversal of removal.

11 Front wing -
removal and refitting

1 Jack up the front of the car and support on axle stands. Apply the handbrake.
2 Remove the front bumper (Section 30) and the appropriate front wheel.
3 Remove the fastenings and withdraw the plastic shield from beneath the wing.
4 Unscrew the bolts securing the wing to the front door pillar and sill.
5 Using a suitable drill, drill the heads from the retaining rivets (Fig. 10.2).
6 Using a hair dryer, soften the sealant

10.3 Releasing a radiator side clip

9.6 Bonnet release cable on the left-hand side of the bulkhead

beneath the wing upper edge then withdraw the wing.
7 Clean away the old sealant.
8 Refitting is a reversal of removal, using new sealant.

12 Tailgate support struts -
removal and refitting

1 With the tailgate open, unhook the parcel shelf support cords and support the tailgate in the raised position using a stout length of wood, or an assistant.
2 Remove the rear light cluster as described in Chapter 11.
3 Using a screwdriver, carefully lever out the locking retainer at the strut ball end fittings (photos).
4 Withdraw the strut from the ball pegs and remove it from the car.
5 No attempt must be made to dismantle the strut or expose it to high temperatures, as it contains gas at high pressure.
6 Refitting is a reversal of removal.

Fig. 10.2 Front wing retaining rivet locations (Sec 11)

10

12.3A Prising out the tailgate support strut locking retainer from the tailgate

12.3B Tailgate support strut mounting on the body

13.6 Tailgate hinge bolt

13 Tailgate - removal and refitting

1 Disconnect the support struts from the tailgate as described in the previous Section.
2 Remove the inner trim panel then disconnect the battery leads as described in Chapter 11, and disconnect the wiring for the

Fig. 10.3 Removing the number plate terminal block (Sec 13)

Fig. 10.4 Removing the wiring and washer pipe from the tailgate (Sec 13)

rear screen wiper, heated rear window and rear number plate lights. If necessary the number plate terminal block can be released from the tailgate inner panel by squeezing the extension with a pair of pliers (Fig. 10.3).
3 Disconnect the rear screen washer pipe.
4 Withdraw the wiring and pipe from the top corners of the tailgate taking care not to damage them.
5 Remove the rear headlining trim panel by prising out the centre cap and removing the screw, then disengaging the panel from the retaining clips.
6 With the help of an assistant support the tailgate then unscrew the hinge bolts from inside the car (photo).
7 Refitting is a reversal of removal, but tape the wiring together temporarily to facilitate inserting it through the holes in the top corners of the tailgate. A length of string can be used to pull the wiring through. Adjust the lock and striker as described in Section 14.

14 Tailgate lock - removal, refitting and adjustment

1 Open the tailgate and remove the trim panel.
2 Unscrew the retaining bolts and withdraw the lock (photo). If necessary, unclip and remove the private lock.
3 Refitting is a reversal of removal, but check

14.2 Tailgate lock

that the tailgate is held firmly against the weatherseal when shut. If necessary loosen the bolt and adjust the position of the striker as required (photo).

15 Windscreen - removal and refitting

The windscreen is bonded in place with special mastic, and special tools are required to cut free the old unit and fit the new unit together with cleaning solutions and primers. It is therefore recommended that this work be entrusted to a Renault dealer or windscreen replacement specialist.

16 Tailgate heated rear window - removal and refitting

1 Remove the rear wiper arm and blade as described in Chapter 11.
2 Remove the inner moulding from the bottom of the window by extracting the screws from the special expanding clips.
3 Disconnect the wiring at the connectors on either side of the window.
4 If the window is broken, cover the floor area with a blanket and use adhesive tape to hold the remaining fragments together.

14.3 Tailgate lock striker

Fig. 10.5 Releasing the heated rear window rubber seal from the tailgate (Sec 16)

Fig. 10.6 Pull the cord to locate the seal lip on the tailgate flange (Sec 16)

5 Using a blunt tool push the inner lip of the rubber seal to the outside of the flange starting at one of the top corners and working downwards (Fig. 10.5). Have an assistant support it as it comes free.

6 Reverse the rubber seal from the window then thoroughly clean the edges of the tailgate aperture and also the window glass if this is to be refitted.

7 Fit a new rubber seal around the window and place a suitable length of strong cord in the body flange groove of the seal with its ends overlapping at the top centre of the window. When fitting the window with the tailgate open, the cord ends will then be at the bottom.

8 With the help of an assistant place the window in position from the outside with the cord ends inside. Insert the heating element connectors through the holes provided. Have the assistant press on the window from the outside then start pulling one end of the cord so that the seal lip locates over the inside of the flange.

9 When the top centre of the window is reached repeat the procedure for the other side until the complete inner lip is located on the flange.

10 Reconnect the wiring and refit the inner moulding, wiper arm and blade.

17 Front door interior trim panel - removal and refitting

1 Remove the external mirror quarter trim panel. Where the mirror is remotely controlled, the panel is retained by one screw on its lower edge and the panel must be lifted to release it from the bracket. Where a standard mirror is fitted prise out the panel to release the retaining pegs.

2 Prise out the bottom edge of the upper trim strip then lift it over the locking knob and remove it (photo).

3 Using a Torx key remove the screws and withdraw the map pocket. Also remove the bracket (photos).

4 Fully close the window on manually operated windows and note the position of the regulator handle. Pull the handle direct from the splines and remove the bezel - the handle is only a press fit on the splines (photo).

5 Remove the screw then slightly lift the interior remote door handle and withdraw the finger plate (photos).

6 Using a wide blade screwdriver release the clips securing the interior trim panel to the door. Do not lever on the panel itself

17.2 Removing the upper trim strip

17.3A Removing a map pocket retaining screw

17.3B Removing the map pocket bracket

17.4 Pull the window regulator handle from the splines

17.5A Remove the screw . . .

17.5B . . . and withdraw the remote door handle finger plate

10

17.6A Releasing the door interior trim panel clips

17.6B Trim panel clip

17.7 Peel back the plastic sheet

otherwise the attachment may break, but position the blade close to the plastic pin of the clip (photos).

7 If the trim panel has been removed for access to the door internal components, peel back the plastic sheet as necessary (photo).

18 Front door - removal, refitting and adjustment

1 On models having electrically-operated windows, electromechanical door locks or door mounted speakers remove the interior trim panel, as described in Section 17, and disconnect the wiring multi-plug connectors. Remove the wiring harness from the door.

2 Release the door check strap by driving out the retaining pin with a drift (photo).
3 Support the door on blocks or with the help of an assistant.
4 Prise out the two caps covering each hinge pin, using a screwdriver (photo).
5 Using a cranked metal rod of suitable diameter as a drift, drive out the upper and lower hinge pins.
6 With the hinge pins removed, carefully lift off the door.
7 Refitting is a reversal of removal, but check that it is correctly aligned with the surrounding bodywork with an equal clearance around its edge. Adjustment is made by bending the hinges as the latter are welded in position. Only attempt to bend the hinge arm welded to the front pillar, and use a block of wood and a mallet or a

suitable claw lever. Check that the striker enters the lock centrally, and if necessary loosen it with a Torx key, re-position and re-tighten (photo).

19 Front door lock and exterior handle - removal and refitting

1 Open the door and wind the window fully up.
2 Remove the interior trim panel, as described in Section 17.
3 If the car is fitted with electro-mechanical door locks, reach inside the door and disconnect the wiring connector from the lock solenoid or motor.
4 Remove the Torx screw and withdraw the remote interior handle (photo). Unhook it from the control rod.

18.2 Door check strap

18.4 Front door hinge

Fig. 10.7 Use a block of wood and a mallet to bend the door hinge arm (Sec 18)

Fig. 10.8 The door striker is adjustable (Sec 18)

18.7 Front door striker

19.4 Removing the remote interior handle

19.5 Disconnect the private lock and exterior handle control rods from the locks (three-door models)

19.6A Remove the screw . . .

19.6B . . . and unhook the exterior door handle (three-door models)

5 Reach through the aperture and disconnect the private lock and exterior handle control rods from the lock (photo).

6 Remove the screw securing the exterior door handle to the edge of the door (three-door models) or outside (four-door models), withdraw the handle and unhook the control rod (photos).

7 Remove the lock mounting screws then withdraw the lock from the door. Disconnect the locking knob and interior door handle control rods (photos).

8 To remove the private lock pull out the retaining plate and withdraw the lock outwards together with the control rod (photos).

9 Refitting is a reversal of removal.

19.7A Unscrew the mounting screws . . .

Fig. 10.9 Front door lock and solenoid on models with central locking (Sec 19)

19.7B . . . and withdraw the front door lock

19.7C Front door lock removed from the door

19.8A Pull out the retaining plate . . .

19.8B . . . and withdraw the private lock

10

Fig. 10.10 Front door window regulator (Sec 20)

Fig. 10.11 Front door glass to channel fitting dimension on three-door models (Sec 20)

Fig. 10.12 Front door glass to channel fitting dimension on five-door models (Sec 20)

20 Front door glass and regulator - removal and refitting

1 Remove the interior trim panel as described in Section 17.
2 With the window fully down remove the inner wiper strip taking care not to break it as it is fragile.
3 Prise out the window channel and outer wiper strip.
4 Raise the window so that the front support bolt is aligned with the hole provided, then support the window and unscrew both bolts (photo).
5 Lower the regulator then lift the glass and withdraw it from the outside.
6 On models with electrically-operated windows disconnect the wiring from the motor and unscrew the motor mounting nuts.
7 Drill out the retaining rivets and withdraw the regulator mechanism through the aperture (photo).
8 Refitting is a reversal of removal, but use new pop rivets to secure the mechanism. Centralize the glass in the fully closed position before fully tightening the support bolts. Where necessary refit the lower channel to the glass in accordance with Figs 10.11 or 10.12.

21 Rear door interior trim panel - removal and refitting

1 Prise out the bottom edge of the upper trim strip then lift it over the locking knob and remove it.
2 Fully close the window and note the position of the regulator handle. Pull the handle direct from the splines and remove the bezel - the handle is only a press fit on the splines.
3 Remove the screw then slightly lift the interior remote door handle and withdraw the finger plate.
4 Using a wide blade screwdriver release the clips securing the interior trim panel to the door. Do not lever on the panel itself otherwise the attachment may break, but position the blade close to the plastic pin of the clip.
5 If the trim panel has been removed for access to the door internal components, peel back the plastic sheet as necessary.

20.4 Front door glass support bolts

20.7 Window regulator retaining rivet near the winder

Fig. 10.13 Bolt-on type hinges for the rear doors on five-door models (Sec 22)

Fig. 10.14 Remove the top screw (1) and bottom bolt (2) securing the rear door glass intermediate channel (C) (Sec 24)

Fig. 10.15 Removing the intermediate channel (C) and fixed window (Sec 24)

22 Rear door - removal and refitting

The procedure is identical to that for the front door described in Section 18 with the exception of the reference to wiring. Note that replacement hinges supplied by Renault are of the bolt type and in this case, adjustment is by movement of the hinges within the limits of the bolt holes and by the use of shims.

23 Rear door lock and exterior handle - removal and refitting

1 Remove the interior trim panel as described in Section 21.
2 Remove the Torx screw and withdraw the remote interior handle. Unhook it from the control rod.
3 Pull out the retaining plate and release the locking knob and lever inside the panel. Also release the rod from the clip.
4 Remove the lock mounting screws then withdraw the lock assembly from inside the door.
5 To remove the exterior handle unscrew the bolt from inside the door and withdraw the handle and packing from the outside.
6 Refitting is a reversal of removal.

24 Rear door glass and regulator - removal and refitting

1 Remove the interior trim panel as described in Section 21.
2 With the window fully down remove the outer wiper strip and mouldings followed by the inner strips.
3 Unscrew the bottom bolt and top screw then withdraw the intermediate channel followed by the fixed window (if applicable) by tilting them forward.

4 Raise the window so that the support bolts are aligned with the holes provided then unscrew both bolts while supporting the window.
5 Lift the window glass, tilt it forwards and withdraw it from the outside. Recover the channel.
6 Drill out the retaining rivets and withdraw the regulator mechanism through the aperture.
7 Refitting is a reversal of removal, but where necessary refit the lower channel to the glass in accordance with Fig. 10.16.

25 Interior rear view mirror - removal and refitting

1 To remove the interior rear view mirror slide it up from the base.
2 Refitting is a reversal of removal.
3 The mirror base is bonded to the windscreen. If it becomes detached or if the windscreen is being renewed, fit the base using the following procedure.
4 Clean the inside of the windscreen and the

Fig. 10.16 Rear door glass to channel fitting dimension (Sec 24)

base of the mirror with trichloroethylene or a similar solvent and allow it to air dry.
5 Apply a strip of adhesive tape to the outside of the windscreen so that its top edge is 45 mm (1.77 in) below the seal lower edge. Measure the width of the windscreen and then mark its centre on the tape. The base of the mirror should be positioned centrally, with the tape mark as a reference, and with its top edge level with the top edge of the tape.
6 Obtain a quantity of Loctite 312 from a Renault dealer and then spray the activator onto the inside of the glass in the bonding zone.
7 Allow the activator to dry, then apply the adhesive to the mirror base. Immediately place the mirror base against the glass and hold it firmly for at least one minute. The adhesive will be fully set after approximately one hour.

26 Exterior rear view mirror - removal and refitting

Standard mirror

1 Prise the quarter trim panel from the inside of the front door so that the retaining pegs are released from the holes (photo).
2 Unscrew the mounting bolt and withdraw

26.1 Removing the quarter trim panel from the standard exterior mirror

10

26.4A Remove the screw . . .

26.4B . . . and lift the quarter trim panel from the remote control exterior mirror

27.1 Front seat rail rear mounting

27.2 Front seat rail front mounting

27.5 Rear seat cushion support bracket and slot

27.6 Rear seat backrest hinge bracket mounting

the mirror assembly from the outside of the door. Recover the collar.

3 Refitting is a reversal of removal.

Remote control mirror

4 Remove the screw from the lower edge of the quarter trim panel, lift the panel and release it from the bracket (photos).

5 Unscrew the screws securing the remote control bracket to the door.

6 Unscrew the ring nut and separate the bracket from the control knob.

7 Prise the grommet from the door then unscrew the mounting bolt and withdraw the mirror assembly, control knob and wires from the outside. Recover the collar.

8 Refitting is a reversal of removal.

27 Front and rear seats -
removal and refitting

Front seat

1 Adjust the seat fully forward then unscrew the Torx screws securing the seat rails at the rear (photo).

2 Adjust the seat fully back and unscrew the Torx screws securing the seat rails at the front (photo).

3 Remove the seat from the car.

4 Refitting is a reversal of removal.

Rear seat

5 Lift the cushion(s) and tilt forward then lift to release the brackets from the slots in the floor (photo).

6 Unlock the top of the backrest then unbolt the hinge brackets from the floor (photo).

7 Remove the cushion and backrest from the car.

8 Refitting is a reversal of removal.

28 Opening rear quarter
window - removal and refitting

1 Open the window then use a screwdriver to prise the retaining forks on the hinges out to the rear.

2 Remove the hinge bases and covers together with the seals.

3 With the catch open pull the window forwards so that the base on the window is released from the notches on the catch. Withdraw the window from the car leaving the catch and hinges attached to the body. These can be removed separately if required.

4 Refitting is a reversal of removal, but make sure that the seals are fitted correctly to the bases.

Fig. 10.17 Prise the retaining fork (1) from the base (2) on the opening rear quarter window (Sec 28)

Fig. 10.18 Pull the window forwards to release the base (4) from the notches (5) on the catch (3) (Sec 28)

29.1 Front seat belt flexible stalk mounting

29.3A Front seat anchor bolt on the inner seal

29.3B Unhook the front seat belt slide rail on three-door models

29 Seat belts -
removed and refitting

Front flexible stalks

1 Prise off the cap then unbolt the stalk from the floor (photo).
2 Refitting is a reversal of removal, but make sure that the stalk faces directly forward and tighten the bolt to the specified torque.

Front bolts

3 Unscrew the anchor bolt from the inner sill and, on three-door models unhook the slide rail (photos).
4 Unscrew the bolt securing the guide to the door pillar.
5 Remove the screws and prise back the sill

29.5 Removing the sill trim

29.6A Unscrew the bolt . . .

trim sufficient to gain access to the inertia reel (photo).
6 Unscrew the bolt and withdraw the inertia reel (photos).
7 Refitting is a reversal of removal, but tighten the bolts to the specified torque.

Rear bolts

8 Lift the rear seat cushion then unbolt the flexible stalk(s) or centre lap belt from the floor.
9 Remove the cover then unbolt the inertia reels from the side panel.
10 Remove the cover and unbolt the guide from the corner panel.
11 Refitting is a reversal of removal, but tighten the bolts to the specified torque.

30 Bumpers -
removal and refitting

Front bumper

1 Where applicable remove the foglights from the front bumper as described in Chapter 11.
2 Apply the handbrake then jack up the front of the car and support on axle stands.
3 Unscrew the bolts securing the bumper to the front body frame and withdraw it from the car (photo). If necessary unbolt and remove the mounting brackets. Remove the impact blocks.
4 Refitting is a reversal of removal.

29.6B . . . and withdraw the inertia reel

Rear bumper

5 Unscrew the side and bottom mounting bolts and withdraw the bumper from the car. If necessary unbolt and remove the mounting brackets. Remove the impact blocks.
6 Refitting is a reversal of removal.

31 Roof console -
removal and refitting

1 Disconnect the battery negative lead as described in Chapter 11.
2 Using a screwdriver prise out the roof console switch and light panel then disconnect the wiring multi-plug.
3 Remove the two retaining screws from the panel recess.
4 Release the console by pressing it down from the head lining then disconnect the wiring from the infra-red receiver.
5 Refitting is a reversal of removal.

32 Facia panel -
removal and refitting

1 Disconnect the battery system lead as described in Chapter 11.
2 Remove the instrument panel as described in Chapter 11.

10

30.3 Front bumper mounting bolt

Fig. 10.19 Front bumper components (Sec 30)

Fig. 10.20 Rear bumper components (Sec 30)

Fig. 10.21 Facia panel removal sequence (Sec 32)

3 Where the gear lever is integral with the centre console, prise up the rubber gaiter and remove the two console retaining screws.

4 Remove the screws on either side of the console by the vents (photo).

5 Remove the choke control and knob as described in Chapter 3.

6 Remove the headlight level adjusting knob where fitted.

7 Lift the ashtray and unscrew the two retaining screws in the recess. Withdraw the assembly and disconnect the wiring (photos).

8 Remove the heater controls as described in Section 35.

9 Remove the upper and lower trim panels on either side of the facia.

10 Remove the steering column as described in Chapter 9.

11 Remove the facia switches with reference to Chapter 11.

12 Unhook the centre console and disconnect the wiring as applicable (photos).

13 Unscrew the lower facia retaining screws (photo).

14 Remove the clock or trip computer, and the fusebox as described in Chapter 11.

15 Disconnect all remaining wiring from the facia.

16 Lift the right of the facia panel to release it

32.4 Removing the centre console retaining screws

32.7A Remove the screws . . .

32.7B . . . then withdraw the ashtray assembly and disconnect the wiring

32.12A Unhook the centre console . . .

32.12B . . . and disconnect the wiring

32.13 Removing the facia lower retaining screws

from the plastic clip, then the centre section from the centre clip and the left of the panel from the left clip (photo). If necessary use a flat blade lever to prise the panel from the clips which are located on the front edge.
17 Withdraw the facia panel from the bulkhead and remove it from the car.
18 Refitting is a reversal of removal.

33 Heater fan motor -
removal and refitting

1 Disconnect the battery negative lead as described in Chapter 11.
2 Remove the plastic sheet from the plenum chamber on the bulkhead.

33.3 Showing the heater fan grille cover

33.4 The fan and motor is pulled direct from the casing

3 Extract the clips and withdraw the grille cover from the heater inlet (photo).
4 Pull the fan and motor direct from the casing (photo).
5 Check the condition of the motor terminals and the socket clips in the casing, and clean if necessary.
6 Refitting is a reversal of removal, but make sure that the motor terminals locate correctly in the socket clips.

34 Heater -
removal and refitting

1 Remove the facia panel as described in Section 32, however there is no need to remove the heater controls, but instead depress the two clips located under the control panel and push the panel into the facia without disconnecting the cables. Carry out this after having removed the ashtray and the screw at the top of the ashtray aperture.
2 Drain the cooling system as described in Chapter 2.
3 Working in the engine compartment locate the heater hoses on the bulkhead and identify them for position (photo). Loosen the clips and disconnect them.
4 Unbolt the heater casing from the bulkhead and withdraw it together with the controls. Disconnect the wiring.
5 Release the plastic clips and carefully slide

34.3 Heater hoses on the bulkhead

32.16 Lift the facia panel from the plastic clips

the heater matrix from the casing. Clean any debris from it by hosing or using an air line.
6 Disconnect the controls if necessary with reference to Section 35.
7 The two halves of the casing may be separated if necessary by releasing the metal clips.
8 Refitting is a reversal of removal, but refill the cooling system with reference to Chapter 2.

Fig. 10.22 Heater fan motor terminals (1) and socket clips (2) (Sec 33)

10

Fig. 10.23 Heater components (Sec 34)

1 Grille
2 Plastic cover
3 Fan and motor

4 Control panel
5 Heater casing

6 Matrix
7 Wiring harness

35 Heater control cables -
removal, refitting and adjustment

1 Disconnect the battery negative lead as described in Chapter 11.
2 Remove the centre console and ashtray with reference to Section 32. Remove the screw from the top of the ashtray aperture.
3 Depress the two clips located under the control panel and push the panel into the facia so that it can be removed through the ashtray aperture.
4 Unscrew the facia lower retaining screws with reference to Section 32 then lift it slightly.
5 Unclip and disconnect the control cables from the side of the heater, disconnect the wiring, and withdraw the control panel and cables from the car.
6 Refitting is a reversal of removal, but before fitting the outer cable clips, adjust the control knobs to distribute cool air as shown in Fig. 10.25 and position the levers as shown with the special dots aligned where applicable.

Fig. 10.24 Heater control cable removal (Sec 35)

1 Ash tray retaining screws
2 Panel retaining screw

3 Clip locations
4 Control panel

Fig. 10.25 Heater control cable adjustment (Sec 35)

Chapter 11 Electrical system

For modifications, and information applicable to later models, see Supplement at end of manual

Contents

Degrees of difficulty

Easy, suitable for novice with little experience	**Fairly easy,** suitable for beginner with some experience	**Fairly difficult,** suitable for competent DIY mechanic	**Difficult,** suitable for experienced DIY mechanic	**Very difficult,** suitable for expert DIY or professional

Specifications

System type .... 12 volt, negative earth

Battery
Type .... Low maintenance or maintenance-free "sealed for life"
Capacity .... 30, 35, 40, 50, 65 or 70 Amp hr according to model

Alternator
Type and output (at 6000 rpm):
    Ducellier 516058 .... 48 Amp
    Paris-Rhone A13N104 .... 48 Amp
    Paris-Rhone A14N87 .... 70 Amp

Starter motor
Type and current (locked pinion):
    Ducellier 534042 pre-engaged .... 350 Amp
    Ducellier 534043 pre-engaged .... 340 Amp
    Paris-Rhone D9E771 pre-engaged .... 460 Amp
    Paris-Rhone D9E76 pre-engaged .... 420 Amp

Wiper blades .... Champion X-4503 (front) and X-4103 (rear)

11

Bulbs (typical)

	Wattage
Headlamp:	
Standard bulb	45/40
Halogen bulb	60/55
Front foglamp	55
Front sidelight	4
Direction indicators	21
Stop/tail	21/5
Reversing lamp	21
Rear foglamp	21
Rear number plate lamp	5
Interior lamp	10
Instrument panel illumination	1.2 or 2

Torque wrench settings

	Nm	lbf ft
Battery terminal clamp - positive	5	4
Battery terminal clamp - negative	3	2
Battery retaining clamp bolt	10	7

1 General description

The electrical system is of the 12 volt negative earth type, and consists of a battery, alternator, starter motor and related electrical accessories, components and wiring.

The battery, charged by the alternator which is belt-driven from the crankshaft pulley, provides a steady amount of current for the ignition, starting, lighting and other electrical circuits. The battery may be a low maintenance type or a maintenance-free "sealed for life" type, according to model.

The starter motor is of the pre-engaged type incorporating an integral solenoid. On starting, the solenoid moves the drive pinion into engagement with the flywheel ring gear before the starter motor is energised. Once the engine has started, a one-way clutch prevents the motor armature being driven by the engine until the pinion disengages from the flywheel.

Further details of the major electrical systems are given in the relevant Sections of this Chapter.

⚠ **Caution: Before carrying out any work on the vehicle electrical system, read through the precautions given in "Safety first!" at the beginning of this manual and in Section 2 of this Chapter.**

2 Electrical system - precautions

It is necessary to take extra care when working on the electrical system to avoid damage to semiconductor devices (diodes and transistors), and to avoid the risk of personal injury. In addition to the precautions given in "Safety first"! at the beginning of this manual, observe the following items when working on the system.

1 *Always remove rings, watches, etc before working on the electrical system.* Even with the battery disconnected, capacitive discharge could occur if a component live terminal is earthed through a metal object. This could cause a shock or nasty burn.

2 *Do not reverse the battery connections.* Components such as the alternator or any other having semiconductor circuitry could be irreparably damaged.

3 If the engine is being started using jump leads and a slave battery, connect the batteries *positive to positive* and *negative to negative.* This also applies when connecting a battery charger.

4 Never disconnect the battery earth terminals, or alternator wiring when the engine is running.

5 The battery leads and alternator wiring must be disconnected before carrying out any electric welding on the car.

3 Routine maintenance

At the intervals specified in the "Routine maintenance" section in the front of the manual carry out the following procedures.

1 Check the operation of all the electrical equipment, ie wipers, washers, lights, direction indicators, horn etc. Refer to the appropriate Sections of this Chapter if any components are found to be inoperative.

2 Visually check all accessible wiring connectors, harnesses and retaining clips for security, or any signs of chafing or damage. Rectify any problems encountered.

3 Check the alternator drivebelt for cracks, fraying or damage. Renew the belt if worn or, if satisfactory, check and adjust the belt tension. These procedures are covered in Chapter 2.

4 Check the condition of the wiper blades and if they are cracked or show signs of deterioration, renew them, as described in Section 34 of this Chapter. Check the

operation of the windscreen and tailgate washers, and adjust the nozzle setting if necessary.

5 Top up the battery, on models where this is necessary, using distilled water until the tops of the cell plates are just submerged. Clean the battery terminals and case and, if necessary, check the battery condition using the procedures described in Section 4.

6 Top up the washer fluid reservoir and check the security of the pump wires and water pipes.

7 It is advisable to have the headlamp aim adjusted using optical beam setting equipment.

8 While carrying out a road test, check the operation of all the instruments and warning lights and the operation of the direction indicator self-cancelling mechanism.

4 Battery - general

1 According to model the battery may be of the low maintenance type in which the cell covers may be removed to allow periodic topping-up in the conventional way, or of the maintenance-free type which do not require topping-up. The maintenance-free battery has a sealed top cover which must not under any circumstances be removed. If the seals are broken the battery warranty will be invalidated.

2 On low maintenance batteries, periodically lift off the cover and check the electrolyte level. The tops of the cell plates should be just covered by the electrolyte. If not, add distilled or demineralized water until they are. Do not add extra water with the idea of reducing the intervals of topping-up. This will merely dilute the electrolyte and reduce charging and current retention efficiency.

3 If the electrolyte level needs an excessive amount of replenishment but no leaks are apparent, it could be due to over-charging as a result of the battery having been run down

and then left to recharge from the vehicle rather than an outside source. If the battery has been heavily discharged for one reason or another, it is best to have it continuously charged at a low amperage for a period of many hours. If it is charged from the car's system under such conditions, the charging will be intermittent and greatly varied in intensity. This does not do the battery any good at all. If the battery needs topping-up frequently, even when it is known to be in good condition and not too old, then the voltage regulator should be checked to ensure that the charging output is being correctly controlled. An elderly battery, however, may need topping-up more than a new one, because it needs to take in more charging current. Do not worry about this, provided it gives satisfactory service.

4 Keep the battery clean and dry all over by wiping it with a dry cloth. A dirty or damp top surface could cause tracking between the two terminal posts with consequent draining of power.

5 Periodically remove the battery and check the support tray clamp and battery terminal connections for signs of corrosion - usually indicated by a whitish green crystalline deposit. Wash this off with clean water to which a little ammonia or washing soda has been added. Then treat the terminals with petroleum jelly and the battery mounting with suitable protective paint to prevent further corrosive action.

6 On maintenance-free batteries access to the cells is not possible and only the overall condition of the battery can be checked using a voltmeter connected across the two terminals. On the low maintenance type a hydrometer can be used to check the condition of each individual cell. The table in the following Section gives the hydrometer readings for the various states of charge. A further check can be made when the battery is undergoing a charge. If, towards the end of the charge, when the cells should be "gassing" (bubbling), one cell appears not to be, this indicates the cell or cells in question are probably breaking down and the life of the battery is limited.

5 Battery - charging

1 In winter when a heavy demand is placed on the battery, such as when starting from cold and using more electrical equipment, it may be necessary to have the battery fully charged from an external source. *Note that both battery leads must be disconnected before charging in order to prevent possible damage to any semiconductor electrical components.*

2 The terminals of the battery and the leads of the charger must be connected positive to positive and negative to negative.

6.2 A plastic knob is provided to loosen the battery negative terminal clamp

3 Charging is best done overnight at a "trickle" rate of 1 to 1.5 amps. Alternatively, on low maintenance batteries, a 3 to 4 amp rate can be used over a period of 4 hours or so. Check the specific gravity in the latter case and stop the charge when the reading is correct. Maintenance-free batteries should not be charged in this way due to their design and construction. It is strongly recommended that you seek the advice of a Renault dealer on the suitability of various types of charging equipment before using them on maintenance-free batteries.

4 The specific gravities for hydrometer readings on low maintenance batteries are as follows:

Fully discharged	Electrolyte temperature	Fully charged
1.098	38°C (100°F)	1.268
1.102	32°C (90°F)	1.272
1.106	27°C (80°F)	1.276
1.110	21°C (70°F)	1.280
1.114	16°C (60°F)	1.284
1.118	10°C (50°F)	1.288
1.122	4°C (40°F)	1.292
1.126	-1.5°C (30°F)	1.296

6 Battery - removal and refitting

1 The battery is located in the engine compartment on the right-hand side of the bulkhead. First check that all electrical

7.2A Wiring to the alternator regulator

6.4 Battery retaining clamp bolt

components are switched off in order to avoid a spark occurring as the negative lead is disconnected.

2 Loosen the plastic knob on the negative terminal clamp (photo) lift the clamp and lead from the terminal and place it on the bulkhead. This is the terminal to disconnect before working on any electrical component on the car.

3 Loosen the nut on the positive terminal clamp, lift the clamp and lead from the terminal and place it on the bulkhead.

4 Unscrew the extended clamp bolt and move the clamp to one side (photo).

5 Lift the battery from the tray keeping it upright and taking care not to touch clothing.

6 Clean the battery terminals posts, clamps, tray and battery casing.

7 Refitting is a reversal of removal, but always connect the positive terminal clamp first and the negative terminal clamp last.

7 Alternator - removal and refitting

1 Disconnect the battery negative terminal.

2 Make a note of the electrical lead locations at the rear of the alternator and disconnect them (photos).

3 Slacken the alternator adjusting arm nut and bolt and the mounting nut and through-bolt, push the alternator towards the engine and slip off the drivebelt (photos).

7.2B Disconnecting the alternator output lead

7.3A Loosen the alternator adjustment bolt . . .

7.3B . . . and push in the alternator to remove the drivebelt

7.4A Alternator mounting bolt

4 Remove the alternator mounting and adjustment nuts and bolts then withdraw the alternator from the engine (photos).

5 Refitting is the reverse sequence of removal, but before tightening the adjustment and mounting bolts tension the drivebelt, as described in Chapter 2.

8 Alternator - fault finding and rectification

1 If the ignition warning fails to illuminate when the ignition is switched on, first check the wiring connections at the rear of the alternator for security. If satisfactory, check that the warning lamp bulb has not blown and is secure in its holder. If the lamps stills fails to illuminate check the continuity of the warning lamp feed wire from the alternator to the bulb holder. If all is satisfactory, the alternator is at fault and should be renewed or taken to an automobile electrician for testing and repair.

2 If the ignition warning lamp illuminates when the engine is running, ensure that the drivebelt is correctly tensioned (see Chapter 2), and that the connections on the rear of the alternator are secure. If all is so far satisfactory, check the alternator brushes and commutator, as described in Section 9. If the fault still persists, the alternator should be renewed, or taken to an automobile electrician for testing and repair.

7.4B Alternator removed from the engine

3 If the alternator output is suspect even though the warning lamp functions correctly, the regulated voltage may be checked as follows:

4 Connect a voltmeter across the battery terminals and then start the engine.

5 Increase the engine speed until the reading on the voltmeter remains steady. This should be between 13.5 and 14.8 volts.

6 Switch on as many electrical accessories as possible and check that the alternator maintains the regulated voltage at between 13.5 and 1 4.8 volts.

7 If the regulated voltage is not as stated, the fault may be due to a faulty diode, a severed phase or worn brushes, springs or commutator. The brushes and commutator may be attended to, as described in Section 9, but if the fault still persists the alternator should be renewed, or taken to an automobile electrician for testing and repair.

9 Alternator brushes - removal, inspection and refitting

Note: *Owing to the specialist knowledge and equipment required to test and repair an alternator accurately, it is recommended that, if the performance is suspect the alternator be taken to an automobile electrician who will have the facilities for such work. It is, however, a relatively simple task to attend to the brush gear and this operation is described below. The work may be carried out without removing the unit from the engine.*

1 Disconnect the battery negative terminal.

2 Note the locations of the wiring connectors and leads at the rear of the alternator and disconnect them. If preferred the alternator can be completely removed to provide easier working conditions.

Fig. 11.1 Exploded views of Paris-Rhone (top) and Ducellier (bottom) alternators (Secs 7 to 9)

9.3 Removing the alternator rear cover

9.4A Unscrew the retaining bolts . . .

9.4B . . . and withdraw the regulator and brush box

3 Unbolt and remove the rear cover if required (photo).

4 Undo the two small bolts or nuts securing the regulator and brush box assembly to the rear of the alternator. Lift off the regulator and brush box, disconnect the electrical leads, noting their locations, then remove the regulator and brush box assembly from the alternator (photos).

5 Check that the brushes stand proud of their holders and are free to move without sticking. If necessary clean them with a petrol-moistened cloth. Check that the brush spring pressure is equal for both brushes and gives reasonable tension. If in doubt about the condition of the brushes and springs compare them with new parts at a Renault parts dealer.

9.5 Removing the cover when separating the regulator from the brush box

9.6 Alternator slip rings

The regulator can be separated from the brush box after removing the cover if necessary (photo).

6 Clean the slip rings with a petrol-moistened cloth, then check for signs of scoring, burning or severe pitting. If evident the slip rings should be attended to by an automobile electrician (photo).

7 Refitting the regulator and brush box assembly is the reverse sequence to removal.

10 Starter motor - testing in the car

1 If the starter motor fails to operate, first check the condition of the battery by switching on the headlamps. If they glow brightly then gradually dim after a few seconds, the battery is in an uncharged condition.

2 If the battery is satisfactory, check the starter motor main terminal and the engine earth cable for security. Check the terminal connections on the solenoid, located on the side of the starter motor.

3 If the starter still fails to turn, use a voltmeter, or 12 volt test lamp and leads, to ensure that there is battery voltage at the solenoid main terminal (containing the cable from the battery positive terminal).

4 With the ignition switched on and the

ignition key in position D check that voltage is reaching the solenoid terminal with the spade connector, and also the starter main terminal beneath the end cover.

5 If there is no voltage reaching the spade connector there is a wiring or ignition switch fault. If voltage is available, but the starter does not operate, then the starter or solenoid is likely to be at fault.

11 Starter motor - removal and refitting

1 Disconnect the battery negative terminal.

2 Remove the air cleaner as described in Chapter 3.

3 On non-Turbo models remove the protective metal shield from the starter motor by unscrewing the bolt at the cylinder block and the nut on the exhaust manifold (photos). On Turbo models disconnect the exhaust pipe flange and unbolt the retaining bracket (Fig. 11.2).

4 Disconnect the battery supply cable and solenoid feed wire from the starter solenoid terminals (photo). On Turbo models unbolt the cable support.

5 Undo the bolt securing the starter motor support bracket to the rear facing side of the cylinder block.

11.3A Starter motor shield bottom mounting

11.3B Starter motor shield top mounting

11

11.4 Battery supply (+) cable (1) and solenoid feed wire (2) to the starter solenoid

Fig. 11.2 Starter motor location on Turbo models (Sec 11)

1 Retaining bracket
2 Battery cable and support
3 Starter motor support bracket

Fig. 11.3 The starter motor bolt locating dowel (B) must be positioned in hole (A) (Sec 11)

6 Undo the three bolts securing the starter motor to the transmission bellhousing and withdraw the starter from the engine. Note the position of the locating dowel in the upper rear bellhousing bolt hole and make sure that it is in place when refitting.

7 Refitting the starter motor is the reverse sequence to removal, but tighten the bellhousing bolts before the support bracket bolt. On Turbo models tighten the exhaust pipe flange bolts as described in Chapter 3.

12 Starter motor - overhaul

Note: *Overhaul of the starter motor is normally confined to inspection and, if necessary, renewal of the brush gear components. Due to the limited availability of replacement parts, any other faults occurring on the starter usually result in renewal of the complete motor. However, for those wishing to dismantle the starter motor, this Section may be used as a guide. The procedure is essentially similar for all motor types and any minor differences can be noted by referring to the accompanying illustrations.*

1 Remove the starter motor from the car, as described in the previous Section.

2 Undo the two nuts and remove the mounting support bracket from the rear of the motor.

3 Undo the nut and disconnect the lead from the solenoid terminal.

4 Where fitted, remove the cap plate on the rear cover and the bolt and washers between rear cover and armature.

5 Tap out the engaging lever pivot pin from the drive end housing.

6 Undo the nuts securing the solenoid to the drive end housing.

7 Undo the through-bolts and withdraw the yoke, armature, solenoid and engaging lever as an assembly from the drive end housing.

8 Withdraw the solenoid and engaging lever, remove the rear cover with brushes, then slide the armature out of the yoke.

9 Slip the brushes out of their brush holders to release the rear cover.

10 If the pinion/clutch assembly is to be removed, drive the stop collar up the armature shaft and extract the circlip. Slide the stop collar and pinion clutch assembly off the armature.

Fig. 11.4 Exploded views of Ducellier (top) and Paris-Rhone (bottom) starter motors (Sec 12)

```
        1   2   3   4   5   6

       [■] [■] [■] [■] [■] [■]

 7   8   9  10  11  12      13  14  15  16  17  18

[■] [■] [■] [■] [■] [■]      [■]       [■] [■] [■]
```

Fig. 11.5 Fuse location and function chart - typical (Sec 13)

No	Amps	Function		No	Amps	Function
				Alternative		
1	15	Cigar lighter* – windscreen wipers		1	–	Not used
2	–	Not used		2	–	Not used
3	7,5	Stop switch		3	20	Door locks
		Reversing light		4	–	Not used
4	15-20*	Heated rear screen		5	30	LH window winder
		Rear screen wiper/washer*		6	30	RH window winder
5	20	Heater fan		7	7.5	Rear foglights
6	5	Clock-radio		8	5	RH sidelights
7	7.5	Rear foglight*		9	5	LH sidelights
8	5	Front RH sidelight and RH rear		10	10	Direction indicator lights
		light control lighting		11	5	Windscreen wiper 'park'
9	5	Front LH sidelight and LH rear		12	10	Clock – interior light – infra-red
		light				remote control
10	10	Direction indicator flasher unit		13	10 or 15	
11	5	Windscreen wiper park posiiton				Cigar lighter – windscreen wiper
12	10	Clock – interior light		14	5	Control box – (driving school car)
		Infra-red remote control		15	7.5	Stoplight – reverse light
13	–	Not used		16	15	Rear screen demister
14	–	Not used			or 20	Rear screen wiper
15	20	Electric door locking system*		17	20	Heating ventilator
16	–	Not used		18	5	Clock – car radio
17	30	LH window winder				
18	30	RH window winder				

11 With the starter motor now completely dismantled, clean all the components with paraffin or a suitable solvent and wipe dry.
12 Check that all the brushes protrude uniformly from their holders and that the springs all provide moderate tension. Check that the brushes move freely in their holders and clean them with a petrol-moistened rag if there is any tendency to stick. If in doubt about the brush length or condition, compare them with new components and renew if necessary. Note that new field brushes must be soldered to their leads.
13 Check the armature shaft for distortion and the commutator for excessive wear, scoring or burrs. If necessary, the commutator may be lightly skimmed in a lathe and then polished with fine glass paper.
14 Check the pinion/clutch assembly, drive end housing, engaging lever and solenoid for wear or damage. Make sure that the clutch permits movement in one direction only and renew the unit if necessary.
15 Accurate checking of the armature, commutator and field coil windings and insulation requires the use of special test equipment. If the starter motor was inoperative when removed from the car and the previous checks have not highlighted the problem, then it can be assumed that there is a continuity or insulation fault and the unit should be renewed.
16 If the starter is in a satisfactory condition, or if a fault has been traced and rectified, the unit can be reassembled using the reverse of the dismantling procedure.

13 Fuses and relays - general

1 The fuses and relays are located below the passenger side glovebox. Access is gained by prising open the lid. Symbols on the reverse of the lid indicate the circuits protected by the fuses, and four spare fuses are supplied together with a plastic clip to remove and fit them (photo).
2 To remove a fuse fit the clip then pull it direct from the holder. The wire within the fuse is clearly visible and it will be broken if the fuse is blown.
3 Always renew a fuse with one of an identical rating. Never renew a fuse more than once without tracing the source of the trouble. The fuse rating is stamped on top of the fuse.
4 The various relays can be removed from their respective locations by carefully pulling them upwards and out.
5 If a system controlled by a relay becomes inoperative and the relay is suspect, operate the system and if the relay is functioning it should be possible to hear it click as it is energized. If this is the case the fault lies with the components or wiring of the system. If the relay is not being energized then the relay is not receiving a main supply voltage or a switching voltage, or the relay itself is faulty.

13.1 Fuse and relay holder with lid open

Fig. 11.6 Relay locations (Sec 13)

4 Mounting screw locations
5 Windscreen wiper timer
6 Lighting warning buzzer
7 Lock timer
8 Direction indicator flasher unit
9 Rear foglight relay
10 Main beam relay (not UK)
11 Dipped beam relay (not UK)
12 Rear screen wiper delay

11

14.2A Fuse and relay holder surround removal

14.2B Fuse and relay holder with surround removed

16.2 Removing the instrument panel visor

16.3 Removing the instrument panel top corner screws

16.5A Removing a multi-plug connector from the instrument panel

14 Fuse and relay holder - removal and refitting

1 Disconnect the battery negative terminal.
2 Remove the surround and lid by unscrewing the two screws using a Torx key (photos).
3 Remove the mounting screws, lower the holder and disconnect the wiring.
4 Refitting is a reversal of removal.

15 Direction indicator and hazard flasher system - general

1 The flasher unit is located on the fuse and relay holder below the passenger glovebox.
2 Should the flashers become faulty in operation, check the bulbs for security and make sure that the contact surfaces are not corroded. If one bulb blows or is making a poor connection due to corrosion, the system will not flash on that side of the car.
3 If the flasher unit operates in one direction and not the other, the fault is likely to be in the bulbs, or wiring to the bulbs. If the system will not flash in either direction, operate the hazard flashers. If these function, check the appropriate fuse and renew it if blown. If the fuse is satisfactory, renew the flasher unit.

16 Instrument panel - removal and refitting

1 Disconnect the battery negative terminal.
2 Pull the visor straight up from its location over the instrument panel (photo).
3 Remove the retaining screws from the top corners (photo).
4 Lift the instrument panel to release it from the clips, and withdraw it sufficiently to gain access to the rear of the panel. Unless the panel has previously been removed it will be held firmly by the clips, and additional upwards pressure can be provided by removing the lower steering column shroud and pressing up the panel with the fingers.
5 Disconnect the speedometer cable and multi-plug connectors then withdraw the instrument panel from the facia (photos).
6 Refitting is a reversal of removal.

17 Instrument panel - dismantling and reassembly

1 Prise the plastic hooks outwards and remove the front cover (photos).
2 To remove the speedometer extract the two screws from the front and rear of the unit.
3 To remove the coolant temperature

16.5B Instrument panel aperture in the facia

17.1A Front view of the instrument panel

17.1B Rear view of the instrument panel

18.3A Removing the lighting and direction indicator switch retaining screws

18.3B Unscrew the facia-to-steering column lower . . .

18.3C . . . and upper screws

indicator extract the printed circuit nuts and the two retaining screws.

4 To remove the fuel gauge extract the printed circuit nuts and the two retaining screws.

5 To remove the tachometer extract the single rear screw and the two front screws.

6 To remove the oil level indicator first remove the tachometer then extract the printed circuit nuts and the two retaining screws.

7 Reassembly of the instrument panel is a reversal of the dismantling procedure.

18 Steering column switches - removal and refitting

1 Disconnect the battery negative terminal.

2 Remove the steering wheel and steering column lower shroud with reference to Chapter 9.

3 To remove the lighting and direction indicator switch undo the switch retaining screws using a Torx key, and the screws securing the facia to the steering column (photos). Remove the steering column upper mounting bolts and loosen the lower mounting nuts, then withdraw the switch and disconnect the wiring.

4 To remove the windscreen wiper switch

undo the retaining screws, withdraw the switch and disconnect the wiring (photos).

5 Ignition switch removal is described in Chapter 12.

6 Refitting is a reversal of removal.

19 Switch (facia) - removal and refitting

1 All the facia mounted switches are held in position by plastic tags on the switch casing and the tags are designed with sloping edges to facilitate direct removal from the facia. Before removing a switch disconnect the battery negative terminal.

2 Ease out the switch then disconnect the multi-plug connector (photos). If the switch proves to be tight press it out from behind after removing the steering column lower shroud.

3 Refitting is a reversal of removal.

20 Clock/trip computer - removal and refitting

1 Disconnect the battery negative terminal.

2 Carefully ease the unit from the facia then disconnect the multi-plug connector (photo).

3 Refitting is a reversal of removal.

18.4A Remove the retaining screws . . .

18.4B . . . and withdraw the windscreen wiper switch

19.2A Removing the hazard warning light switch

19.2B Removing the rear window wiper/washer switch

20.2 Removing the clock

11

22.3 Removing the courtesy lamp pillar switch

23.1 Pull off the headlamp bulb wiring connector . . .

23.2 . . . release the clip . . .

21 Cigarette lighter - removal and refitting

1 Disconnect the battery negative terminal.
2 Lift the ashtray lid and remove the lower retaining screws.
3 Withdraw the ashtray assembly and disconnect the wiring.
4 Unscrew the ring nut and withdraw the cigarette lighter from the ashtray.
5 Refitting is a reversal of removal.

23.3 . . . and withdraw the bulb

Fig. 11.7 Headlamp bulb fittings (Sec 23)

1 Wiring connector
2 Clip for halogen type bulb
3 Double clips for conventional bulb

22 Courtesy lamp pillar switches - removal and refitting

1 Disconnect the battery negative terminal.
2 Open the door and locate the front courtesy lamp switch on the door pillar.
3 Remove the retaining screw and withdraw the switch (photo).
4 Disconnect the supply wire and tie a loose knot in it to prevent it dropping into the pillar. Remove the switch.
5 Refitting is a reversal of removal.

23 Headlamp bulb - renewal

1 Open the bonnet and pull the wiring connector from the rear of the headlamp (photo).
2 If conventional bulbs are fitted, spring back the two wire retaining clips. If halogen bulbs are fitted, release the ends of the wire retaining clip and pivot the clip clear (photo).
3 The bulb can now be withdrawn from its location in the lens assembly (photo). Take care not to touch the bulb glass with your fingers; if touched, clean the bulb with methylated spirit.
4 Fit the new bulb using a reversal of the removal procedure, but make sure that the

24.1 Pull off the front sidelight bulb wiring connector . . .

stud or tabs on the bulb support is correctly located in the lens assembly.

24 Front sidelight bulb - renewal

1 Open the bonnet and pull the wiring connector from the sidelight bulbholder on the rear of the headlamp (photo).
2 Pull the bulbholder and bulb from the grommet in the lens assembly (photo).
3 Fit the new bulb using a reversal of the removal procedure.

25 Front direction indicator bulb - renewal

1 Open the bonnet and locate the wire spring positioned below the rear of the headlamp. Pull the spring rearwards to release it from the bracket then withdraw the direction indicator lamp forwards (photos).
2 Disconnect the wiring if necessary.
3 Turn the bulbholder a quarter turn anti-clockwise to release it from the lamp (photo).
4 Depress and twist the bulb to remove it from the bulbholder.
5 Fit the new bulb using a reversal of the removal procedure.

24.2 . . . and remove the bulbholder and bulb

25.1A Release the spring . . .

25.1B . . . withdraw the direction indicator
lamp . . .

25.3 . . . and remove the bulb and
bulbholder

26 Front foglamp bulb - renewal

1 Undo the two screws securing the lens glass to the lamp body and carefully withdraw the lens.
2 Disconnect the two wires at the bulbholder terminals, release the retaining spring clip and lift out the bulbholder.
3 Lift and pull the bulb to remove it from the holder.
4 Refit the bulb and lens assembly using the reverse of this procedure. Ensure that the new bulb is held with a piece of cloth or tissue paper and clean the bulb glass with methylated spirit if it is touched with the fingers.

27 Headlamp lens assembly - removal and refitting

1 Remove the headlamp bulb (Section 23), sidelight bulb (Section 24) and direction indicator bulb (Section 25).
2 Remove the radiator grille as described in Chapter 10.
3 Unscrew the four mounting nuts and withdraw the headlamp lens assembly forwards (photos).
4 Refitting is a reversal of removal, but finally

adjust the headlamp aim as described in the following Section.

28 Headlamp aim - adjustment

1 Accurate adjustment of the headlamp aim can only be done using optical beam setting equipment and this work should therefore be carried out by a Renault dealer or service station with the necessary facilities. For reference, the location of the beam adjusting screws are shown in the accompanying photos (photos).
2 The headlamps incorporate a two position adjustment to compensate for "laden" or "unladen" conditions. On some models this is a remote control on the facia panel, but on other models a knob is provided on the rear of the headlamp lens assembly.

29 Side marker bulb (five-door models) - renewal

1 Reach up under the front wing and pull the bulbholder from the rear of the lamp.
2 Remove the bulb from the bulbholder.
3 Fit the new bulb using a reversal of the removal procedure.

Fig. 11.8 Front foglamp components
(Sec 26)

1 Bulbholder and lens   4 Wiring
2 Bulb   5 Screws
3 Lamp body

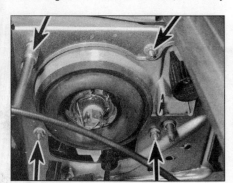

27.3A Unscrewing the four mounting nuts
for the headlamp lens assembly

27.3B Headlamp lens assembly removed
from the car

Fig. 11.9 Headlamp adjuster (B) for "laden"
or "unladen" conditions (Sec 28)

30.1 Unscrew the plastic knob . . .

30.2 . . . and release the rear lamp cluster upper tag

30.3 Slide the wiring connector from the terminal contacts

30.4A Squeeze the plastic clips . . .

30.4B . . . and remove the bulbholder

30.4C Rear lamp unit with bulbholder removed

30.5 Removing a rear lamp cluster bulb

30 Rear lamp cluster bulbs - renewal

1 Open the tailgate then working through the access hole on the appropriate side of the luggage compartment unscrew the plastic knob retaining the bottom of the cluster (photo).
2 Withdraw the bottom of the cluster and lower it to release the upper tag (photo).
3 Slide the wiring connector from the terminal contacts (photo).
4 Squeeze the plastic clips together and separate the bulbholder from the lamp (photos).
5 Depress and twist the appropriate bulb to remove it (photo). The upper bulb is for the tail light and stop light, the middle bulb is for the direction indicator, and the bottom bulb is for the foglight on the left-hand side and the reversing light on the right-hand side.
6 Fit the new bulb using a reversal of the removal procedure. Check the security of the earth bolt on the body before refitting the lamp (photo).

31 Rear number plate lamp bulb - renewal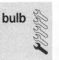

1 Prise the lamp from the tailgate using a screwdriver (photo).
2 Release the lens cover from the base (photo).

30.6 Earth bolt positioned beneath the rear lamp unit location

31.1 Prising the rear number plate lamp from the tailgate

31.2 Removing the lens cover from the rear number plate lamp base

32.1 Prise off the lens cover for access to the bulbs in the roof console

3 Remove the festoon type bulb from the spring contacts.
4 Fit the new bulb using a reversal of the removal procedure, but check the tension of the spring contacts and if necessary bend them so that they firmly contact the bulb end caps.

32 Interior light bulb - renewal

1 Prise the lens cover from the roof console or side interior lights as applicable (photo).
2 Remove the festoon type bulb from the spring contacts.
3 Fit the new bulb making sure that it is firmly held by the spring contacts then refit the lens cover.

33 Instrument panel illumination bulbs - renewal

1 Remove the instrument panel as described in Section 16.
2 Turn the appropriate bulbholder a quarter turn to align the shoulders with the slots, then remove it from the instrument panel and extract the bulb (photos).

34.5 Lift the hinged cover for access to the wiper arm retaining nut

33.2A Large type bulb removal from the instrument panel

3 Fit the new bulb using a reversal of the removal procedure.

34 Wiper blades and arms - removal and refitting

Wiper blades

1 The wiper blades should be renewed when they no longer clean the windscreen or tailgate window effectively.
2 Lift the wiper arm away from the window.
3 Release the catch on the arm, turn the blade through 90° and withdraw the blade from the arm fork (photo).
4 Insert the new blade into the arm, making sure it locates securely.

Wiper arms

5 To remove a wiper arm, lift the hinged cover and unscrew the retaining nut (photo).
6 Using a screwdriver, carefully prise the arm off the spindle.
7 Before refitting the arm switch the wipers on and off, allowing them to return to the "park" position.
8 Refit the arm to the spindle, with the arm and blade positioned at the bottom edge of the screen in the normal "parked" position.
9 Refit and tighten the retaining nut and close the hinged cover.

35.2 Removing the bonnet sealing rubber

33.2B Small type bulb removal from the instrument panel

35 Windscreen wiper motor and linkage - removal and refitting

1 Remove the wiper arms as described in Section 34 and the washer reservoir as described in Section 37.
2 Remove the bonnet sealing rubber (photo) and the plastic cover from the bulkhead plenum chamber.
3 Disconnect the battery negative terminal.
4 At the wiper arm spindles, withdraw the rubber washers (photo), unscrew the nuts and remove the plain and rubber washers.
5 Disconnect the motor wiring multi-plug.

34.3 Removing the wiper blade from the arm

35.4 Removing the wiper arm spindle rubber washer

11

35.6 Wiper motor and linkage centre mounting bolt

35.8 Wiper crank arm to the motor driveshaft nut

35.9 Wiper motor mounting bolts

Fig. 11.10 Exploded view of the windscreen wiper linkage (Sec 35)

1 Spindles
2 Frame
3 Wiper blade
4 Linkage arms
5 Crank arm
6 Wiper arm
7 Wiper arm retaining nut and washers

6 Unscrew the centre mounting bolt together with the plain and rubber washers (photo).

7 Push the spindles through their location holes then withdraw the linkage and motor as an assembly from the bulkhead.

8 Unscrew the nut securing the crank arm to the motor driveshaft and remove the arm (photo).

9 Unbolt and remove the wiper motor from the linkage centre bracket (photo).

10 Refitting is a reversal of removal, but position the crank arm as follows. Operate the motor temporarily so that it stops at the parked position. For safety disconnect the battery negative terminal before proceeding. Fit the crank arm to the motor driveshaft in the position shown in Fig. 11.11 so that all three linkage pivots are in line.

36 Tailgate wiper motor - removal and refitting

1 Disconnect the battery negative terminal.

2 Remove the wiper arm, as described in Section 34.

3 Open the tailgate and remove the cover panel (one screw) to gain access to the motor (photo).

4 Lift off the rubber washer, then undo the nut securing the motor spindle to the tailgate. Lift off the remaining washers and spacers.

Fig. 11.11 Windscreen wiper crank arm, "parked" position (Sec 35)

4 Nut
5 Crank arm
6 Motor mounting bolts
7 Spindle arm pivots

36.3 Removing the tailgate wiper motor cover panel

36.5 Tailgate wiper motor and wiring multi-plug (arrowed)

37.2 Windscreen/tailgate washer reservoir

37.3 Washer reservoir mounting bolt (1) and pipe clip (2)

5 Disconnect the motor wiring multi-plug, undo the retaining bolts and withdraw the motor assembly from inside the tailgate (photo).

6 The motor and gearbox assembly cannot be dismantled for repair or overhaul as replacement parts are not available separately.

7 Refitting is the reverse sequence to removal.

37 Windscreen/tailgate washer reservoir and pumps - removal and refitting

1 Disconnect the battery negative terminal.

2 Pull the wiring connectors from the pump(s) and minimum level sender as applicable and identify them for location (photo).

3 Unscrew the mounting nut, withdraw the reservoir and disconnect the pipes noting their location (photo).

4 Pull the pump(s) from the location in the

reservoir and remove the sealing grommets. Drain any remaining water.

5 Refitting is a reversal of removal, but make sure that the reservoir extension is located in the hole provided in the bulkhead bracket (photo).

38 Horn - removal and refitting

1 Either one or two horns are fitted to the body front valance behind the front bumper (photo). To remove it jack up the front of the car and support on axle stands. Apply the handbrake.

2 Disconnect the battery negative terminal then disconnect the horn supply lead.

3 Unscrew the nut securing the horn to the mounting bracket and remove it from the car.

4 If the horn is inoperative, check for a supply voltage to it by connecting a test bulb

between the electrical lead and a good earth. With the ignition switched on, depress the horn button and the test bulb should light. If the bulb fails to light, check for a blown fuse. If the fuse is satisfactory there is a fault in the wiring or multi-function switch. If the bulb lights, the horn is faulty and the horn will have to be renewed.

5 Refitting the horn is the reverse sequence to removal.

39 Speedometer cable - removal and refitting

1 Refer to Section 17, and remove the instrument panel sufficiently to allow the speedometer cable to be disconnected.

2 Where a trip computer is fitted disconnect the sender unit from the upper and lower cable sections.

3 Release the bulkhead grommet and pull the cable through into the engine compartment.

4 Release the cable from its retaining clips in the engine compartment.

5 At the rear of the transmission, withdraw the shaped wire clip securing the cable to the transmission through the engine mounting bracket. Withdraw the cable and remove it from the engine compartment (photo).

6 Refitting is the reverse sequence of removal, but ensure that the transmission retaining clip is located as shown in Fig. 11.13.

37.5 Washer reservoir location extension

Fig. 11.12 Trip computer sender unit fitted between the upper and lower speedometer cables (Sec 39)

Fig. 11.13 Correct position of the speedometer cable retaining clip in the engine mounting bracket (Sec 39)

38.1 Horn location behind the front bumper

39.5 Removing the speedometer cable

11

Fig. 11.14 Oil level sensor (C) located in the sump (Sec 40)

40 Engine oil level indicator - general

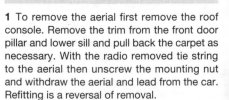

1 On models so equipped, a gauge is provided on the instrument panel to inform the driver of the level of oil in the sump.
2 The gauge is controlled by an electronic circuit located in the instrument panel which receives information from a sensor located in the sump. The sensor contains a high resistance wire whose thermal conductivity alters according to its depth of immersion in the oil.
3 If the engine develops a fault the following test can be carried out to isolate the component concerned.
4 Remove the sensor from the sump by disconnecting the two wires and unscrewing the unit from its mounting.

5 Using an ohmmeter, check the resistance across the sensor terminals. A reading on the ohmmeter should be shown. If not, the sensor is faulty and should be renewed.
6 If the sensor is satisfactory, remove the instrument panel, as described in Section 17, and check the continuity of the wires from the sensor wiring connectors to the appropriate terminals in the instrument panel multi-plug. If there is no continuity, trace the wiring until the break or poor connection is found and make the necessary repair.
7 If the wiring is satisfactory the fault lies with the indicator gauge or the electronic circuit and these can only accurately be checked by substitution.
8 Refit any removed components using the reverse of the removal sequence.

41 Electro-mechanical door locks - general

1 A central door locking system may be fitted as standard equipment or optional according to model. The system enables all the doors to be locked or unlocked by locking or unlocking either of the front doors. When inside the car all the doors can be locked or unlocked by depressing the switch on the centre console.
2 A safety device consisting of an inertia switch and thermal cut-out automatically unlocks all the doors in the event of impact or heat build-up.
3 The system may also be operated by remote control using a small hand held infra-red transmitter. The transmitter signal is decoded by a receiver mounted on the roof console and this activates the electro-mechanical system to lock or unlock the doors.
4 The transmitter is powered by three 1.5 volt alkaline type batteries which have a life of approximately 12 months. The batteries can

be renewed after undoing the transmitter case screw and opening the case to gain access.
5 In the event of a fault occurring in the system it is recommended that you seek the advice of a dealer as specialist knowledge and equipment are necessary for accurate fault diagnosis.

42 Radio - removal and refitting

1 Disconnect the battery negative terminal.
2 On some models it may be necessary to remove the centre console as described in Chapter 10.
3 Prise the radio from the centre console in order to release the retaining springs (photo).
4 Withdraw the radio and disconnect the aerial and wiring (photo).
5 Refitting is a reversal of removal.

43 Radio aerial and speakers - removal and refitting

1 To remove the aerial first remove the roof console. Remove the trim from the front door pillar and lower sill and pull back the carpet as necessary. With the radio removed tie string to the aerial then unscrew the mounting nut and withdraw the aerial and lead from the car. Refitting is a reversal of removal.
2 The speakers may be either mounted on the rear shelf or in the front doors. To remove the shelf type disconnect the wiring and remove the retaining screws, clips or nuts. To remove the door mounted type first remove the trim panel then drill out the rivets and disconnect the wiring (photo). Refitting is a reversal of removal using new rivets where necessary.

42.3 Removing the radio from the centre console

42.4 Showing radio wiring connections and aerial socket (arrowed)

43.2 The door mounted speaker is riveted to the inner panel

Fault finding - electrical system

Starter fails to turn engine

- ☐ Battery discharged or defective
- ☐ Battery terminal and/or earth leads loose
- ☐ Starter motor connections loose
- ☐ Starter solenoid faulty
- ☐ Starter brushes worn or sticking
- ☐ Starter commutator dirty or worn
- ☐ Starter field coils earthed

Starter turns engine very slowly

- ☐ Battery discharged
- ☐ Starter motor connections loose
- ☐ Starter brushes worn or sticking

Starter noisy

- ☐ Pinion or flywheel ring gear teeth badly worn
- ☐ Mounting bolts loose

Battery will not hold charge for more than a few days

- ☐ Battery defective internally
- ☐ Battery terminals loose
- ☐ Alternator drivebelt slipping
- ☐ Alternator or regulator faulty
- ☐ Short circuit

Ignition light stays on

- ☐ Alternator faulty
- ☐ Alternator drivebelt broken

Ignition light fails to come on

- ☐ Warning bulb blown
- ☐ Indicator light open circuit
- ☐ Alternator faulty

Fuel or temperature gauge gives no reading

- ☐ Wiring open circuit
- ☐ Sender unit faulty

Fuel or temperature gauge give maximum reading all the time

- ☐ Wiring short circuit
- ☐ Gauge faulty

Lights inoperative

- ☐ Bulb blown
- ☐ Fuses blown
- ☐ Battery discharged
- ☐ Switch faulty
- ☐ Wiring open circuit
- ☐ Bad connection due to corrosion

Failure of component motor

- ☐ Commutator dirty or burnt
- ☐ Armature faulty
- ☐ Brushes sticking or worn
- ☐ Armature bearings dry or misaligned
- ☐ Field coils faulty
- ☐ Fuse blown
- ☐ Wiring loose or broken

Failure of an individual component

- ☐ Wiring loose or broken
- ☐ Fuse blown
- ☐ Bad circuit connection
- ☐ Switch faulty
- ☐ Component faulty

Notes

Chapter 12 Supplement:
Revisions and information on later models

Contents

12

Degrees of difficulty

| Easy, suitable for novice with little experience | | Fairly easy, suitable for beginner with some experience | | Fairly difficult, suitable for competent DIY mechanic | | Difficult, suitable for experienced DIY mechanic | | Very difficult, suitable for expert DIY or professional | |

1 Introduction

1 This Supplement contains information which is additional to, or a revision of, material in the first eleven Chapters. Much of it is concerned with the 1721 cc engine and associated items fitted to the GTX models introduced in 1987, but some of the information applies to all models. The 1390 cc, C3J engine, fitted to later Campus and Prima models, is also included.

2 The Sections in the Supplement follow the same order as the Chapters to which they relate. The Specifications are all grouped together for convenience, but they too follow Chapter order.

3 It is recommended that, before any operation is undertaken, reference be made to the appropriate Section(s) of the Supplement. In this way, changes to procedures or components can be noted before referring to the main Chapters.

4 In addition to the vehicle identification number on the chassis plate, prefix and suffix number have been added to assist model identification. Make a note of all numbers when buying spare parts from your supplier.

Specifications

These Specifications are revisions of, or supplementary to, those at the beginning of the preceding Chapters

Engine type C1G (1237 cc)

General

Type	Four-cylinder, in-line, overhead valve
Bore	71.5 mm
Stroke	77.0 mm
Capacity	1237 cc
Compression ratio	9.2 : 1

Other data as for C1C engine (Chapter 1)

Under-bonnet view of Renault 5 GTX (1721 cc) with power steering

1 Power steering fluid reservoir
2 Brake fluid reservoir
3 Suspension strut mounting
4 Screen washer reservoir
5 Fuel filter
6 Engine oil filler cap
7 Camshaft drivebelt cover

8 Steering fluid supply pipe
9 Alternator
10 Steering fluid high-pressure pipe
11 Oil filter
12 Fuel vapour separator
13 Radiator top hose

14 Engine oil dipstick
15 Oil separator
16 Cooling fan
17 Carburettor cooling duct
18 Radiator sealing cap
19 Expansion tank filler cap

20 Distributor
21 Idle speed adjusting hole
22 Air cleaner
23 Fast idle actuator vacuum valve
24 Battery cover

Engine type C3J (1390 cc)

General

Type	Four cylinder, in-line overhead valve
Bore	75.8 mm
Stroke	77.0 mm
Capacity	1390 cc
Compression ratio	9.0 : 1
Maximum power output (typical)	43kW (60 bhp) at 4750 rpm
Maximum torque (typical)	100 Nm (74 lbf ft) at 3000 rpm

Torque wrench settings

	Nm	lbf ft
Connecting rod (big-end) cap bolts	45	33

Other data as for C1C engine (Chapter 1)

12

Engine type F2N (1721 cc)

General

Type	Four-cylinder, in-line, overhead cam
Bore	81.0 mm
Stroke	83.5 mm
Capacity	1721 cc
Compression ratio	10.0 : 1
Firing order	1-3-4-2 (No 1 at flywheel end)

Crankshaft

Number of main bearings	5
Main bearing journal diameter:	
New	54.795 mm
Undersize	54.545 mm
Crankpin journal diameter:	
New	48.000 mm
Undersize	47.750 mm
Crankshaft endfloat	0.07 to 0.23 mm
Thrust washer thicknesses	2.30, 2.35, 2.40, 2.45 and 2.50 mm

Connecting rods

Endfloat on crankshaft	0.22 to 0.40 mm

Pistons

Fitted direction	"V" or arrow on crown towards flywheel
Gudgeon pin fit:	
In piston	Hand-push
In connecting rod	Interference
Gudgeon pin length	$65.0 {}^{+0}_{-0.3}$ mm
Gudgeon pin outside diameter	21.0 mm
Piston clearance in bore	0.023 to 0.047 mm

Piston rings

Number	Three (two compression, one oil control)
Compression ring thickness:	
Top ring	1.75 mm
Second ring	2.00 mm
Oil control ring thickness	3.0 mm
End gaps	Supplied preset

Camshaft

Drive	Toothed belt
Number of bearings	5
Endfloat	0.048 to 0.133 mm

Auxiliary shaft

Bush diameter	
Inner	39.5 mm
Outer	40.5 mm
Endfloat	0.07 to 0.15 mm

Cylinder head

Height	169.5 ± 0.2 mm
Maximum permitted warp	0.05 mm
Refinishing limit	No refinishing permitted

Tappets

Diameter	$35.00 {}^{-0.00}_{-0.04}$ mm

Valves

Stem diameter	8.0 mm
Head diameter	
Inlet	38.1 mm
Exhaust	32.5 mm
Seat included angle:	
Inlet	120°
Exhaust	90°
Seat width in cylinder head	1.7 ± 0.2 mm
Valve head-to-cylinder head recess depth	0.8 to 1.1 mm

Valve guides

Outside diameter (nominal):
- Production . . . . 13.0 mm
- Repair . . . . 13.3 mm

Bore diameter in cylinder head . . . . 0.1 mm less than outside diameter
Fitted height above joint face . . . . 43.0 ± 0.2 mm

Valve springs

Free height . . . . 44.9 mm

Valve timing

At theoretical clearance of 0.40 mm inlet, 0.50 mm exhaust:
- Inlet opens . . . . 4° BTDC
- Inlet closes . . . . 40° ABDC
- Exhaust opens . . . . 40° BBDC
- Exhaust closes . . . . 4° ATDC

Valve clearances (cold)

Inlet . . . . 0.20 mm (0.008 in)
Exhaust . . . . 0.40 mm (0.016 in)

Lubrication system

Oil pump:
- Gear-to-body clearance . . . . 0.02 mm maximum
- Gear endfloat . . . . 0.085 mm maximum

Oil pressure (at 80°C):
- At 1000 rpm . . . . 2.0 bar (29 lbf/in²)
- At 3000 rpm . . . . 3.5 bar (51 lbf/in²)

Oil capacity (including filter) . . . . 5.2 litres (9.2 pints) approx.
Oil filter . . . . Champion F102

Torque wrench settings

	Nm	lbf ft
Cylinder head bolts:		
Stage 1	30	22
Stage 2	37	52
Stage 3	Wait three minutes, then slacken	
Stage 4	20	15
Stage 5	Angle-tighten a further 123°	
Main bearing cap bolts	65	48
Big-end bearing cap bolts	50	37
Flywheel retaining bolts	55	41
Camshaft bearing cap bolts:		
6 mm diameter	10	7
8 mm diameter	20	15
Camshaft sprocket bolt	50	37
Idler roller bolt	20	15
Tensioner roller nut	40	30
Auxiliary shaft sprocket bolt	50	37
Crankshaft pulley bolt	95	70
Oil pump bolts:		
6 mm diameter	10	7
8 mm diameter	20	15
Sump bolts	15	11
Piston cooling jet bolts	30	22
Engine mounting nuts and bolts	40	30

Fuel and exhaust systems - non-Turbo carburettor models

Carburettor application

C1G (1237 cc engine) . . . . Solex 32 BIS or Zenith 32 IF 2
C2J (later 1397 cc) engine:
- Manual transmission . . . . Weber 32 DRT 21.100
- Automatic transmission . . . . Weber 32 DRT 8

F2N (1721 cc) engine . . . . Solex 28/34 Z10 or 32/34 Z13

12

Carburettor data

Zenith 32 IF 2:

Type identification number	V10517
Venturi	24
Main jet	130
Idling jet	58
Air compensating jet	90 x 200
Pneumatic enrichment jet	100
Accelerator pump stroke	27 mm (1.06 in)
Accelerator pump jet	50
Accelerator pump delivery tube setting	60 mm (2.36 in)
Needle valve	1.25
Float height dimension	13.65 mm (0.537 in)
Auxiliary jet	60
Auxiliary jet tube setting	6.0 mm (0.24 in)
Defuming valve setting	2.0 mm (0.08 in)
Initial throttle opening (fast idle)	0.8 mm (0.032 in)
Idle speed	650 ± 25 rpm
CO mixture	1.5 ± 0.5%

Solex 32 BIS:

	869	907
Type identification number	869	907
Venturi	24	24
Main jet	115	120
Air compensating jet	155	125
Idling jet	38	42
Enrichener	52	40
Needle valve	1.3	1.3
Accelerator pump jet	40	40
Initial throttle opening (fast idle)	0.75 mm (0.03 in) or 20°	0.75 mm (0.03 in) or 20° 30'
Defuming valve setting	3 mm (0.12 in)	3 mm (0.12 in)

Weber 32 DRT 21.100:

	Primary	Secondary
Venturi	23	24
Main jet	110	105
Air compensating jet	230	135
Idling jet	55	70
Emulsifier	F58	F56
Needle valve	1.75	
Float height dimension	8 mm (0.32 in)	
Float travel dimension	13 mm (0.51 in)	
Accelerator pump jet	45	
Initial throttle opening (fast idle)	0.8 mm (0.032 in)	
Pneumatic part-opening setting	3.5 mm (0.14 in)	
Defuming valve throttle opening	Not applicable	
Idling speed	700 ± 50 rpm	
CO mixture	1.5 ± 0.5%	
Fast idling speed *	1050 ± 50 rpm	

* Models with power steering

Weber 32 DRT 8:

	Primary	Secondary
Venturi	23	24
Main jet	107	105
Air compensating jet	220	135
Idling jet	52	70
Emulsifier	F58	F56
Needle valve	1.75	
Float height dimension	8 mm (0.32 in)	
Float travel dimension	13 mm (0.51 in)	
Accelerator pump jet	50	
Initial throttle opening (fast idle)	0.9 mm (0.035 in)	
Pneumatic part-opening setting	3.5 mm (0.14 in)	
Defuming valve throttle opening	0.3 mm (0.012 in)	
Idling speed (in "D")	600 ± 25 rpm	
CO mixture	1.0 ± 0.5%	
Fast idling speed *	1050 ± 50 rpm	

* Models with power steering

Solex 28/34 Z10:	Primary	Secondary
Venturi	20	27
Main jet	97.5	145
Idling jet	46 (49*)	50
Air compensating jet	200	190
Econostat	-	120
Enrichener	50	
Accelerator pump injector	40	35
Needle valve	1.8	
Float level	33.5 mm (1.32 in)	
Initial throttle opening (fast idle)	1.0 mm (0.039 in) or 25° 30'	
Defuming valve setting	2 mm (0.08 in)	
Pneumatic part-opening setting	2.2 mm (0.09 in)	
Idling speed	800 ± 50 rpm	
Fast idling speed *	1050 ± 50 rpm	
CO mixture	1.5 ± 0.5%	

* Models with power steering

Solex 32/34 Z13:	Primary	Secondary
Venturi	24	27
Main jet	115	137.5
Idling jet	43	50
Air compensating jet	165	190
Econostat	-	120
Enrichener	50	-
Accelerator pump injector	40	35
Needle valve	1.8	
Float level	33.5 mm (1.32 in)	
Initial throttle opening (fast idle)	0.75 mm (0.03 in) or 22° 30'	
Defuming valve setting	0.3 mm (0.012 in)	
Pneumatic part-opening setting	3.5 mm (0.14 in)	
Idling speed	800 ± 50 rpm	
Fast idling speed	1050 ± 50 rpm	
CO mixture.	1.5 ± 0.5%	

* Models with power steering

Air cleaner element
1237 cc models	Champion W145
1721 cc models	Champion type not available

Fuel and exhaust systems - non-Turbo fuel injection models

General
System type:	
1390 cc (C3J) engine	Single point with catalyst
Fuel octane requirement	Unleaded - 91 RON (Regular), 95 RON (Premium) or 98 RON (Super)

Fuel pump
Type	Electrical driven
Delivery	0.83 litre per minute
Pressure	1.00 ± 0.2 bar

Fuel injector
Operating voltage	12 volts
Resistance	1.4 ohms (approx.)

Inlet air temperature sensor
	20°C	70°C
Resistance	3400 ohms	450 ohms

Coolant temperature sensor
	20°C	70°C
Resistance	3400 ohms	450 ohms

Ignition system

General
System type:	
1237 cc (C1G)	Integrated electronic system (as fitted to 1397 cc engines)
1390 cc (C3J)	Fully electronic, computer controlled
1721 cc (F2N)	As C1G, but with distributor rotor mounted directly on camshaft

12

Spark plugs*

Type:

1237 cc	Champion N9YCC or N281YC
1390 cc	Champion C9YC or RC9YCC
1721 cc	Champion N7YCC or N279YC
Electrode gap	0.8 mm (0.32 in)

* Information on spark plug types and electrode gaps is as recommended by Champion Spark Plug. Where alternative types are used, refer to the manufacturer's recommendations

HT leads

1237 cc, 1390 cc and 1721 cc models	Champion type not available

Clutch

Disc diameter

1721 cc models	200 mm (7.9 in)

Manual gearbox

Designation

1237 cc models	JB3 (5-speed) or JB4 (4-speed)
1390 cc models	JB5 (5-speed)
1721 cc models	JB3

Ratios - JB3

1st	3.091 : 1
2nd	1.842 : 1
3rd	1.320 : 1
4th	0.967 : 1
5th	0.758 : 1
Reverse	3.545 : 1
Final drive:	
Non-Turbo models	3.733 : 1 (56/15)
Turbo models	3.563 : 1 (57/16)

Ratios - JB5

1st	3.7 : 1
2nd	2.1 : 1
3rd	1.3 : 1
4th	1.0 : 1
5th	0.8 : 1
Reverse	3.6 : 1
Final drive	3.6 to 4.2 : 1

Suspension and steering

Power steering

Fluid type	Dexron type ATF

Tyres

Tyre size (1721 cc models)	165/65 R13T	
Tyre pressures (bar/lbf/in^2):	**Front**	**Rear**
1721 cc models	2.2/32	2.2/32
Automatic transmission models	2.1/31	2.2/32

Torque wrench setting - front suspension	Nm	lbf ft
Lower suspension arm pivot -Turbo models from June 1987	90	66

General dimensions, weights and capacities

Dimensions (Renault Extra)

Length	3982 mm (156.8 in)
Width	1588 mm (62.5 in)
Height	1765 mm (69.5 in)
Wheelbase	2580 mm (101.6 in)

Weights (Renault Extra)

	Extra 1.1	Extra 1.4
Kerb weight	790 kg (1742 lb)	810 kg (1786 lb)
Payload (including driver)	525 kg (1157 lb)	575 kg (1268 lb)
Maximum towing weight:		
Braked	600 kg (1323 lb)	700 kg (1543 lb)
Unbraked	395 kg (871 lb)	405 kg (893 lb)
Maximum roof load	60 kg (132 lb)	60 kg (132 lb)

Weights (1721 cc models)

Kerb weight:	
3-door	775 kg (1709 lb)
5-door	840 kg (1852 lb)

Capacities

Engine oil (including filter) - 1721 cc models	5.2 litres (9.2 pints) approx.
Power steering fluid	1.1 litres (1.9 pints) approx.
Load space - Renault Extra	2.6 m³ (91.8 cu ft)

---

3   Routine maintenance

Maintenance intervals - all models

1 The intervals specified in the schedule at the beginning of the manual are for vehicles working under average conditions. In adverse conditions maintenance should be more frequent. Adverse conditions include:

Operating in extreme of climate
Operation in dusty conditions (e.g. on unmade roads)
Predominantly short journeys
Full-time towing

Engine oil change interval - Turbo models

2 On models where the turbocharger is not water-cooled, the engine oil must be changed every 3000 miles (say 5000 km) or three months, whichever comes first.
3 On models with a water-cooled turbo charger the specified oil change interval is 6000 miles (10 000 km) or six months.
4 On all turbod models the oil filter must be renewed every 6000 miles (10 000 km) or six months.

Brake fluid renewal - all models

5 The renewal of brake fluid as a maintenance task is no longer specified by Renault. The reason stated is that modern fluid in a well-designed system does not deteriorate to a significant extent.
6 The conscientious DIY mechanic may prefer to continue renewing the brake fluid periodically. In any event, the fluid must be renewed when new calipers or wheel cylinders are fitted, or if the hydraulic system is drained for any other reason.

Maintenance schedule - 1721 cc models

7 The schedule at the beginning of the manual applies equally to these models, with the following additional task.

8 Renew the camshaft drivebelt every 72 000 miles (say 120 000 km). See Section 6 of this Chapter for details.

Automatic transmission models - additional maintenance

9 When the transmission fluid is renewed at the 30 000 mile (50 000 km) service, the filter screen inside the transmission must be renewed. See Section 15 of this Chapter.

Power steering - maintenance

10 Check the steering fluid level every 6000 miles (10 000 km). See Section 18.
11 On models with a separate drivebelt for the steering pump, check the tension and condition of the drivebelt at the same interval.

---

4   Engine - C1G (1237 cc) OHV

Engine splash guards - general

1 Later models are fitted with the engine splash guards (Fig. 12.1). When operations requiring access to the underside of the engine are carried out, the splash guards will need to be removed.

Engine C1G (1237 cc) - description

2 This engine was added to the range in July 1987. Mechanically it is identical to the other OHV engines described in Chapter 1.

H.19482

Fig. 12.1 Engine and spare wheel splash guards (Sec 4)

12

Fig. 12.2 Cutaway view of the 1721 cc engine (Sec 6A)

Fig. 12.3 Sectional view of the 1721 cc engine (Sec 6A)

Engine - removal and refitting (models with power steering)

3 On these models the alternator and the steering pump must be removed before engine removal. Refer to Section 18.

Engine - removal and refitting (Turbo models)

4 On Turbo models the removal of the engine alone is no longer recommended; instead, it should be removed with the gearbox.

Cylinder liners - incorrect protrusion after reassembly

5 If, after the reassembly procedure given in Chapter 1, Section 27, the liner protrusion cannot be brought into tolerance, a new set of liners should be fitted to establish if it is the liners or the cylinder block which is at fault.

6 If the new liners cannot be brought into tolerance, the cylinder block is probably at fault. Consult a Renault dealer for further guidance.

Engine/gearbox locating dowels - all models

7 The length of the dowels which locate the engine/gearbox mating areas may vary with model and year. The variation is not great - roughly 2.5 mm (0.1 in). If fitting a different engine or gearbox, therefore, make sure that the lengths of the dowels correspond to the depths of the recesses into which they fit. Obtain new dowels if necessary.

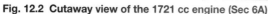

5   Engine - C3J (1390 cc) OHV

Engine - description

1 This engine was added to the Campus and Prima models during 1990. It was originally fitted to the Renault 19. Based on the existing OHV 'C' type engine, that is already covered, it is fitted with a Bendix/Renix Single Point fuel injection system. This model is also fitted with a catalytic converter, therefore must only be operated with unleaded fuel.

Engine - general

2 The engine repair procedures are as described in Chapter 1. However references to the carburettor should be replaced with fuel injection, as described in Section 9.

6   Engine - F2N (1721 cc) OHC

PART A: GENERAL

Description

1 This engine became available in the Renault 5 range in July 1987. It is a well-proven unit of conventional design which has already been used in several larger Renault models.

2 The engine is of four-cylinder in-line overhead camshaft type. Like the overhead valve engines it is mounted transversely at the front of the car. The crankshaft runs in five shell-type main bearings, with thrust washers fitted to No 2 main bearing to control endfloat.

3 The connecting rods are attached to the crankshaft by horizontally split shell-type big-end bearings, and to the pistons by gudgeon pins which are an interference fit in the small-end bushes. The pistons are of aluminium alloy, with three piston rings each. The crowns of the pistons are recessed to form the combustion chambers.

4 The cylinder bores are formed directly in the cylinder block. There are six possible bore sizes and pistons and bores are matched in production.

5 The overhead camshaft runs directly in the cylinder head, where it is secured by five bearing caps. It is driven from the crankshaft by a toothed rubber belt (the camshaft drive belt). The cam lobes bear on shims carried in inverted bucket type tappets, the other ends of the tappets bearing on the valve stems. Valve clearances are determined by shim thickness. The valves are mounted vertically in the cylinder head and are each closed by a single spring.

6 The camshaft drivebelt also drives an auxiliary shaft which in turn drives the oil pump via a skew gear. The oil pump feeds oil to an externally mounted disposable filter, from where it passes to the main oil gallery and then to the crankshaft, auxiliary shaft and

Fig. 12.4 Lubrication circuit of the 1721 cc engine. Detail shows piston cooling oil jets (Sec 6A)

6A.16 Removing a camshaft cover nut

6A.18 Measuring a valve clearance

camshaft. Oil jets at the bottom of each bore squirt oil onto the pistons to lubricate and cool them.

7 The camshaft drives the fuel pump by means of an eccentric and a plunger. The distributor rotor is attached directly to the tail of the camshaft.

Routine maintenance

8 Refer to Chapter 1, Section 2.
9 At the intervals specified in Section 3 of this Chapter the camshaft drivebelt must be renewed. This is necessary because if the belt breaks or slips in service, extensive engine damage may occur. The operation is described later in this Section.

Major operations possible with the engine in the car

10 The following operations can be carried out without removing the engine:
a) Removal and refitting of the camshaft drivebelt
b) Removal and refitting of the camshaft

c) Removal and refitting of the cylinder head
d) Removal and refitting of the sump
e) Removal and refitting of the oil pump
f) Renewal of the crankshaft front oil seal
g) Removal and refitting of the piston/connecting rod assemblies
h) Removal and refitting of the engine mountings

Major operations requiring engine removal

11 The following operations can only be carried out after engine removal:
a) Removal and refitting of the flywheel
b) Removal and refitting of the crankshaft and main bearings
c) Renewal of the crankshaft rear oil seal
d) Removal and refitting of the auxiliary shaft

Valve clearances - checking and adjustment

12 This is not specified as a routine maintenance operation. It should only be

necessary after component renewal, or if noise or compression loss give rise to suspicion that the clearances are incorrect. The clearances are checked with the engine cold.
13 Disconnect the battery earth lead.
14 Remove the air cleaner (Section 8).
15 Unbolt the fuel vapour separator from the front of the engine, but do not disconnect the hoses from it.
16 Remove the six nuts which secure the camshaft cover (photo). Lift the fuel pipe cluster slightly and remove the cover and gasket.
17 Using a spanner on the crankshaft pulley bolt, turn the crankshaft until both cam lobes for No 1 cylinder (flywheel end) are pointing obliquely upwards, and the timing mark on the flywheel is aligned with the "O" mark on the gearbox housing.
18 With the engine in this position, measure and record the clearance between the base of No 1 cylinder exhaust valve cam lobe and the tappet shim beneath it. (The exhaust valve cam lobe is the one nearest the flywheel.) Insert various thicknesses of feeler blade until a firm sliding fit is obtained (photo). This thickness is the clearance for No 1 exhaust valve.
19 Repeat the measurement and recording on the second cam from the flywheel end. This gives No 1 inlet valve clearance.
20 Turn the crankshaft half a turn in the normal direction of rotation so that the cam

12

Fig. 12.5 Cam lobe identification (Sec 6A)

A Inlet   E Exhaust

6A.24 Shim thickness engraved on the underside

lobes for No 3 cylinder are pointing obliquely upwards. Measure and record the clearances for these two valves. On cylinders 1 and 2 the exhaust valves are nearer the flywheel, while on cylinders 3 and 4 the inlet valves are nearer (Fig. 12.5).

21 Turn the crankshaft a further half a turn and deal with No 4 cylinder, then half a turn again for No 2.

22 Compare the clearances recorded with those given in the Specifications. If the clearances are as specified, commence reassembly. Otherwise, adjust the clearances as follows.

23 With the cam lobes in the same position as for checking, depress a tappet with a C-spanner or a stout screwdriver. Only press on the edge of the tappet. Flick the shim out of the top of the tappet with a small screwdriver

and remove it with long-nosed pliers. Release the tappet.

24 The correct thickness of shim must now be calculated. First the thickness of the old shim must be known. It is engraved on the underside (photo), but ideally the actual thickness should be measured using a micrometer or vernier gauge. This will take account of any wear.

25 The required shim thickness can now be calculated as shown in this example:

Specified clearance (A) = 0.4 mm
Measured clearance (B) = 0.28 mm
Original shim thickness (C) = 3.95 mm
Shim thickness required = C - A + B = 3.83 mm
The closest shim thicknesses available are

3.80 and 3.85 mm, giving clearances of 0.43 mm and 0.38 mm respectively.

26 Lubricate a new shim of the required thickness. Depress the tappet and insert the shim, marked side downwards. Release the tappet and check that the shim is properly located, and that the notches in the top of the tappet are at right-angles to the camshaft.

27 Repeat the operations on the adjacent tappet, if necessary, then proceed to the other valves, each time turning the crankshaft to position the cam lobes upwards. Do not turn the crankshaft while shims are missing from tappets, as the cam lobes may jam in them.

28 When all the required shims have been fitted, turn the crankshaft through several complete turns, then check all the clearances again.

29 Refit the camshaft cover, using a new gasket if necessary, and secure it with the six nuts.

30 Refit the fuel vapour separator and the air cleaner. Reconnect the battery.

Crankcase ventilation system - description

31 The layout of the system is shown in Fig.12.6. Its operation is as described in Chapter 1, Section 23.

32 Check the condition and security of the hoses from time to time, and make sure that the restrictors are not blocked. Blockages or leakage in the system can cause idling problems and (by raising the pressure in the crankcase) oil leaks.

PART B: REMOVAL AND DISMANTLING

Method of engine removal

1 The engine and gearbox must be removed together and separated on the bench. They are removed upwards out of the engine bay as described in the following paragraphs.

Engine - removal with gearbox

2 Jack up the front of the vehicle and support it on axle stands. Remove the front wheels. Also remove the bonnet.

3 Disconnect the battery earth lead.

4 Remove the air cleaner (see Section 8).

5 Disconnect the throttle and choke cables from the carburettor.

6 Disconnect the following items of wiring (photos):
a) Ignition coil-to-distributor HT lead
b) Ignition unit LT and TDC sensor connectors
c) Two multi-plugs on the left-hand inner wing
d) Carburettor heater and idle cut-off connectors
e) Vacuum valve electrical connectors (models with power steering)

7 Remove the carburettor cooling duct, if fitted.

8 Disconnect the clutch cable.

Fig. 12.6 Crankcase ventilation system - 1721 cc engine (Sec 6A)

1 Oil separator
2 Hose
3 Air cleaner
4 Hose
5 Hose (to carburettor base)
6 3-way union
7 Restrictor (1.7 mm)
8 Restrictor (7 mm)

6B.6A Disconnecting the ignition unit multi-plugs . . .

6B.6B . . . two plugs on the inner wing . . .

6B.6C . . . and the vacuum valve connectors (power steering models)

9 Disconnect the vacuum hoses from the carburettor and inlet manifold, making identifying marks if necessary to aid refitting.
10 Disconnect the fuel supply hose from the fuel pump (photo), and the fuel return hose from the pipe cluster on top of the engine.
11 Unbolt the earth strap from below the fuel pump (photo).
12 Drain the engine oil, the gearbox oil and the coolant.
13 Remove the radiator (Chapter 2, Section 7).
14 On models with power steering, clamp the reservoir-to-pump hose. Disconnect the wiring from the pressure switch. Prepare for fluid spillage, then disconnect the supply hose and the high pressure pipe from the pump. Allow the high pressure pipe to drain, then move it aside. Cover the open pipes and unions to keep dirt out.
15 Disconnect the small hose from the expansion tank, and the large hose which runs from the tank to the water pump pipe. Unclip the tank and move it aside.
16 Disconnect the heater hose from the T-piece behind the distributor (photo).
17 Disconnect the temperature sensor wiring (photo).
18 Disconnect the speedometer cable from the gearbox.
19 Disconnect the track rod end balljoints and the suspension arm lower balljoints on both sides. Refer to Chapter 9 if necessary.
20 Remove the three bolts which secure the

6B.10 Disconnecting the fuel supply hose from the pump

6B.11 The unit (arrowed) which secures the earth strap

left-hand driveshaft to the gearbox. Swing the left-hand stub axle carrier outwards and disconnect the driveshaft from the gearbox.
21 Drive out the roll pin which holds the right-hand driveshaft sections together. Swing the right-hand stub axle carrier outwards and separate the driveshaft sections.
22 Unbolt the gearchange linkage at the gearbox. Be careful not to lose the spacer.
23 Remove the two nuts, springs and sleeves which secure the exhaust downpipe to the manifold. Lower the downpipe.
24 Disconnect the starter motor feed wire from the solenoid. Access is very poor, but an alternative procedure is to disconnect the wire at the battery, remove the bulkhead grommet and feed the wire through so that it can be removed with the engine.

25 Unclip the HT lead bracket from the left-hand lifting eye (photo).
26 Attach lifting tackle to the two lifting eyes. The chain or rope should be shorter to the right-hand eye than to the left, so that when the unit is hanging freely the engine will be slightly higher than the gearbox.
27 Take the weight of the engine/gearbox unit, then unbolt the mountings. These are positioned as follows:
a) Left-hand front
b) Right-hand front
c) Rear centre
d) Front centre (movement limiter)

28 Check that no attachments have been overlooked, then lift the engine and gearbox out of the engine bay. An assistant should

6B.16 Disconnecting the heater hose

6B.17 Disconnecting the coolant temperature sensor

6B.25 Unclipping the HT lead bracket from the lifting eye

12

6B.28 Lifting out the engine and gearbox

6B.31 Removing the flywheel cover plate and bracing bar

6B.33 Removing an engine-to-gearbox bolt. This one has a thick spacer washer

guide the unit as it is lifted to make sure that nothing is trapped or fouled (photo).

Engine - separation from gearbox

29 Remove the starter motor, its heat shield and its wiring.
30 Make a TDC mark on the engine if wished - see Chapter 1, Section 8, paragraph 3.
31 Unbolt the flywheel cover plate and bracing bar from the base of the engine (photo).
32 Unbolt the TDC sensor and bracket.
33 Remove the remaining bolts which secure the engine to the gearbox (photo). Have an assistant steady the engine. Pull the gearbox off the engine, being careful not to allow the weight to hang on the input shaft.

Engine dismantling - general

34 Refer to Chapter 1, Section 9, paragraphs 1 to 9.
35 Operations which can be carried out with the engine in the car are described as if this were the case. If the engine has been removed, many of the preliminary steps can be ignored.

Ancillary components - removal

36 Refer to Chapter 1, Section 10. On models with power steering, also remove the steering pump.

Camshaft drivebelt - removal

37 Disconnect the battery negative lead.
38 Remove the right-hand front roadwheel. Also remove the splash guard in the right-

hand wheel arch (photo). This will give access to the crankshaft pulley.
39 Remove the alternator/water pump drivebelt.
40 Using a spanner on the crankshaft pulley bolt turn the crankshaft until the timing marks on the camshaft sprocket and on the flywheel are aligned with the pointer on the camshaft drivebelt cover and the TDC (O) mark on the bellhousing (photos).
41 Have an assistant prevent the crankshaft turning by jamming the flywheel ring-gear teeth with a large screwdriver or a tyre lever. Slacken the crankshaft pulley bolt. Remove the bolt and the pulley (photo).
42 Check that the timing marks are still aligned. If they are not, temporarily refit the pulley and bolt and turn the crankshaft to realign them.

6B.38 Removing the wheel arch splash guard

6B.40A Camshaft sprocket mark aligned with pointer . . .

6B.40B . . . and flywheel mark aligned with "O" line

6B.41 Removing the crankshaft pulley

6B.43A Removing the camshaft drivebelt cover clip

6B.43B Removing the camshaft drivebelt cover. The 5 screw holes are arrowed

6B.44 Mark the cover in line with the mark on the sprocket (arrowed)

6B.45 Camshaft drivebelt run - engine removed. Tensioner nut is arrowed (A) - on some engines it is in idler position (B)

Fig. 12.7 Restraining the camshaft sprocket with an old camshaft drivebelt (Sec 6B)

43 Remove the spring clip and the five Torx screws which secure the front of the camshaft drivebelt cover. Access to some of the screws is very tight, and a short cranked key will be needed to undo them. Remove the cover (photos).

44 Paint or scribe a mark on the camshaft sprocket cover in line with the timing mark on the sprocket. This will be useful for initial setting during reassembly. If the original camshaft drivebelt is to be re-used, make marks on the belt and the sprockets so that it can be refitted in exactly the same position (photo).

45 Slacken the belt tensioner nut, move the tensioner to release the belt and nip up the nut again (photo). Slide the belt off the sprockets and rollers and remove it.

Camshaft and tappets - removal 𝄽𝄽𝄽𝄽𝄽

46 Remove the camshaft drivebelt as described earlier in this Section.

47 Disconnect the HT leads and remove the distributor cap and rotor arm (Section 12). Remove the rotor arm shield.

48 Remove the air cleaner (Section 8).

49 Unbolt the fuel vapour separator from the front of the engine, but do not disconnect the hoses from it.

50 Remove the six nuts which secure the camshaft cover. Lift the fuel pipe cluster slightly and remove the cover and gasket.

51 Remove the fuel pump (Section 8).

52 Prevent the camshaft sprocket from

turning by gripping it with a strap wrench or with an old camshaft drivebelt (Fig. 12.7). Undo the camshaft sprocket bolt and remove the bolt and sprocket. Recover the Woodruff key if it is loose.

53 Remove the sprocket backing plate (photo).

54 Make identifying marks on the camshaft bearing caps so that they can be refitted in the same positions and the same way round.

55 Progressively slacken the bearing cap bolts until the valve spring pressure is released. Remove the bolts, and the bearing caps themselves (photos).

56 Lift out the camshaft with its oil seals (photo).

57 Remove the tappets, each with its shim (photo). Place them in a compartmented box, or on a sheet of card marked into eight

sections, so that they may be refitted to their original locations. Write down the shim thicknesses - they will be needed later if any of the valve clearances are incorrect.

Cylinder head - removal 𝄽𝄽𝄽𝄽𝄽

58 Disconnect the battery negative lead.

59 Drain the cooling system.

60 Remove the air cleaner (Section 8).

61 Disconnect the HT leads and remove the distributor cap.

62 Remove the camshaft drivebelt as described earlier in this Section.

63 Disconnect the wiring from the temperature sensor on the rear of the cylinder head.

64 Identify the various fuel hoses and disconnect them. Unbolt and remove the fuel vapour separator and the fuel pipe cluster.

6B.53 Camshaft sprocket backing plate

6B.55A Camshaft bearing cap and bolts

6B.55B Removing the No 1 (flywheel end) camshaft bearing cap

6B.56 Lifting out the camshaft

6B.57 Removing a tappet

12

6B.68 Coolant pipe bracket bolts (arrowed)

6B.86 Unbolting the oil pump

6B.93 Refitting the front oil seal carrier plate. Make sure zone C is not blocked by sealant

65 Disconnect the throttle and choke cables from the carburettor.

66 Identify and disconnect the vacuum hoses from the carburettor and inlet manifold.

67 Disconnect the heater and crankcase ventilation hoses from the cylinder head.

68 Remove the two bolts which secure the coolant pipe bracket to the rear of the cylinder head (photo).

69 Disconnect the radiator top hose from the thermostat housing.

70 Remove the two nuts, springs and spacers which secure the exhaust downpipe to the manifold. Lower the downpipe.

71 Remove the six nuts which secure the camshaft cover. Remove the cover and gasket.

72 Unbolt the camshaft drivebelt backplate from the cylinder head.

73 Slacken the cylinder head bolts progressively, half a turn at a time, in the reverse of the tightening sequence (Fig.12.10). When the tension has been released, remove the bolts.

74 Lift off the head, complete with manifolds and carburettor. If it is stuck, tap it upwards using a hammer and a block of wood. Do not try to rotate the head to free it, as it is located by two dowels. Do not try to free it by prising between the mating faces, as damage may result.

75 Remove the head gasket and clean the mating faces.

Cylinder head - dismantling

76 If not already done, remove the following components:
a) *Carburettor and manifolds*
b) *Fuel pump*
c) *Temperature gauge sender*
d) *Camshaft and tappets*
e) *Thermostat (see Section 7)*

77 Now remove the valves and associated components as described in Chapter 1, Section 13, paragraphs 2 to 5. Note however that on this engine the inlet valves are Nos 2, 4, 5 and 7, and the exhaust valves Nos 1, 3, 6 and 8.

78 Remove the oil seals from the tops of the valve guides.

Sump - removal

79 Jack up the vehicle and support it on axle stands at a height convenient for working underneath.

80 Drain the engine oil, then refit and tighten the drain plug.

81 Remove any splash guards or undertrays impeding access to the sump

82 Unbolt and remove the flywheel cover plate and bracing bar.

83 Remove the sump-to-crankcase bolts. Tap the sump with a wooden or plastic mallet to free it, and remove it.

84 Clean the inside of the sump. Remove old jointing compound from the sump and crankcase mating faces.

Oil pump - removal

85 Remove the sump as just described.

86 Remove the four bolts which secure the oil pump (photo). Withdraw the pump from its driveshaft.

Crankshaft front oil seal - renewal

87 Remove the camshaft drivebelt as described earlier in this Section. Also remove the drivebelt backplate.

88 Remove the sump.

89 Withdraw the crankshaft sprocket, preferably using a puller or by careful levering. Recover the Woodruff key.

90 Remove the bolts which secure the oil seal carrier plate to the crankcase. Remove the plate and seal.

91 Prise or tap the old oil seal out of the plate, being careful not to damage the seal housing. Remove old jointing compound from the plate and from the crankcase.

92 Fit a new seal, lips inwards, and tap it home with a tube or a piece of wood so that it is flush with the outer face of the plate.

93 Apply jointing sealant (CAF 4/60 THIXO or equivalent) to the plate mating face. Liberally lubricate the oil seal lips with clean engine oil. Make sure that the oilway in the top section of the plate is not blocked by sealant (photo).

94 Fit the oil seal carrier to the engine. Insert and tighten the retaining bolts, except for the two nearest the seal, which also secure the camshaft drivebelt backplate.

95 Refit the remaining components in the reverse order to removal. Apply a little sealant to the threads of the backplate bolts nearest the seal, as they penetrate into the crankcase. Remember that if the camshaft drivebelt has been contaminated with oil it must be renewed.

Pistons, connecting rods and big-end bearings - removal

96 Remove the sump, the oil pump and the cylinder head. If applicable, also remove the oil level sensor.

97 Turn the crankshaft to bring No 1 big-end cap (flywheel end) within reach. Make punch or paint marks on one side of the cap and the connecting rod so that they may be refitted in the same position and the same way round.

98 Remove the big-end cap bolts and withdraw the cap and shell. Push the connecting rod up the bore, recovering its shell if it is loose. Withdraw the piston and connecting rod from the top of the block.

99 Repeat the procedure on the other three pistons and rods. Keep the bearing shells with their respective caps and rods if they are to be re-used.

Engine mountings - renewal

100 Refer to Chapter 1, Section 22. The procedures are basically the same.

Flywheel - removal

101 With the engine removed, separate it from the gearbox and remove the clutch.

102 Prevent the crankshaft from turning by jamming the flywheel ring gear teeth. Slacken all the flywheel retaining bolts.

103 Remove the bolts and lift off the flywheel. Be careful, it is heavy. Obtain new bolts for reassembly.

Crankshaft and main bearings - removal

104 Remove the front oil seal carrier, the pistons and connecting rods and the flywheel. Invert the engine or place it on its side.

105 Check that the main bearing caps carry identification numbers. If not, mark them as was done for the big-end caps.

6B.109A Oil jet and retaining bolt

6B.109B Oil jet in position in the crankcase

6B.110 Fitting a crankshaft rear oil seal -
note the piece of plastic used to protect
the seal

106 Remove the main bearing cap bolts. A hexagonal bit will be needed for No 1 bearing cap bolts. Withdraw the bearing caps and the bearing shell lower halves. Keep the shells with their respective caps if they are to be re-used.

107 Carefully lift out the crankshaft complete with rear oil seal.

108 Recover the thrust washers from each side of No 2 main bearing, and the bearing shell upper halves from the crankcase. Again, identify the shell positions for refitting if necessary.

109 The cooling oil jets at the lower end of each cylinder bore may be unbolted and removed for cleaning if necessary (photos).

Crankshaft rear oil seal - renewal

110 Refer to Chapter 1, Section 21. Protect the lips of the new seal by wrapping a thin piece of flexible plastic round the crankshaft (photo). Remove the plastic once the seal is fitted.

Auxiliary shaft - removal

111 With the engine removed from the vehicle, remove the camshaft drivebelt.

112 Restrain the auxiliary shaft sprocket with a strap wrench or by clamping an old camshaft drivebelt round it. Remove the sprocket bolt and washer.

113 Pull or carefully lever the sprocket off the auxiliary shaft. Recover the Woodruff key if it is loose.

114 Remove the camshaft drivebelt backplate.

115 Remove the four bolts which secure the auxiliary shaft oil seal carrier. Remove the carrier, oil seal and gasket.

116 From above the shaft remove the two bolts which secure the oil pump drivegear cover plate. Remove the plate and withdraw the drivegear using a long bolt (12 mm x 150) or a tapered piece of wood such as a chopstick.

117 Remove the two bolts and washer which secure the auxiliary shaft retaining plate. Remove the plate and lift out the shaft (photos).

118 Remove the old oil seal from the carrier. Clean the seal recess and fit a new seal, lips inwards.

PART C: EXAMINATION AND RENOVATION

Examination and renovation - general

1 Refer to Chapter 1, Section 24.

Oil pump - examination and renovation

2 Refer to Chapter 1, Section 25. Note the different construction and location of the pressure relief valve on this pump (Fig. 12.8). Note also that as well as gear-to-body clearance, the gear endfloat must be measured (Fig. 12.9). Desired values are given in the Specifications.

Crankshaft and main bearings - examination and renovation

3 Refer to Chapter 1, Section 26. The thrust washers on this engine are fitted not to the centre bearing but to No 2.

Cylinder bores and crankcase - examination and renovation

4 The cylinder bores on this engine are formed directly in the block, as opposed to the wet liners used on the smaller engines. They must be examined for taper, ovality, scoring and scratches.

5 Examine the tops of the bores. A wear ridge will be found marking the top limit of piston

Fig. 12.8 Exploded view of the oil pump
(Sec 6C)

Fig. 12.9 Measuring the oil pump gear
endfloat (B) (Sec 6C)

6B.117A Removing the auxiliary shaft
retaining plate . . .

6B.117B . . . and the auxiliary shaft itself

12

6C.13 Marks on piston crown show fitting direction and grade

travel. The size of this ridge will give a good idea of the extent of wear. With very worn bores a high rate of oil consumption will have been experienced, accompanied by blue smoke from the exhaust.

6 For an accurate assessment of bore wear an inside dial gauge will be needed. Use this to measure the bore diameter just below the wear ridge, and again at the bottom of the bore, which is not subject to wear. If the difference between the two measurements is greater than 0.15 mm (0.006 in), this would normally be considered grounds for a rebore and new pistons.

7 Special oil control rings and pistons can be obtained if it is felt that the expense of a rebore is unjustified, but it must be said that the improvement effected by such products is sometimes short-lived.

8 If new rings or pistons are being fitted to old bores, it is essential to roughen the bore walls slightly with fine abrasive paper or a "glaze buster" hone in an electric drill. The aim is to produce a cross-hatch pattern (not vertical).

9 The wear ridge at the top of the bore should be removed using a tool sold for the purpose, or alternatively the top piston rings may be of stepped construction ("ridge dodger" pattern). If plain rings are used and the ridge is not removed, there is a risk of the top ring hitting the ridge and breaking.

10 If a rebore is carried out, it is normal for the engineering works concerned to supply the oversize pistons required.

11 Thoroughly examine the crankcase for cracks and other damage. Probe all oilways and waterways with a piece of wire to make sure they are unobstructed.

Pistons and connecting rods - examination and renovation

12 Refer to Chapter 1, Section 28, paragraphs 1 to 6.

13 The pistons fitted in production are individually matched to their bores. If renewing a single piston, therefore, ensure that the replacement carries the same grade markings on the crown as the piston being replaced (photo).

Camshaft and tappets - examination and renovation 🔧🔧🔧

14 Examine the camshaft bearing surfaces and cam lobes for wear ridges, pitting or scoring. Renew the camshaft if evident.

15 Renew the oil seals at the ends of the camshaft as a matter of course. On some models the distributor rotor arm is glued to the end of the camshaft and will be broken during removal, while on other models it can be removed without damage. Lubricate the lips of the new seals before fitting them, and store the camshaft so that its weight is not resting on the seals.

16 Examine the camshaft bearing surfaces in the cylinder head and bearing caps. Deep scoring or other damage means that the cylinder head must be renewed.

17 Inspect the tappet buckets and shims for scoring, pitting and wear ridges. Renew as necessary. Some scuffing and discoloration of the tappets is acceptable provided they are not actually scored.

Auxiliary shaft and bearings - examination and renovation 🔧🔧🔧

18 Examine the auxiliary shaft and the oil pump driveshaft for pitting, scoring or wear ridges on the bearing surfaces, and for chipping or wear of the gear teeth. Renew as necessary.

19 Examine the auxiliary shaft bearings in the cylinder block for evidence of wear. Renewal is not a DIY job and should be carried out by a Renault dealer or other specialist.

20 Renew the auxiliary shaft oil seal as a matter of course.

Camshaft drivebelt, sprockets and idlers - examination and renovation 🔧🔧🔧

21 Examine the belt carefully for signs of cracking, fraying or general wear, particularly at the roots of the teeth. The belt should be renewed as a matter of course at the time of major overhaul. A belt which has been contaminated with oil or grease must also be renewed.

22 Examine the sprockets for cracks, chips

or burrs. They are quite fragile, and will crack or break if treated roughly. Small burrs must be removed with a fine file or an oil stone if they are in an area which will contact the belt. Cracks or chips mean that the sprockets must be renewed.

23 Spin the tensioner and idler rollers and check for roughness or shake. Renew them if necessary.

Flywheel - examination and renovation

24 Refer to Chapter 1, Section 31.

Cylinder head and pistons - decarbonising, valve grinding and renovation

25 Refer to Chapter 1, Section 32, paragraphs 1 to 10. Note however that resurfacing of this cylinder head is not permitted. If distortion exceeds the specified limit, the head must be renewed.

26 Examine the valve springs. Measure their free height and compare it with that specified. Renew the springs if they are distorted or not of the correct height, or as a matter of course if they have been in service for a high mileage.

27 Renew the valve stem oil seals as a matter of course.

PART D: REASSEMBLY AND REFITTING

Engine reassembly - general

1 Refer to Chapter 1, Section 33.

Auxiliary shaft - refitting 🔧🔧🔧

2 Lubricate the shaft with clean engine oil and slide it into position. Fit the retaining plate, curved edge away from the crankshaft, and secure it with the two bolts.

3 Lubricate the oil pump drivegear and refit it. Refit the cover plate, using a new O-ring, and secure it.

4 Lubricate the lips of the oil seal. Place a new gasket on the dowels on the cylinder block and refit the oil seal carrier, being careful not to damage the seal lips (photos). Fit and tighten the four bolts. (If no gasket was found during dismantling, seal the joint with CAF 4/60 THIXO sealant or equivalent.)

6D.4A Auxiliary shaft gasket positioned on the dowels

6D.4B Auxiliary shaft oil seal carrier

6D.11 Plain main bearing shells go in the caps

6D.12 Fit the thrust washers to No 2 main bearing. Note that the oil grooves face outwards

6D.15 Fitting a main bearing cap

5 Refit the camshaft drivebelt backplate. Apply a little sealant to the two bolts nearest the crankshaft front oil seal, as they protrude into the crankcase.

6 Refit the Woodruff key (if removed) and the sprocket. Fit the bolt and washer, restrain the sprocket and tighten the bolt to the specified torque.

7 Refit the camshaft drivebelt.

Crankshaft and main bearings - refitting

8 Refit the cooling oil jets if they were removed, noting their correct positioning (see detail in Fig.12.4).

9 Before refitting the crankshaft it is necessary to determine the thickness of No 1 bearing cap side seals. Place the cap in position without any seals and secure it with the two bolts. Insert twist drills or other rods of known diameter into the side seal grooves to establish the size of the groove. If the diameter of the largest rod which will fit is less than or equal to 5 mm (0.197 in), a side seal 5.1 mm (0.201 in) thick is needed. If the groove is larger than 5 mm, a side seal 5.3 mm (0.209 in) thick is needed. Remove the cap, obtain the necessary seals and proceed as follows.

10 Clean the backs of the bearing shells and their recesses in the crankcase and bearing caps. Clean any protective coating off new shells using white spirit or paraffin.

11 If the old bearing shells are being re-used, refit them to their original positions. If using

new shells, fit the plain shells to the bearing caps (photo) and the shells with oil holes and grooves to the crankcase. Press the shells into their recesses, ensuring that the tag on each shell engages with the notch in the recess.

12 Using a little grease, stick the thrust washers to each side of No 2 main bearing in the crankcase. The thrust washer grooves must face outwards (photo).

13 Lubricate the lips of a new rear oil seal and fit it to the rear of the crankshaft, lips inwards. Be careful not to damage the seal lips.

14 Liberally lubricate the bearing shells in the cylinder block with clean engine oil. Lower the crankshaft into position and inject clean oil into the oilways.

15 Fit the bearing caps, with the exception of No 1, to their previously noted positions, making sure they are the right way round (photo). Insert the bearing cap bolts and tighten them hand-tight.

16 Using a dial gauge or feeler blades, check the crankshaft endfloat while levering it back and forth (photos). Endfloat limits are given in the Specifications. If the endfloat is incorrect, the crankshaft and thrust washers must be removed and thrust washers of a different thickness obtained.

17 Fit the selected side seals to No 1 main bearing cap. The grooves in the seals must face outward (photo). Position the seals so that approximately 0.2 mm (0.008 in) protrudes from the cap at the crankcase mating face.

18 Apply a little sealant (CAF 4/60 THIXO

or equivalent) to the crankcase mating area of the cap. Lubricate the side seals.

19 Place the retaining bolts through the holes in the cap. Lower the cap into position, making sure that the bearing shell and the side seals are not displaced, and start the bolts two or three turns into their threads. These will now serve as guide studs.

20 Push the cap firmly into place. When it is nearly home, check that the side seals are still protruding, then push it fully home and tighten the bolts hand-tight.

21 If the rear oil seal is proud of the cap, drive it in flush or recess it slightly (see Chapter 1, Section 21).

22 Tighten the main bearing cap bolts to the specified torque. Check that the crankshaft is free to turn.

23 Trim off the ends of No 1 cap side seals flush with the cylinder block face (photo).

6D.16A Checking the crankshaft endfloat using a dial gauge

6D.16B Checking crankshaft endfloat using feeler blades

6D.17 Side seal fitted to No 1 bearing cap

6D.23 Trim the seals flush with the block

12

6D.30 Fitting a piston

6D.31A Fit the big-end bearing cap . . .

6D.31B . . . and tighten the retaining bolts

24 Refit the remaining components in the reverse order to removal.

Flywheel - refitting

25 Clean the flywheel and crankshaft mating areas.
26 Fit the flywheel to the crankshaft. It will only fit in one position, as the bolt hole positions are not symmetrical.
27 Apply thread-locking compound to the new bolts. Fit the bolts, jam the ring gear and tighten the bolts to the specified torque.

Pistons, connecting rods and big-end bearings - refitting

28 Clean the backs of the bearing shells and the recesses in the rods and caps. Dirt here will cause tight spots and perhaps early failure. If new shells are being fitted, clean off any protective coating using white spirit or paraffin.
29 Press the shells into their correct positions in the rods and caps. Oil them liberally.
30 Oil No 1 piston and its bore. Fit a ring compressor to the piston. Make sure that the piston is the right way round (arrow or "V" mark on crown facing the flywheel end) and that No 1 crankpin is at its lowest point. Insert the piston into the bore, tapping it out of the ring compressor with a hammer handle and guiding the connecting rod onto the crankpin (photo).

31 Fit the big-end cap, making sure it is the right way round. Insert the bolts and tighten them to the specified torque (photos).
32 Check that the crankshaft turns freely, then repeat the procedure on the remaining pistons.
33 Refit the cylinder head, the oil level sensor, the oil pump and the sump, as detailed elsewhere in this Section.

Oil pump - refitting

34 Lubricate the pump with clean engine oil if it is dry.
35 Engage the pump on the driveshaft and fit it to the crankcase. Secure it with the four bolts, tightened to the specified torque.
36 Refit the sump, as detailed below.

Sump - refitting

37 Apply a bead of jointing sealant (CAF 4/60 THIXO or equivalent) to the sump mating face.
38 Offer the sump to the engine and secure it with the bolts. Tighten the bolts in diagonal sequence to the specified torque.
39 Refit the cover plate and bracing bar, and any undertrays or splash guards which were removed.
40 Make sure the drain plug is tight, then lower the vehicle and refill the engine with oil.

Cylinder head - reassembly

41 Using a socket or box spanner, fit new oil seals to the valve guides (photos).
42 Refit the valves, springs etc. as described

in Chapter 1, Section 41, paragraphs 1 to 4.
43 Refit the thermostat, the tappets and camshaft, the temperature gauge sender (use some sealant on the threads), the fuel pump, the manifolds and the carburettor (using new gaskets).

Cylinder head - refitting

44 Check that the threads of the cylinder head bolts are clean. Mop any oil out of the bolt holes.
45 Check that No 1 piston is at TDC, and that the timing mark on the camshaft sprocket is aligned with the mark on the backplate.
46 Fit a new cylinder head gasket to the block, locating it over the dowels. Make sure it is the right way up.
47 Lower the cylinder head onto the block, engaging it over the dowels.
48 Lightly oil the cylinder head bolts, both on their threads and under their heads. Insert the bolts and tighten them finger-tight.
49 Following the sequence in Fig. 12.10, tighten the bolts to the torque specified for Stage 1. Repeat the sequence and tighten to the torque specified for Stage 2.
50 Wait three minutes, then progressively slacken all the bolts in the reverse of the tightening sequence. This is Stage 3.
51 Again following the tightening sequence, tighten the bolts to the torque specified for Stage 4.
52 Final tightening is carried out by turning each bolt through the angle specified for

6D.41A Using a socket or tube . . .

6D.41B . . . fit the valve stem oil seals to the guides (arrowed)

Fig. 12.10 Cylinder head bolt tightening sequence (Sec 6D)

Stage 5. Measure the angle using a commercially available gauge (photo), or make up a cardboard template cut to the angle required.

53 Reattach the camshaft drivebelt backplate to the cylinder head.

54 Refit the camshaft drivebelt, then check the valve clearances.

55 Refit the remaining components in the reverse order to removal, using a new camshaft cover gasket if necessary.

Camshaft and tappets - refitting

56 Oil the tappets and fit them to the bores from which they were removed. Fit the correct shim, numbered side downwards, to each tappet.

57 Oil the camshaft bearings. Place the camshaft with its oil seals onto the cylinder head. The oil seals must be positioned so that they are flush with the cylinder head faces.

58 Refit the camshaft bearing caps to their original locations, applying a little sealant to the end caps where they meet the cylinder head.

59 Apply sealant to the threads of the bearing cap bolts. Fit the bolts and tighten them progressively to the specified torque.

60 Refit the sprocket backing plate.

61 Insert the Woodruff key if it was removed. Refit the camshaft sprocket and its bolt. Restrain the sprocket and tighten the bolt to the specified torque.

62 Refit the camshaft drivebelt and check the valve clearances as described in this Section.

63 Refit the remaining components in the reverse order to removal, using a new camshaft cover gasket if necessary.

Camshaft drivebelt - refitting

64 Check that the timing mark on the flywheel is aligned with the TDC (O) line on the gearbox, and that the mark on the camshaft sprocket is aligned with the mark on the backplate.

65 Fit the belt over the sprockets and rollers. If the old belt is being refitted, observe the alignment marks made during dismantling. If a new belt is being fitted, observe the arrow showing the running direction, and the two lines on the belt which align with the mark on the camshaft sprocket and the notch in the crankshaft sprocket backplate (Fig. 12.11). The auxiliary shaft sprocket has no timing mark.

66 Slacken the tensioner nut. Move the tensioner to give roughly the correct belt tension and nip up the nut.

67 Temporarily refit the crankshaft pulley and its bolt. Turn the crankshaft through two full turns in the normal direction of rotation and check that the timing marks are still aligned. If not, the belt must be removed and the procedure recommenced.

68 Slacken the tensioner nut again. Move the tensioner to set the belt tension accurately and retighten the nut to the specified torque. Belt tension is correct when firm finger pressure, applied midway between the

6D.52 Tightening the cylinder head bolts using an angle gauge

auxiliary shaft sprocket and the tensioner roller, will deflect the belt by 7.5 mm (0.3 in). There is a removable section in the belt cover through which the check may be made.

69 Remove the crankshaft pulley again. Refit and secure the front section of the belt cover, then refit the pulley and tighten its bolt to the specified torque. An assistant will have to jam the ring gear teeth while this is done.

70 Refit and tension the alternator/water pump drivebelt.

71 Refit the splash guard and the roadwheel. Remember to carry out final tightening of the wheel bolts after lowering the vehicle.

72 Reconnect the battery.

Engine - attachment to gearbox

73 Refit and centralise the clutch (Chapter 5, Section 2).

74 Put a smear of molybdenum grease or copper-based anti-seize compound on the gearbox input shaft splines.

75 Make sure the locating dowels are in position. Have an assistant steady the engine and offer the gearbox to it, engaging the input shaft with the clutch. Turn the crankshaft slightly if necessary to enable the splines to mate. Do not allow the weight of the gearbox to hang on the input shaft.

76 Fit and tighten the engine-to-gearbox bolts.

77 Refit the TDC sensor and bracket, the flywheel cover plate and bracing bar, and the starter motor with its wiring and heat shield.

Engine - refitting with gearbox

78 Engine and gearbox refitting is a reversal of the removal procedure described earlier in this Section. Remember to refill the engine and gearbox with oil, and the cooling system with coolant. On models with power steering, refill and bleed the system as described in Section 18.

Engine - adjustments after major overhaul

79 Refer to Chapter 1, Section 46, but ignore paragraph 4 - there is no need to retighten the cylinder head bolts on this engine.

80 After the running-in period it is advisable to change the engine oil and filter, and to check the valve clearances if new components have been fitted in this area.

Fig. 12.11 Camshaft drivebelt run. Details show alignment of lines on belt with camshaft and crankshaft sprocket backplate marks (Sec 6D)

1 Crankshaft pulley
2 Auxiliary shaft sprocket
3 Camshaft sprocket
A Arrows showing belt running direction

7 Cooling system

Description - later Turbo models

1 The arrangement shown in Chapter 2 (Fig.2.1) was modified to that shown in Fig. 12.12. In the new arrangement the return from the expansion tank goes to the water pump instead of to the radiator.

2 Further modifications were made with the introduction of the water-cooled turbocharger. These are shown in Figs.12.13 and 12.14.

Description - 1721 cc models

3 The layout of the cooling system components is shown in Fig.12.15.

Draining and refilling - 1721 cc models

4 The procedures are similar to those described in Chapter 2, Sections 3 and 5, but note the following points:
a) The cylinder block drain plug is on the rear face of the engine, next to the oil pressure switch (photo)
b) There are no bleed screws in this system

12

Fig. 12.12 Cooling system schematic - later Turbo models with air-cooled turbocharger (Sec 7)

1 Engine	5 Temperature switch	11 Carburettor base
2 Radiator	7 Water pump	heater
3 Expansion tank	8 Manifold	G Restrictor (3 mm)
4 Heater matrix	10 Bleed screws	T Thermostat

Fig. 12.13 Cooling system schematic - early arrangement for Turbo models with water-cooled turbocharger (13) (Sec 7)

For key see Fig. 12.12

Fig. 12.14 Cooling system schematic - later arrangement for Turbo-models with water-cooled turbocharger (13) (Sec 7)

V Degassing unit   See also key to Fig. 12.12

Fig. 12.15 Cooling system schematic - 1721 cc models (Sec 7)

1 Engine	6 Oil cooler	T Thermostat
2 Radiator	8 Restrictor (8 mm)	For symbols see key
3 Expansion tank	9 Restrictor (3 mm)	to Fig. 12.12
4 Heater matrix		

7.4 Coolant drain plug (arrowed) next to oil pressure switch on 1721 cc engine

Water pump (1721 cc models) - removal and refitting

5 Disconnect the battery negative lead.
6 Drain the cooling system (Chapter 2, Section 3).
7 Remove the alternator/water pump drivebelt as described later in this Section.
8 Restrain the pulley with a strap wrench. Undo the three bolts and remove the pulley (photo).
9 Remove the nine bolts which secure the pump to the block (Fig. 12.16). Remove the pump - if it is stuck, tap it with a wooden or plastic mallet.
10 Remove the remains of the pump gasket from the mating faces.
11 Refit by reversing the removal operations, using a new gasket (photo). The gasket must be fitted dry. Adjust the drivebelt tension on completion.

Thermostat (1721 cc models) - removal and refitting

12 The thermostat is located in a housing on the left-hand end of the cylinder head.
13 Remove the carburettor cooling duct (if fitted).
14 Drain approximately 1 litre (nearly 2 pints) of coolant - see Chapter 2, Section 3.
15 Release the hose clip and pull the radiator top hose off the thermostat housing.
16 Remove the three bolts, withdraw the thermostat housing, and remove the thermostat and sealing ring (photo).

7.11 Refitting the water pump

7.8 Water pump and pulley - 1721 cc engine

17 Refit by reversing the removal operations, using a new sealing ring.

Oil cooler (1721 cc models) - removal and refitting

18 The oil cooler is located between the oil filter and the cylinder block. Commence removal by removing the oil filter.
19 Drain the cooling system, or depressurise it by removing the expansion tank cap, and clamp the hoses leading to and from the cooler.
20 Disconnect the hoses from the oil cooler.
21 Undo the central nut and remove the oil cooler.
22 Refit by reversing the removal operations, using new seals and gaskets and a new oil filter.

Drivebelt (later models) - renewal and adjustment

23 The procedure given in Chapter 2, Section 12, still holds good, but account must be taken of the following points.
24 On 1397 cc models with power steering there are two drivebelts (Fig. 12.17). The outer belt drives the steering pump and the inner belt drives the alternator and the water pump.
25 Adjustment of belt tension on 1721 cc models is by means of an adjuster screw on the alternator slide bracket. The belt routing on such models with power steering is as shown (photo). It will be noted that the water pump is driven by the back of the belt, and that an idler roller is fitted.

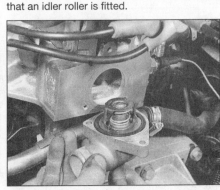

7.16 Removing the thermostat - 1721 cc engine

Fig. 12.16 Water pump securing bolts (arrowed) on 1721 cc model (Sec 7)

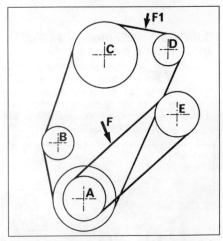

Fig. 12.17 Drivebelt runs - 1397 cc models with power steering (Sec 7)

A Crankshaft pulley
B Tensioner roller
C Water pump pulley
D Alternator pulley
E Power steering pump pulley
F Tension checking point
F1 Tension checking point

7.25 Drivebelt run - 1721 cc engine with power steering. Tensioner screw is arrowed

12

8.7 Three nuts and one screw which secure the air cleaner lid

8.10 Fitting a new air cleaner element

8.12 Disconnecting the cold air trunking from its intake

8 Fuel and exhaust system - non-Turbo carburettor models

Cold start difficulties - 956 cc and 1108 cc engines

1 Check that, when the choke control lever is fully "on", the end of the slot in the choke operating flap cam is against the eccentric spindle (Fig. 12.18). If this is not the case, check the choke cable operation and adjustment (Chapter 3, Section 11).

Fig. 12.18 Carburettor correctly set for cold start - no clearance between cam (1) and spindle (2) (Sec 8)

2 If difficulty is still experienced on the 1108 cc engine, especially after it has been stopped for a long period, this may be due to fuel evaporating from the float chamber. The remedy, if it is felt worthwhile, is to fit an electrically-operated idle circuit cut-off solenoid, and to make sure that the defuming valve is fully closed at idle. The solenoid may be purchased from a Renault dealer.

Fuel smells in passenger compartment - Weber 32 DRT and Solex 28/34 Z10 carburettors

3 Under some conditions, fuel smells may be noticed in the passenger compartment on models fitted with the above carburettors. The smell is caused by vapour escaping from the carburettor venting system, and may be remedied as follows.

4 On the Weber 32 DRT carburettor, fit tubing between the float chamber vent and the air filter housing (Fig 12.19).

5 On the Solex carburettor, fit tubing between the float chamber vent and the left-hand wheel arch, drilling a hole in the blanking cover to accept the tubing (Fig. 12.20). The tubing must run smoothly downwards, with no kinks or bends.

6 Early versions of the Solex carburettor (before October 1987) do not have a suitable external vent, in which case the carburettor must be renewed. Consult a Renault dealer.

Air cleaner element (1721 cc engine) - renewal

7 Remove the screw and the three nuts from the air cleaner lid (photo).

8 Release the spring clips round the edge of the lid and remove the lid.

9 Remove the old element. Clean inside the housing and lid, being careful not to sweep debris into the carburettor.

10 Fit the new element (photo), then refit and secure the lid.

Air cleaner (1721 cc engine) - removal and refitting

11 Remove the three nuts from the air cleaner lid.

12 Release the hot and cold air pick-up trunking from the air intakes (photo).

13 Lift the air cleaner body. Disconnect the breather hose, then remove the air cleaner and trunking (photos).

14 Refit by reversing the removal operations.

Fuel pump (1721 cc engine) - removal and refitting

15 The procedure is described in Chapter 3, Section 5, but with the following differences:

Fig. 12.20 Carburettor venting hose - Solex Z10 carburettor (Sec 8)

Fig. 12.19 Carburettor venting - Weber 32 DRT (Sec 8)

A Float chamber vent   B Air cleaner housing   C Air cleaner element
D Angled connector   E Rubber tubing

8.13A Disconnect the breather hose . . .

8.13B . . . and remove the air cleaner

8.16 Fuel vapour separator

a) *The fuel pump is mounted on the rear of the cylinder head, not on the block*
b) *The pump is secured by two nuts*
c) *There is no fuel return connection on the pump*

Fuel vapour separator (all models with Solex carburettor) - general

16 A fuel vapour separator (sometimes called an anti-percolation device) is fitted to all 1721 cc models, and may also be fitted to other engines equipped with a Solex carburettor (photo). It is placed between the fuel pump and the carburettor, and prevents problems arising from fuel vaporisation when the engine is hot. Fig. 12.21 shows the fuel vapour separator and its connections.

17 If a vapour separator is to be fitted to a model which did not originally have one, the carburettor needle valve must be changed from the 1.6 mm originally fitted to 1.3 mm.

Fig. 12.21 Fuel vapour separator and associated components (OHV engine shown) (Sec 8)

1 *Vapour separator*
2 *Fuel filter*
3 *Fuel pump*
4 *Blanking stub*
5 *Fuel hoses (to carburettor)*
6 *Fuel return hose*
7 *Engine lifting eye*
8 *Fuel hose (tank-to-pump)*
A *To carburettor*
B *To fuel tank*

Additionally, the fuel return connection on the fuel pump must be blanked off, since this function is now carried out by the vapour separator.

18 The three hose connections to the vapour separator are inlet (from fuel pump), outlet (to carburettor) and return (to tank). Identify the hoses if they have to be disconnected for any reason.

8.19A Solex Z10 carburettor

1 *Fast idle actuator (power steering)*
2 *Idle cut-off solenoid*
3 *Choke vacuum actuator*
4 *Heater*

8.19C Solex Z10 carburettor (continued)

1 *Fuel inlet strainer*
2 *Fuel inlet*
3 *Crankcase ventilation connection*

Solex carburettor (1721 cc engine) - description

19 The Solex carburettor fitted to the 1721 cc engine is a twin throat downdraught unit, with sequential operation of the throttle valves. It is very similar in operating principles to the Weber 32 DRT described in Chapter 3, Section 14 (photos).

8.19B Solex Z10 carburettor (continued)

1 *Idle jet*
2 *Idle speed adjusting screw*
3 *Accelerator pump*
4 *Enrichment device*
5 *Defuming valve*
6 *Float chamber vent*

8.19D Solex Z10 carburettor (continued)

1 *Idle mixture adjustment screw*
2 *Fast idle adjustment screw*
3 *Secondary throttle stop screw (do not touch)*

12

8.24 Carburettor cooling trunking

8.25A Carburettor temperature sensor

8.25B Line fuse for the carburettor cooling system

Fig. 12.22 Idle adjustment points - Solex 32/34 Z13 (Sec 8)

A Idle speed   B Idle mixture
C Fast idle actuator (power steering)

8.27A Adjusting the idle speed - Z10 carburettor

20 All versions of this carburettor have an idle cut-off solenoid valve which interrupts the idle mixture circuit when the ignition is switched off, so preventing running-on. If this valve is disconnected or defective, the engine will idle roughly or not at all.

21 The idle mixture circuit also incorporates an electrical heater to improve fuel vaporisation when cold. This system supersedes the coolant heating of the carburettor base found on other models.

22 Later versions of the carburettor (32/34 Z13) have the opening of the secondary throttle valve controlled by a vacuum diaphragm instead of mechanically.

Carburettor cooling system (1721 cc engine) - description

23 Depending on model and year, the following system may be fitted. Its purpose is to prevent fuel vaporisation occurring in the carburettor in the minutes following engine switch-off, if when running in very hot conditions.

24 A small additional shroud is fitted to the radiator cooling fan. Trunking is fitted to the shroud and discharges under the air cleaner, so blowing air over the carburettor when the fan is turning (photo).

25 A temperature sensor adjacent to the carburettor starts the fan when necessary. The electrical feed is taken directly from the alternator live terminal, a line fuse being fitted in the feed wire (photos).

26 As with the ordinary cooling function, the fan may start after the engine has stopped, even with the ignition switched off.

Idle speed and mixture adjustment - 1721 cc engine

27 Refer to Chapter 3, Section 15, for the procedure. The locations of the idle speed and mixture screws are shown in the accompanying photos for the 28/34 Z10 carburettor, and in Fig.12.22 for the 32/34 Z13 carburettor (photos).

Solex carburettor (1721 cc engine) - removal and refitting

28 Disconnect the battery negative lead.

29 Remove the air cleaner as described in this Section.

30 Disconnect the wiring from the carburettor heater and the idle cut-off solenoid (photo).

31 Unsnap the throttle link rod balljoint (photo).

32 Disconnect the choke cable (photos).

33 Slacken the hose clip and disconnect the fuel inlet hose (photo).

34 Identify and disconnect the vacuum hoses from the carburettor (photo).

35 Disconnect the crankcase ventilation hose from the base of the carburettor (photo).

36 Remove the four Allen screws from the

8.27B Adjusting the idle mixture - Z10 carburettor

8.30 Disconnecting the idle cut-off solenoid

8.31 Unclipping the throttle link

Fig. 12.23 Heater details - Solex 28/34 Z10 (Sec 8)

1 *Roll pin*
2 *Insulator*
3 *Terminal*
4 *Heater disc*
5 *Securing plate*
a *Tongue*
b *Roll pin slot*

top of the carburettor. Recover the washers from the bases of the screws (photos).

37 Lift off the carburettor and recover the gasket from the manifold (photo).

38 Refit by reversing the removal operations, using a new gasket.

Solex carburettor (1721 cc engine) - cleaning

Note: *The carburettor seen in the photographs is a Solex 28/34 Z10. The 32/34 Z13 fitted to later models is very similar, the main difference being that the secondary throttle valve is opened by a vacuum actuator instead of mechanically.*

39 With the carburettor removed from the engine, thoroughly clean it externally with paraffin or a degreasing solvent.

40 Unscrew and remove the fuel inlet strainer (photo).

41 Unscrew the idling jet from the carburettor cover (photo).

42 Remove the heater securing plate screw. Remove the plate and withdraw the roll pin with the insulator, the terminal and the heater disc (photos). Be careful with the heater disc, it is fragile.

8.32A Disconnecting the choke control inner cable . . .

8.32B . . . and unclipping the outer cable

8.33 Disconnecting the fuel inlet hose

8.34 Carburettor vacuum hoses

8.35 Disconnecting the crankcase ventilation hose

8.36A Four Allen screws (arrowed) which secure the carburettor

8.36B Recover the washers from the bases of the screws

8.37 Removing the carburettor

8.40 Removing the fuel inlet strainer

12

8.41 Removing the idling jet

8.42A Remove the screw and plate . . .

8.42B . . . and withdraw the heater assembly

8.43 Disconnecting the defuming valve link

8.44A Five screws (arrowed) which secure the cover

8.44B Removing the carburettor cover

8.45 Removing the float pivot pin

8.46 Removing the idle circuit filter

8.47 Removing the accelerator pump injector

8.48 Removing an air correction jet/emulsion tube assembly

8.49A Unscrewing a main jet

8.49B Removing a main jet from the well

8.54 Checking the float level

8.56 Fast idle adjustment screw

8.59 Fast idle actuator solenoid valve and vacuum reservoir

43 Prise the defuming valve link rod out of the plastic bush (photo).
44 Remove the five screws which secure the carburettor cover. Lift off the cover with the floats and the choke vacuum actuator attached (photos).
45 Remove the float pivot pin (photo). Remove the floats, the needle valve and the gasket.
46 Remove the idle circuit filter from the carburettor body (photo).
47 Pull the accelerator pump injector assembly from the body (photo).
48 Unscrew and remove the air correction jet emulsion tube assemblies (photo).
49 Remove the main jets from the bottom of the emulsion tube wells by unscrewing them (photos).
50 If a complete overhaul is being undertaken, remove the various diaphragm covers so that the diaphragms can be renewed.
51 Clean out any sediment from the float chamber, and blow through all passages with low-pressure compressed air.
52 Reassemble in the reverse order to dismantling, using new gaskets, O-rings etc. and carrying out the adjustments described in the following paragraphs (when appropriate).

Pay attention to the correct fitting of the heater components - if the insulator is misplaced, there is a risk of a short-circuit.

Solex carburettor (1721 cc engine) - overhaul adjustment

53 Refer to Chapter 3, Section 17, paragraphs 1 to 4.

Float level adjustment

54 With the carburettor cover reassembled (including the gasket), invert the cover and measure the distance from the gasket to the furthest point of the floats (photo). The correct value is given in the Specifications. Adjust if necessary by carefully bending the float arms.

Defuming valve adjustment

55 Invert the reassembled carburettor. Open the throttle until the defuming valve just closes. In this position, the throttle valve opening should correspond to the value given in the Specifications. Adjust if necessary at the point shown (Fig.12.24 or 12.25).

Initial throttle opening (fast idle)

56 With the carburettor still inverted, operate the choke linkage to close the choke flap. Measure the throttle valve opening, which should be as specified. Adjust if necessary by turning the screw which bears on the fast idle cam (photo).

Choke pneumatic part-opening adjustment

57 Operate the choke linkage to close the choke flap. Push the operating rod as far as it will go into the choke vacuum actuator. In this position measure the choke flap opening, which should be as specified. Adjust if necessary by means of the screw in the centre of the vacuum actuator.

Secondary throttle link adjustment (32/34 Z13 only)

58 The link rod between the throttle vacuum actuator and the secondary throttle lever should be adjusted so that there is a small amount of play (A in Fig.12.26) in both the fully closed and fully open positions.

Fast idle actuator (models with power steering) - description and adjustment

59 On models with power steering, a vacuum-operated actuator raises the idle speed if the steering is turned to full lock, so preventing stalling. The vacuum feed to the actuator is via a solenoid valve which is controlled by a pressure-operated switch in the high-pressure hydraulic pipe (photo).
60 Before commencing adjustment, the

Fig. 12.24 Defuming valve adjustment - Solex 28/34 Z10 (Sec 8)
A Gauge rod (measuring throttle valve gap)
B Adjustment screw

Fig. 12.25 Defuming valve adjustment - Solex 32/34 Z13 (Sec 8)
A Gauge rod
B Adjustment screw

Fig. 12.26 Throttle actuator link rod adjustment - Solex 32/34 Z13 (Sec 8)
A See text

engine must be at normal operating temperature and the idle speed and mixture must be correctly adjusted.

61 With the engine idling and the steering straight ahead, unplug the wiring connector from the pressure switch. Bridge the female terminals of the connector with a paper clip or a short length of stiff wire. Do not allow the bridge to touch earth (vehicle metal) (photo).

62 With the terminals bridged, idle speed should rise to the value given in the Specifications. Adjust if necessary by means of the adjusting screw on the fast idle actuator see Fig. 12.22 or (photo).

63 When adjustment is correct, stop the engine and remake the original electrical connections.

Fuel gauge sender unit - checking

64 With the sender unit removed as described in Chapter 3, Section 8, connect an ohmmeter across terminals 1 and 3. Check that the resistance varies in an approximately linear fashion between 7 ohms with the float in the highest (full) position and 280 ohms in the lowest (empty) position.

8.61 Bridging the pressure switch connector terminals with a paper clip

8.62 Adjusting the fast idle actuator

9 Fuel and exhaust systems - fuel injection models (C3J engine)

General information and precautions

1 This section deals with the fuel injection system and associated components fitted to the C3J model.

2 The fuel pump on all fuel injection models is electric; it is located inside the fuel tank. As with the carburettor models, fuel circulates continuously when the pump is operating, excess fuel being returned to the tank.

3 The exhaust system is conventional. On most models, it incorporates a catalytic converter, to reduce emissions of toxic gases.

4 The catalytic converter and other emission control components are described later.

⚠️ **Warning: Many of the procedures in this Section require the removal of fuel lines and connections, which may result in some fuel spillage (depressurise the fuel system before disconnecting any fuel lines or hoses). Before carrying out any operation on the fuel system, refer to the precautions given in "Safety first!" at the beginning of this manual, and follow them implicitly. Petrol is a highly-dangerous and volatile liquid, and the precautions necessary when handling it cannot be overstressed.**

5 Note that the components used in this single-point injection system may be sourced from a number of different manufacturers, including Bosch, Weber, GM and Renix.

6 The system can be considered as a halfway stage between a conventional fixed-jet carburettor and an electronically-controlled multi-point injection system. As with a carburettor, fuel metering and vaporisation take place in one unit (the throttle housing), and the fuel/air mixture is then distributed to the cylinders via the inlet manifold. As with any modern petrol injection system, fuel metering is controlled electronically by a ECU, which receives information from various sensors. The ECU also controls the idle speed, and manages the emission control and ignition systems.

7 The main advantage of single-point injection over a carburettor is that the injection system allows much more precise control over the air-fuel ratio (mixture) under all operating conditions. This control is necessary to keep exhaust emissions to a minimum, and for the correct operation and long life of the catalytic converter. Additional benefits from the driver's point of view are improved fuel economy under all operating conditions, and better driveability when cold.

8 The system is best understood if considered in two parts: the fuel supply and the control sub-systems.

Fuel supply

9 The fuel supply sub-system consists of an electric fuel pump immersed in the tank, a fuel filter, a fuel pressure regulator and a fuel injector. These last two items are located in the throttle housing.

10 Fuel passes from the pump through the filter to the throttle housing, where it enters the fuel pressure regulator. The pressure regulator maintains a constant fuel pressure at the injector, relative to the pressure in the throttle body upstream of the throttle plate. Excess fuel is returned to the tank. Fuel is therefore circulating all the time that the pump is running, which ensures a constant supply of cool fuel, and reduces problems with vapour-locks.

11 The fuel injector consists of a needle valve, which is opened by an electromagnet and closed by a spring. The electromagnet is controlled by the injection ECU. When the valve is open, fuel is sprayed from the injector onto the throttle plate. Because the relative fuel pressure is constant, the quantity of fuel injected varies directly according to the opening time.

12 The electrical feed to the fuel pump is via a relay controlled by the injection ECU. The pump is only energised when the engine is running, or when the starter motor is operating. Some procedures in this Chapter require the pump to be running when the engine is stopped. This is achieved by bridging two terminals in the relay socket (see paragraph 27).

Control

13 The injection control sub-system consists of the injection ECU and its associated sensors and actuators. As mentioned previously, the ECU also controls the emission control and ignition systems; there is some overlap between these functions.

14 The ECU is located at the front right-hand corner of the engine compartment. It receives signals from sensors which monitor the following functions:

Coolant temperature.
Inlet manifold pressure (MAP sensor).
Engine speed (flywheel sensor).
Throttle position/full-load/no-load (throttle switch/sensor).
Inlet air temperature.
Exhaust gas oxygen content (oxygen sensor).

15 The oxygen sensor is properly part of the emission control system, and further details are given in Sections 11. The engine speed/position sensor is covered in Section 12.

16 Outputs from the ECU control the operation of the following components:

Fuel pump (via the fuel pump relay).
Fuel injector.
Idle speed control motor.
Evaporative emission control solenoid valve.
Ignition power module.

17 The ECU processes the information from the various sensors, to determine the quantity of fuel which must be injected to suit operating conditions at any given moment. For this purpose, the volume of inlet air is calculated from the engine speed and throttle position signals, with a correction being made for inlet air temperature. Extra enrichment is provided at full-load and during warm-up.

9.26 Fuel system pressure check

A Fuel feed pipe   B Fuel return pipe

9.27 Fuel pump relay location (arrowed) in auxiliary fusebox

9.37 Disconnecting the hot-air hose from the air cleaner inlet

Compensation is also made for the effect of changes in battery voltage.

18 In the no-load condition (throttle in idle position), the ECU cuts off injection at engine speeds above idle. At idle, the engine speed is controlled by the ECU sending signals to the idle speed control motor incorporated in the throttle housing. The motor opens or closes the throttle butterfly, to maintain a constant idle speed regardless of engine temperature or additional loads (alternator, power steering pump, etc.). There is no need for periodic adjustment of idle speed or mixture, even to compensate for long-term factors such as engine wear. The system is also self-correcting for changes in altitude.

19 When stopping the engine, the idle speed control motor first closes the throttle completely, then opens it again in readiness for the next start. This means that, with the engine stopped, there will be more slack in the accelerator cable than with the engine idling.

Unleaded petrol - general information

20 Refer to Specifications for details of unleaded petrol usage. Note that this model must be operated on unleaded petrol at all times; leaded petrol *must not* be used, as it will damage the catalytic converter.

21 Note that there is no requirement to adjust the ignition timing when operating the engine on different types of petrol.

Fault finding

Note: *Refer to the precautions given at the biginning of this Section, before attempting to carry out any fault diagnosis.*

22 In the event of a fault developing, the amount of diagnostic work possible for the home mechanic is limited. Renault technicians use dedicated test equipment, which can find a fault quickly and precisely. Initial fault-finding checks should concentrate on external factors such as a blocked fuel filter, loose or corroded electrical connections, and loose or

damaged vacuum hoses. Remember also that incorrect adjustment of the accelerator cable can affect operation of the fuel injection system, especially at idle.

23 If it appears that the fault is in one of the sensors or in the ECU, it will probably be more satisfactory to consult a Renault dealer or other specialist, rather than to embark on a hit-and-miss programme of component renewal.

Fuel system pressure - check

Note: *Refer to the warning at the beginning of this Section before starting work.*

24 Depressurise the fuel system, remembering to refit the fuel pump fuse.

25 Remove the air cleaner or air duct, as applicable, from the top of the throttle housing.

26 Connect a pressure gauge (range 0 to 3 bars) into the fuel feed pipe where it enters the throttle housing, using a T-piece (see illustration).

27 Make the fuel pump run by bridging terminals 3 and 5 of the fuel pump relay (located in the ECU case or in the auxiliary fusebox in the engine compartment - see Chapter 11) (see illustration). The fuel pump relay can be distinguished by the thick leads connected to terminals 3 (red or red/white lead) and 5 (brown or white lead).

28 Note the pressure shown on the gauge. It should correspond to the regulated fuel pressure given in the Specifications.

29 Momentarily pinch the fuel return pipe. Note the pressure registered on the gauge: this must correspond to the unregulated pressure given in the Specifications.

30 If the pressure readings are low, check the pump delivery to see whether the fault is in the pump or the pressure regulator. Also check the fuel filter(s). If the readings are high, the fault can only be in the pressure regulator.

31 Remove the bridge from the fuel pump relay. Depressurise the fuel system and disconnect the pressure gauge, then remake the original connections.

Depressurising the system

Note: *Refer to the warning at the beginning of this Section before proceeding.*

32 Fuel lines may contain fuel under pressure, even though the engine is not running. Depressurisation of the fuel system is therefore necessary before undertaking any work which will involve opening a fuel line or union, otherwise fuel under pressure could spray out onto hot engine components.

33 Remove the fuel pump fuse, which is the 30 amp fuse located in the under-bonnet (auxiliary) fusebox.

34 Try to start the engine. It may run briefly and die, or it may not start at all. Operate the starter motor a couple more times, to ensure that all fuel pressure has been relieved.

35 Switch off the ignition, and refit the fuel pump fuse.

Air cleaner housing assembly - removal and refitting

36 Remove the air cleaner filter element as described in Chapter 1.

37 Disconnect the air inlet hose and hot-air hose from the air cleaner inlet (photo). Where applicable, also disconnect the breather hose.

38 Unscrew and remove the mounting bolt and nuts, noting the arrangement of the rubber spacers, washers and sleeves (photos).

9.38A Remove the right hand mounting bolt (arrowed) . . .

9.38B . . . front mounting nut (arrowed) . . .

9.38C . . . and top mounting nuts (arrowed)

9.44 Accelerator cable end securing
clip (1) and adjustment ferrule (2)

39 Withdraw the air cleaner body from the engine.
40 Refitting is a reversal of removal.

Accelerator cable - removal, refitting and adjustment

41 The procedure is as described for carburettor models in Chapter 3, noting the following points.
42 Ignore any references to a carburettor.
43 On single-point fuel injection models, to improve access where necessary, remove the air cleaner assembly or the air duct, as applicable, from the top of the throttle housing.
44 The end of the cable may be secured to the throttle sector arm by a clip. It may also be necessary to remove the locknut before sliding the adjustment ferrule from its bracket (photo).
45 The bracket retaining the adjustment ferrule may be attached to the throttle housing or manifold.
46 Note that there will be more free-play in the cable with the engine stopped, than when the engine is idling. This is because when the engine stops, the idle speed control motor closes the throttle, then partially opens it ready for the next start. For this reason, it is wise to re-check the cable free-play with the engine idling.

Fuel pump and sender unit - testing, removal and refitting

Note: *Refer to the warning at the beginning of this Section before starting work.*

Testing the pump

47 Carry out a pressure check as described in paragrahs 24 to 31.
48 Disconnect the fuel return pipe from the throttle housing or injector rail, as applicable. Connect a length of flexible hose to the return union, and place the other end of the hose in a measuring jar (capacity 2 litres approx.).
49 Make the fuel pump run by bridging terminals 3 and 5 of the fuel pump relay as described in paragraph 27.
50 Note the quantity of fuel delivered in exactly one minute (single-point system) or

30 seconds (multi-point system). Correct values are given in the Specifications.
51 Remove the bridge from the fuel pump relay. Return the pumped fuel to the tank, or put it in a suitable sealed container.
52 If delivery is low, check that full battery voltage is available at the pump relay contacts, and at the pump itself. (Refer to the pump removal procedure for details of the pump wiring connector location). A 1 volt drop in supply voltage will result in a drop of approximately 10% in delivery.
53 If the supply voltage is correct, but delivery is still low, there are two possible reasons. Either there is a blockage somewhere in the supply line (including the main fuel filter and the pump pick-up filter), or the pump is defective. If the pump is defective, it must be renewed.
54 On completion, remake the original fuel pipe connections.

Fuel pump and sender unit renewal

Note: *The fuel pump is an integral unit with fuel gauge sender.*

55 Depressurise the fuel system as described in earlier in this Section.
56 Proceed as described in Chapter 3 for the fuel gauge sender unit on carburettor models. Note the wiring connections, before disconnecting, for correct replacement.
57 When refitting, ensure that the fuel hoses wires are correctly reconnected.

Fuel injection system - component testing

58 Renault dealers use dedicated test equipment (test box XR25) which plugs into the diagnostic socket provided on the main fuse/relay box in the facia. This equipment provides a rapid and comprehensive diagnosis of the complete system. It is the only means of checking the operation of the ECU.
59 Limited testing of individual components is still possible. The information in the following paragraphs is given as a guide to the owner who wishes to carry out preliminary checks if a fault develops. However, it may still be necessary to enlist the help of a Renault dealer or other specialist for positive diagnosis of a fault.

60 Where the use of an electrical multi-meter is called for, this should be a modern digital type, with an internal resistance of at least 10 Megohms. *Do not* use analogue (moving pointer) meters, which may have an unacceptably-low internal resistance.
61 No meaningful testing is possible on the idle speed control motor, the throttle sensor, the manifold pressure (MAP) sensor, the road speed sensor (when fitted), or the ECU itself.
62 Before testing individual components, make sure that all system electrical connections are clean and secure, and that all fuel, air and vacuum hoses are in good condition. Also remember that problems with idle speed regulation may simply be due to incorrect accelerator cable adjustment.
63 Where a component is found to be defective, it must be renewed as described in the following paragraphs.

Inlet air temperature sensor

64 The sensor is an integral with fuel injector.
65 Remove the air cleaner or the air duct from the top of the throttle housing.
66 Disconnect the sensor wiring plug (photo and illustration).
67 Use an ohmmeter across the sensor terminals to measure the resistance of the sensor. Typical values which can be expected are given in the Specifications.
68 Use a hairdryer or a fan heater to raise the temperature of the sensor, and check that the resistance of the sensor falls as it warms up.

9.66A Inlet air temperature sensor wiring
plug (arrowed) - Weber type

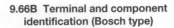

9.66B Terminal and component identification (Bosch type)

1 *Inlet air temperature sensor*
2 *Fuel pressure regulator*
3 *Fuel return connection*
4 *Fuel feed connection*
5 *Idle speed control motor*
6 *Fuel injector*
A *Inlet air temperature sensor/fuel injector wiring connector*
A1 *Inlet air temperature sensor*
A2 *Injector +*
A3 *Injector -*
A4 *Inlet air temperature sensor*
B *Idle speed motor/idle switch connector*
B1 *Motor feed*
B2 *Motor feed*
B3 *Idle switch*
B4 *Idle switch*

9.84 Top view of the throttle housing

Coolant temperature sensor

69 This sensor is located on the left hand end of the cylinder head.

70 Disconnect the multi-plug from the sensor unit.

71 Using an ohmmeter, measure the resistance of the sensor, and compare it with the typical values given in the Specifications. If the value obtained is greatly different from that specified, the sensor is probably defective.

Fuel injector

72 Remove the air cleaner, or air duct, as appropriate, from the top of the throttle body.

73 The resistance of the injector winding can be checked at the injector wiring connector, using an ohmmeter between the appropriate terminals.

74 Typical values for the resistance are given in the Specifications. If the resistance is significantly different from that specified, remove the plug from the top of the sensor, and repeat the measurement at the terminals of the injector itself.

75 If the resistance is now correct, there was a fault in the wiring between the wiring connector and the injector. If the resistance is still incorrect, the injector is defective.

76 If it is suspected that dirt or gum in the injector is impairing performance, the use of a

proprietary cleaning additive in the fuel tank may be effective.

Fuel pressure regulator

77 Testing of the fuel pressure regulator is included in the fuel pressure check, described earlier.

Fuel injection system components - removal and refitting

Note: *Special test equipment may be required for initial setting-up after renewal of some components described in this Section. Read through the procedures carefully before starting work, to see what is involved. Also refer to the warning note at the beginning of this Section. A number of different types of throttle housing may be fitted, including Bosch, Weber, and GM. Although the components differ in detail, the general procedures given below can be used for all types.*

Air duct

78 An air duct is fitted to the top of the throttle housing, which is connected to the main air cleaner via the inlet air trunking.

79 Disconnect the hoses from the air duct, noting their locations to aid refitting.

80 Loosen the hose clip, and disconnect the inlet air trunking from the air duct.

81 Remove the screws securing the air duct to the throttle housing, then lift off the air duct and recover the gasket.

82 Refit by reversing the removal operations, making sure that the hoses are connected correctly. Use a new gasket if necessary on the top of the throttle housing.

Throttle housing

83 Depressurise the fuel system as described earlier, then disconnect the battery negative lead.

84 Remove the air cleaner or the air duct, as applicable, from the top of the throttle housing (photo).

85 Disconnect all relevant wiring plugs (throttle position sensor, fuel injector, idle speed control motor) from the throttle housing.

86 Disconnect the fuel supply and return lines, making identification marks for reference when refitting (photo). Be prepared for fuel spillage.

87 Where applicable, disconnect any vacuum and breather hoses from the throttle housing, noting their locations.

88 Disconnect the accelerator cable.

89 Remove the securing screws or nuts (as applicable), and lift the throttle housing from the inlet manifold (photo). Recover the gasket.

90 The two halves of the housing can be separated by removing the two securing screws (photo).

91 Refit by reversing the removal operations, using new gaskets.

9.86 Fuel supply and return hose connections (arrowed)

9.89 Two of the throttle housing securing nuts (arrowed)

9.90 Throttle housing upper-to-lower section securing screws (arrowed)

12

9.107A Remove the securing screw. . .

9.107B . . . and withdraw the injector clamp bracket

9.109 Fuel injector clamp bracket screws (arrowed)

92 Ensure that all wiring plugs and hoses are correctly reconnected.

Inlet air temperature sensor

93 The sensor is screwed into the top of the inlet manifold.
94 Disconnect the battery negative lead.
95 Unclip the sensor wiring connector from its bracket, and separate the two halves of the connector.
96 Unscrew the sensor, and withdraw it from the manifold.
97 Refitting is a reversal of removal.

Coolant temperature sensor

98 The sensor is located on the left-hand end of the cylinder head.
99 Drain the cooling system with reference to Chapter 2. Alternatively, remove the

9.112 Disconnecting the wiring plug (arrowed) from the idle speed control motor (Bosch type shown)

expansion tank cap to depressurise the system, and have the new sensor or a suitable bung to hand.
100 Disconnect the multi-plug and unscrew the sensor.
101 Apply a little sealant to the sensor threads, and screw it into position. Reconnect the multi-plug.
102 Top-up or refill the cooling system as necessary.

Fuel injector

103 Depressurise the fuel system as described earlier.
104 Remove the air cleaner or the air duct, as applicable, from the top of the throttle body.
105 Disconnect the battery negative lead.
106 Squeeze the securing lugs, and disconnect the wiring plug from the fuel injector.
107 Remove the Torx-type securing screw, and withdraw the injector clamp bracket (photos).
108 Carefully withdraw the injector from the throttle housing.
109 Refitting is a reversal of removal, bearing in mind the following points:
(a) *Use new injector seals.*
(b) *The injector wiring socket should point towards the clamp bracket screw hole.*
(c) *Ensure that the clamp bracket engages with the slot below the wiring socket in the injector.*
(d) *Coat the threads of the clamp bracket screw with thread-locking compound.*
(e) *The injector clamp bracket is secured by two screws (photo).*

(f) *Note the location of the collar below the clamp bracket.*

Idle speed control motor

110 Remove the air cleaner or the air duct, as applicable.
111 Where necessary, for improved access to the motor securing screws, remove the securing screws and lift the throttle housing.
112 Disconnect the motor wiring plug (photo).
113 Remove the securing nuts and withdraw the motor (photo).
114 Refitting is a reversal of removal, but on completion, the initial position of the throttle must be set as follows.
115 Using a suitable shim or feeler blades, bridge the gap between the throttle lever and the motor plunger.
116 Switch the ignition on for a few seconds, then switch it off again. Remove the shim or blades, then switch on and off again.
117 Run the engine and check that the idle speed and quality are satisfactory.

Fuel pressure regulator

118 Depressurise the fuel system as described earlier.
119 Disconnect the battery negative lead.
120 Note the location of all components before removal, to ensure correct relocation.
121 Remove the air cleaner or the air duct, as applicable, from the top of the throttle housing.
122 Unscrew the three pressure regulator cover securing screws, and carefully remove the cover (photos).

9.113 Two of the idle speed control motor securing nuts

9.122A Removing the fuel pressure regulator cover

9.122B Fuel pressure regulator cover securing screws (arrowed)

9.123 Fuel pressure regulator components

123 Recover the spring seat and spring assembly, and lift out the diaphragm (see illustration).
124 Refitting is a reversal of removal, but ensure that the diaphragm is correctly located in the groove in the throttle housing, and coat the threads of the cover securing screws with suitable thread-locking compound before fitting.
125 The pressure regulator is located under the left-hand side of the throttle housing.

Throttle position sensor

126 To gain access, remove the idle speed

control motor, as described previously in this Section.
127 Release the sensor wiring connector from its bracket, and separate the two halves of the connector.
128 Remove the two securing screws, and withdraw the sensor from its bracket (photo).
129 Refitting is a reversal of removal, but refit the idle speed control motor as described previously in this Section.

ECU (Electronic control unit)

130 The ECU is located in a protective plastic casing in the engine compartment, in front of the right-hand suspension turret.
131 Disconnect the battery negative lead.
132 Unclip the retaining strap, then remove the casing from its location (photo).
133 Where applicable, unclip the casing cover, then disconnect the ECU wiring plug.
134 Where applicable, remove the securing bolts, and withdraw the ECU from the casing.
135 Refitting is a reversal of removal, ensuring that the wiring plug is securely reconnected.

Manifold absolute pressure (MAP) sensor

136 Unclip the MAP sensor from its bracket on the bulkhead, then disconnect the multi-plug and the vacuum hose (photo).
137 Refit by reversing the removal operations.

---

10 Fuel and exhaust systems - Turbo models

Description (later models)

1 During 1986, a water-cooled turbocharger superseded the air-cooled one previously fitted. Operating principles are unchanged, and the precautions listed in Chapter 3, Section 22, still apply.
2 A schematic diagram of the later system is given in Fig. 12.27.

Turbocharger (water-cooled) - removal and refitting

3 The procedure is as described in Chapter 3, Section 27, with the following additional operations.
4 Depressurise the cooling system by removing the expansion tank cap. Clamp the turbo coolant feed hose and disconnect it. Also disconnect the output hose which connects the turbocharger to the expansion tank.
5 After refitting, release the feed hose clamp and top up the cooling system.

Auxiliary fuel tank and pump - description of operation

6 The operation of the auxiliary fuel supply should be understood in order to avoid problems after running out of fuel or after draining the main tank.
7 The auxiliary tank is at a lower level than the main tank. When filling with fuel, the fuel flows down the filler pipe into the auxiliary tank, then through the connecting pipe into the main tank. A flap at the end of the connecting pipe prevents fuel running back out of the main tank into the auxiliary tank.
8 In normal operation fuel is drawn from the main tank by the main fuel pump. When the level in the main tank falls to a certain amount, the auxiliary fuel pump runs for 40 seconds to transfer fuel from the auxiliary to the main tank. At the same time the "low level" warning light illuminates for 5 seconds. The auxiliary pump will only operate when the engine is running or when the starter motor is cranking.
9 If the vehicle is allowed to run out of fuel, more than 10 litres (over 2 gallons) will have to be put into the filler before any appears in the main tank. If this is not possible, the engine will have to be cranked continuously on the starter for at least 60 seconds in order to energise the auxiliary pump and transfer enough fuel to the main tank.
10 To avoid a similar problem after intentional draining of the main tank, a few litres of fuel can be added via the fuel gauge sender aperture when refitting.

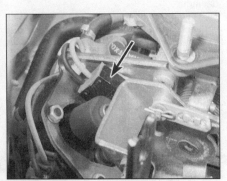
9.128 Throttle position sensor (arrowed)

9.132 Unclipping the ECU casing cover

9.136 Unclip the MAP sensor from its bracket

12

Fig. 12.27 **Water-cooled turbocharger schematic (Sec 10)**

1 Air cleaner
2 Compressor
3 Wastegate actuator
4 Wastegate
5 Turbine
6 Safety pressure switch
7 Intercooler
8 Fuel pressure regulator
9 Carburettor
10 Anti-percolation system switch
11 Anti-percolation fan
12 Boost pressure gauge
13 Ignition unit
14 Radiator and fan
15 Oil filter
16 Oil cooler
17 Non-return valve
18 T-pieces
19 Enriching devices
20 Coolant jacket
21 Solenoid valve
22 Pinking detector

Key:
⇨ Air at atmospheric pressure
⇛ Pressurised air intake
⇨ Pressurised and cooled air intake
⇏ Air-fuel mixture
➨ Exhaust gases

Fig. 12.28 **Water-cooled turbocharger removal (Sec 10)**

4 Exhaust clamp
5 Oil return pipe
6 Coolant feed hose (clamped)
T Wastegate rod (do not stress)

11 Emission control systems - fuel injection (C3J models)

General information and precautions

Evaporative emission control

1 The purpose of the evaporative emission control system is to minimise emissions of fuel vapour. The fuel tank filler cap and hoses form part of this system. The rest of the system varies according to model, as follows.

Fuel injection engines

2 Fuel vapour which forms when the engine is not running is stored in a charcoal canister located under the right-hand headlight. With the engine running, vapour is drawn into the inlet manifold, and fresh air is drawn into the canister. A solenoid valve and a calibrated bleeding valve control the rate at which this happens. The system operates in conjunction with a vacuum valve located on the inlet manifold.

Crankcase emission control

3 This system ensures that there is always a partial vacuum in the crankcase, and so prevents pressure which could cause oil contamination, fume emission and oil leakage past seals.

4 The layout of the crankcase ventilation system varies according to model.

5 When the engine is idling, or under partial load conditions, the high depression in the inlet manifold draws the crankcase fumes (diluted by air from the air cleaner side of the throttle valve) through the calibrated restrictor and into the combustion chambers.

6 The crankcase ventilation hoses and restrictors should be periodically cleaned to ensure correct operation of the system.

Exhaust emission control

7 The system comprises an oxygen sensor and a catalytic converter. These components ensure a very low level of toxic emissions in the exhaust gas.

Oxygen sensor - general

8 The oxygen sensor (also known as a "lambda" sensor, from the symbol used to indicate air/fuel ratio) is located in the exhaust manifold or front pipe (depending on model). It provides a signal to the injection computer which varies according to the oxygen content of the exhaust gas. The computer uses the varying signal to calculate the amount of fuel which must be injected to ensure efficient combustion and low emission levels.

Catalytic converter - general

9 The catalytic converter is located in the exhaust system, at the end of the front section furthest from the manifold. It contains a ceramic honeycomb structure coated with a precious metal compound. This compound acts as a catalyst in the conversion of carbon monoxide (CO) to carbon dioxide (CO_2), and unburned hydrocarbons (HC_x) to water and carbon dioxide (H_2O and CO_2).

Catalytic converter - precautions

10 For long life and satisfactory operation of the catalytic converter, certain precautions must be observed. These are as follows.

11 Only use unleaded fuel. Leaded fuel will poison the catalyst and the oxygen sensor.

12 Do not run the engine for long periods if it is misfiring. Unburnt fuel entering the catalytic converter can cause it to overheat, resulting in permanent damage. For the same reason, do not try to start the engine by pushing or towing the car, nor crank it on the starter motor for long periods.

13 Do not strike or drop the catalytic converter. The ceramic honeycomb which forms part of its internal structure may be damaged.

14 Always renew seals and gaskets upstream of the catalytic converter whenever they are disturbed.

15 Remember that the catalytic converter gets hotter than the rest of the exhaust system. Avoid parking over long grass, undergrowth or similar material which could catch fire or be damaged.

Exhaust gas recirculation system

16 Under certain engine running conditions, a vacuum-operated valve located on the inlet manifold allows a small amount of exhaust gas to be recirculated from the exhaust manifold directly into the inlet manifold via a metal pipe.

11.27 Carbon canister hoses (arrowed) - viewed from above

11.44 Oxygen sensor (arrowed) located in the exhaust manifold

11.55 Vacuum valve (arrowed) located on rear of inlet manifold

Emission control system components - testing and renewal

Testing

17 The operating principle of the system is that the solenoid valve should be open only when the engine is warm and at part-throttle conditions.

18 Bring the engine to normal operating temperature, then switch it off. Connect a vacuum gauge (range 0 to 1000 mbars) into the hose between the canister and the restrictor. Connect a voltmeter to the solenoid valve terminals.

19 Start the engine and allow it to idle. There should be no vacuum shown on the gauge, and no voltage present at the solenoid.

20 If manifold vacuum is indicated although no voltage is present, check that the restrictor is of the correct size. If it is, the solenoid valve is stuck open.

21 If voltage is present at idle, there is a fault in the wiring or the computer.

22 Depress the accelerator slightly. Voltage should appear momentarily at the solenoid terminals, and manifold vacuum be indicated on the gauge.

23 If vacuum is not indicated even though voltage is present, either there is a leak in the hoses, or the valve is not opening.

24 If no voltage appears, there is a fault in the wiring or the computer.

Canister renewal

25 The canister is located under the right-hand front wheel arch.

26 Where applicable, remove the wheel arch splash shield for access to the canister.

27 Working in the engine compartment, disconnect the two hoses from the top of the canister, noting their locations (photo).

28 Working under the front wing, release the two rubber straps securing the canister, and withdraw it from the mounting bracket.

29 Dispose of the old canister safely, bearing in mind that it may contain liquid fuel and/or fuel vapour.

30 Refit by reversing the removal operations. Make sure that the hoses are connected correctly.

Solenoid valve renewal

31 The valve may be mounted on a bracket on the inlet manifold or next to the injection computer, depending on model.

32 Unclip or unbolt (as applicable) the valve from its bracket.

33 Disconnect the hoses from the solenoid valve, marking them if necessary for reference when reassembling.

34 Disconnect the multi-plug from the valve, and withdraw it.

35 Refit by reversing the removal operations. Make sure that the hoses are connected correctly.

Crankcase emission control

36 There is no specific test procedure for the crankcase emission control system. If problems are suspected (sometimes indicated by oil contamination of the air cleaner element), check that the hoses are clean internally, and that the restrictors are not blocked or missing.

37 This is self-evident. Mark the various hoses before disconnecting them, if there is any possibility of confusion on reassembly.

Exhaust emission control - testing

38 An exhaust gas analyser (CO meter) will be needed. The ignition system must be in good condition, the air cleaner element must be clean, and the engine must be in good mechanical condition.

39 Bring the engine to normal operating temperature, then connect the exhaust gas analyser in accordance with the equipment maker's instructions.

40 Allow the engine to idle, and check the CO level (Chapter 1 Specifications). Repeat the check at 2500 to 3000 rpm. If the CO level is within the specified limits, the system is operating correctly.

41 If the CO level is higher than specified, try the effect of disconnecting the oxygen sensor wiring. If the CO level rises when the sensor is disconnected, this suggests that the oxygen sensor is OK and that the catalytic converter is faulty. If disconnecting the sensor has no effect, this suggests a fault in the sensor.

42 If a digital voltmeter is available, the oxygen sensor output voltage can be measured (terminal C of the sensor multi-plug, or terminal 35 of the computer multi-plug). Voltage should alternate between 625 to 1100 mV (rich mixture) and 0 to 100 mV (lean mixture).

43 Before renewing either component, run the car using several tankfuls of unleaded fuel, if there is any possibility that leaded fuel has been used in error. Repeat the test to see if the CO level has reduced.

Oxygen sensor - renewal

44 The oxygen sensor may be located in the exhaust manifold or in the exhaust front section, depending on model (photo).

45 Where necessary for access, apply the handbrake, then jack up the front of the vehicle and support securely on axle stands.

46 Disconnect the sensor wiring plug.

47 Where applicable, unclip the heat shield.

48 Unscrew the sensor from the exhaust manifold or front pipe, as applicable, and remove it.

49 Clean the threads in the exhaust pipe or manifold, and the threads of the sensor (if it is to be refitted).

50 Note that if the sensor wires are broken, the sensor must be renewed. No attempt should be made to repair them.

51 Apply high-temperature anti-seize compound to the sensor threads. Screw the sensor in by hand, then tighten it fully.

52 Where applicable, refit the heat shield.

53 Reconnect the sensor wiring plug.

Catalytic converter - renewal

54 The catalytic converter is renewed in the same way as any other part of the exhaust system. Refer to Chapter 3.

Exhaust gas recirculation system

Vacuum valve renewal

55 The valve is located on the rear of the inlet manifold (photo).

56 Disconnect the hose from the valve.

57 Unscrew the two securing screws, and withdraw the valve. Recover the gasket.

58 Refit by reversing the removal operations, using a new gasket.

12

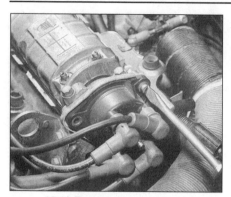

12.4A Remove the screws . . .

12.4B . . . and lift off the distributor cap

12.7 Removing the rotor arm

Gas pipe renewal

59 Unscrew the two bolts securing the pipe to the exhaust manifold. Recover the washers and gasket.
60 Unscrew the union from the inlet manifold, and withdraw the pipe.
61 Fit the new pipe using a reversal of the removal procedure. Fit a new gasket.

12 Ignition system

Description - 1721 cc models

1 The ignition system fitted to 1721 cc models is almost identical to the fully electronic system described in Chapter 4. An additional feature is the provision of an oil temperature sensor, mounted next to the oil filter. This enables the computer module to adjust the ignition timing in response to engine temperature.
2 The distributor on these models is mounted on the left-hand end of the cylinder head. The rotor arm is fitted directly to the end of the camshaft.

Description - 1390 cc (C3J) fuel injection models

3 A modified version of the electronic system, described in Chapter 4, is fitted to these models. One computer having control over both the fuel injection and the ignition systems.
4 Operation of both systems is similar. An engine speed/position sensor, bolted to the flywheel housing, provides signals indicating engine speed and crankshaft angular position. A manifold vacuum (MAP) sensor provides a signal varying with inlet manifold vacuum, which is an indication of load. The signals are processed by a computer, and used to determine the moment when ignition must occur. The computer controls an amplifier which drives the ignition coil.
5 High-tension voltage passes from the coil to the distributor rotor arm, and from there to the appropriate spark plug. The distributor has no other function than the distribution of HT; speed- and load-related advance are handled by the computer. There is no means of adjusting ignition timing, short of changing the computer or the sensors.
6 The ignition module consists of the amplifier and the ignition coil, mounted together. The computer is shared with the fuel injection system, and is described in detail in earlier Sections of this Chapter. The same applies to the manifold vacuum (MAP) sensor.

Precautions

7 The following precautions must be observed, to prevent damage to the ignition system components, and to reduce risk of personal injury:
(a) Ensure that the ignition is switched off before disconnecting any of the ignition wiring.
(b) Ensure that the ignition is switched off before connecting or disconnecting any ignition test equipment, such as a timing light.
(c) Do not connect a suppression condenser or test light to the ignition coil negative terminal.
(d) Do not connect any test appliance or stroboscopic timing light requiring a 12-volt supply to the ignition coil positive terminal.
(e) Do not allow an HT lead to short out or spark against the computer control unit body.
(f) Do not earth the coil primary or secondary circuits.
(g) When carrying out welding operations on the vehicle using electric welding equipment, the battery and alternator should be disconnected.
(h) Although the underbonnet-mounted modules will tolerate normal underbonnet conditions, they can be adversely affected by excess heat or moisture. If using welding equipment or pressure washing equipment in the vicinity of an electronic module, take care not to direct heat, or jets of water or steam, at the module. If this cannot be avoided, remove the module from the vehicle, and protect its wiring plug with a plastic bag.
(i) Do not attempt to improvise fault diagnosis procedures using a test light or multimeter, as irreparable damage could be caused to the module.
(j) After working on ignition system/engine management system components, ensure that all wiring is correctly reconnected before reconnecting the battery or switching on the ignition.

⚠ **Warning: The voltages produced by the electronic ignition system are considerably higher than those produced by conventional systems. Extreme care must be taken when working on the system with the ignition switched on. Persons with surgically-implanted cardiac pacemaker devices should keep well clear of the ignition circuits, components and test equipment.**

Ignition system - testing

8 There is little that can be done by way of testing the control circuitry without special test equipment. The following paragraphs provide suggestions for preliminary checks which can be made without such equipment.

Engine turns normally, but fails to start
9 Check the HT leads, distributor cap and spark plugs as described in Chapter 4.
10 Remove the connectors from the ignition amplifier, and check the terminals for corrosion. If necessary, remove and refit the connectors several times in order to clean the terminals. If they are very dirty, scrape the terminals with a suitable instrument.
11 Check that the wiring on the engine speed/position sensor is secure, refer to paragraphs 30 to 33.
12 Disconnect the coil terminals, and check the resistance of the windings using an ohmmeter. Consult your dealer for values.

Engine misfires
13 Check the HT leads, distributor cap and spark plugs as described in Chapter 4.
14 Check the engine speed/position sensor as described earlier.
15 If no improvement is produced, consult a Renault dealer or other specialist.

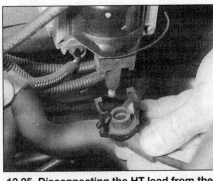

12.25 Disconnecting the HT lead from the coil

12.27 Ignition module securing nut (A) and suppression condenser

12.32 Removing the speed/position sensor from the top of the transmission bellhousing

Distributor cap (1721 cc models) - removal and refitting

16 Disconnect the ignition coil-to-distributor HT lead from the cap.

17 Remove the three screws which secure the cap and lift off the cap (photos). If it is wished to remove the cap completely, identify the plug leads and disconnect them from the cap.

18 Refit by reversing the removal operations.

Rotor arm (1721 cc models) - removal and refitting

18 Remove the distributor cap.

19 On some models the rotor arm may now simply be pulled off (photo). On other models it is glued to the camshaft, and will almost certainly be broken during removal. The necessary adhesive should be purchased from a Renault dealer along with the new rotor arm.

20 Clean off the remains of the old adhesive, if applicable, and glue the new arm in position. If the rotor arm was not glued to the camshaft, refit it and press it home.

21 Refit the distributor cap.

Distributor types (later models) - general

22 Marelli and Femsa distributors are fitted to certain later engines in the Renault 5 range. At the time of writing little information was available on these distributors, except for ignition timing settings, which are the same as for the Ducellier distributor; see Specifications at the beginning of this Chapter or Chapter 4 (as applicable).

Transistor assistance unit (later 1108 cc C1E engines) - general

23 On later 1108 cc C1E engines, a modified transistor assistance unit is fitted which has only one wiring socket; the diagnostic socket no longer being incorporated. Therefore the information given in Section 13 of Chapter 4 regarding the bypassing of the unit is no longer applicable. The dwell angle can only be checked by a Renault dealer with access to specialised test equipment.

24 When checking or adjusting the ignition timing, note that the dynamic setting procedure remains unchanged from that described in Chapter 4, Section 8. When statically setting the ignition timing, it is not recommended that a 12 volt test lamp is connected to the distributor LT terminal due to the possible risk of damage to the transistor assistance unit. Static adjustment should be carried out by eye, with the ignition switched off, so that the contact breaker points are just opening when the appropriate flywheel notch aligns with the notch on the clutch bellhousing. This method will be sufficient to allow the engine to be started, after which the ignition timing can be accurately set dynamically.

Ignition module (C3J - fuel injection models) - removal and refitting

Note: The ignition coil is not renewable separately on fuel injection models.

25 Disconnect the battery negative lead. Release the securing lugs, and disconnect the HT lead from the coil (photo).

26 Disconnect the two multi-plugs from the module.

27 Remove the two nuts which secure the module. Note that one of them also secures the radio interference suppression condenser (photo).

28 Remove the ignition module.

29 Refit by reversing the removal operations.

Engine speed/position sensor (C3J - fuel injection models) - removal and refitting

30 Disconnect the speed/position sensor connector from the bottom of the ignition module or computer, as applicable.

31 Where necessary, for improved access, remove the air cleaner assembly as described in Chapter 3, and unbolt any hose or wiring brackets obscuring the sensor.

32 Unbolt and remove the sensor from the aperture at the top of the transmission bellhousing (photo).

33 Refitting is a reversal of removal. It is important to use only the special shouldered bolts to attach the sensor to the bellhousing, as these determine the correct clearance from the flywheel.

13 Clutch

Clutch assembly - removal and refitting (Turbo and 1721 cc models)

1 On the above models, the engine and gearbox must be removed together and then separated on the bench for access to the clutch.

Clutch release fork - later models

2 On later models the release fork spring shown in Chapter 5 is no longer fitted - the fork simply sits on the pivot stud.

Clutch cable - greasing of trunnion

3 In order that the trunnion and cable guide operate correctly and keep the clutch cable in alignment, the trunnion and cable guide should be kept coated with a general purpose lithium-based grease (Fig. 12.29).

Fig. 12.29 Clutch cable trunnion greasing area (A) (Sec 13)

12

Fig. 12.30 Adjustment of later type gear lever (Sec 14)

Y See text

Fig. 12.31 Early (1) and later (2) types of synchro spring (Sec 14)

14 Manual gearbox

Removal and refitting - Turbo and 1721 cc models

1 On the above models, the gearbox cannot be removed independently of the engine. The engine and gearbox must be removed together and then separated on the bench.

Gearchange mechanism (later models) - general

2 During 1989, a modified gearchange mechanism was introduced. The new mechanism incorporates a locking ring just below the gear knob which must be raised before reverse gear can be selected.

3 Accurate adjustment of the mechanism requires a special tool to be fitted to the gearchange lever on the gearbox to lock it into first gear. As a rough guide, however, adjustment is correct when with first gear selected, gap "Y" (Fig. 12.30) is between 2 and 5 mm (0.08 and 0.20 in). Adjustment is carried out by slackening the clamp nut and bolt at the base of the gear lever and turning the selector rod one way or the other.

Synchroniser unit springs - modifications

4 Two types of synchroniser spring have been fitted (Fig. 12.31)

5 Early type springs can be used to replace later ones, provided that the same type of spring is used in any one synchro unit. However, later type springs must not be used in place of early ones.

Differential (models with electronic speedometer) - dismantling and reassembly

6 On models with an electronic speedometer, a sensor ring wheel and spring are fitted instead of a speedometer drivegear.

7 Two types of spring have been used (Fig. 12.32). The first type of spring can be fitted in place of the second type, but not vice versa.

8 To remove the second type of spring, prise its tabs out of the groove on the differential case (Fig. 12.33). Use a new spring when reassembling, driving it home with a tube of suitable diameter and making sure that the tabs engage in the groove.

15 Automatic transmission

Filter screen renewal

1 This operation is carried out at time of routine renewal of transmission fluid. Begin by draining the fluid (Chapter 6, Section 20).

Fig. 12.32 First type (left) and second type (right) of speedometer sensor ring springs (Sec 14)

Fig. 12.33 Prising the spring tabs out of the groove (Sec 14)

Fig. 12.34 Raise the transmission to the height shown for fluid-pan removal (Sec 15)

2 Remove the nut which secures the transmission mounting on the left-hand side of the vehicle.
3 Support the transmission with a jack placed under the differential housing. Raise the jack to give a clearance of approximately 135 mm (5.3 in) between the transmission fluid pan and the crossmember (Fig. 12.34).
4 Clean the fluid pan and the transmission so that no dirt will be introduced. Remove the fluid pan securing bolts. Remove the fluid pan, the filter screen and gasket.
5 Clean the inside of the fluid pan. Remove the magnets and clean them, then refit them to the pan in their correct positions

Fig. 12.37 O-rings (T) must be renewed when refitting fluid cooler - later models (Sec 15)

Fig. 12.35 Correct positioning of magnets inside fluid pan (Sec 15)

(Fig. 12.35) with the ridged faces against the pan.
6 Fit a new filter screen and gasket, then refit the fluid pan.
7 Lower the jack, secure the transmission mounting and fill the transmission with fresh fluid.

Oil leakage from dipstick tube

8 Oil leakage from the top of the dipstick tube can be cured by fitting a modified dipstick which incorporates a small expansion chamber in its top. The modified dipstick has a green handle.

Transmission fluid cooler assembly (later models) - general

9 On later models, a modified fluid cooler assembly is fitted to the top of the transmission unit.
10 To remove the cooler, drain the cooling system (Chapter 2) then slacken the retaining clips and disconnect both coolant hoses from the cooler. Undo the two bolts securing the cooler to the top of the transmission unit and remove it, noting the O-rings fitted on each side of the cooler mounting bolt holes (Fig. 12.37). Plug the cooler and transmission unions to prevent the entry of dirt.
11 On refitting, position a new O-ring on each side of the fluid cooler mounting bolt

Fig. 12.38 Sectional view of later type driveshaft inboard joint (Sec 16)

1 Yoke	5 Bellows
2 Spider	6 Clip
3 Metal cover	7 Shaft
4 Clip	

Fig. 12.36 Modified transmission fluid cooler location - later models (Sec 15)

holes and tighten the mounting bolts evenly and progressively to the specified torque wrench setting.
12 On completion refill the cooling system (Chapter 2) then check and, if necessary, top up the transmission fluid level (Chapter 6). Start the engine and check the cooler for signs of fluid leakage before taking the vehicle on the road.

16 Driveshafts

New driveshafts - fitting

1 New driveshafts are supplied with cardboard protectors over the bellows. These protectors must be left in place until fitting is complete, then removed by hand. Do not use sharp-ended tools to remove the protectors, as there is a risk of damaging the bellows.

Driveshaft bellows - renewal (general)

2 The rubber bellows at the outboard end of each driveshaft have been superseded by bellows made of a thermoplastic material. These later bellows cannot be expanded to pass over the driveshaft yoke, so the inboard bellows will have to be removed and the driveshaft dismantled as described in Chapter 7, Sections 5 or 6, or as follows in this Section.

Right-hand driveshaft inner bellows (later models) - removal

3 Two types of driveshaft joint have been used at the right-hand inner position. The first type is known as GT62 - the bellows renewal procedure is given in Chapter 7, Section 5. The second type (Fig. 12.38) is known as RC 490, for which the bellows renewal procedure is as follows.
4 Remove the driveshaft (Chapter 7, Section 3).

12

Fig. 12.39 Removing the circlip which secures the spider (Sec 16)

5 Release the staking which secures the metal casing to the yoke.

6 Cut the bellows retaining clip. Cut open the bellows and remove as much grease as possible.

7 Remove the yoke by tapping the metal casing off it, using a brass or copper drill. Be careful that the rollers do not fall off the trunnions - they must not be interchanged.

8 Remove the circlip (if fitted) which secures the spider to the driveshaft (Fig. 12.39). Make identification marks between the spider and the shaft for use when refitting.

9 Press or pull the spider off the driveshaft - see Chapter 7, Section 5, paragraph 6.

10 Remove the bellows, metal casing and insert. Clean and examine the shaft and spider (Chapter 7, Section 5, paragraphs 8 to 10).

11 To the driveshaft fit a new retaining clip, new bellows, the insert and the metal casing.

Fig. 12.40 Venting the driveshaft bellows (Sec 16)

A = 156 ± 1 mm

12 Refit the spider, observing the alignment marks, and press it home.

13 Refit the securing circlip, if one was found. On versions without a circlip, secure the spider by opening the splines in three places.

14 Using the grease supplied in the repair kit, lubricate the yoke, the spider and the inside of the bellows. All the grease must be used.

15 Fit the yoke to the spider. Fit the bellows and insert to the metal casing, then slide the casing onto the yoke. Secure the casing by staking it in three places.

16 Insert a thin blunt instrument, such as a knitting needle, between the end of the bellows and the driveshaft so that air can escape. Move the joint in or out to achieve a dimension "A" as shown in Fig. 12.40.

17 Without disturbing the joint or the bellows, remove the knitting needle and fit the new retaining clip.

18 Refit the driveshaft (Chapter 7, Section 3).

17 Braking system

Rear brake drum (all models) - renewal

1 Later type rear brake drums have a larger locating area for the bearing than early types (Fig. 12.41). Only later type drums are supplied as spares. If an early type drum is

Fig. 12.41 Brake drum bearing locating area (Sec 17)

X (early type) = 2.5 mm
X (later type) = 4.5 mm

being replaced by a later type, proceed as follows.

2 Remove the brake backplate bolts one at a time. Discard the shakeproof washer. Apply thread-locking compound to the tapping in the suspension arm (not to the bolt threads), then refit and tighten the bolt. This is necessary to prevent the new drum fouling the bolt heads.

Rear brake shoes (later Bendix type) - removal and refitting

3 Remove the brake drum (Chapter 8, paragraphs 1 to 10).

4 Note the initial fitted positions of the springs and the adjuster strut (photo).

5 Remove the shoe steady spring cups by depressing them and turning through 90°. Remove the cups, springs and pins.

6 Pull the shoes apart by hand and draw them off the wheel cylinder and bottom pivot. Be careful not to damage the wheel cylinder rubber boots. Allow the springs to draw the shoes together again.

7 Unhook the handbrake cable from the trailing shoe lever and remove the shoes with springs and strut (photo).

8 Remove the bottom spring.

9 Unhook the top spring from the leading shoe and withdraw it from the strut. The adjuster wheel, thread and spring will come away with the shoe (photos).

17.4 Later type Bendix rear brake assembly

17.7 Disconnecting the handbrake cable

17.9A Unhook the top spring . . .

17.9B . . . and withdraw the leading shoe

17.10 Spring and strut engagement in the trailing shoe

17.12 Right-hand adjuster strut is marked "D" (arrowed)

10 Unhook the springs and the strut from the trailing shoe (photo).

11 If necessary, transfer the handbrake lever from the old trailing shoe to the new one.

12 Clean the adjuster strut, paying particular attention to the wheel and threads. Note that left-hand and right-hand struts are not interchangeable - they are marked "G" (gauche) and "D" (droit) respectively (photo).

13 Reassemble the shoes, strut and springs (photo).

14 Engage the handbrake cable in the lever. Pull the shoes apart and fit the assembly to the backplate, again being careful not to damage the wheel cylinder.

15 Refit the steady pins, springs and cups.

16 Turn the adjuster wheel to expand or contract the strut until the brake drum will just pass over the shoes.

17 Refit the brake drum (Chapter 8, Section 6, paragraph 26 onwards).

Rear brakes (later Bendix type) - correction of noise or drag

18 If rear brake drag or noise is a problem on models fitted with the later type Bendix brakes, renew the handbrake return spring and the adjuster strut bracket (Fig. 12.42). The latest versions of both these components have been modified - later springs are yellow or green where the early ones were white. Later brackets are green where the early ones were yellow.

19 When excessive heating has occurred as a result of drag, it is advisable to renew the wheel cylinder and/or hub bearings - consult a Renault dealer for further advice.

Rear wheel cylinder (later models) - overhaul

20 On models where the rear wheel cylinder incorporates a pressure regulating valve, the cylinder cannot be overhauled. In case of leakage or other malfunction it must be renewed.

Master cylinder (1721 cc models) - removal and refitting

21 On these models the master cylinder reservoir is remote from the cylinder itself. Commence removal by clamping the reservoir-to-master cylinder hoses (or by emptying the reservoir) and disconnect the hoses from the cylinder. Be careful not to spill brake fluid on the paintwork.

22 The procedure is now as described in Chapter 8, Section 13.

Pressure regulating valve (later models) - description

23 On most later models the pressure regulating function is carried out by a valve incorporated in each rear wheel cylinder (photo).

24 The combined wheel cylinder/regulating valve assembly cannot be repaired. If either part malfunctions it must be renewed.

Handbrake - adjustment

25 When carrying out the handbrake adjustment procedure in Chapter 8, Section 19, it is imperative that there is no tension in the handbrake cable at the start of proceedings.

26 Adjustment of the handbrake with tension in the cable will result in faulty operation of the automatic adjuster and excessive footbrake pedal travel.

27 Under no circumstances should these symptoms be remedied by further adjustment of the handbrake, which will only make matters worse.

28 The handbrake is not a "wear take-up" system, and should only need adjusting after the brake linings, handbrake cables or handbrake lever have been renewed.

Erratic servo operation - Turbo models

29 Lack of servo effort of Turbo models, especially when the engine is cold, may be due to the non-return valve in the inlet manifold jamming. Renew this valve before suspecting a fault in the servo itself.

17.13 Shoes, springs and strut reassembled

17.23 Rear wheel cylinder/pressure regulating valve components

Fig. 12.42 To cure brake drag or noise, renew the spring (B) and the bracket (C) (Sec 17)

D (early type) = 12 mm
D (modified type) = 10 mm
F Handbrake lever

12

18.9 Topping-up the power steering fluid

18.11 Disconnecting the high-pressure pipe from the steering pump

18 Suspension and steering

Front suspension strut (later Turbo models) - dismantling and reassembly

1 On Turbo models from June 1987, a modified strut with an inclined top mounting is fitted.
2 Dismantling and reassembly are still as described in Chapter 9, Section 6, but on reassembly the dimension to which the spring must be compressed is 400 mm (15.8 in).

Rear suspension bushes (enclosed bar rear axle) - modification

3 The plastic bushes fitted originally have been superseded by needle roller races. Some suspension arm dimensions have changed slightly at the same time.
4 The new races are not a direct replacement for the old bushes, but special kits of parts are available.
5 A press and various special mandrels are needed for the fitting of the races and their tracks. The operation should therefore be carried out by a Renault dealer or a suitable workshop.

Power steering - description

6 Available on certain models, power steering reduces the effort required to turn the steering wheel by means of hydraulic assistance. Hydraulic pressure is produced by a pump, belt-driven from the crankshaft pulley, and is applied to one side or the other of a hydraulic ram inside the steering gear. The direction and amount of assistance is determined by a rotary valve on the steering gear pinion shaft.
7 If power assistance is lost for any reason, the vehicle can still be steered but considerably more effort will be required.
8 To prevent the engine stalling under sudden load from the steering pump at idle (for example when parking) a pressure-sensitive switch in the steering hydraulic system operates a fast idle device on the carburettor.

Adjustment of this system is covered in Section 8.

Power steering - maintenance

9 Routine maintenance is confined to inspecting the pipes, hoses and unions in the system for leaks, and checking the fluid level in the reservoir. The fluid level should be between the two lines on the reservoir. Top up if necessary with the specified grade of automatic transmission fluid (photo). Be careful not to introduce dirt into the system, and do not overfill. Frequent need for topping-up must be due to a leak, which should be investigated.

Power steering pump - removal and refitting

10 Remove the drivebelt(s) and the alternator.
11 Clamp the reservoir-to-pump hose, then disconnect the high-pressure pipe and the supply hose from the pump (photo). Be prepared for fluid spillage.

Fig. 12.43 Steering pump mounting bolts (arrowed) - 1397 cc model (Sec 18)

A Pivot bolt   B Belt tension adjuster

12 Undo the mounting bolts (Fig. 12.43) and remove the pump.
13 Refit by reversing the removal operations. Tension the drivebelt(s), then bleed the steering hydraulic circuit as follows.

Power steering circuit - bleeding

14 This procedure is only required after component renewal, or if the fluid level has become very low due to leakage.
15 Top up the reservoir to the maximum level line with the specified fluid. Turn the steering wheel from lock to lock and top up further if required.
16 Start the engine and again turn the steering from lock to lock. Stop the engine and top up the reservoir again to the maximum line.

Fig. 12.44 Power steering gear peripheral components (Sec 18)

Fig. 12.45 Steering column intermediate shaft length - models with power steering (Sec 18)

L = 401 mm ± 1 mm (RHD) or 381 ± 1 mm (LHD)

Fig. 12.46 Later type door hinge (Sec 19)

B Hinge pin   C Bush

Power steering gear - removal and refitting

17 Refer to Chapter 9, Section 26, but note the following additional operations.

18 On 1397 cc models, disconnect the gearchange linkage from the gearbox or the selector linkage from the automatic transmission.

19 On all models, clamp both hoses at the steering fluid reservoir. Disconnect the fluid supply and return pipes from the steering gear and remove them. Be prepared for fluid spillage.

20 After unbolting the steering gear from its mountings but before removing it, remove the pipes which connect the ram with the rotary valve. Plug the openings to keep dirt out.

Fig. 12.47 Adjust door striker so that lock bolt engages in area A (Sec 19)

21 After refitting, bleed the steering hydraulic circuit as previously described.

Power steering gear - overhaul

22 Overhaul of the power steering gear should be left to specialists. Purchase of a new or reconditioned unit is probably the most satisfactory course of action.

Steering column intermediate shaft length - power steering

23 On models with power steering, the intermediate shaft checking dimension is as shown (Fig. 12.45).

19 Bodywork and fittings

Front door interior trim panel (later models) - removal and refitting

1 On later models a plastic sheet is not fitted inside the door. A bead of sealant round the edge of the trim panel is used instead. This sealant must be cut using a sharp knife when removing the panel, and fresh sealant used during reassembly.

Door hinges (later models) - modification

2 The type of door hinge shown in Chapter 10, Section 18, has been replaced by that shown here (Fig. 12.46). The hinge pin is

removed not by driving it out, but by unscrewing it.

3 A door with the new hinge can be fitted to an old hinge mount if the pin hole is drilled out to accept the new bushes.

Door striker - adjustment

4 In addition to the adjustment given in Chapter 10, Section 18, the door striker is also adjustable fore-and-aft by using shims under the door striker.

5 The shims should be placed between the thrust washer and the plastic washer, and be of such thickness that the door lock bolt engages as near to the centre of the door striker as possible (Fig. 12.47).

Steering lock/ignition switch (all models) - removal and refitting

6 Disconnect the battery negative lead.

7 Remove the steering column lower shroud.

8 Remove the two nuts and two bolts which secure the steering column brackets, and the two Torx screws which secure the facia to the column. Lower the column slightly.

9 Follow the ignition switch wiring back behind the facia and disconnect it.

10 Remove the lock securing screw (photo).

11 Insert the ignition key and turn it to position "G". Depress the retaining lugs and withdraw the lock/switch assembly (photos).

12 Refit by reversing the removal operations.

19.10 Steering lock securing screw

19.11A Depress the lugs (arrowed) . . .

19.11B . . . and withdraw the lock and switch

12

Fig. 12.48 Wiring harness heat shield (A) (Sec 20)

Fig. 12.49 Exhaust downpipe mounting bar (A) and starter support bracket (B) (Sec 20)

Fig. 12.50 Centring dowel (A) must be in place on bolt (B) (Sec 20)

20 Electrical system

Starter motor (Turbo models) - removal and refitting

Note: *The procedure given here is in clarification of that given in Chapter 11, Section 11.*

1 Remove the hoses for the air scoop and air filter.

2 Remove the air filter.

3 Remove the turbo heat shield.

4 Refer to Fig. 12.48 and remove the electrical harness heat shield.

5 Undo and remove the bolts securing the starter, and the starter support bracket from the rear of the starter.

6 Remove the exhaust downpipe mounting bar (Fig. 12.49).

7 Disconnect the starter electrical connections and withdraw the starter from behind the front right-hand roadwheel.

8 Refitting is a reversal of this procedure, but make sure the centering dowel is still in place in the starter securing bolt hole (Fig. 12.50).

9 The turbo heat shield must be refitted.

Headlamp dim-dip system - general

10 Most UK market models covered by this manual will be fitted with the "dim-dip" headlamp system required by current legislation. This system causes the headlamp dipped beams to illuminate at reduced intensity if the sidelights and the ignition are both switched on.

11 The resistor is mounted in the right-hand scuttle (photo).

Electronic speedometer - general

12 The sensor for the electronic speedometer is mounted in the differential housing, as for the cable-driven type, and is secured by a retainer and a bolt (Fig. 12.51).

13 In the event of malfunction, first check that the sensor wiring connector is making good contact. If the condition of the

20.11 Dim-dip resistor

connector is suspect, cut the wires on either side of it and remake the connection by soldering the wires, matching the colours. Insulate the joints from each other with tape.

14 To remove the sensor, disconnect the electrical lead, remove the bolt from the retainer and pull the sensor from the housing.

15 Make sure the O-ring is in good condition, and lubricate it with gearbox oil before refitting.

16 Further fault tracing should be done by a Renault dealer, who will have the necessary test equipment to determine if a fault lies in the sensor, the wiring or the instrument itself.

Fig. 12.51 Electronic speedometer sensor (Sec 20)

| 1 Bolt | 3 Sensor |
| 2 Retainer | 4 O-ring |

Key to wiring diagram circuits

	TC - TL - TS	TC - TL - TS with rear screen wiper	GTL - GTS	GTS with infra red receiver	TSE	TSE with car-borne computer
AEI ignition	11	12	11	12	17	17
Assisted ignition	13	15	13	15	-	-
Battery charge indicator	5	10	11	15	4	4
Brake pad wear warning light	5	8	6	9	7	7
Cigar lighter	8	8	13	9	18	18
Clock	1	1	1	12	17	17
Cooling fan motor	8	8	8	8	17	17
Direction indicator lights	1	1	2	2	3	3
Door locks	-	-	-	14	16	16
External temperature sensor	-	-	-	12	-	17
Feed to car radio	5	5	5	5	16	16
Flowmeter	-	-	-	12	-	17
Fuel gauge	5	8	11	12	18	17
Glovebox illumination	-	-	-	-	18	18
Handbrake	5	8	6	9	7	7
Hazard warning lights	1	1	2	2	3	3
Headlight main beam	1	1	2	2	3	3
Headlight dipped beam	1	1	2	2	3	3
Heating	10	10	10	10	18	18
Horn	3	3	3	3	3	3
Identification plate lights + switches	10	10	13	13	18	18
Interior lights	10	10	10	14	16	16
Minimum coolant level indicator	-	-	-	-	4	4
Minimum fuel level indicator	-	-	-	12	-	17
Minimum windscreen washer fluid level	-	-	-	-	7	7
Nivocode	5	8	6	9	7	7
Oil level probe	-	11	12	17	17	
Oil pressure switch (minimum level and pressure)	5	8	11	15	17	17
Rear foglight	-	8	-	15	-	-
Rear screen defroster	1	1	6	9	7	7
Rear screen wiper/washer	-	6	6	9	7	7
Registration plate light	1	1	2	2	3	3
Reversing lights	-	8	8	15	4	4
Revolution counter	-	-	11	12	17	17
Sidelights	1	1	2	2	3	3
Speed sensor	-	-	-	12	-	17
Standard ignition	10	14	-	-	-	-
Start flap	5	10	6	9	4	4
Starter	5	10	11	15	4	4
Stop-lights	5	8	8	15	4	4
Temperature switch	5	10	6	9	4	4
Trip computer	-	-	-	12	-	17
Window winder	-	-	-	14	16	16
Windscreen wiper/washer	6	6	6	9	7	7

Wire No. — Basic colour of wire (orange)

This wire goes to component 41

This wire goes to component 40

133-Or/N2-41   133-Or/N2-40

40   41

Wire end colour (black)

Wire section and diameter mark

Wire identification diagram

13

Wire colours

B Blue	C Clear	M Brown	R Red	V Green
Bc White	G Grey	N Black	S Salmon pink	Vi Violet
Be Beige	J Yellow	Or Orange		

Wire diameters

No	mm	No	mm	No	mm	No	mm
1	0.7	4	1.2 and 1.4	7	2.5	10	5.0
2	0.9	5	1.6	8	3.0	11	7.0
3	1.0	6	2.0	9	4.5	12	8.0

List of components

1 LH sidelight and/or direction indicator
2 RH sidelight and/or direction indicator
7 LH headlight
8 RH headlight
9 LH horn
10 RH horn
12 Alternator
13 LH front earth
14 RH front earth
15 Starter
16 Battery
17 Engine cooling fan motor
18 Ignition coil (or mounting)
19 Distributor
20 Windscreen washer pump
21 Oil pressure switch
22 No. 1 thermal switch on radiator
24 LH front brake
25 RH front brake
26 Windscreen wiper motor
27 Nivocode or ICP (pressure drop indicator)
28 Heating-ventilating fan motor
29 Instrument panel
30 Connector No.1 - instrument panel
32 Connector No.3 - instrument panel
33 Connector No.4 - instrument panel
34 Hazard warning lights switch
35 Rear screen demister switch
36 Heating fan resistances or rheostat
37 LH window switch
38 RH window switch
40 LH front door pillar switch
41 RH front door pillar switch
42 LH window motor
43 RH window motor
45 Junction block - front harness accessories plate
46 Junction block - front harness accessories plate
47 Junction block - front harness accessories plate
52 Stoplights switch
53 Ignition-starter-anti-theft switch
55 Glove compartment illumination
56 Cigar lighter
57 Feed to car radio
58 Windscreen washer/wiper switch
59 Lights and direction indicators switch
60 Direction indicators switch or connector
61 Before ignition terminal

64 Handbrake switch
65 Fuel gauge tank unit
66 Rear screen demister
67 Luggage compartment illumination
68 LH rear light assembly
69 RH rear light assembly
70 Licence plate lights
71 Choke "On" warning light switch
72 Reversing lights switch
73 Rear light assembly earth
74 Flasher unit
75 Heating fan switch
76 Instrument panel lighting rheostat
77 Diagnostic socket
78 Rear screen wiper motor
79 Rear screen washer pump
80 Junction block - front and engine harnesses
81 Junction block No. 1 - rear harness
83 Junction block - heating wiring harness
86 Lights reminder relay
97 Bodyshell earth
99 Dashboard earth
106 Rear foglight switch
109 Speed sensor
110 Engine cooling fan motor relay
114 Windscreen wiper timer relay
123 Clock
129 Front foglight switch
135 LH front door lock solenoid
136 RH front door lock solenoid
139 Centre front interior light
144 Junction block - interior lights harness
146 Temperature or thermal switch
150 LH front speaker
151 RH front speaker
152 Electro-magnetic locks central switch
164 Electric petrol pump
171 Rear screen wiper/washer switch
172 Impulse generator
174 RH headlight wiper motor
175 LH headlight wiper motor
176 Headlight wipers timer relay
184 Luggage compartment light switch
185 Glove compartment light switch
187 Speedo drive relay (petrol pump)
209 Engine oil level indicator
211 RH rear speaker panel
212 LH rear speaker panel
214 No. 1 front additional lights relay
215 RH front foglight
216 LH front foglight

220 Junction block - ventilation compartment, harness
230 Ignition starter box
231 Junction block - tailgate harness
239 No. 2 petrol pump
241 Horn compressor
247 Junction block - additional lights switch harness
273 Flowmeter
274 Wire joint No. 1
276 Engine earth
286 Wire joint No. 2
289 Wire joint No. 3
290 Wire joint No. 4
296 Horn compressor relay
306 Unlocking remote control
308 No. 2 junction - rear harness
319 Ignition cut-out relay
321 AEI module
340 "Driving aid" computer
341 External temperature sensor
342 Headlight washer solenoid valve
386 Antipercolation motor fan
409 Junction block - registration plate iight harnesses
422 Junction No. 3 - door locking/unlocking harnesses
423 Junction No. 4 - door locking/unlocking harnesses
432 Junction RH front and dashboard harnesses
433 Junction LH front and dashboard harnesses
438 Wire joint No. 5
439 Wire joint No. 6
440 Wire joint No. 7
441 Wire joint No. 8
447 Coolant level detector
454 Junction - headlight wiper harness
460 Wire joint No. 9
461 Wire joint No. 10
462 Door locking timer relay
464 Wire joint No. 11
467 Wire joint No. 12
476 Windscreen washer fluid level detector
484 Wire joint No. 13
487 Wire joint No. 14
493 Petrol pump relay
494 Wire joint No. 15
518 RH front pillar earth
521 Antipercolation relay
560 Antipercolation sensor

Wiring diagram circuit 1

Wiring diagram circuit 2

Wiring diagram circuit 3

Wiring diagram circuit 4

Wiring diagram circuit 5

Wiring diagram circuit 6

Wiring diagram circuit 7

Wiring diagram circuit 8

Wiring diagram circuit 9

Wiring diagram circuit 10

Wiring diagram circuit 11

Wiring diagram circuit 12

Wiring diagram circuit 13

Wiring diagram circuit 14

Wiring diagram circuit 15

Wiring diagram circuit 16

Wiring diagram circuit 17

Wiring diagram circuit 18

This is a guide to getting your vehicle through the MOT test. Obviously it will not be possible to examine the vehicle to the same standard as the professional MOT tester. However, working through the following checks will enable you to identify any problem areas before submitting the vehicle for the test.

Where a testable component is in borderline condition, the tester has discretion in deciding whether to pass or fail it. The basis of such discretion is whether the tester would be happy for a close relative or friend to use the vehicle with the component in that condition. If the vehicle presented is clean and evidently well cared for, the tester may be more inclined to pass a borderline component than if the vehicle is scruffy and apparently neglected.

It has only been possible to summarise the test requirements here, based on the regulations in force at the time of printing. Test standards are becoming increasingly stringent, although there are some exemptions for older vehicles. For full details obtain a copy of the Haynes publication Pass the MOT! (available from stockists of Haynes manuals).

An assistant will be needed to help carry out some of these checks.

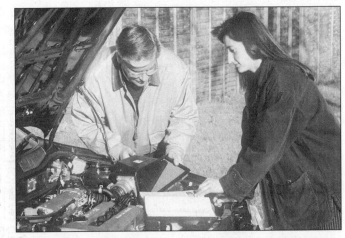

The checks have been sub-divided into four categories, as follows:

1 Checks carried out **FROM THE DRIVER'S SEAT**

2 Checks carried out **WITH THE VEHICLE ON THE GROUND**

3 Checks carried out **WITH THE VEHICLE RAISED AND THE WHEELS FREE TO TURN**

4 Checks carried out on **YOUR VEHICLE'S EXHAUST EMISSION SYSTEM**

---

1 Checks carried out **FROM THE DRIVER'S SEAT**

Handbrake

☐ Test the operation of the handbrake. Excessive travel (too many clicks) indicates incorrect brake or cable adjustment.

☐ Check that the handbrake cannot be released by tapping the lever sideways. Check the security of the lever mountings.

☐ Check that the brake pedal is secure and in good condition. Check also for signs of fluid leaks on the pedal, floor or carpets, which would indicate failed seals in the brake master cylinder.

☐ Check the servo unit (when applicable) by operating the brake pedal several times, then keeping the pedal depressed and starting the engine. As the engine starts, the pedal will move down slightly. If not, the vacuum hose or the servo itself may be faulty.

Steering wheel and column

☐ Examine the steering wheel for fractures or looseness of the hub, spokes or rim.

☐ Move the steering wheel from side to side and then up and down. Check that the steering wheel is not loose on the column, indicating wear or a loose retaining nut. Continue moving the steering wheel as before, but also turn it slightly from left to right.

☐ Check that the steering wheel is not loose on the column, and that there is no abnormal

Footbrake

☐ Depress the brake pedal and check that it does not creep down to the floor, indicating a master cylinder fault. Release the pedal, wait a few seconds, then depress it again. If the pedal travels nearly to the floor before firm resistance is felt, brake adjustment or repair is necessary. If the pedal feels spongy, there is air in the hydraulic system which must be removed by bleeding.

movement of the steering wheel, indicating wear in the column support bearings or couplings.

Windscreen and mirrors

☐ The windscreen must be free of cracks or other significant damage within the driver's field of view. (Small stone chips are acceptable.) Rear view mirrors must be secure, intact, and capable of being adjusted.

290mm

Seat belts and seats

Note: *The following checks are applicable to all seat belts, front and rear.*

☐ Examine the webbing of all the belts (including rear belts if fitted) for cuts, serious fraying or deterioration. Fasten and unfasten each belt to check the buckles. If applicable, check the retracting mechanism. Check the security of all seat belt mountings accessible from inside the vehicle.

☐ The front seats themselves must be securely attached and the backrests must lock in the upright position.

Doors

☐ Both front doors must be able to be opened and closed from outside and inside, and must latch securely when closed.

2 Checks carried out WITH THE VEHICLE ON THE GROUND

Vehicle identification

☐ Number plates must be in good condition, secure and legible, with letters and numbers correctly spaced – spacing at (A) should be twice that at (B).

☐ The VIN plate and/or homologation plate must be legible.

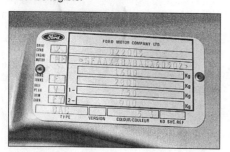

Electrical equipment

☐ Switch on the ignition and check the operation of the horn.

☐ Check the windscreen washers and wipers, examining the wiper blades; renew damaged or perished blades. Also check the operation of the stop-lights.

☐ Check the operation of the sidelights and number plate lights. The lenses and reflectors must be secure, clean and undamaged.

☐ Check the operation and alignment of the headlights. The headlight reflectors must not be tarnished and the lenses must be undamaged.

☐ Switch on the ignition and check the operation of the direction indicators (including the instrument panel tell-tale) and the hazard warning lights. Operation of the sidelights and stop-lights must not affect the indicators - if it does, the cause is usually a bad earth at the rear light cluster.

☐ Check the operation of the rear foglight(s), including the warning light on the instrument panel or in the switch.

Footbrake

☐ Examine the master cylinder, brake pipes and servo unit for leaks, loose mountings, corrosion or other damage.

☐ The fluid reservoir must be secure and the fluid level must be between the upper (A) and lower (B) markings.

☐ Inspect both front brake flexible hoses for cracks or deterioration of the rubber. Turn the steering from lock to lock, and ensure that the hoses do not contact the wheel, tyre, or any part of the steering or suspension mechanism. With the brake pedal firmly depressed, check the hoses for bulges or leaks under pressure.

Steering and suspension

☐ Have your assistant turn the steering wheel from side to side slightly, up to the point where the steering gear just begins to transmit this movement to the roadwheels. Check for excessive free play between the steering wheel and the steering gear, indicating wear or insecurity of the steering column joints, the column-to-steering gear coupling, or the steering gear itself.

☐ Have your assistant turn the steering wheel more vigorously in each direction, so that the roadwheels just begin to turn. As this is done, examine all the steering joints, linkages, fittings and attachments. Renew any component that shows signs of wear or damage. On vehicles with power steering, check the security and condition of the steering pump, drivebelt and hoses.

☐ Check that the vehicle is standing level, and at approximately the correct ride height.

Shock absorbers

☐ Depress each corner of the vehicle in turn, then release it. The vehicle should rise and then settle in its normal position. If the vehicle continues to rise and fall, the shock absorber is defective. A shock absorber which has seized will also cause the vehicle to fail.

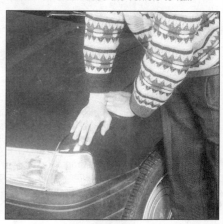

Exhaust system

☐ Start the engine. With your assistant holding a rag over the tailpipe, check the entire system for leaks. Repair or renew leaking sections.

3 Checks carried out **WITH THE VEHICLE RAISED AND THE WHEELS FREE TO TURN**

Jack up the front and rear of the vehicle, and securely support it on axle stands. Position the stands clear of the suspension assemblies. Ensure that the wheels are clear of the ground and that the steering can be turned from lock to lock.

Steering mechanism

☐ Have your assistant turn the steering from lock to lock. Check that the steering turns smoothly, and that no part of the steering mechanism, including a wheel or tyre, fouls any brake hose or pipe or any part of the body structure.
☐ Examine the steering rack rubber gaiters for damage or insecurity of the retaining clips. If power steering is fitted, check for signs of damage or leakage of the fluid hoses, pipes or connections. Also check for excessive stiffness or binding of the steering, a missing split pin or locking device, or severe corrosion of the body structure within 30 cm of any steering component attachment point.

Front and rear suspension and wheel bearings

☐ Starting at the front right-hand side, grasp the roadwheel at the 3 o'clock and 9 o'clock positions and shake it vigorously. Check for free play or insecurity at the wheel bearings, suspension balljoints, or suspension mountings, pivots and attachments.
☐ Now grasp the wheel at the 12 o'clock and 6 o'clock positions and repeat the previous inspection. Spin the wheel, and check for roughness or tightness of the front wheel bearing.

☐ If excess free play is suspected at a component pivot point, this can be confirmed by using a large screwdriver or similar tool and levering between the mounting and the component attachment. This will confirm whether the wear is in the pivot bush, its retaining bolt, or in the mounting itself (the bolt holes can often become elongated).

☐ Carry out all the above checks at the other front wheel, and then at both rear wheels.

Springs and shock absorbers

☐ Examine the suspension struts (when applicable) for serious fluid leakage, corrosion, or damage to the casing. Also check the security of the mounting points.
☐ If coil springs are fitted, check that the spring ends locate in their seats, and that the spring is not corroded, cracked or broken.
☐ If leaf springs are fitted, check that all leaves are intact, that the axle is securely attached to each spring, and that there is no deterioration of the spring eye mountings, bushes, and shackles.

☐ The same general checks apply to vehicles fitted with other suspension types, such as torsion bars, hydraulic displacer units, etc. Ensure that all mountings and attachments are secure, that there are no signs of excessive wear, corrosion or damage, and (on hydraulic types) that there are no fluid leaks or damaged pipes.
☐ Inspect the shock absorbers for signs of serious fluid leakage. Check for wear of the mounting bushes or attachments, or damage to the body of the unit.

Driveshafts (fwd vehicles only)

☐ Rotate each front wheel in turn and inspect the constant velocity joint gaiters for splits or damage. Also check that each driveshaft is straight and undamaged.

Braking system

☐ If possible without dismantling, check brake pad wear and disc condition. Ensure that the friction lining material has not worn excessively, (A) and that the discs are not fractured, pitted, scored or badly worn (B).

☐ Examine all the rigid brake pipes underneath the vehicle, and the flexible hose(s) at the rear. Look for corrosion, chafing or insecurity of the pipes, and for signs of bulging under pressure, chafing, splits or deterioration of the flexible hoses.
☐ Look for signs of fluid leaks at the brake calipers or on the brake backplates. Repair or renew leaking components.
☐ Slowly spin each wheel, while your assistant depresses and releases the footbrake. Ensure that each brake is operating and does not bind when the pedal is released.

☐ Examine the handbrake mechanism, checking for frayed or broken cables, excessive corrosion, or wear or insecurity of the linkage. Check that the mechanism works on each relevant wheel, and releases fully, without binding.

☐ It is not possible to test brake efficiency without special equipment, but a road test can be carried out later to check that the vehicle pulls up in a straight line.

Fuel and exhaust systems

☐ Inspect the fuel tank (including the filler cap), fuel pipes, hoses and unions. All components must be secure and free from leaks.

☐ Examine the exhaust system over its entire length, checking for any damaged, broken or missing mountings, security of the retaining clamps and rust or corrosion.

Wheels and tyres

☐ Examine the sidewalls and tread area of each tyre in turn. Check for cuts, tears, lumps, bulges, separation of the tread, and exposure of the ply or cord due to wear or damage. Check that the tyre bead is correctly seated on the wheel rim, that the valve is sound and

properly seated, and that the wheel is not distorted or damaged.

☐ Check that the tyres are of the correct size for the vehicle, that they are of the same size and type on each axle, and that the pressures are correct.

☐ Check the tyre tread depth. The legal minimum at the time of writing is 1.6 mm over at least three-quarters of the tread width. Abnormal tread wear may indicate incorrect front wheel alignment.

Body corrosion

☐ Check the condition of the entire vehicle structure for signs of corrosion in load-bearing areas. (These include chassis box sections, side sills, cross-members, pillars, and all suspension, steering, braking system and seat belt mountings and anchorages.) Any corrosion which has seriously reduced the thickness of a load-bearing area is likely to cause the vehicle to fail. In this case professional repairs are likely to be needed.

☐ Damage or corrosion which causes sharp or otherwise dangerous edges to be exposed will also cause the vehicle to fail.

4 Checks carried out on YOUR VEHICLE'S EXHAUST EMISSION SYSTEM

Petrol models

☐ Have the engine at normal operating temperature, and make sure that it is in good tune (ignition system in good order, air filter element clean, etc).

☐ Before any measurements are carried out, raise the engine speed to around 2500 rpm, and hold it at this speed for 20 seconds. Allow

the engine speed to return to idle, and watch for smoke emissions from the exhaust tailpipe. If the idle speed is obviously much too high, or if dense blue or clearly-visible black smoke comes from the tailpipe for more than 5 seconds, the vehicle will fail. As a rule of thumb, blue smoke signifies oil being burnt (engine wear) while black smoke signifies unburnt fuel (dirty air cleaner element, or other carburettor or fuel system fault).

☐ An exhaust gas analyser capable of measuring carbon monoxide (CO) and hydrocarbons (HC) is now needed. If such an instrument cannot be hired or borrowed, a local garage may agree to perform the check for a small fee.

CO emissions (mixture)

☐ At the time of writing, the maximum CO level at idle is 3.5% for vehicles first used after August 1986 and 4.5% for older vehicles. From January 1996 a much tighter limit (around 0.5%) applies to catalyst-equipped vehicles first used from August 1992. If the CO level cannot be reduced far enough to pass the test (and the fuel and ignition systems are otherwise in good condition) then the carburettor is badly worn, or there is some problem in the fuel injection system or catalytic converter (as applicable).

HC emissions

☐ With the CO emissions within limits, HC emissions must be no more than 1200 ppm (parts per million). If the vehicle fails this test at idle, it can be re-tested at around 2000 rpm; if the HC level is then 1200 ppm or less, this counts as a pass.

☐ Excessive HC emissions can be caused by oil being burnt, but they are more likely to be due to unburnt fuel.

Diesel models

☐ The only emission test applicable to Diesel engines is the measuring of exhaust smoke density. The test involves accelerating the engine several times to its maximum unloaded speed.

Note: *It is of the utmost importance that the engine timing belt is in good condition before the test is carried out.*

☐ Excessive smoke can be caused by a dirty air cleaner element. Otherwise, professional advice may be needed to find the cause.

Introduction

A selection of good tools is a fundamental requirement for anyone contemplating the maintenance and repair of a motor vehicle. For the owner who does not possess any, their purchase will prove a considerable expense, offsetting some of the savings made by doing-it-yourself. However, provided that the tools purchased meet the relevant national safety standards and are of good quality, they will last for many years and prove an extremely worthwhile investment.

To help the average owner to decide which tools are needed to carry out the various tasks detailed in this manual, we have compiled three lists of tools under the following headings: *Maintenance and minor repair, Repair and overhaul*, and *Special*. Newcomers to practical mechanics should start off with the *Maintenance and minor repair* tool kit, and confine themselves to the simpler jobs around the vehicle. Then, as confidence and experience grow, more difficult tasks can be undertaken, with extra tools being purchased as, and when, they are needed. In this way, a *Maintenance and minor repair* tool kit can be built up into a *Repair and overhaul* tool kit over a considerable period of time, without any major cash outlays. The experienced do-it-yourselfer will have a tool kit good enough for most repair and overhaul procedures, and will add tools from the *Special* category when it is felt that the expense is justified by the amount of use to which these tools will be put.

Maintenance and minor repair tool kit

The tools given in this list should be considered as a minimum requirement if routine maintenance, servicing and minor repair operations are to be undertaken. We recommend the purchase of combination spanners (ring one end, open-ended the other); although more expensive than open-ended ones, they do give the advantages of both types of spanner.

- [ ] *Combination spanners: 8, 9, 10, 11, 12, 13, 14, 15, 16, 17, 19, 21, 22, 24 & 26 mm*
- [ ] *Adjustable spanner - 35 mm jaw (approx)*
- [ ] *Gearbox/engine sump drain plug key*
- [ ] *Set of feeler gauges*
- [ ] *Spark plug spanner (with rubber insert)*
- [ ] *Spark plug gap adjustment tool*
- [ ] *Brake bleed nipple spanner*
- [ ] *Screwdrivers: Flat blade and cross blade – approx 100 mm long x 6 mm dia*
- [ ] *Combination pliers*
- [ ] *Hacksaw (junior)*
- [ ] *Tyre pump*
- [ ] *Tyre pressure gauge*
- [ ] *Grease gun*
- [ ] *Oil can*
- [ ] *Oil filter removal tool*
- [ ] *Fine emery cloth*
- [ ] *Wire brush (small)*
- [ ] *Funnel (medium size)*

Repair and overhaul tool kit

These tools are virtually essential for anyone undertaking any major repairs to a motor vehicle, and are additional to those given in the *Maintenance and minor repair* list. Included in this list is a comprehensive set of sockets. Although these are expensive, they will be found invaluable as they are so versatile - particularly if various drives are included in the set. We recommend the half-inch square-drive type, as this can be used with most proprietary torque wrenches. If you cannot afford a socket set, even bought piecemeal, then inexpensive tubular box spanners are a useful alternative.

The tools in this list will occasionally need to be supplemented by tools from the *Special* list:

- [ ] *Sockets (or box spanners) to cover range in previous list*
- [ ] *Reversible ratchet drive (for use with sockets) (see illustration)*
- [ ] *Extension piece, 250 mm (for use with sockets)*
- [ ] *Universal joint (for use with sockets)*
- [ ] *Torque wrench (for use with sockets)*
- [ ] *Self-locking grips*
- [ ] *Ball pein hammer*
- [ ] *Soft-faced mallet (plastic/aluminium or rubber)*
- [ ] *Screwdrivers:*
  Flat blade - long & sturdy, short (chubby), and narrow (electrician's) types
  Cross blade - Long & sturdy, and short (chubby) types
- [ ] *Pliers:*
  Long-nosed
  Side cutters (electrician's)
  Circlip (internal and external)
- [ ] *Cold chisel - 25 mm*
- [ ] *Scriber*
- [ ] *Scraper*
- [ ] *Centre-punch*
- [ ] *Pin punch*
- [ ] *Hacksaw*
- [ ] *Brake hose clamp*
- [ ] *Brake bleeding kit*
- [ ] *Selection of twist drills*
- [ ] *Steel rule/straight-edge*
- [ ] *Allen keys (inc. splined/Torx type) (see illustrations)*
- [ ] *Selection of files*
- [ ] *Wire brush*
- [ ] *Axle stands*
- [ ] *Jack (strong trolley or hydraulic type)*
- [ ] *Light with extension lead*

Special tools

The tools in this list are those which are not used regularly, are expensive to buy, or which need to be used in accordance with their manufacturers' instructions. Unless relatively difficult mechanical jobs are undertaken frequently, it will not be economic to buy many of these tools. Where this is the case, you could consider clubbing together with friends (or joining a motorists' club) to make a joint purchase, or borrowing the tools against a deposit from a local garage or tool hire specialist. It is worth noting that many of the larger DIY superstores now carry a large range of special tools for hire at modest rates.

The following list contains only those tools and instruments freely available to the public, and not those special tools produced by the vehicle manufacturer specifically for its dealer network. You will find occasional references to these manufacturers' special tools in the text of this manual. Generally, an alternative method of doing the job without the vehicle manufacturers' special tool is given. However, sometimes there is no alternative to using them. Where this is the case and the relevant tool cannot be bought or borrowed, you will have to entrust the work to a franchised garage.

- [ ] *Valve spring compressor (see illustration)*
- [ ] *Valve grinding tool*
- [ ] *Piston ring compressor (see illustration)*
- [ ] *Piston ring removal/installation tool (see illustration)*
- [ ] *Cylinder bore hone (see illustration)*
- [ ] *Balljoint separator*
- [ ] *Coil spring compressors (where applicable)*
- [ ] *Two/three-legged hub and bearing puller (see illustration)*

Sockets and reversible ratchet drive

Spline bit set

Tools and Working Facilities

Spline key set

Valve spring compressor

Piston ring compressor

Piston ring removal/installation tool

Cylinder bore hone

Three-legged hub and bearing puller

Micrometer set

Vernier calipers

Dial test indicator and magnetic stand

Compression testing gauge

Clutch plate alignment set

Brake shoe steady spring cup removal tool

- ☐ Impact screwdriver
- ☐ Micrometer and/or vernier calipers **(see illustrations)**
- ☐ Dial gauge **(see illustration)**
- ☐ Universal electrical multi-meter
- ☐ Cylinder compression gauge **(see illustration)**
- ☐ Clutch plate alignment set **(see illustration)**
- ☐ Brake shoe steady spring cup removal tool **(see illustration)**
- ☐ Bush and bearing removal/installation set **(see illustration)**
- ☐ Stud extractors **(see illustration)**
- ☐ Tap and die set **(see illustration)**
- ☐ Lifting tackle
- ☐ Trolley jack

Buying tools

For practically all tools, a tool factor is the best source, since he will have a very comprehensive range compared with the average garage or accessory shop. Having said that, accessory shops often offer excellent quality tools at discount prices, so it pays to shop around.

Remember, you don't have to buy the most expensive items on the shelf, but it is always advisable to steer clear of the very cheap tools. There are plenty of good tools around at reasonable prices, but always aim to purchase items which meet the relevant national safety standards. If in doubt, ask the proprietor or manager of the shop for advice before making a purchase.

Care and maintenance of tools

Having purchased a reasonable tool kit, it is necessary to keep the tools in a clean and serviceable condition. After use, always wipe off any dirt, grease and metal particles using a clean, dry cloth, before putting the tools away. Never leave them lying around after they have been used. A simple tool rack on the garage or workshop wall for items such as screwdrivers and pliers is a good idea. Store all normal spanners and sockets in a metal box. Any measuring instruments, gauges, meters, etc, must be carefully stored where they cannot be damaged or become rusty.

Take a little care when tools are used. Hammer heads inevitably become marked, and screwdrivers lose the keen edge on their blades from time to time. A little timely attention with emery cloth or a file will soon restore items like this to a good serviceable finish.

Working facilities

Not to be forgotten when discussing tools is the workshop itself. If anything more than routine maintenance is to be carried out, some form of suitable working area becomes essential.

It is appreciated that many an owner-mechanic is forced by circumstances to remove an engine or similar item without the benefit of a garage or workshop. Having done this, any repairs should always be done under the cover of a roof.

Wherever possible, any dismantling should be done on a clean, flat workbench or table at a suitable working height.

Any workbench needs a vice; one with a jaw opening of 100 mm is suitable for most jobs. As mentioned previously, some clean dry storage space is also required for tools, as well as for any lubricants, cleaning fluids, touch-up paints and so on, which become necessary.

Another item which may be required, and which has a much more general usage, is an electric drill with a chuck capacity of at least 8 mm. This, together with a good range of twist drills, is virtually essential for fitting accessories.

Last, but not least, always keep a supply of old newspapers and clean, lint-free rags available, and try to keep any working area as clean as possible.

Bush and bearing removal/installation set

Stud extractor set

Tap and die set

General Repair Procedures

Whenever servicing, repair or overhaul work is carried out on the car or its components, it is necessary to observe the following procedures and instructions. This will assist in carrying out the operation efficiently and to a professional standard of workmanship.

Joint mating faces and gaskets

When separating components at their mating faces, never insert screwdrivers or similar implements into the joint between the faces in order to prise them apart. This can cause severe damage which results in oil leaks, coolant leaks, etc upon reassembly. Separation is usually achieved by tapping along the joint with a soft-faced hammer in order to break the seal. However, note that this method may not be suitable where dowels are used for component location.

Where a gasket is used between the mating faces of two components, ensure that it is renewed on reassembly, and fit it dry unless otherwise stated in the repair procedure. Make sure that the mating faces are clean and dry, with all traces of old gasket removed. When cleaning a joint face, use a tool which is not likely to score or damage the face, and remove any burrs or nicks with an oilstone or fine file.

Make sure that tapped holes are cleaned with a pipe cleaner, and keep them free of jointing compound, if this is being used, unless specifically instructed otherwise.

Ensure that all orifices, channels or pipes are clear, and blow through them, preferably using compressed air.

Oil seals

Oil seals can be removed by levering them out with a wide flat-bladed screwdriver or similar implement. Alternatively, a number of self-tapping screws may be screwed into the seal, and these used as a purchase for pliers or some similar device in order to pull the seal free.

Whenever an oil seal is removed from its working location, either individually or as part of an assembly, it should be renewed.

The very fine sealing lip of the seal is easily damaged, and will not seal if the surface it contacts is not completely clean and free from scratches, nicks or grooves.

Protect the lips of the seal from any surface which may damage them in the course of fitting. Use tape or a conical sleeve where possible. Lubricate the seal lips with oil before fitting and, on dual-lipped seals, fill the space between the lips with grease.

Unless otherwise stated, oil seals must be fitted with their sealing lips toward the lubricant to be sealed.

Use a tubular drift or block of wood of the appropriate size to install the seal and, if the seal housing is shouldered, drive the seal down to the shoulder. If the seal housing is unshouldered, the seal should be fitted with its face flush with the housing top face (unless otherwise instructed).

Screw threads and fastenings

Seized nuts, bolts and screws are quite a common occurrence where corrosion has set in, and the use of penetrating oil or releasing fluid will often overcome this problem if the offending item is soaked for a while before attempting to release it. The use of an impact driver may also provide a means of releasing such stubborn fastening devices, when used in conjunction with the appropriate screwdriver bit or socket. If none of these methods works, it may be necessary to resort to the careful application of heat, or the use of a hacksaw or nut splitter device.

Studs are usually removed by locking two nuts together on the threaded part, and then using a spanner on the lower nut to unscrew the stud. Studs or bolts which have broken off below the surface of the component in which they are mounted can sometimes be removed using a proprietary stud extractor. Always ensure that a blind tapped hole is completely free from oil, grease, water or other fluid before installing the bolt or stud. Failure to do this could cause the housing to crack due to the hydraulic action of the bolt or stud as it is screwed in.

When tightening a castellated nut to accept a split pin, tighten the nut to the specified torque, where applicable, and then tighten further to the next split pin hole. Never slacken the nut to align the split pin hole, unless stated in the repair procedure.

When checking or retightening a nut or bolt to a specified torque setting, slacken the nut or bolt by a quarter of a turn, and then retighten to the specified setting. However, this should not be attempted where angular tightening has been used.

For some screw fastenings, notably cylinder head bolts or nuts, torque wrench settings are no longer specified for the latter stages of tightening, "angle-tightening" being called up instead. Typically, a fairly low torque wrench setting will be applied to the bolts/nuts in the correct sequence, followed by one or more stages of tightening through specified angles.

Locknuts, locktabs and washers

Any fastening which will rotate against a component or housing in the course of tightening should always have a washer between it and the relevant component or housing.

Spring or split washers should always be renewed when they are used to lock a critical component such as a big-end bearing retaining bolt or nut. Locktabs which are folded over to retain a nut or bolt should always be renewed.

Self-locking nuts can be re-used in non-critical areas, providing resistance can be felt when the locking portion passes over the bolt or stud thread. However, it should be noted that self-locking stiffnuts tend to lose their

effectiveness after long periods of use, and in such cases should be renewed as a matter of course.

Split pins must always be replaced with new ones of the correct size for the hole.

When thread-locking compound is found on the threads of a fastener which is to be re-used, it should be cleaned off with a wire brush and solvent, and fresh compound applied on reassembly.

Special tools

Some repair procedures in this manual entail the use of special tools such as a press, two or three-legged pullers, spring compressors, etc. Wherever possible, suitable readily-available alternatives to the manufacturer's special tools are described, and are shown in use. Unless you are highly-skilled and have a thorough understanding of the procedures described, never attempt to bypass the use of any special tool when the procedure described specifies its use. Not only is there a very great risk of personal injury, but expensive damage could be caused to the components involved.

Environmental considerations

When disposing of used engine oil, brake fluid, antifreeze, etc, give due consideration to any detrimental environmental effects. Do not, for instance, pour any of the above liquids down drains into the general sewage system, or onto the ground to soak away. Many local council refuse tips provide a facility for waste oil disposal, as do some garages. If none of these facilities are available, consult your local Environmental Health Department for further advice.

With the universal tightening-up of legislation regarding the emission of environmentally-harmful substances from motor vehicles, most current vehicles have tamperproof devices fitted to the main adjustment points of the fuel system. These devices are primarily designed to prevent unqualified persons from adjusting the fuel/air mixture, with the chance of a consequent increase in toxic emissions. If such devices are encountered during servicing or overhaul, they should, wherever possible, be renewed or refitted in accordance with the vehicle manufacturer's requirements or current legislation.

OIL CARE

FOLLOW THE CODE

OIL BANK LINE
0800 66 33 66

Note: It is antisocial and illegal to dump oil down the drain. To find the location of your local oil recycling bank, call this number free.

Introduction

The vehicle owner who does his or her own maintenance according to the recommended schedules should not have to use this section of the manual very often. Modern component reliability is such that, provided those items subject to wear or deterioration are inspected or renewed at the specified intervals, sudden failure is comparatively rare. Faults do not usually just happen as a result of sudden failure, but develop over a period of time. Major mechanical failures in particular are usually preceded by characteristic symptoms over hundreds or even thousands of miles. Those components which do occasionally fail without warning are often small and easily carried in the vehicle.

With any fault finding, the first step is to decide where to begin investigations. Sometimes this is obvious, but on other occasions a little detective work will be necessary. The owner who makes half a dozen haphazard adjustments or replacements may be successful in curing a fault (or its symptoms), but he will be none the wiser if the fault recurs and he may well have spent more time and money than was necessary. A calm and logical approach will be found to be more satisfactory in the long run. Always take into account any warning signs or abnormalities that may have been noticed in the period preceding the fault – power loss, high or low gauge readings, unusual noises or smells, etc – and remember that failure of components such as fuses or spark plugs may only be pointers to some underlying fault.

The pages which follow here are intended to help in cases of failure to start or breakdown on the road. There is also a Fault Diagnosis Section at the end of each Chapter which should be consulted if the preliminary checks prove unfruitful. Whatever the fault, certain basic principles apply. These are as follows:

Verify the fault. This is simply a matter of being sure that you know what the symptoms are before starting work. This is particularly important if you are investigating a fault for someone else who may not have described it very accurately.

Don't overlook the obvious. For example, if the vehicle won't start, is there petrol in the tank? (Don't take anyone else's word on this particular point, and don't trust the fuel gauge either!) If an electrical fault is indicated, look for loose or broken wires before digging out the test gear.

Cure the disease, not the symptom. Substituting a flat battery with a fully charged one will get you off the hard shoulder, but if the underlying cause is not attended to, the new battery will go the same way. Similarly, changing oil-fouled spark plugs for a new set will get you moving again, but remember that the reason for the fouling (if it wasn't simply an incorrect grade of plug) will have to be established and corrected.

Don't take anything for granted. Particularly, don't forget that a 'new' component may itself be defective (especially if it's been rattling round in the boot for months), and don't leave components out of a fault diagnosis sequence just because they are new or recently fitted. When you do finally diagnose a difficult fault, you'll probably realise that all the evidence was there from the start.

Electrical faults

Electrical faults can be more puzzling than straightforward mechanical failures, but they are no less susceptible to logical analysis if the basic principles of operation are understood. Vehicle electrical wiring exists in extremely unfavourable conditions – heat, vibration and chemical attack and the first things to look for are loose or corroded connections and broken or chafed wires, especially where the wires pass through holes in the bodywork or are subject to vibration.

All metal-bodied vehicles in current production have one pole of the battery 'earthed', ie connected to the vehicle bodywork, and in nearly all modern vehicles it is the negative (–) terminal. The various electrical components – motors, bulb holders, etc – are also connected to earth, either by means of a lead or directly by their mountings. Electric current flows through the component and then back to the battery via the bodywork. If the component mounting is loose or corroded, or if a good path back to the battery is not available, the circuit will be incomplete and malfunction will result. The engine and/or gearbox are also earthed by means of flexible metal straps to the body or subframe; if these straps are loose or missing, starter motor, generator and ignition trouble may result.

Assuming the earth return to be satisfactory, electrical faults will be due either to component malfunction or to defects in the current supply. Individual components are dealt with in Chapter 11. If supply wires are broken or cracked internally this results in an open-circuit, and the easiest way to check for this is to bypass the suspect wire temporarily with a length of wire having a crocodile clip or suitable connector at each end. Alternatively, a 12V test lamp can be used to verify the presence of supply voltage at various points along the wire and the break can be thus isolated.

If a bare portion of a live wire touches the bodywork or other earthed metal part, the electricity will take the low-resistance path thus formed back to the battery: this is known as a short-circuit. Hopefully a short-circuit will blow a fuse, but otherwise it may cause burning of the insulation (and possibly further short-circuits) or even a fire. This is why it is inadvisable to bypass persistently blowing fuses with silver foil or wire.

Spares and tool kit

Most vehicles are supplied only with sufficient tools for wheel changing; the *Maintenance and minor repair* tool kit detailed in *Tools and working facilities,* with the addition of a hammer, is probably sufficient for those repairs that most motorists would consider attempting at the roadside. In addition a few items which can be fitted without too much trouble in the event of a breakdown should be carried. Experience and available space will modify the list below, but the following may save having to call on professional assistance:

☐ *Spark plugs, clean and correctly gapped*
☐ *HT lead and plug cap – long enough to reach the plug furthest from the distributor*
☐ *Distributor rotor, condenser and contact breaker points (if applicable)*
☐ *Drivebelt(s) — emergency type may suffice*
☐ *Spare fuses*
☐ *Set of principal light bulbs*
☐ *Tin of radiator sealer and hose bandage*
☐ *Exhaust bandage*
☐ *Roll of insulating tape*
☐ *Length of soft iron wire*
☐ *Length of electrical flex*
☐ *Torch or inspection lamp (can double as test lamp)*
☐ *Battery jump leads*
☐ *Tow-rope*
☐ *Ignition waterproofing aerosol*
☐ *Litre of engine oil*
☐ *Sealed can of hydraulic fluid*
☐ *Emergency windscreen*
☐ *Wormdrive clips*
☐ *Tube of filler paste*

If spare fuel is carried, a can designed for the purpose should be used to minimise risks of leakage and collision damage. A first aid kit and a warning triangle, whilst not at present compulsory in the UK, are obviously sensible items to carry in addition to the above. When touring abroad it may be advisable to carry additional spares which, even if you cannot fit them yourself, could save having to wait while parts are obtained. The items below may be worth considering:

☐ *Clutch and throttle cables*
☐ *Cylinder head gasket*
☐ *Alternator brushes*
☐ *Tyre valve core*

One of the motoring organisations will be able to advise on availability of fuel, etc, in foreign countries.

Engine will not start

Engine fails to turn when starter operated

☐ Flat battery (recharge use jump leads or push start)
☐ Battery terminals loose or corroded
☐ Battery earth to body defective
☐ Engine earth strap loose or broken
☐ Starter motor (or solenoid) wiring loose or broken
☐ Automatic transmission selector in wrong position, or inhibitor switch faulty
☐ Ignition/starter switch faulty
☐ Major mechanical failure (seizure)
☐ Starter or solenoid internal fault (see Chapter 11)

Starter motor turns engine slowly

☐ Partially discharged battery (recharge, use jump leads, or push start)
☐ Battery terminals loose or corroded
☐ Battery earth to body defective

☐ Engine earth strap loose
☐ Starter motor (or solenoid) wiring loose
☐ Starter motor internal fault (see Chapter 11)

Starter motor spins without turning engine

☐ Flywheel gear teeth damaged or worn
☐ Starter motor mounting bolts loose

Engine turns normally but fails to start

☐ Damp or dirty HT leads and distributor cap (crank engine and check for spark)
☐ No fuel in tank (check for delivery at carburettor)

☐ Choke fault
☐ Fouled or incorrectly gapped spark plugs (remove, clean and regap)
☐ Other ignition system fault (see Chapter 4)
☐ Other fuel system fault (see Chapter 3)
☐ Poor compression (see Chapter 1)
☐ Major mechanical failure (eg camshaft drive)

Engine fires but will not run

☐ Insufficient choke (cold engine)
☐ Air leaks at carburettor or inlet manifold
☐ Fuel starvation (see Chapter 3)
☐ Ballast resistor defective, or other ignition fault (see Chapter 4)

A simple test lamp is useful for checking electrical faults

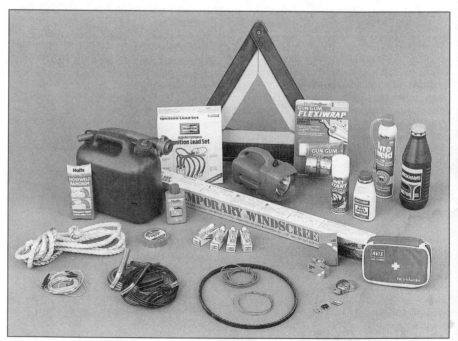

Carrying a few spares may save you a long walk!

Engine cuts out and will not restart

Engine cuts out suddenly – ignition fault

☐ Loose or disconnected LT wires
☐ Wet HT leads or distributor cap (after traversing water splash)
☐ Coil failure (check for spark)
☐ Other ignition fault (see Chapter 4)

Engine misfires before cutting out – fuel fault

☐ Fuel tank empty
☐ Fuel pump defective or filter blocked (check for delivery)
☐ Fuel tank filler vent blocked (suction will be evident on releasing cap)
☐ Carburettor needle valve sticking
☐ Carburettor jets blocked (fuel contaminated)
☐ Other fuel system fault (see Chapter 3)

Engine cuts out – other causes

☐ Serious overheating
☐ Major mechanical failure (eg camshaft drive)

Crank engine and check for a spark. Note use of insulated tool

Engine overheats

Ignition (no-charge) warning light illuminated

☐ Slack or broken drivebelt — retension or renew (Chapter 2)

Ignition warning light not illuminated

☐ Coolant loss due to internal or external leakage (see Chapter 2)
☐ Thermostat defective
☐ Low oil level
☐ Brakes binding
☐ Radiator clogged externally or internally
☐ Electric cooling fan not operating correctly
☐ Engine waterways clogged
☐ Ignition timing incorrect or automatic advance malfunctioning
☐ Mixture too weak
Note: *Do not add cold water to an overheated engine or damage may result*

Low engine oil pressure

Note: *Low oil pressure in a high-mileage engine at tickover is not necessarily a cause for concern. Sudden pressure loss at speed is far more significant. In any event check the gauge or warning light sender before condemning the engine.*

Gauge reads low or warning light illuminated with engine running

☐ Oil level low or incorrect grade
☐ Defective gauge or sender unit
☐ Wire to sender unit earthed

☐ Engine overheating
☐ Oil filter clogged or bypass valve defective
☐ Oil pressure relief valve defective
☐ Oil pick-up strainer clogged
☐ Oil pump worn or mountings loose
☐ Worn main or big-end bearings

Engine noises

Pre-ignition (pinking) on acceleration

☐ Incorrect grade of fuel
☐ Ignition timing incorrect
☐ Distributor faulty or worn
☐ Worn or maladjusted carburettor
☐ Excessive carbon build-up in engine

Whistling or wheezing noises

☐ Leaking vacuum hose
☐ Leaking carburettor or manifold gasket
☐ Blowing head gasket

Tapping or rattling

☐ Incorrect valve clearances
☐ Worn valve gear
☐ Worn timing chain or belt
☐ Broken piston ring (ticking noise)

Knocking or thumping

☐ Unintentional mechanical contact (eg fan blades)
☐ Worn drivebelt
☐ Peripheral component fault (generator, water pump, etc)
☐ Worn big-end bearings (regular heavy knocking, perhaps less under load)
☐ Worn main bearings (rumbling and knocking, perhaps worsening under load)
☐ Piston slap (most noticeable when cold)

Conversion Factors

Length (distance)

Inches (in)	25.4	= Millimetres (mm)	x 0.0394	= Inches (in)
Feet (ft)	0.305	= Metres (m)	x 3.281	= Feet (ft)
Miles	1.609	= Kilometres (km)	x 0.621	= Miles

Volume (capacity)

Cubic inches (cu in; in³)	x 16.387	= Cubic centimetres (cc; cm³)	x 0.061	= Cubic inches (cu in; in³)
Imperial pints (Imp pt)	x 0.568	= Litres (l)	x 1.76	= Imperial pints (Imp pt)
Imperial quarts (Imp qt)	x 1.137	= Litres (l)	x 0.88	= Imperial quarts (Imp qt)
Imperial quarts (Imp qt)	x 1.201	= US quarts (US qt)	x 0.833	= Imperial quarts (Imp qt)
US quarts (US qt)	x 0.946	= Litres (l)	x 1.057	= US quarts (US qt)
Imperial gallons (Imp gal)	x 4.546	= Litres (l)	x 0.22	= Imperial gallons (Imp gal)
Imperial gallons (Imp gal)	x 1.201	= US gallons (US gal)	x 0.833	= Imperial gallons (Imp gal)
US gallons (US gal)	x 3.785	= Litres (l)	x 0.264	= US gallons (US gal)

Mass (weight)

Ounces (oz)	x 28.35	= Grams (g)	x 0.035	= Ounces (oz)
Pounds (lb)	x 0.454	= Kilograms (kg)	x 2.205	= Pounds (lb)

Force

Ounces-force (ozf; oz)	x 0.278	= Newtons (N)	x 3.6	= Ounces-force (ozf; oz)
Pounds-force (lbf; lb)	x 4.448	= Newtons (N)	x 0.225	= Pounds-force (lbf; lb)
Newtons (N)	x 0.1	= Kilograms-force (kgf; kg)	x 9.81	= Newtons (N)

Pressure

Pounds-force per square inch (psi; lbf/in²; lb/in²)	x 0.070	= Kilograms-force per square centimetre (kgf/cm²; kg/cm²)	x 14.223	= Pounds-force per square inch (psi; lbf/in²; lb/in²)
Pounds-force per square inch (psi; lbf/in²; lb/in²)	x 0.068	= Atmospheres (atm)	x 14.696	= Pounds-force per square inch (psi; lbf/in²; lb/in²)
Pounds-force per square inch (psi; lbf/in²; lb/in²)	x 0.069	= Bars	x 14.5	= Pounds-force per square inch (psi; lbf/in²; lb/in²)
Pounds-force per square inch (psi; lbf/in²; lb/in²)	x 6.895	= Kilopascals (kPa)	x 0.145	= Pounds-force per square inch (psi; lbf/in²; lb/in²)
Kilopascals (kPa)	x 0.01	= Kilograms-force per square centimetre (kgf/cm²; kg/cm²)	x 98.1	= Kilopascals (kPa)
Millibar (mbar)	x 100	= Pascals (Pa)	x 0.01	= Millibar (mbar)
Millibar (mbar)	x 0.0145	= Pounds-force per square inch (psi; lbf/in²; lb/in²)	x 68.947	= Millibar (mbar)
Millibar (mbar)	x 0.75	= Millimetres of mercury (mmHg)	x 1.333	= Millibar (mbar)
Millibar (mbar)	x 0.401	= Inches of water (inH₂O)	x 2.491	= Millibar (mbar)
Millimetres of mercury (mmHg)	x 0.535	= Inches of water (inH₂O)	x 1.868	= Millimetres of mercury (mmHg)
Inches of water (inH₂O)	x 0.036	= Pounds-force per square inch (psi; lbf/in²; lb/in²)	x 27.68	= Inches of water (inH₂O)

Torque (moment of force)

Pounds-force inches (lbf in; lb in)	x 1.152	= Kilograms-force centimetre (kgf cm; kg cm)	x 0.868	= Pounds-force inches (lbf in; lb in)
Pounds-force inches (lbf in; lb in)	x 0.113	= Newton metres (Nm)	x 8.85	= Pounds-force inches (lbf in; lb in)
Pounds-force inches (lbf in; lb in)	x 0.083	= Pounds-force feet (lbf ft; lb ft)	x 12	= Pounds-force inches (lbf in; lb in)
Pounds-force feet (lbf ft; lb ft)	x 0.138	= Kilograms-force metres (kgf m; kg m)	x 7.233	= Pounds-force feet (lbf ft; lb ft)
Pounds-force feet (lbf ft; lb ft)	x 1.356	= Newton metres (Nm)	x 0.738	= Pounds-force feet (lbf ft; lb ft)
Newton metres (Nm)	x 0.102	= Kilograms-force metres (kgf m; kg m)	x 9.804	= Newton metres (Nm)

Power

Horsepower (hp)	x 745.7	= Watts (W)	x 0.0013	= Horsepower (hp)

Velocity (speed)

Miles per hour (miles/hr; mph)	x 1.609	= Kilometres per hour (km/hr; kph)	x 0.621	= Miles per hour (miles/hr; mph)

Fuel consumption*

Miles per gallon (mpg)	x 0.354	= Kilometres per litre (km/l)	x 2.825	= Miles per gallon (mpg)

It is common practice to convert from miles per gallon (mpg) to litres/100 kilometres (l/100km), where mpg x l/100 km = 282

Temperature

Degrees Fahrenheit = (°C x 1.8) + 32   Degrees Celsius (Degrees Centigrade; °C) = (°F - 32) x 0.56

Buying spare parts

Spare parts are available from many sources, for example: Renault garages, other garages and accessory shops, and motor factors. Our advice regarding spare parts is as follows:

Officially appointed Renault garages: These will be the best source of parts which are peculiar to your car and are otherwise not generally available (eg, complete cylinder heads, internal gearbox components, badges, interior trim etc). It is also the only place at which you should buy parts if your car is still under warranty; non-Renault components may invalidate the warranty. To be sure of obtaining the correct parts it will always be necessary to give the storeman your car's vehicle identification number, and if possible to take the old part along for positive identification. Remember that many parts are available on a factory exchange scheme - any parts returned should always be clean. It obviously makes good sense to go straight to the specialists on your car for this type of part as they are best equipped to supply you.

Other garages and accessory shops: These are often very good places to buy materials and components needed for the maintenance of your car (eg, oil filters, spark plugs, bulbs, fan belts, oils and greases, touch-up paint, filler paste etc). They also sell general accessories, usually have convenient opening hours, charge lower prices and can often be found not far from home.

Motor factors: Good factors will stock all of the more important components which wear out relatively quickly (eg, clutch components, pistons, valves, exhaust systems, brake cylinders/pipes/hoses/seals/shoes and pads etc). Motor factors will often provide new or reconditioned components on a part exchange basis - this can save a considerable amount of money.

Vehicle identification numbers

Modifications are a continuing and unpublicised process in vehicle manufacture quite apart from their major model changes. Spare parts manuals and lists are compiled on a numerical basis, the individual vehicle numbers being essential for correct identification of the component required.

When ordering parts it will usually be necessary to quote the numbers on the oval plate under all circumstances and often those on the manufacturer's plate. If engine or gearbox parts are being ordered the engine plate or gearbox plate numbers will be needed. The paint code may be required if the colour of the car is not easily described. All these numbers with the exception of those on the gearbox plate are located in readily visible places in the engine compartment. The gearbox plate is affixed to the transmission housing. The vehicle type numbers and corresponding details are as follows:

Prefix	Body type
B	Five-door
C	Three-door
F	Van 'Extra'
S	Van

Type	Engine code	Engine capacity
400	C1C	956 cc
401	C1E	1108 cc
402	C1J	1397 cc
403	C2J	1397 cc
405	C1J	1397 cc (Turbo)
40F	C1G	1237 cc
40G	F2N	1721 cc

The oval plate may also be positioned on the front right-hand side of the engine compartment

A Oval Plate   B Manufacturer's plate   C Engine number plate   D Paint code

A

ABS (Anti-lock brake system) A system, usually electronically controlled, that senses incipient wheel lockup during braking and relieves hydraulic pressure at wheels that are about to skid.

Air bag An inflatable bag hidden in the steering wheel (driver's side) or the dash or glovebox (passenger side). In a head-on collision, the bags inflate, preventing the driver and front passenger from being thrown forward into the steering wheel or windscreen.

Air cleaner A metal or plastic housing, containing a filter element, which removes dust and dirt from the air being drawn into the engine.

Air filter element The actual filter in an air cleaner system, usually manufactured from pleated paper and requiring renewal at regular intervals.

Air filter

Allen key A hexagonal wrench which fits into a recessed hexagonal hole.

Alligator clip A long-nosed spring-loaded metal clip with meshing teeth. Used to make temporary electrical connections.

Alternator A component in the electrical system which converts mechanical energy from a drivebelt into electrical energy to charge the battery and to operate the starting system, ignition system and electrical accessories.

Alternator (exploded view)

Ampere (amp) A unit of measurement for the flow of electric current. One amp is the amount of current produced by one volt acting through a resistance of one ohm.

Anaerobic sealer A substance used to prevent bolts and screws from loosening. Anaerobic means that it does not require oxygen for activation. The Loctite brand is widely used.

Antifreeze A substance (usually ethylene glycol) mixed with water, and added to a vehicle's cooling system, to prevent freezing of the coolant in winter. Antifreeze also contains chemicals to inhibit corrosion and the formation of rust and other deposits that

would tend to clog the radiator and coolant passages and reduce cooling efficiency.

Anti-seize compound A coating that reduces the risk of seizing on fasteners that are subjected to high temperatures, such as exhaust manifold bolts and nuts.

Anti-seize compound

Asbestos A natural fibrous mineral with great heat resistance, commonly used in the composition of brake friction materials. Asbestos is a health hazard and the dust created by brake systems should never be inhaled or ingested.

Axle A shaft on which a wheel revolves, or which revolves with a wheel. Also, a solid beam that connects the two wheels at one end of the vehicle. An axle which also transmits power to the wheels is known as a live axle.

Axle assembly

Axleshaft A single rotating shaft, on either side of the differential, which delivers power from the final drive assembly to the drive wheels. Also called a driveshaft or a halfshaft.

B

Ball bearing An anti-friction bearing consisting of a hardened inner and outer race with hardened steel balls between two races.

Bearing

Bearing The curved surface on a shaft or in a bore, or the part assembled into either, that permits relative motion between them with minimum wear and friction.

Big-end bearing The bearing in the end of the connecting rod that's attached to the crankshaft.

Bleed nipple A valve on a brake wheel cylinder, caliper or other hydraulic component that is opened to purge the hydraulic system of air. Also called a bleed screw.

Brake bleeding

Brake bleeding Procedure for removing air from lines of a hydraulic brake system.

Brake disc The component of a disc brake that rotates with the wheels.

Brake drum The component of a drum brake that rotates with the wheels.

Brake linings The friction material which contacts the brake disc or drum to retard the vehicle's speed. The linings are bonded or riveted to the brake pads or shoes.

Brake pads The replaceable friction pads that pinch the brake disc when the brakes are applied. Brake pads consist of a friction material bonded or riveted to a rigid backing plate.

Brake shoe The crescent-shaped carrier to which the brake linings are mounted and which forces the lining against the rotating drum during braking.

Braking systems For more information on braking systems, consult the *Haynes Automotive Brake Manual*.

Breaker bar A long socket wrench handle providing greater leverage.

Bulkhead The insulated partition between the engine and the passenger compartment.

C

Caliper The non-rotating part of a disc-brake assembly that straddles the disc and carries the brake pads. The caliper also contains the hydraulic components that cause the pads to pinch the disc when the brakes are applied. A caliper is also a measuring tool that can be set to measure inside or outside dimensions of an object.

Glossary of Technical Terms

Camshaft A rotating shaft on which a series of cam lobes operate the valve mechanisms. The camshaft may be driven by gears, by sprockets and chain or by sprockets and a belt.

Canister A container in an evaporative emission control system; contains activated charcoal granules to trap vapours from the fuel system.

Canister

Carburettor A device which mixes fuel with air in the proper proportions to provide a desired power output from a spark ignition internal combustion engine.

Carburettor

Castellated Resembling the parapets along the top of a castle wall. For example, a castellated balljoint stud nut.

Castellated nut

Castor In wheel alignment, the backward or forward tilt of the steering axis. Castor is positive when the steering axis is inclined rearward at the top.

Catalytic converter A silencer-like device in the exhaust system which converts certain pollutants in the exhaust gases into less harmful substances.

Catalytic converter

Circlip A ring-shaped clip used to prevent endwise movement of cylindrical parts and shafts. An internal circlip is installed in a groove in a housing; an external circlip fits into a groove on the outside of a cylindrical piece such as a shaft.

Clearance The amount of space between two parts. For example, between a piston and a cylinder, between a bearing and a journal, etc.

Coil spring A spiral of elastic steel found in various sizes throughout a vehicle, for example as a springing medium in the suspension and in the valve train.

Compression Reduction in volume, and increase in pressure and temperature, of a gas, caused by squeezing it into a smaller space.

Compression ratio The relationship between cylinder volume when the piston is at top dead centre and cylinder volume when the piston is at bottom dead centre.

Constant velocity (CV) joint A type of universal joint that cancels out vibrations caused by driving power being transmitted through an angle.

Core plug A disc or cup-shaped metal device inserted in a hole in a casting through which core was removed when the casting was formed. Also known as a freeze plug or expansion plug.

Crankcase The lower part of the engine block in which the crankshaft rotates.

Crankshaft The main rotating member, or shaft, running the length of the crankcase, with offset "throws" to which the connecting rods are attached.

Crankshaft assembly

Crocodile clip See Alligator clip

D

Diagnostic code Code numbers obtained by accessing the diagnostic mode of an engine management computer. This code can be used to determine the area in the system where a malfunction may be located.

Disc brake A brake design incorporating a rotating disc onto which brake pads are squeezed. The resulting friction converts the energy of a moving vehicle into heat.

Double-overhead cam (DOHC) An engine that uses two overhead camshafts, usually one for the intake valves and one for the exhaust valves.

Drivebelt(s) The belt(s) used to drive accessories such as the alternator, water pump, power steering pump, air conditioning compressor, etc. off the crankshaft pulley.

Accessory drivebelts

Driveshaft Any shaft used to transmit motion. Commonly used when referring to the axleshafts on a front wheel drive vehicle.

Driveshaft

Drum brake A type of brake using a drum-shaped metal cylinder attached to the inner surface of the wheel. When the brake pedal is pressed, curved brake shoes with friction linings press against the inside of the drum to slow or stop the vehicle.

Drum brake assembly

E

EGR valve A valve used to introduce exhaust gases into the intake air stream.

EGR valve

Electronic control unit (ECU) A computer which controls (for instance) ignition and fuel injection systems, or an anti-lock braking system. For more information refer to the *Haynes Automotive Electrical and Electronic Systems Manual.*

Electronic Fuel Injection (EFI) A computer controlled fuel system that distributes fuel through an injector located in each intake port of the engine.

Emergency brake A braking system, independent of the main hydraulic system, that can be used to slow or stop the vehicle if the primary brakes fail, or to hold the vehicle stationary even though the brake pedal isn't depressed. It usually consists of a hand lever that actuates either front or rear brakes mechanically through a series of cables and linkages. Also known as a handbrake or parking brake.

Endfloat The amount of lengthwise movement between two parts. As applied to a crankshaft, the distance that the crankshaft can move forward and back in the cylinder block.

Engine management system (EMS) A computer controlled system which manages the fuel injection and the ignition systems in an integrated fashion.

Exhaust manifold A part with several passages through which exhaust gases leave the engine combustion chambers and enter the exhaust pipe.

Exhaust manifold

F

Fan clutch A viscous (fluid) drive coupling device which permits variable engine fan speeds in relation to engine speeds.

Feeler blade A thin strip or blade of hardened steel, ground to an exact thickness, used to check or measure clearances between parts.

Feeler blade

Firing order The order in which the engine cylinders fire, or deliver their power strokes, beginning with the number one cylinder.

Flywheel A heavy spinning wheel in which energy is absorbed and stored by means of momentum. On cars, the flywheel is attached to the crankshaft to smooth out firing impulses.

Free play The amount of travel before any action takes place. The "looseness" in a linkage, or an assembly of parts, between the initial application of force and actual movement. For example, the distance the brake pedal moves before the pistons in the master cylinder are actuated.

Fuse An electrical device which protects a circuit against accidental overload. The typical fuse contains a soft piece of metal which is calibrated to melt at a predetermined current flow (expressed as amps) and break the circuit.

Fusible link A circuit protection device consisting of a conductor surrounded by heat-resistant insulation. The conductor is smaller than the wire it protects, so it acts as the weakest link in the circuit. Unlike a blown fuse, a failed fusible link must frequently be cut from the wire for replacement.

G

Gap The distance the spark must travel in jumping from the centre electrode to the side

Adjusting spark plug gap

electrode in a spark plug. Also refers to the spacing between the points in a contact breaker assembly in a conventional points-type ignition, or to the distance between the reluctor or rotor and the pickup coil in an electronic ignition.

Gasket Any thin, soft material - usually cork, cardboard, asbestos or soft metal - installed between two metal surfaces to ensure a good seal. For instance, the cylinder head gasket seals the joint between the block and the cylinder head.

Gasket

Gauge An instrument panel display used to monitor engine conditions. A gauge with a movable pointer on a dial or a fixed scale is an analogue gauge. A gauge with a numerical readout is called a digital gauge.

H

Halfshaft A rotating shaft that transmits power from the final drive unit to a drive wheel, usually when referring to a live rear axle.

Harmonic balancer A device designed to reduce torsion or twisting vibration in the crankshaft. May be incorporated in the crankshaft pulley. Also known as a vibration damper.

Hone An abrasive tool for correcting small irregularities or differences in diameter in an engine cylinder, brake cylinder, etc.

Hydraulic tappet A tappet that utilises hydraulic pressure from the engine's lubrication system to maintain zero clearance (constant contact with both camshaft and valve stem). Automatically adjusts to variation in valve stem length. Hydraulic tappets also reduce valve noise.

I

Ignition timing The moment at which the spark plug fires, usually expressed in the number of crankshaft degrees before the piston reaches the top of its stroke.

Inlet manifold A tube or housing with passages through which flows the air-fuel mixture (carburettor vehicles and vehicles with throttle body injection) or air only (port fuel-injected vehicles) to the port openings in the cylinder head.

J

Jump start Starting the engine of a vehicle with a discharged or weak battery by attaching jump leads from the weak battery to a charged or helper battery.

L

Load Sensing Proportioning Valve (LSPV) A brake hydraulic system control valve that works like a proportioning valve, but also takes into consideration the amount of weight carried by the rear axle.

Locknut A nut used to lock an adjustment nut, or other threaded component, in place. For example, a locknut is employed to keep the adjusting nut on the rocker arm in position.

Lockwasher A form of washer designed to prevent an attaching nut from working loose.

M

MacPherson strut A type of front suspension system devised by Earle MacPherson at Ford of England. In its original form, a simple lateral link with the anti-roll bar creates the lower control arm. A long strut - an integral coil spring and shock absorber - is mounted between the body and the steering knuckle. Many modern so-called MacPherson strut systems use a conventional lower A-arm and don't rely on the anti-roll bar for location.

Multimeter An electrical test instrument with the capability to measure voltage, current and resistance.

N

NOx Oxides of Nitrogen. A common toxic pollutant emitted by petrol and diesel engines at higher temperatures.

O

Ohm The unit of electrical resistance. One volt applied to a resistance of one ohm will produce a current of one amp.

Ohmmeter An instrument for measuring electrical resistance.

O-ring A type of sealing ring made of a special rubber-like material; in use, the O-ring is compressed into a groove to provide the sealing action.

O-ring

Overhead cam (ohc) engine An engine with the camshaft(s) located on top of the cylinder head(s).

Overhead valve (ohv) engine An engine with the valves located in the cylinder head, but with the camshaft located in the engine block.

Oxygen sensor A device installed in the engine exhaust manifold, which senses the oxygen content in the exhaust and converts this information into an electric current. Also called a Lambda sensor.

P

Phillips screw A type of screw head having a cross instead of a slot for a corresponding type of screwdriver.

Plastigage A thin strip of plastic thread, available in different sizes, used for measuring clearances. For example, a strip of Plastigage is laid across a bearing journal. The parts are assembled and dismantled; the width of the crushed strip indicates the clearance between journal and bearing.

Plastigage

Propeller shaft The long hollow tube with universal joints at both ends that carries power from the transmission to the differential on front-engined rear wheel drive vehicles.

Proportioning valve A hydraulic control valve which limits the amount of pressure to the rear brakes during panic stops to prevent wheel lock-up.

R

Rack-and-pinion steering A steering system with a pinion gear on the end of the steering shaft that mates with a rack (think of a geared wheel opened up and laid flat). When the steering wheel is turned, the pinion turns, moving the rack to the left or right. This movement is transmitted through the track rods to the steering arms at the wheels.

Radiator A liquid-to-air heat transfer device designed to reduce the temperature of the coolant in an internal combustion engine cooling system.

Refrigerant Any substance used as a heat transfer agent in an air-conditioning system. R-12 has been the principle refrigerant for many years; recently, however, manufacturers have begun using R-134a, a non-CFC substance that is considered less harmful to the ozone in the upper atmosphere.

Rocker arm A lever arm that rocks on a shaft or pivots on a stud. In an overhead valve engine, the rocker arm converts the upward movement of the pushrod into a downward movement to open a valve.

Rotor In a distributor, the rotating device inside the cap that connects the centre electrode and the outer terminals as it turns, distributing the high voltage from the coil secondary winding to the proper spark plug. Also, that part of an alternator which rotates inside the stator. Also, the rotating assembly of a turbocharger, including the compressor wheel, shaft and turbine wheel.

Runout The amount of wobble (in-and-out movement) of a gear or wheel as it's rotated. The amount a shaft rotates "out-of-true." The out-of-round condition of a rotating part.

S

Sealant A liquid or paste used to prevent leakage at a joint. Sometimes used in conjunction with a gasket.

Sealed beam lamp An older headlight design which integrates the reflector, lens and filaments into a hermetically-sealed one-piece unit. When a filament burns out or the lens cracks, the entire unit is simply replaced.

Serpentine drivebelt A single, long, wide accessory drivebelt that's used on some newer vehicles to drive all the accessories, instead of a series of smaller, shorter belts. Serpentine drivebelts are usually tensioned by an automatic tensioner.

Serpentine drivebelt

Shim Thin spacer, commonly used to adjust the clearance or relative positions between two parts. For example, shims inserted into or under bucket tappets control valve clearances. Clearance is adjusted by changing the thickness of the shim.

Slide hammer A special puller that screws into or hooks onto a component such as a shaft or bearing; a heavy sliding handle on the shaft bottoms against the end of the shaft to knock the component free.

Sprocket A tooth or projection on the periphery of a wheel, shaped to engage with a chain or drivebelt. Commonly used to refer to the sprocket wheel itself.

Starter inhibitor switch On vehicles with an

automatic transmission, a switch that prevents starting if the vehicle is not in Neutral or Park.

Strut See MacPherson strut.

T

Tappet A cylindrical component which transmits motion from the cam to the valve stem, either directly or via a pushrod and rocker arm. Also called a cam follower.

Thermostat A heat-controlled valve that regulates the flow of coolant between the cylinder block and the radiator, so maintaining optimum engine operating temperature. A thermostat is also used in some air cleaners in which the temperature is regulated.

Thrust bearing The bearing in the clutch assembly that is moved in to the release levers by clutch pedal action to disengage the clutch. Also referred to as a release bearing.

Timing belt A toothed belt which drives the camshaft. Serious engine damage may result if it breaks in service.

Timing chain A chain which drives the camshaft.

Toe-in The amount the front wheels are closer together at the front than at the rear. On rear wheel drive vehicles, a slight amount of toe-in is usually specified to keep the front wheels running parallel on the road by offsetting other forces that tend to spread the wheels apart.

Toe-out The amount the front wheels are closer together at the rear than at the front. On front wheel drive vehicles, a slight amount of toe-out is usually specified.

Tools For full information on choosing and using tools, refer to the *Haynes Automotive Tools Manual.*

Tracer A stripe of a second colour applied to a wire insulator to distinguish that wire from another one with the same colour insulator.

Tune-up A process of accurate and careful adjustments and parts replacement to obtain the best possible engine performance.

Turbocharger A centrifugal device, driven by exhaust gases, that pressurises the intake air. Normally used to increase the power output from a given engine displacement, but can also be used primarily to reduce exhaust emissions (as on VW's "Umwelt" Diesel engine).

U

Universal joint or U-joint A double-pivoted connection for transmitting power from a driving to a driven shaft through an angle. A U-joint consists of two Y-shaped yokes and a cross-shaped member called the spider.

V

Valve A device through which the flow of liquid, gas, vacuum, or loose material in bulk may be started, stopped, or regulated by a movable part that opens, shuts, or partially obstructs one or more ports or passageways. A valve is also the movable part of such a device.

Valve clearance The clearance between the valve tip (the end of the valve stem) and the rocker arm or tappet. The valve clearance is measured when the valve is closed.

Vernier caliper A precision measuring instrument that measures inside and outside dimensions. Not quite as accurate as a micrometer, but more convenient.

Viscosity The thickness of a liquid or its resistance to flow.

Volt A unit for expressing electrical "pressure" in a circuit. One volt that will produce a current of one ampere through a resistance of one ohm.

W

Welding Various processes used to join metal items by heating the areas to be joined to a molten state and fusing them together. For more information refer to the *Haynes Automotive Welding Manual.*

Wiring diagram A drawing portraying the components and wires in a vehicle's electrical system, using standardised symbols. For more information refer to the *Haynes Automotive Electrical and Electronic Systems Manual.*

Note: *References throughout this index relate to Chapter•page number*

Preserving Our Motoring Heritage

< *The Model J Duesenberg Derham Tourster. Only eight of these magnificent cars were ever built – this is the only example to be found outside the United States of America*

Almost every car you've ever loved, loathed or desired is gathered under one roof at the Haynes Motor Museum. Over 300 immaculately presented cars and motorbikes represent every aspect of our motoring heritage, from elegant reminders of bygone days, such as the superb Model J Duesenberg to curiosities like the bug-eyed BMW Isetta. There are also many old friends and flames. Perhaps you remember the 1959 Ford Popular that you did your courting in? The magnificent 'Red Collection' is a spectacle of classic sports cars including AC, Alfa Romeo, Austin Healey, Ferrari, Lamborghini, Maserati, MG, Riley, Porsche and Triumph.

A Perfect Day Out

Each and every vehicle at the Haynes Motor Museum has played its part in the history and culture of Motoring. Today, they make a wonderful spectacle and a great day out for all the family. Bring the kids, bring Mum and Dad, but above all bring your camera to capture those golden memories for ever. You will also find an impressive array of motoring memorabilia, a comfortable 70 seat video cinema and one of the most extensive transport book shops in Britain. The Pit Stop Cafe serves everything from a cup of tea to wholesome, home-made meals or, if you prefer, you can enjoy the large picnic area nestled in the beautiful rural surroundings of Somerset.

> *John Haynes O.B.E., Founder and Chairman of the museum at the wheel of a Haynes Light 12.*

< *Graham Hill's Lola Cosworth Formula 1 car next to a 1934 Riley Sports.*

The Museum is situated on the A359 Yeovil to Frome road at Sparkford, just off the A303 in Somerset. It is about 40 miles south of Bristol, and 25 minutes drive from the M5 intersection at Taunton.
Open 9.30am - 5.30pm (10.00am - 4.00pm Winter) 7 days a week, *except Christmas Day, Boxing Day and New Years Day*
Special rates available for schools, coach parties and outings Charitable Trust No. 292048